ARM Assembly Language

Programming & Architecture

Second Edition

Muhammad Ali Mazidi

Sarmad Naimi

Sepehr Naimi

Shujen Chen

www.NicerLand.com

To contact authors, use the following email address:

Sepehr.Naimi@gmail.com

Visit our website at

https://nicerland.com/

ISBN-13: 978-1-970054-86-6

ISBN-10: 1-970054-86-7

"Regard man as a mine

rich in gems of inestimable value.

Education can, alone,

cause it to reveal its treasures,

and enable mankind to benefit therefrom."

Baha'u'llah

Dedication

To the faculty, staff, and students of BIHE university for their dedication and steadfastness.

Table of Contents

Preface to Second Edition

The ARM processor is becoming the dominant CPU architecture in the computer industry. It is already the leading architecture in cell phones and tablet computers. With such a large number of companies producing ARM chips, it is certain that the architecture will move to the laptop, desktop and high-performance computers presently dominated by x86 architecture from Intel and AMD. Currently the PIC and AVR microcontrollers dominate the 8-bit microcontroller market. The ARM architecture will have a major impact in this area too as designers become more familiar with its architecture. This book is intended as an introduction to ARM assembly language programming and architecture. We assume no prior background in assembly language programming with other CPUs. However, we urge you to study Chapter 0 covering the fundamentals of digital systems such as hexadecimal numbers, various types of memory, memory and I/O interfacing, and memory address decoding. Chapter 0 is available free of charge on our website https://nicerland.com/eduFiles/AVR/Tutorials/Chapter0_v17.pdf

Universities and colleges

This book is intended for both academic and industry readers. The answers to review questions at end of each section are provided at end of the chapter. If you are a professor using this book for a university course you can contact us to receive the solutions to the end-of-chapter problems.

This book covers the assembly language programming of the ARM chip. The ARM assembly language is standard regardless of who makes the chip. The ARM licensees are free to implement the on-chip peripherals (ADC, Timers, I/O, ...) as they choose. Since the ARM peripherals are not standard among the various vendors, we have dedicated a separate book to each vendor. See our web site for ARM peripheral programming books for various vendors. These books use C language to program the peripherals.

Finally, we would like to thank professors Elias Kougianos (of UNT.edu), Shahram Rohani, and Clyde Knight for their suggestions.

Contact us at the following email address:

NicerBooks@gmail.com

, and please place ARM book in subject line of your email.

New to This Edition

In this second edition, we moved some sections around in Chapter 6 to improve the flow of materials. We also added new chapters of 8 and 9. Chapter 8 examines the Thumb instructions. Chapter 9 shows the programming of floating-point unit (FPU) coprocessor in ARM.

Keil and GCC tutorials

We have used the Keil Compiler for the programs throughout this book. See our website for Keil tutorial for ARM. If you are interested in using the GNU Compiler (GCC) we have provided a tutorial for it using Raspberry Pi. See our web site:

https://nicerland.com/

On the above web site, you can also find the source codes and Power Points for the book.

Chapter 1: The History of ARM and Microcontrollers

In Section 1.1 we look at the history of microcontrollers then we introduce some of the available microcontrollers. The history of ARM is provided in Section 1.2.

Section 1.1: Introduction to Microcontrollers

The evolution of Microprocessors and Microcontrollers

In early computers, CPUs were designed using a number of vacuum tubes. The vacuum tube was bulky and consumed a lot of electricity. The invention of transistors, followed by the IC (Integrated Circuit), provided the means to put a CPU on printed circuit boards. The advances in IC technology allowed putting the entire CPU on a single IC chip. This IC was called a *microprocessor*. Some of the microprocessors are the x86 family of Intel used widely in desktop computers, and the 68000 of Motorola. The microprocessors do not contain RAM, ROM, or I/O peripherals. As a result, they must be connected externally to RAM, ROM and I/O, as shown in Figure 1-1.

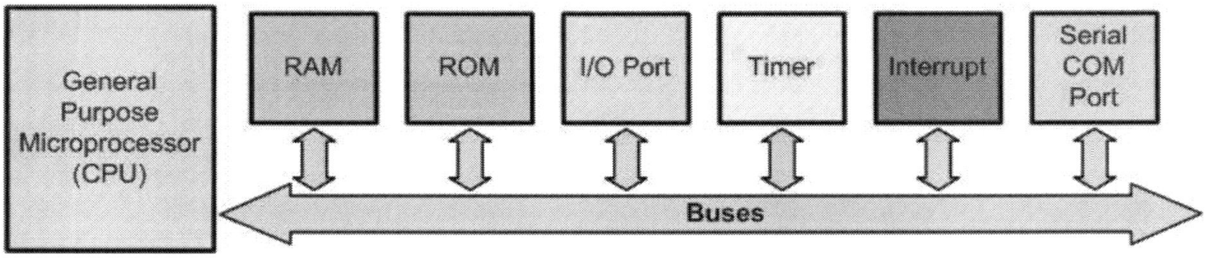

Figure 1- 1: A Computer Made by General Purpose Microprocessor

In the next step, the different parts of a system, including CPU, RAM, ROM, and I/Os, were put together on a single IC chip and it was called *microcontroller*. SOC (System on Chip) and MCU (Micro Controller Unit) are other names used to refer to microcontrollers. Figure 1-2 shows the simplified view of the internal parts of microcontrollers.

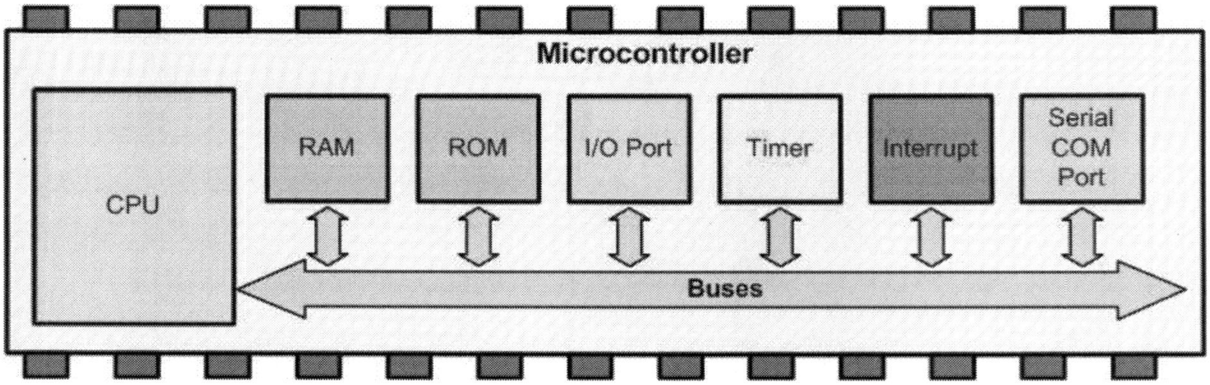

Figure 1- 2: Simplified View of the Internal Parts of Microcontrollers (SOC)

Since the microcontrollers are cheap and small, they are widely used in many devices.

Types of Computers

Typically, computers are categorized into 3 groups: desktop computers, servers, and embedded systems.

Desktop computers, including PCs, tablets, and laptops, are general purpose computers. They can be used to play games, read and edit articles, and do any other task just by running the proper application programs. The desktop computers use microprocessors.

In contrast, embedded systems are special-purpose computers. In embedded system devices, the software application and hardware are embedded together and are designed to do a specific task. For example, the Kindle, digital camera, vacuum cleaner, mp3 player, mouse, keyboard, and printer, are some examples of embedded systems. In most cases embedded systems run a fixed program and contain a microcontroller. It is interesting to note that embedded systems are the largest class of computers though they are not normally considered as computers by the general public.

Servers are the fast computers which might be used as web hosts, database servers, and in any application in which we need to process a huge amount of data such as weather forecasting. Similar to desktop computers, servers are made of microprocessors but, multiple processors are usually used in each server. Both servers and desktop computers are connected to a number of embedded system devices such as mouse, keyboard, disk controller, Flash stick memory and so on.

A Brief History of the Microcontrollers

In the 1980s and 1990s, Intel and Motorola dominated the field of microprocessors and microcontrollers. Intel had the x86 (8088/86, 80286, 80386, 80486, and Pentium). Motorola (now Freescale) had the 68xxx (68000, 68010, 68020, etc.). Many embedded systems used Intel's 32-bit chips of x86 (386, 486, Pentium) and Motorola's 32-bit 68xxx for high-end embedded products such as routers. For example, Cisco routers used 68xxx for the CPU. At the low end, the 8051 from Intel and 68HC11 from Motorola were the dominant 8-bit microcontrollers. With the introduction of PIC from Microchip and AVR from Atmel, they became major players in the 8-bit market for microcontroller. At the time of this writing, PIC and AVR are the leaders in terms of volume for 8-bit microcontrollers. In the late 1990s, the ARM microcontroller started to challenge the dominance of Intel and Motorola in the 32-bit market. Although both Intel and Motorola used RISC features to enhance the performance of their microprocessors, due to the need to maintain compatibility with legacy software, they could not make a clean break and start over. Intel used massive amounts of gates to keep up the performance of x86 architecture and that in turn increased the power consumption of the x86 to a level unacceptable for battery-powered embedded products. Meanwhile Freescale (Motorola) streamlined the instructions of the 68xxx CPU and created a new line of microprocessors called ColdFire, while at the same time worked with IBM to design a new RISC processor called PowerPC. While both PowerPC and Coldfire are still alive and being used in the 32-bit market, it is ARM which has become the leading microcontroller in the 32-bit market.

Currently Available Microcontrollers

There are many microcontrollers available in the market. Some of them are listed in Table 1-1.

32-bit
ARM, AVR32 (Atmel/Microchip), ColdFire (Freescale/NXP), MIPS32, PIC32 (Microchip), PowerPC, TriCore (Infineon), SuperH, RX (Renesas)
16-bit
MSP430 (TI), HCS12 (NXP), PIC24 (Microchip), dsPIC (Microchip), RL78 (Renesas)
8-bit
8051, AVR (Atmel), HCS08 (NXP), PIC16, PIC18

Table 1-1: Some Microcontrollers

Introduction to some 32-bit microcontrollers

x86: The x86 and Pentium processors are based on the 32-bit architecture of the 386. Although both Intel and AMD are pushing the x86 into the embedded market, due to the high power consumption of these chips, the embedded market has not embraced the x86. Intel is working hard to make a low-power version of the 386 called Atom available for the embedded market.

PIC32: It is based on the MIPS architecture and is getting some attention due to the fact it shares some of the peripherals with the PIC24/PIC18 chips and also using the MPLAB for IDE. Microchip hopes the free MPLAB IDE and engineers' knowledge of the 8-bit PIC will attract embedded developers to the PIC32 as they move to 32-bit systems for their high end embedded products.

ColdFire: The NXP (formerly Freescale, Motorola) is based on the venerable 680x0 (68000, 68010) popular in the 1980s and 1990s. They streamlined the 68000 instructions to make it more RISC-type architecture and is the top seller of 32-bit processors from the Freescale. In recent years Freescale revamped and redesigned the 8-bit HCS08 (from the 6808) to share some of the peripherals with ColdFire and are pushing them under the name Flexis. They hope engineers use the HCS08 at the low-end and move to Coldfire for high-end of the embedded products with minimum learning curve.

PowerPC: This was developed jointly by IBM and Freescale. It was used in the Apple Mac for a few years. Then Apple switched to x86 for a while and currently is using ARM in all their products. Nowadays, both Freescale and IBM market the PowerPC for the high-end of the embedded systems.

How to choose a microcontroller

The following two factors can be important in choosing a microcontroller:

- ***Chip characteristics:*** Some of the factors in choosing a microcontroller chip are clock speed, power consumption, price, and on-chip memories and peripherals.
- ***Available resources:*** Other factors in choosing a microcontroller include the IDE compiler, legacy software, and multiple sources of production.

Review Questions

1. True or false. Microcontrollers are normally less expensive than microprocessors.

2. When comparing a system board based on a microcontroller and a general- purpose microprocessor, which one is cheaper?

3. A microcontroller normally has which of the following devices on-chip?

   (a) RAM (b) ROM (c) I/O (d) all of the above

4. A general-purpose microprocessor normally needs which of the following devices to be attached to it?

   (a) RAM (b) ROM (c) I/O (d) all of the above

5. An embedded system is also called a dedicated system. Why?

6. What does the term embedded system mean?

7. Why does having multiple sources of a given product matter?

Section 1.2: The ARM Family History

In this section, we look at the ARM and its history.

A brief history of the ARM

The ARM came out of a company called Acorn Computers in United Kingdom in the 1980s. Professor Steve Furber of Manchester University worked with Sophie Wilson to define the ARM architecture and instructions. The VLSI Technology Corp. produced the first ARM chip in 1985 for Acorn Computers and was designated as Acorn RISC Machine (ARM). Unable to compete with x86 (8088, 80286, 80386, ...) PCs from IBM and other personal computer makers, the Acorn was forced to push the ARM chip into the single-chip microcontroller market for embedded products. That is when Apple Corp. got interested in using the ARM chip for the PDA (personal digital assistants) products. This renewed interest in the chip led to the creation of a new company called ARM (Advanced RISC Machine). This new company bet its entire fortune on selling the rights to this new CPU to other silicon manufacturers and design houses. Since the early 1990s, an ever increasing number of companies have licensed the right to make the ARM chip. See Table 1-2 for the major milestones of the ARM.

Also see *http://www.arm.com/about/company-profile/milestones.php* for the list.

Table 1- 2: ARM Company milestones (www.ARM.com)

1982

- Acorn produced a computer for BBC named BBC micro. Good sales of the computer motivated Acorn to decide to make its own microprocessor.

1983

- Acorn and VLSI began designing the ARM microprocessor.

1985

- Acorn Computer Group developed the world's first commercial RISC processor. The ARMv1 had 25,000 transistors, and worked with a frequency of 4MHz.

1987

- Acorn's ARM processor debuts as the first RISC processor for low-cost PCs

1989

- Acorn introduced ARMv3 with a frequency of 25MHz. It had a 4KB cache as well.

1990

- Advanced RISC Machines (ARM) spins out of Acorn and Apple Computer's collaboration efforts with a charter to create a new microprocessor standard. VLSI Technology becomes an investor and the first licensee.

1991

- ARM introduced its first embeddable RISC core, the ARM6 solution using ARMv3 architecture.

1992

- GEC Plessey and Sharp licensed ARM technology

1993

- Texas Instruments licensed ARM technology
- ARM introduced the ARM7 core.

1995

- ARM announced the Thumb architecture extension, which gives 32-bit RISC performance at 16-bit system cost and offers industry-leading code density

- ARM launched Software Development Toolkit

1996

- ARM and VLSI Technology introduced the ARM810 microprocessor
- ARM and Microsoft worked together to extend Windows CE to the ARM architecture

1997

- Hyundai, Lucent, Philips, Rockwell and Sony licensed ARM technology
- ARM9TDMI family announced

1998

- HP, IBM, Matsushita, Seiko Epson and Qualcomm licensed ARM technology
- ARM developed synthesizable version of the ARM7TDMI core
- ARM Partners shipped more than 50 million ARM-powered products

1999

- LSI Logic, STMicroelectronics and Fujitsu licensed ARM technology
- ARM announced synthesizable ARM9E processor with enhanced signal processing

2000

- Agilent, Altera, Micronas, Mitsubishi, Motorola, Sanyo, Triscend and ZTEIC licensed ARM technology
- ARM launched SecurCore family for smartcards
- TSMC and UMC became members of ARM Foundry Program

2001

- ARM's share of the 32-bit embedded RISC microprocessor market grew to 76.8 per cent
- ARM announced new ARMv6 architecture
- Fujitsu, Global UniChip, Samsung and Zeevo licensed ARM technology
- ARM acquired key technologies and an embedded debug design team from Noral Micrologics Ltd

2002

- ARM announced that it had shipped over one billion of its microprocessor cores to date

- ARM technology licensed to Seagate, Broadcom, Philips, Matsushita, Micrel, eSilicon, Chip Express and ITRI
- ARM launched the ARM11 micro-architecture
- ARM launches its RealView family of development tools
- Flextronics became the first ARM Licensing Partner program member, allowing it to sub-license ARM technology to its own customers

_2004_

- The ARM Cortex family of processors, based on the ARMv7 architecture, is announced. The ARM Cortex-M3 is announced in conjunction, as the first of the new family of processors
- ARM Cortex-M3 processor announced, the first of a new Cortex family of processor cores
- MPCore multiprocessor launched, the first integrated multiprocessor
- OptimoDE technology launched, the groundbreaking embedded signal processing core

_2005_

- ARM acquired Keil Software
- ARM Cortex-A8 processor announced

_2007_

- Five billionth ARM Powered processor shipped to the mobile device market
- ARM Cortex-M1 processor launched – the first ARM processor designed specifically for implementation on FPGAs
- RealView Profiler for Embedded Software Analysis introduced
- ARM unveils Cortex-A9 processors for scalable performance and low-power designs

_2008_

- ARM announces 10 billionth processors shipment
- ARM Mali-200 GPU Worlds First to achieve Khronos Open GL ES 2.0 conformance at 1080p HDTV resolution

_2009_

- ARM announces 2GHz capable Cortex-A9 dual core processor implementation
- ARM launches its smallest, lowest power, most energy efficient processor, Cortex-M0

_2010_

- ARM launches Cortex-M4 processor for high performance digital signal control
- ARM together with key Partners form Linaro to speed rollout of Linux-based devices

- Microsoft becomes an ARM Architecture Licensee
- ARM & TSMC sign long-term agreement to achieve optimized Systems-on-Chip based on ARM processors, extending down to 20nm
- ARM extends performance range of processor offering with the Cortex-A15 MPCore processor
- ARM Mali becomes the most widely licensed embedded GPU architecture
- ARM Mali-T604 Graphics Processing Unit introduced providing industry-leading graphics performance with an energy-efficient profile

2011

- Microsoft unveils Windows on ARM at CES 2011
- IBM and ARM collaborate to provide comprehensive design platforms down to 14nm
- ARM and UMC extend partnership into 28nm
- Cortex-A7 processor launched
- Big-Little processing announced, linking Cortex-A15 and Cortex-A7 processors
- ARMv8 architecture unveiled at TechCon
- AMP announce license and plans for first ARMv8-based processor
- ARM Mali-T658 GPU launched
- ARM expands R&D presence in Taiwan with Hsinchu Design Center
- ARM and Avnet launch Embedded Software Store (ESS)
- ARM, Cadence and TSMC tape out first 20nm Cortex-A15 multicore processor

2012

- ARM, Gemalto and G&D form joint venture to deliver next-generation mobile security
- First Windows RT (Windows on ARM) devices revealed
- ARM, AMD, Imagination, MediaTek and Texas Instruments founding members of Heterogeneous System Architecture (HAS) Foundation
- ARM and TSMC work together on FinFET process technology for next-generation 64-bit ARM processors
- ARM forms first UK forum to create technology blueprint “Internet of Things” devices
- ARM named one of Britain's Top Employers
- MIT Technology Review named ARM in its list of 50 Most Innovative Companies

Currently the ARM Corp. receives its entire revenue from licensing the ARM to other companies since it does not own state of the art chip fabrication facility. This business model of making money from selling IP (intellectual property) has made ARM one of the most widely used CPU architectures in the world. Unlike Intel or Freescale who define the architecture and fabricate the chip, hundreds of companies who have licensed the ARM IP feel a level playing field when it comes to competing with the originator of the chip.

ARM and Apple

When Steve Jobs came back to run the Apple in 1996, the company was in decline. It had lost the personal computer race that had started 20 years earlier. The introduction of iPod in 2001 changed the fortune of that company more than anything else. Apple had tried to sell a PDA called Newton in the 1990s but was not successful. The Newton was using the ARM processor and it was too early for its time. The iPod used an enhanced version of ARM called ARM7 and became an instant success. iPod brought the attention to the ARM chip that it deserved. Since then Apple has been using the ARM chip in iPhones and iPads. Today, the ARM microcontroller is the CPU of choice for designing cell phone and other hand-held devices. In the future, ARM will make further in-roads into the tablet and laptop PC market now that Microsoft Corp has introduced the ARM version of its Windows operating system.

ARM family variations

Although the ARM7 family is the most widely used version, ARM is determined to push the architecture into the low end of the microcontroller market where 8- and 16-bit microcontrollers have been traditionally dominating. For this reason, they have come up with a microcontroller version of ARM called Cortex. As we will see in future chapters, the Cortex family of ARM microcontrollers maintains compatibility with the ARM7 without sacrificing performance. The ARM architecture is also being pushed into high-performance systems where multicore chips such as Intel Xeon dominate.

Figure 1-3 shows some of the most widely used ARM processors. It should be emphasized that we cannot use the terms ARM family and ARM architecture interchangeably. For example, ARM11 family is based on ARMv6 architecture and ARMv7A is the architecture of Cortex-A family.

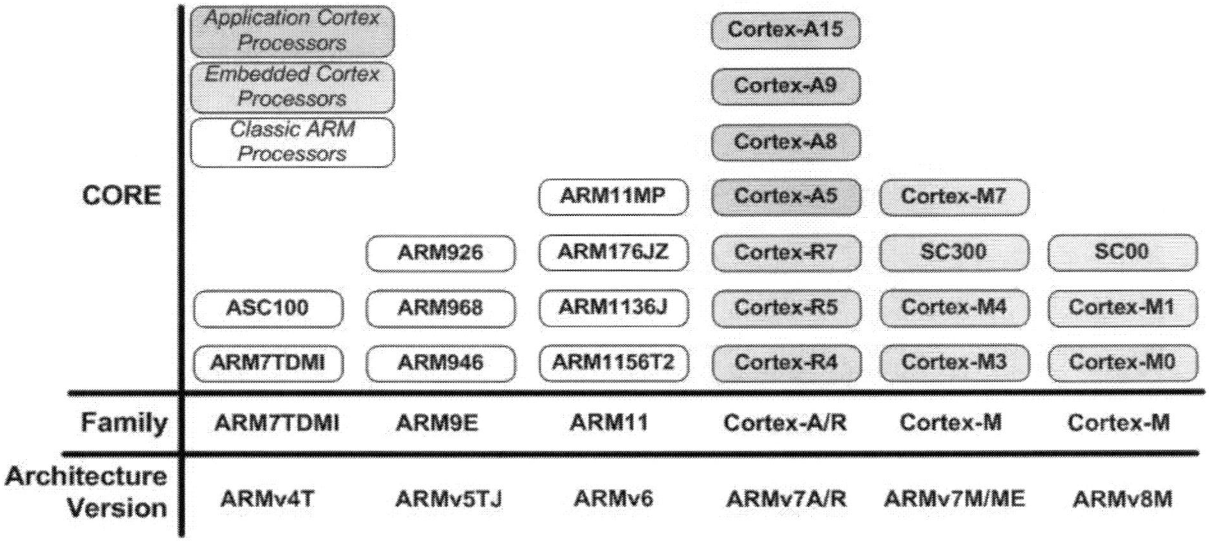

Figure 1- 3: ARM Family and Architecture

One CPU, many peripherals

ARM has defined the details of architecture, registers, instruction set, memory map, and timing of the ARM CPU and holds the copyright to it. The various design houses and semiconductor manufacturers license the IP (intellectual property) for the CPU and can add their own peripherals as they please. It is up to the licensee (design houses and semiconductor manufactures) to define the details of peripherals such as I/O ports, serial port UART, timer, ADC, SPI, DAC, I2C, and so on. As a result, while the CPU instructions and architecture are same across all the ARM chips made by different vendors, their peripherals are not compatible. That means if you write a program for the serial port of an ARM chip made by TI (Texas Instrument), the program might not necessarily run on an ARM chip sold by NXP. This is the only drawback of the ARM microcontroller. The good news is that the manufacturers do provide peripheral libraries or tools for their chips and make the job of programming the peripherals much easier. For example, TI has the TivaWare for Tiva series devices, Freescale (now part of NXP) has Processor Expert, ST Micro has the Cube. Figure 1-4 shows the ARM simplified block diagram and Table 1-3 provides a list of some ARM vendors.

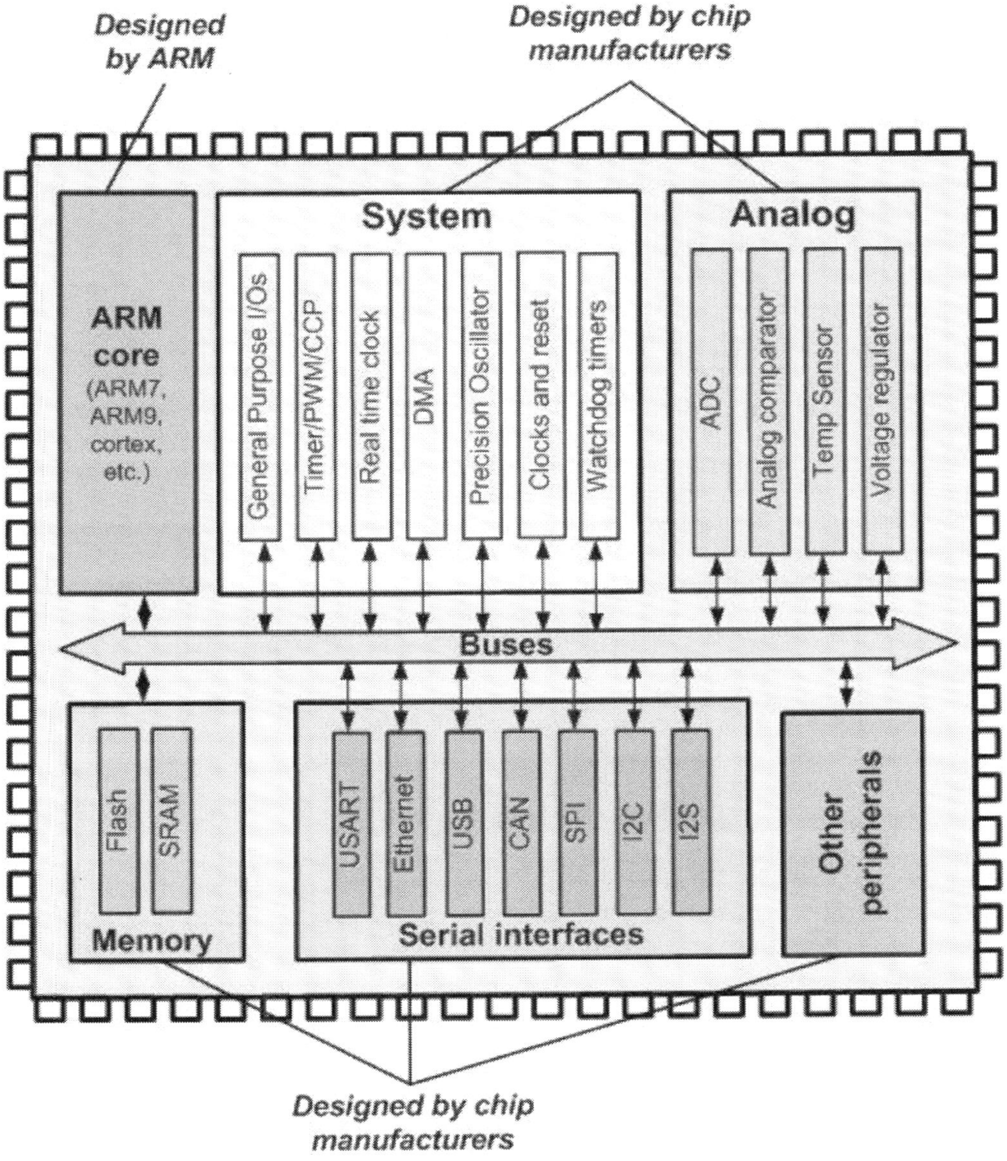

Figure 1- 4: ARM Simplified Block Diagram

Actel	Analog Devices	Atmel
Broadcom	Cypress	Ember
Dust Networks	Energy	Freescale
Fujitso	Nuvoton	NXP
Renesas	Samsung	ST
Toshiba	Texas Instruments	Triad Semiconductor

Table 1- 3: ARM Vendors

Review Questions

1. True or false. The ARM CPU instructions are universal regardless of who makes the chip.
2. True or false. The peripherals of ARM microcontroller are standardized regardless of who makes the chip.
3. An ARM microcontroller normally has which of the following devices on-chip?
   (a) RAM (b) Timer (c) I/O (d) all of the above
4. For which of the followings, ARM has defined standard?

   (a) RAM size (b) ROM size (c) instruction set (d) all of the above

> See the following websites for ARM microcontrollers and ARM trainers:
>
> http://www.ARM.com
>
> https://nicerland.com/

Problems

Section 1.1: Introduction to Microcontrollers

1. True or False. A general-purpose microprocessor has on-chip ROM.
2. True or False. Generally, a microcontroller has on-chip ROM.
3. True or False. A microcontroller has on-chip I/O ports.
4. True or False. A microcontroller has a fixed amount of RAM on the chip.
5. What components are usually put together with the microcontroller onto a single chip?
6. Intel's Pentium chips used in Windows PCs need external ______ and _____ chips to store data and code.
7. List three embedded products attached to a PC.
8. Why would someone want to use an x86 as an embedded processor?
9. Give the name and the manufacturer of some of the most widely used 8-bit microcontrollers.
10. In Question 9, which one has the most manufacture sources?
11. In a battery-based embedded product, what is the most important factor in choosing a microcontroller?

12. In an embedded controller with on-chip ROM, why does the size of the ROM matter?
13. In choosing a microcontroller, how important is it to have multiple sources for that chip?
14. What does the term "third-party support" mean?

Section 1.2: The ARM Family History

15. What does ARM stand for?
16. True or false. In ARM, architectures have the same names as families.
17. True or false. In 1990s, ARM was widely used in microprocessor world.
18. True or false. ARM is widely used in Apple products, like iPhone and iPod.
19. True or false. Currently the Microsoft Windows does not support ARM products.
20. True or false. All ARM chips have standard instructions.
21. True or false. All ARM chips have standard peripherals
22. True or false. The ARM corp. also manufactures the ARM chip.
23. True or false. The ARM IP must be licensed from ARM corp.
24. True or false. A given serial communication program is written for TI ARM chip. It should work without any modification on Freescale ARM chip
25. True or false. A given Assembly language program is written for a given family of ARM Cortex chip. Any other Cortex ARM chip can execute the program.
26. True or false. At the present time, ARM has just one manufacturer.
27. What is the difference between the ARM products of different manufacturers?
28. Name some 32-bit microcontrollers.
29. What is Intel's challenge in decreasing the power consumption of the x86?

Answers to Review Questions

Section 1.1

1. True
2. A microcontroller-based system
3. d
4. d
5. It is dedicated because it does only one type of job.
6. Embedded system means that the application (software) and the processor (hardware such as CPU and memory) are embedded together into a single system.
7. Having multiple sources for a given part means you are not hostage to one supplier. More importantly, competition among suppliers brings about lower cost for that product.

Section 1.2

1. True
2. False
3. d
4. c

Chapter 2: ARM Architecture and Assembly Language Programming

CPUs use registers to store data temporarily and most of the operations involve the registers. To program in assembly language, we must understand the registers of a given CPU and the role they play in processing data. In Section 2.1 we look at the general-purpose registers (GPRs) of the ARM. We demonstrate the use of GPRs with simple instructions such as MOV and ADD. Memory map and memory access of the ARM are discussed in Sections 2.2 and 2.3, respectively. In Section 2.4 we discuss the status register's flag bits and how they are affected by arithmetic instructions. In Section 2.5 we look at some widely used assembly language directives, pseudo-instruction, and data types related to the ARM. In Section 2.6 we examine assembly language and machine language programming and define terms such as mnemonics, opcode, operand, and so on. The process of assembling and creating a ready-to-run program for the ARM is discussed in Section 2.7. Step-by-step execution of an ARM program and the role of the program counter are examined in Section 2.8. Section 2.9 examines some ARM addressing modes. The merits of RISC architecture are examined in Section 2.10. Section 2.11 discusses the Keil IDE.

Section 2.1: The General Purpose Registers in the ARM

ARM microcontrollers have many registers for arithmetic and logic operations. In the CPU, registers are used to store information temporarily. That information could be a piece of data to be processed, or an address pointing to the data to be fetched. All of ARM registers are 32-bit wide. The 32 bits of a register are shown in Figure 2-1. These range from the MSB (most-significant bit) D31 to the LSB (least-significant bit) D0. With a 32-bit data type, any data larger than 32 bits must be broken into 32-bit chunks before it is processed. Although the ARM default data size is 32-bit many assemblers also support the single bit, 8-bit, and 16-bit data types, as we will see in future chapters. The 32-bit data size of the ARM is often referred as "word". In ARM the 16-bit data is referred to as half-word. Therefore, ARM supports byte, half-word (two bytes), and word (four bytes) data types.

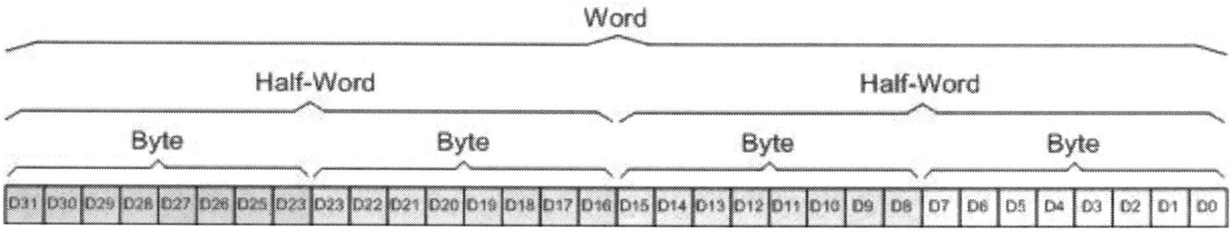

Figure 2- 1: ARM Registers Data Size

In ARM there are 13 general purpose registers. They are R0–R12. See Figure 2-2. All of these registers are 32 bits wide.

The general purpose registers in ARM are the same as the accumulator in other microprocessors. They can be used by all arithmetic and logic instructions. To understand the use of the general purpose registers, we will show it in the context of three simple instructions: MOV, ADD, and SUB. The ARM core has three special function registers of R13, R14, and R15. We will examine their uses in the next section. In some ARM processors, we also have shadow registers in various operating modes designed to speed up the program execution when CPU switches tasks.

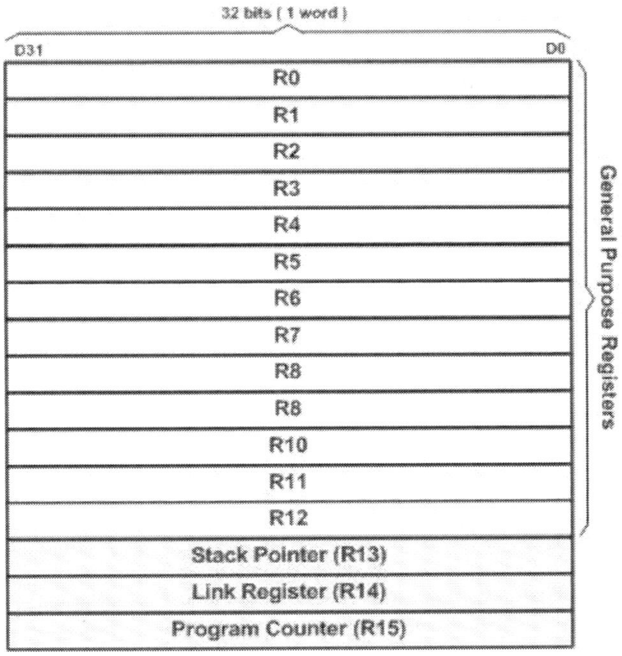

Figure 2- 2: ARM Registers

ARM Instruction Format

The ARM CPU uses the three-part instruction format for most instructions. One of the most common format is:

```
opcode  destination, source1, source2
```

As a RISC machine, ARM instructions operate on the data in the registers with the exception of load and store instructions, which move the data between registers and memory. Depending on the instruction the source2 can be an immediate value. An immediate value is a literal constant that is included as part of the instruction.

MOV instruction

Simply stated, the MOV instruction copies data into register from register to register or from an immediate value. It has the following formats:

```
MOV     Rn, Op2      ; load Rn register with Op2 (Operand2)
                     ; Op2 can be an immediate value
```

Op2 can be a register Rm. Rn or Rm are any of the registers R0 to R15. Op2 can also be an immediate value.

Immediate value is a literal constant encoded in the instruction. In the ARM data processing instructions, the immediate value is an 8-bit value that can be 0–255 in decimal, (00–FF in hex). In addition to the 8-bit value encoded in the instruction, there are four additional bits in the instruction to specify the rotation of the 8-bit value. This will be discussed in Chapter 3.

An immediate value is preceded by a '#' in the instruction.

The following instruction loads R5 with the value of R7.

```
MOV R5, R7          ; copy contents of R7 into R5 (R5 = R7)
```

The following instruction loads the R2 register with a value of 25 (decimal).

```
MOV R2, #25         ; load R2 with 25 (R2 = 25)
```

The following instruction loads the R1 register with the value 0x87 (87 in hex).

```
MOV R1, #0x87       ; copy 0x87 into R1 (R1 = 0x87)
```

Notice the order of the source and destination operands. As you can see, the MOV loads the right operand into the left operand. In other words, the destination register is written first in the instruction.

To write a comment in assembly language we use '; '. It is similar to the use of '//' in C language, which causes the remainder of the line to be ignored by the assembler. For instance, in the above examples the words after '; ' were written to explain the functionality of the instructions to the human reader, and do not have any effects on the execution of the instructions.

When programming the registers of the ARM microcontroller with an immediate value, the following points should be noted:

1. A '#' sign is written in front of an immediate value.
2. If we want to specify an immediate number in hexadecimal, a '0x' is put between '#' and the number, otherwise the number is treated as decimal. For example, in "MOV R1, #50", R1 is loaded with 50 in decimal, whereas in "MOV R1, #0x50", R1 is loaded with 50 in hex (80 in decimal).
3. Eight bits are moved into a 32-bit register after the possible rotation, the remaining 24 bits are loaded with all zeros. For example, in "MOV R1, #0xA5" the result will be R1 = 0x000000A5; that is, R1 = 00000000000000000000000010100101 in binary.
4. If an immediate value cannot be represented by an 8-bit value with even number bits of right rotate, the assembler will flag it as a syntax error.

More on immediate value for MOV instruction

The rules of immediate values discussed so far also apply to the rest of the data processing instructions such as ADD or SUB that comes after this section. For MOV instruction, there are more possibilities to format immediate values.

ADD instruction

The ADD instruction has the following format:

```
ADD   Rd, Rn, Op2 ; ADD Op2 to Rn and store the result in Rd
                  ; Op2 can be immediate value or Register Rm
```

The ADD instruction tells the CPU to add the value of Op2 to Rn and put the result into the Rd (destination) register. As we mentioned before, Op2 can be an immediate value or a register Rm. To add two numbers such as 0x25 and 0x34, one can do any of the following:

```
MOV   R1, #0x25        ; copy 0x25 into R1 (R1 = 0x25)
MOV   R7, #0x34        ; copy 0x34 into R1 (R7 = 0x34)
ADD   R5, R1, R7       ; add value R7 to R1 and put it in R5
                       ; (R5 = R1 + R7)
```

or

```
MOV   R1, #0x25        ; load (copy) 0x25 into R1 (R1 = 0x25)
ADD   R5, R1, #0x34    ; add 0x34 to R1 and put it in R5
                       ; (R5 = R1 + 0x34)
```

Executing the above lines results in R5 = 0x59 (0x59 = 0x25 + 0x34).

SUB instruction

The SUB instruction is like ADD instruction format. It subtracts Op2 from Rn and put the result in Rd (destination).

```
SUB   Rd, Rn, Op2      ; Rd = Rn - Op2
```

To subtract two numbers such as 0x34 and 0x25, one can do the following:

```
MOV   R1, #0x34        ; load 0x34 into R1 (R1 = 0x34)
SUB   R5, R1, #0x25    ; R5 = R1 - 0x25 (R5 = 0x34 - 0x25)
```

The old format

Notice that in most of instructions like ADD and SUB, Rn can be omitted if Rd and Rn are the same. This format is no longer recommended by Unified Assembler Language.

For example, each pair of the following instructions are the same.

```
SUB   R1, R1, #0x25      ; R1=R1-0x25
SUB   R1, #0x25          ; R1=R1-0x25

SUB   R1, R1, R2         ; R1=R1-R2
SUB   R1, R2             ; R1=R1-R2

ADD   R1, R1, #0x25      ; R1=R1+0x25
ADD   R1, #0x25          ; R1=R1+0x25

ADD   R1, R1, R2         ; R1=R1+R2
ADD   R1, R2             ; R1=R1+R2
```

Figure 2-3 shows the general-purpose registers (GPRs) and the ALU in ARM. The effect of arithmetic and logic operations on the status register will be discussed in Section 2.4. In Table 2-1 you see some of the ARM ALU instructions.

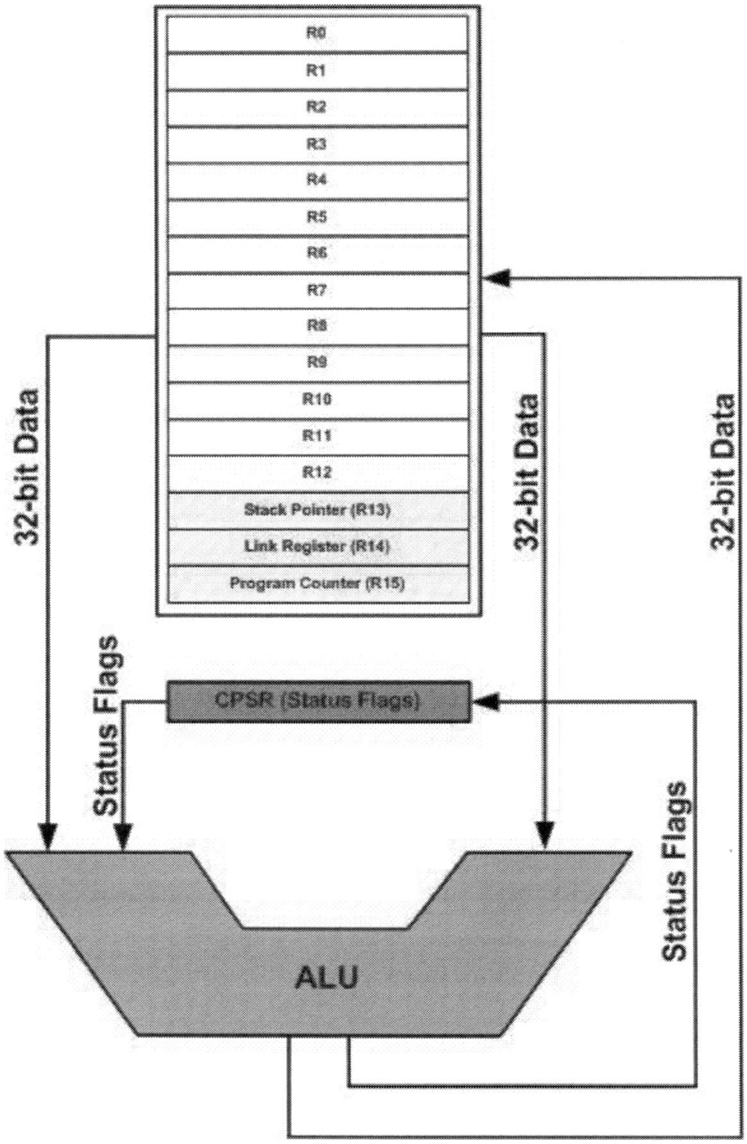

Figure 2- 3: ARM Registers and ALU

Instruction		Description
ADD	**Rd, Rn,Op2***	ADD Rn to Op2 and place the result in Rd
ADC	**Rd, Rn,Op2**	ADD Rn to Op2 with Carry and place the result in Rd
AND	**Rd, Rn,Op2**	AND Rn with Op2 and place the result in Rd
BIC	**Rd, Rn,Op2**	AND Rn with NOT of Op2 and place the result in Rd
CMP	**Rn,Op2**	Compare Rn with Op2 and set the status bits of CPSR**
CMN	**Rn,Op2**	Compare Rn with negative of Op2 and set the status bits
EOR	**Rd, Rn,Op2**	Exclusive OR Rn with Op2 and place the result in Rd
MVN	**Rd,Op2**	Store the negative of Op2 in Rd
MOV	**Rd,Op2**	Move (Copy) Op2 to Rd

ORR	**Rd, Rn,Op2**	OR Rn with Op2 and place the result in Rd
RSB	**Rd, Rn,Op2**	Subtract Rn from Op2 and place the result in Rd
RSC	**Rd, Rn,Op2**	Subtract Rn from Op2 with carry and place the result in Rd
SBC	**Rd, Rn,Op2**	Subtract Op2 from Rn with carry and place the result in Rd
SUB	**Rd, Rn,Op2**	Subtract Op2 from Rn and place the result in Rd
TEQ	**Rn,Op2**	Exclusive-OR Rn with Op2 and set the status bits of CPSR
TST	**Rn,Op2**	AND Rn with Op2 and set the status bits of CPSR
*****	***Op2 can be an immediate 8-bit value #K which can be 0–255 in decimal, (00–FF in hex). Op2 can also be a register Rm. Rd, Rn and Rm are any of the general-purpose registers***	
********	***CPSR is discussed later in this chapter***	
*********	***The instructions are discussed in detail in the next chapters***	

Table 2- 1: ALU Instructions Using GPRs

Review Questions

1. Write instructions to move the value 0x34 into the R2 register.
2. Write instructions to add the values 0x16 and 0xCD. Place the result in the R1 register.
3. True or false. No value can be moved directly into the GPRs.
4. All of the registers in the ARM are _____-bit.

Section 2.2: The ARM Memory Map

In this section we discuss the memory map for ARM family members.

The Special Function Registers in ARM

In ARM the R13, R14, R15, and CPSR (current program status register) registers are called *SFRs (special function registers)* since each one is dedicated to a specific function. The function of each SFR is fixed by the CPU designer at the time of design because it is used for control of the microcontroller or keeping track of specific CPU status. The four SFRs of R13, R14, R15, and CPSR play extremely important roles in the systems with ARM CPU. The R13 is set aside for stack pointer. The R14 is designated as link register which holds the return address when the CPU calls a subroutine and the R15 is the program counter (PC). The PC (program counter) points to the address of the next instruction to be executed as we will see in next section. The CPSR (current program status register) is used for keeping condition flags among other things, as we will see in Section 2.4. In contrast to SFRs, the GPRs (R0-R12) do not have any specific function and are used for storing data or pointer to the memory.

Program Counter in the ARM

One of the most important register in the ARM CPU is the PC (program counter). As we mentioned earlier, the R15 is the program counter. The program counter is used by the CPU to point to the address of the next instruction to be executed. As the CPU fetches the opcode from the program memory, the program counter is incremented automatically to point to the next instruction. The more bits the program counter has, the more memory locations a CPU can access. A 32-bit program counter can access a maximum of 4 gigabytes (2^{32} = 4G) of program memory locations.

The program counter in the ARM family is 32-bit wide. That means ARM CPU can access, a total of 4 gigabytes of locations (memory addresses 0x00000000 to 0xFFFFFFFF). Although these 4 gigabytes of memory space can be allocated to on-chip or off-chip memory; however, at the time of this writing, none of the members of the ARM microcontroller family have the entire 4 gigabytes of on-chip memory populated. See Table 2-2.

Company	Device	Flash (K Bytes)	RAM (K Bytes)	I/O Pins
Atmel	AT91SAM7X512	512	128	62
NXP	LPC2367	512	58	70
ST	STR750FV2	256	16	72
TI	TMS470R1A256	256	12	49
Freescale	MK10DX256VML7	256	64	74

Table 2- 2: On-chip Memory Size for some ARM Chips

Memory space allocation in the ARM

The ARM has 4 gigabytes of directly accessible memory space. This memory space has addresses from 0 to 0xFFFFFFFF. The 4 gigabytes of memory space can be divided into five sections. They are as follows:

1. **On-chip peripheral and I/O registers:** This area is dedicated to registers of peripherals such as timers, serial communication, ADC, and so on. In other words, ARM uses memory-mapped I/O. (See Chapter 0 on the website for discussion of memory-mapped I/O.) The function and address location of each register is fixed by the chip vendor at the time of design. The number of locations set aside for registers depend on the pin numbers and peripheral functions supported by that chip. That number can vary from chip to chip even among members of the same family from the same vendor. Due to the fact that ARM does not define the type and number of I/O peripherals one must not expect to have same address locations for the peripheral registers among various devices.

2. **On-chip data SRAM:** The data RAM space is used for data variables and stack and is accessed by the microcontroller instructions. The ARM microcontrollers' data SRAM size ranges from 2K bytes to several thousand kilobytes depending on the chip. Even within the same family, the size of the data SRAM space varies from chip to chip. Although in many of the ARM microcontrollers embedded systems the SRAM is used only for data; one can also design an ARM-based system in which the RAM is used for both data and program codes. In such systems normally one connects the ARM CPU to external DRAM and the DRAM memory is used for both code and data.

3. **On-chip EEPROM:** A block of memory from 1K bytes to several thousand bytes is set aside for EEPROM memory. The amount and the location of the EEPROM space vary from chip to chip in the ARM microcontrollers. Although in some applications the EEPROM is used for program code storage, it is used most often for saving critical data. Not all ARM chips have on-chip EEPROM.

4. **On-chip Flash ROM:** A block of memory from a few kilobytes to megabytes is set aside for program space. The program space is used to store the program code. In today's ARM microcontroller

chips, the code ROM space is of Flash type memory. The amount and the location of the code ROM space vary from chip to chip in the ARM products. See Table 2-2 and Examples 2-1 and 2-2. The code ROM memory can also be used for storage of static data such as text strings and look-up tables.

Example 2-1

A given ARM chip has the following address assignments. Calculate the space and the amount of memory given to each section.

(a) Address range of 0x00100000 – 0x00100FFF for EEPROM
(b) Address range of 0x40000000 – 0x40007FFF for SRAM
(c) Address range of 0x00000000 – 0x0007FFFF for Flash
(d) Address range of 0xFFFC0000 – 0xFFFFFFFF for peripherals

Solution:

(a) With address space of 0x00100000 to 0x00100FFF, we have 00100FFF – 00100000 + 1 = 1000 bytes. Converting 1000 hex to decimal, we get 4,096, which is equal to 4K bytes.

(b) With address space of 0x40000000 to 0x40007FFF, we have 40007FFF – 40000000 + 1 = 8000 bytes. Converting 8000 hex to decimal, we get 32,768, which is equal to 32K bytes.

(c) With address space of 0x00000000 to 0x0007FFFF, we have 7FFFF – 0 + 1= 80000 bytes. Converting 80000 hex to decimal, we get 524,288, which is equal to 512K bytes.

(d) With address space of 0xFFFC0000 to 0xFFFFFFFF, we have FFFFFFFF–FFFC0000 + 1 = 40000 bytes. Converting 40000 hex to decimal, we get 262,144, which is equal to 256K bytes.

See Figure 2-4.

Example 2-2

Find the address space range of each of the following memory of an ARM chip:

(a) 2 KB of EEPROM starting at address 0x80000000
(b) 16 KB of SRAM starting at address 0x90000000
(c) 64 KB of Flash ROM starting at address 0xF0000000

Solution:

(a) With 2K bytes of on-chip EEPROM memory, we have 2048 bytes (2 × 1024 = 2048). This maps to address locations of 0x80000000 to 0x800007FF.

(b) With 16K bytes of on-chip SRAM memory, we have 16,384 bytes (16 × 1024 = 16,384), and 16,384 locations gives 0x90000000–0x90003FFF.

(c) With 64K we have 65,536 bytes (64 × 1024 = 65,536), therefore, the memory space is 0xF0000000 to 0xF000FFFF.

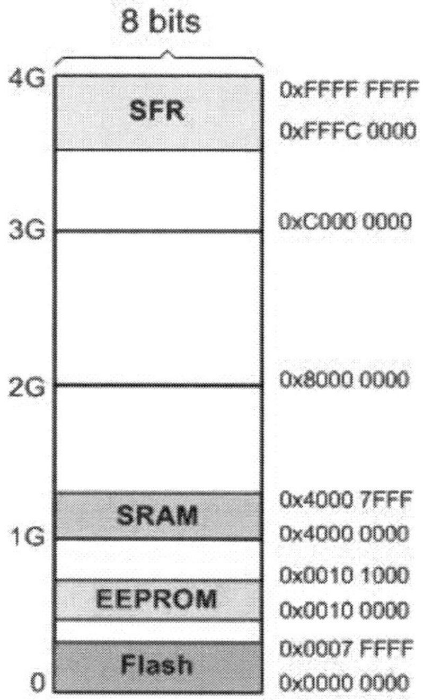

Figure 2- 4: An Example of ARM Memory Allocation

5. **Off-chip DRAM space:** A DRAM memory ranging from few megabytes to several hundred megabytes can be implemented for external memory connection. Many ARM vendors are pushing the ARM11 chip for the high-end of the market such as servers and database computers. In ARM11-based server computers, the external (off-chip) DRAM is used and managed by the operating system while on-chip Flash, EEPROM, and SRAM memories are used for BIOS (basic input output system), POST (power on self-test), and CPU scratch pad, respectively. In such cases the system is not different from x86 computers currently in use, except it uses ARM CPU instead of a Pentium chip from Intel or x86 from AMD. The Microsoft Windows 10 uses ARM motherboard with off-chip DRAM.

Notice the following differences among the on-chip Flash ROM, data SRAM, and EEPROM memories in ARM microcontrollers used for embedded products:

a) The data SRAM is used by the CPU for data variables and stack, whereas the EEPROMs are considered to be memory that one can also add externally to the chip. In other words, while many ARM microcontroller chips have no EEPROM memory, it is very unlikely for an ARM microcontroller to have no on-chip data SRAM.

b) The on-chip Flash ROM is used for program code, while the EEPROM is used most often for critical system data that must not be lost if power is cut off. Remember that data SRAM is volatile memory and its contents are lost if the power to the chip is cut off. Since volatile data SRAM is used for dynamic variables (constantly changing data) and stack. We need EEPROM memory to secure critical system data that does not change very often and will not be lost in the event of power failure.

c) The on-chip Flash ROM is programmed and erased in block size. The block size is 8, 16, 32, or 64 bytes or more depending on the chip technology. That is not the case with EEPROM, since the EEPROM is byte programmable and erasable. Both the EEPROM and Flash memories have limited number of erase/write cycles. While all semiconductor memories have unlimited number of reads (accesses), the number of times that we can erase and write to most of the Flash and EEPROM are limited to around 100,000 times at the time of this writing. Some designs are capable of reaching above 1,000,000 times. We have already seen solid state hard drives used in laptop computers.

Memory mapped I/O in the ARM

Some of the CPU designs had two distinct spaces: the I/O space and memory space. In x86, while all of the I/O ports are accessed using IN and OUT instructions, the memory address space is accessed using the MOV instruction. In the ARM CPU we have only one space and it is memory space and it can be as high as 4 gigabytes. The ARM uses these 4 gigabytes for both memory and I/O space. This mapping of the I/O ports to memory space is called memory mapped I/O and was discussed in Chapter 0 on the website.

Review Questions

1. True or false. The GPR registers are used for storing data and memory addresses.
2. The R0-R12 registers are called______.
3. The GPR registers in ARM are _____-bit.
4. The R13-R15 registers are called _____.
5. The SFR registers in ARM are ______ -bit.

Section 2.3: Load and Store Instructions in ARM

The instructions we have used so far worked with the immediate value and the content of registers. They also used the registers as their destination. We saw simple examples of using MOV, ADD, and SUB earlier in Section 2.1.

The ARM CPU allows direct access to all locations in the memory but they are done with specific instructions. Since these instructions either load the register with data from memory or store the data in the register to the memory, they are called the load/store instructions. This is one of the most important sections in the book for mastering the topic of ARM assembly language programming. Before we embark on studying the load and store instructions of the ARM, we must note the fact that all the instructions of the ARM are 32-bit wide. As we will see in later section, the fixed size instruction is one of the most important characteristics of RISC architecture.

LDR Rd, [Rx] instruction

```
LDR    Rd,[Rx]       ; load Rd with the contents of location pointed
                     ; to by Rx register. Rx contains an address between
                     ; 0x00000000 to 0xFFFFFFFF
```

The LDR instruction tells the CPU to load (read in) one word (32-bit or 4 bytes) of data from a memory location pointed to by Rx to the register Rd. Since each memory location can hold only one byte (ARM is a byte addressable CPU), and the CPU registers are 32-bit wide, the LDR will bring in 4 bytes of data from 4 consecutive memory locations. The locations can be in the SRAM, a Flash memory or I/O registers. For example, the "LDR R2, [R5]" instruction copies the contents of memory locations pointed to by R5 into register R2. Since the R2 register is 32-bit wide, it expects a 32-bit operand in the range of 0x00000000 to 0xFFFFFFFF. That means the R5 register gives the base address of the memory in which it holds the data. Therefore, if R5=0x80000, the CPU will fetch into register R2 the contents of memory locations 0x80000, 0x80001,0x80002, and 0x80003.

The following instruction loads R7 with the contents of location 0x40000200. See Figure 2-5.

```
                     ; assume R5 = 0x40000200
LDR    R7, [R5]      ; load R7 with the contents of memory locations
                     ; 0x40000200-0x40000203
```

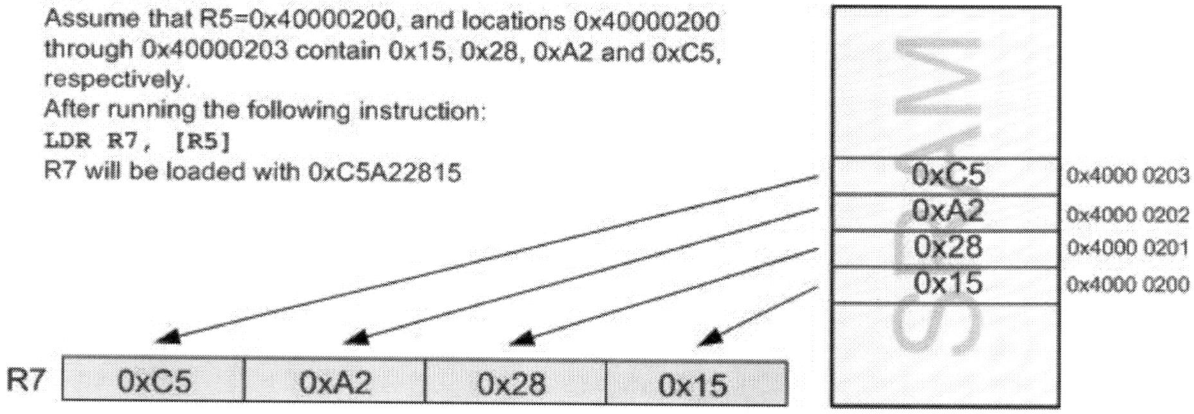

Figure 2-5: Executing the LDR Instruction

STR Rx, [Rd] instruction

```
STR    Rx,[Rd]       ; store register Rx into locations pointed to by Rd
```

The STR instruction tells the CPU to store (copy) the contents of a CPU register to a memory location pointed to by the Rd register. Notice that the source register of STR instruction is placed before the destination register. Obviously since CPU registers are 32-bit wide (4-byte) we need four consecutive memory locations to store the contents of the register. The memory locations must be writable such as SRAM. See Figure 2-6. The "STR R3, [R6]" instruction will copy the contents of R3 into locations pointed to by R6, the locations 0x40000200 through 0x40000203 in the SRAM memory.

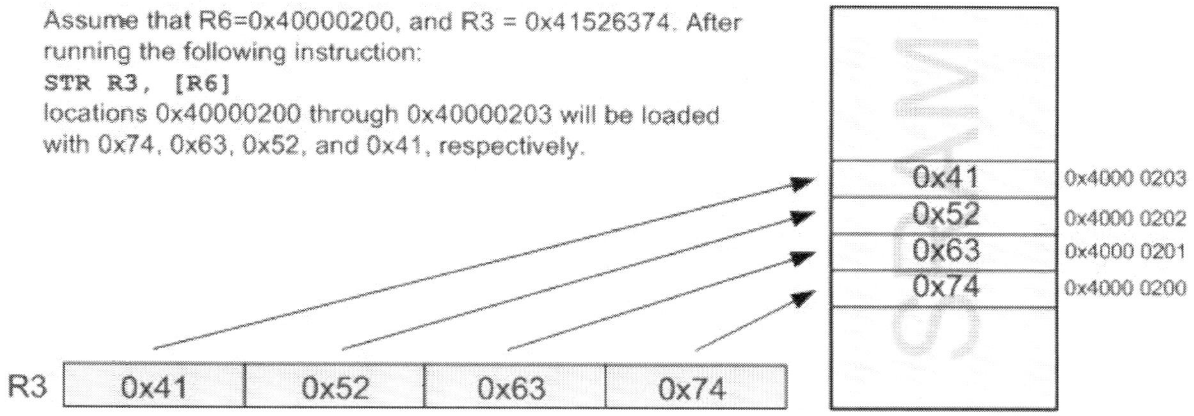

Figure 2-6: Executing the STR Instruction

The following instruction stores the contents of R5 into locations pointed to by R1. Assume 0x40000340 is an address of internal RAM locations and held by register R1.

```
                    ; assume R1 = 0x40000340
STR   R5, [R1]      ; store R5 into locations pointed to by R1.
```

LDRB Rd, [Rx] instruction

The load/store instructions can also operate on smaller data sizes by appending 'B' or 'H' to the opcode.

```
LDRB  Rd, [Rx]      ; load Rd with the contents of the location
                    ; pointed to by Rx register.
```

The LDRB instruction tells the CPU to load (copy) one byte from a memory location pointed to by Rx into the least significant byte of Rd. After this instruction is executed, the least significant byte of Rd will have the same value as the memory location pointed to by Rx. It must be noted that the unused portion (the upper 24 bits) of the Rd register will be filled by all zeros, as shown in Figure 2-7.

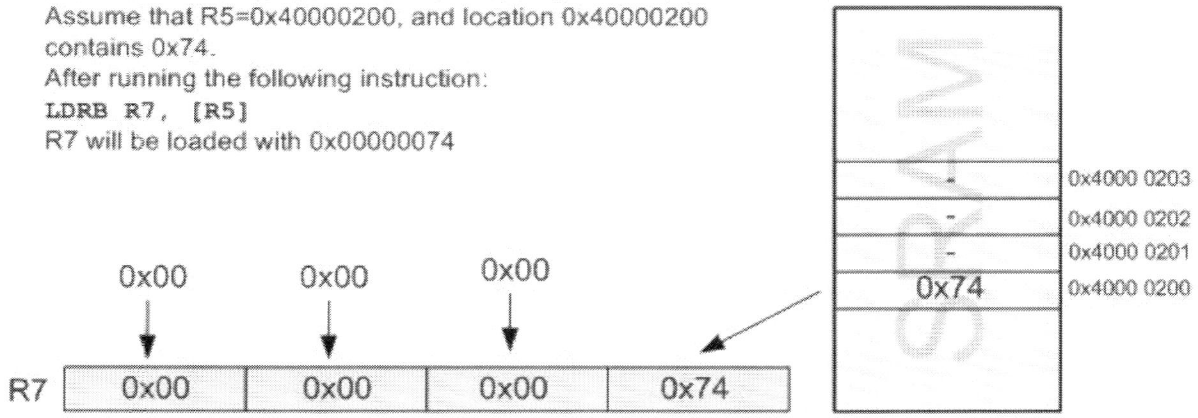

Figure 2- 7: Executing the LDRB Instruction

LDR vs. LDRB

As we mentioned earlier, we can use the LDR instruction to copy the contents of four consecutive memory locations into a 32-bit register. There are situations that we do not need to bring in all 4 bytes of data. An UART register is such a case. The UART registers are generally 8-bit and take only one memory space location (memory mapped I/O). Using LDRB, we can bring into CPU register a single byte of data from UART registers. This is a widely used instruction for accessing the 8-bit peripheral ports.

STRB Rx, [Rd] instruction

```
STRB  Rx, [Rd]     ; store the byte in register Rx into
                   ; memory location pointed to by Rd
```

The STRB instruction tells the CPU to store (copy) the least significant byte of Rx to a memory location pointed to by the Rd register. After this instruction is executed, the memory locations pointed to by the Rd will have the same byte as the lower byte of the Rx, as shown in Figure 2-8.

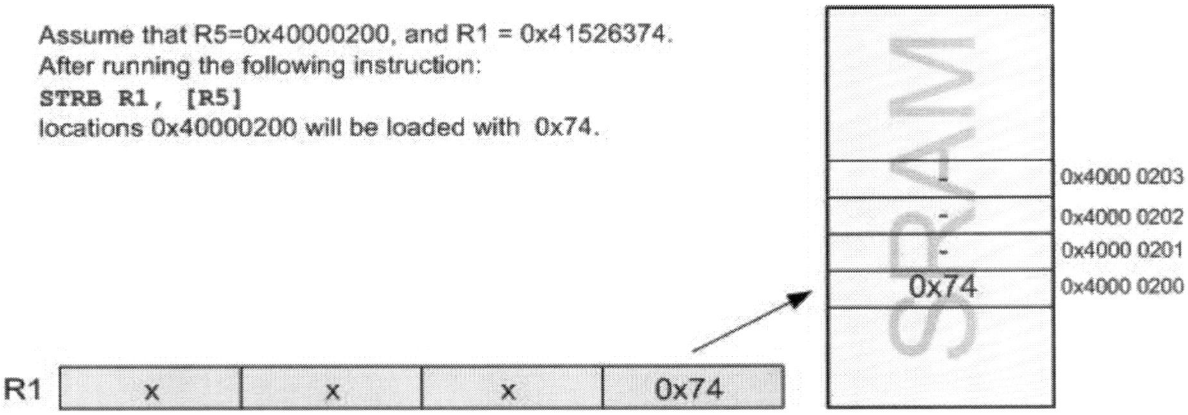

Figure 2- 8: Executing the STRB Instruction

The following program first loads the R1 register with value 0x55, then stores this value into location 0x40000100:

```
                   ; assume R5 = 0x40000100
MOV   R1, #0x55    ; R1 = 0x55 (in hex)
STRB  R1, [R5]     ; copy R1 location pointed to by R5
```

Example 2-3

State the contents of RAM locations 0x92 to 0x96 after the following program is executed:

```
MOV   R1, #0x99    ; R1 = 0x99
MOV   R6, #0x92    ; R6 = 0x92
STRB  R1, [R6]     ; store R1 into location pointed to by R6
                   ; (location 0x92)
ADD   R6, R6, #1   ; R6 = R6 + 1
MOV   R1, #0x85    ; R1 = 0x85
STRB  R1, [R6]     ; store R1 into location pointed to by R6
                   ; (location 0x93)
```

```
ADD   R6, R6, #1  ; R6 = R6 + 1
MOV   R1, #0x3F   ; R1 = 0x3F
STRB  R1, [R6]    ; store R1 into location pointed to by R6

ADD   R6, R6, #1  ; R6 = R6 + 1
MOV   R1, #0x63   ; R1 = 0x63
STRB  R1, [R6]    ; store R1 into location pointed to by R6

ADD   R6, R6, #1  ; R6 = R6 + 1
MOV   R1, #0x12   ; R1 = 0x12
STRB  R1, [R6]
```

Solution:

After the execution of STRB R1, [R6] data memory location 0x92 has value 0x99.
After the execution of STRB R1, [R6] data memory location 0x93 has value 0x85.
After the execution of STRB R1, [R6] data memory location 0x94 has value 0x3F; and so on, as shown in the chart.

Address	Data
0x92	0x99
0x93	0x85
0x94	0x3F
0x95	0x63
0x96	0x12

Example 2-4

State the contents of R2, R1, and memory location 0x20 after the following program:

```
MOV   R2, #0x5    ; load R2 with 5  (R2 = 0x05)
MOV   R1, #0x2    ; load R1 with 2 (R1 = 0x02)
ADD   R2, R1, R2  ; R2 = R1 + R2
ADD   R2, R1, R2  ; R2 = R1 + R2
MOV   R5, #0x20   ; R5 = 0x20
STRB  R2, [R5]    ; store R2 into location pointed to by R5
```

Solution:

The program loads R2 with value 5. Then it loads R1 with value 2. Then it adds the R1 register to R2 twice. At the end, it stores the result in location 0x20 of memory.

After MOV R2, #0x05

Location	Data
R2	5
R1	
0x20	

After MOV R1, #0x02

Location	Data
R2	5
R1	2
0x20	

After ADD R2, R1, R2

Location	Data
R2	7
R1	2
0x20	

After ADD R2, R1, R2

Location	Data
R2	9
R1	2
0x20	

After STRB [R5], R2

Location	Data
R2	9
R1	2
0x20	9

STR vs. STRB

As we mentioned earlier, we can use the STR instruction to copy the content of a 32-bit register into four consecutive memory locations. Some of the peripheral registers are 8-bit and take only one memory space location (memory mapped I/O). Using STRB, we can send a byte of data from register to memory location such as a peripheral register. Again, this is a widely used instruction for accessing the 8-bit peripheral registers.

LDRH Rd, [Rx] instruction

```
LDRH  Rd, [Rx]      ; load Rd with the half-word pointed
                    ; to by Rx register
```

The LDRH instruction tells the CPU to load (copy) half-word (16-bit or 2 bytes) from a memory location pointed to by Rx into the lower 16-bits of Rd Register. After this instruction is executed, the lower 16-bit of Rd will have the same value as two consecutive locations in the memory pointed to by base address of Rx. It must be noted that the unused portion (the upper 16 bits) of the Rd register will be filled with all zeros, as shown in Figure 2-9.

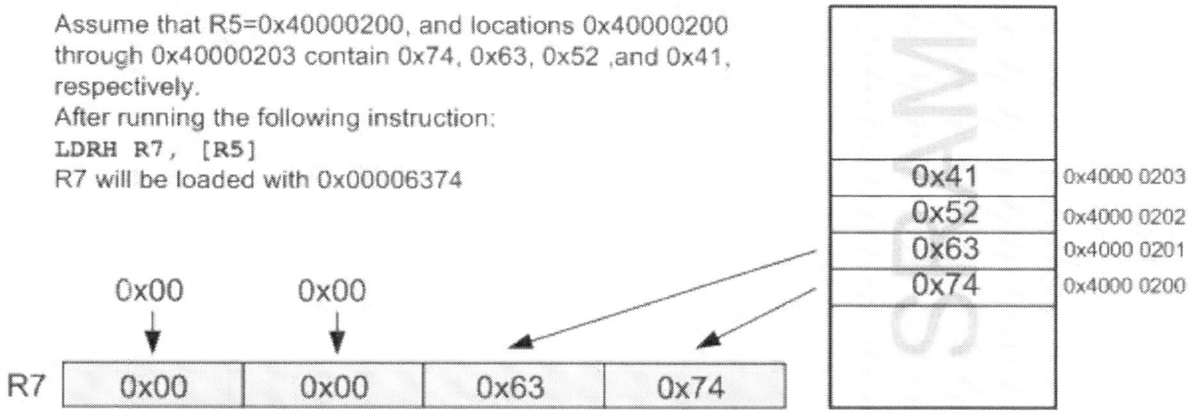

Figure 2- 9: Executing the LDRH Instruction

Table 2-3 compares LDRB, LDRH, and LDR.

Data Size	Bits	Decimal	Hexadecimal	Load instruction used
Byte	8	0 – 255	0 - 0xFF	LDRB
Half-word	16	0 – 65535	0 - 0xFFFF	LDRH
Word	32	$0 - 2^{32}-1$	0 - 0xFFFFFFFF	LDR

Table 2- 3: Unsigned Data Range in ARM and associated Load Instructions

STRH Rx,[Rd] instruction

```
STRH  Rx, [Rd]      ; store half-word (2-byte) in register Rx
                    ; into locations pointed to by Rd
```

The STRH instruction tells the CPU to store (copy) the lower 16-bit contents of the Rx to an address location pointed to by the Rd register. After this instruction is executed, the memory locations pointed to by the Rd will have the same value as the lower 16-bit of Rx Register. The locations are part of the data read/write memory space such as on-chip SRAM. For example, the "STRH R3,[R6]" instruction will copy the 16-bit lower contents of R3 into two consecutive locations pointed to by base register R6. As you can see in Figure 2-10, locations 0x2000 and 0x2001 of the SRAM memory will have the contents of the lower half word of R3 since R6 = 0x2000.

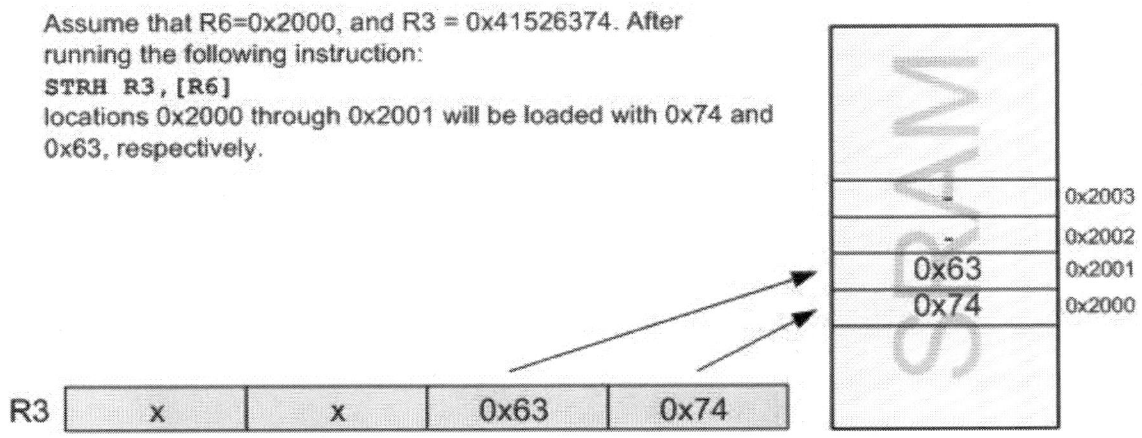

Figure 2- 10: Executing the STRH Instruction

In Table 2-4 you see a comparison between STRB, STRH, and STR.

Data Size	Bits	Decimal	Hexadecimal	Load instruction used
Byte	8	0 – 255	0 - 0xFF	STRB
Half-word	16	0 – 65535	0 - 0xFFFF	STRH
Word	32	$0 - 2^{32}$-1	0 - 0xFFFFFFFF	STR

Table 2-4: Unsigned Data Range in ARM and associated Store Instructions

Review Questions

1. True or false. You can't store an immediate value directly into a memory location.
2. Write instructions to store byte value 0x95 into memory location with address 0x20.
3. Write instructions to store the content of R2 to memory location pointed to by R8.
4. Write instructions to load values from memory locations 0x20–0x23 into R4 register.
5. What is the largest hex value that can be stored in a single byte location in the data memory? What is the decimal equivalent of this value?
6. "LDR R6, [R3]" puts the result in _____.
7. What does "STRB R1, [R2]" do?
8. What is the largest hex value that can be moved into four consecutive locations in the data memory? What is the decimal equivalent of this value?

Section 2.4: ARM CPSR (Current Program Status Register)

Like all other microprocessors, the ARM has a flag register to indicate arithmetic conditions such as the carry bit. The flag register in the ARM is called the *current program status register (CPSR)*. In this section, we discuss various bits of this register and provide some examples of how it is altered. Chapters 3 and 4 show how the flag bits of the status register are used.

ARM current program status register

The status register is a 32-bit register. See Figure 2-11 for the bits of the status register. The bits N, Z, C, and V are called conditional flags, meaning that they indicate some conditions that resulted after an instruction is executed. Each of the conditional flags or the combinations of them can be used to perform a conditional execution, as we will see in Chapter 4.

D31	D30	D29	D28	....	D7	D6	D5	D4	D3	D2	D1	D0
N	Z	C	V	Reserved	I	F	T	M4	M3	M2	M1	M0

Figure 2- 11: CPSR (Current Program Status Register)

The following is a brief explanation of the flag bits of the current program status register (CPSR). The impact of instructions on this register is then discussed.

N, the negative flag

Binary representation of signed numbers uses D31 as the sign bit. The negative flag reflects the result of an arithmetic operation. If the D31 bit of the result is zero, then N = 0 and the result is positive. If the D31 bit is one, then N = 1 and the result is negative. The negative and V flag bits are used for the signed number arithmetic operations and are discussed in Chapter 5.

Z, the zero flag

The zero flag reflects the result of an arithmetic or logic operation. If the result is zero, then Z = 1. Therefore, Z = 0 if the result is not zero. See Chapter 4 to see how we use the Z flag for looping.

C, the carry flag

This flag is set whenever there is a carry out from the D31 bit. This flag bit is affected after a 32-bit addition or subtraction. Chapter 4 shows how the carry flag is used.

V, the overflow flag

This flag is set whenever the result of a signed number operation is too large, causing the high-order bit to overflow into the sign bit. In general, the carry flag is used to detect errors in unsigned arithmetic operations while the overflow flag is used to detect errors in signed arithmetic operations. The C and V flag bits are used for signed number arithmetic operations and are discussed in Chapter 5.

The T flag bit is used to indicate the ARM is in Thumb state. We will discuss this in Chapter 8. The I and F flags are used to enable or disable the interrupt. See the ARM manual.

S suffix and the status register

Most of ARM data processing instructions generate the status flags according to the result. But by default, the status flags of CPSR are not updated. If we need an instruction to update the value of status bits in CPSR, we have to put the 'S' suffix at the end of the opcode. That means, for example, ADDS instead of ADD is used.

ADD instruction and the status register

Next we examine the impact of the SUBS and ADDS instructions on the flag bits C and Z of the status register. Some examples should clarify their meanings. Although all the flag bits C, Z, V, and N are affected by the ADDS and SUBS instruction, we will focus on flags C and Z for now. The other flag bits are discussed in Chapter 5, because they relate only to signed number operations. Examine Example 2-5 to see the impact of the ADDS instruction on selected flag bits. See also Example 2-6 to see the impact of the SUBS instruction on selected flag bits.

Example 2-5

Show the status of the C and Z flags after the addition of

a) 0x0000009C and 0xFFFFFF64 in the following instruction:

```
; assume R1 = 0x0000009C and R2 = 0xFFFFFF64
ADDS   R2, R1, R2     ; add R1 to R2 and place the result in R2
```

b) 0x0000009C and 0xFFFFFF69 in the following instruction:

```
; assume R1 = 0x0000009C and R2 = 0xFFFFFF69
ADDS   R2, R1, R2     ; add R1 to R2 and place the result in R2
```

Solution:

a)

```
    0x0000009C         0000 0000 0000 0000 0000 0000 1001 1100
+   0xFFFFFF64     +   1111 1111 1111 1111 1111 1111 0110 0100
   0x100000000       1 0000 0000 0000 0000 0000 0000 0000 0000
```

C = 1 because there is a carry beyond the D31 bit.

Z = 1 because the R2 (the result) has value 0 in it after the addition.

b)

```
    0x0000009C         0000 0000 0000 0000 0000 0000 1001 1100
+   0xFFFFFF69     +   1111 1111 1111 1111 1111 1111 0110 1001
   0x100000005       1 0000 0000 0000 0000 0000 0000 0000 0101
```

C = 1 because there is a carry beyond the D31 bit.

Z = 0 because the R2 (the result) does not have value 0 in it after the addition. (R2=0x00000005)

Example 2-6

Show the status of the Z flag during the execution of the following program:

```
MOV   R2, #4            ; R2 = 4
MOV   R3, #2            ; R3 = 2
MOV   R4, #4            ; R4 = 4
SUBS  R5, R2, R3        ; R5 = R2 - R3 (R5 = 4 - 2 = 2)
SUBS  R5, R2, R4        ; R5 = R2 - R4 (R5 = 4 - 4 = 0)
```

Solution:

The Z flag is raised when the result is zero. Otherwise, it is cleared (zero). Thus:

After	Value of R5	Z flag
SUBS R5,R2,R3	2	0
SUBS R5,R2,R4	0	1

Not all instructions affect the flags

Some instructions affect all the four flag bits C, Z, V, and N (e.g. ADDS). But some instructions affect no flag bits at all. The branch instructions are in this category. Some instructions affect only some of the flag bits. The logic instructions (e.g. ANDS) are in this category. In general, only data processing instructions affect the status flags.

Table 2-5 shows the instructions and the flag bits affected by them. Appendix A provides a complete list of all the instructions and their associated flag bits.

Instruction	Flags Affected
ANDS	C, Z, N
ORRS	C, Z, N
MOVS	C, Z, N
ADDS	C, Z, N, V
SUBS	C, Z, N, V
B	No flags
Note that we cannot put S after B instruction.	

Table 2- 5: Flag Bits Affected by Different Instructions

Flag bits and decision making

Most of the ARM instructions may be executed conditionally based on the status of the flag bits in CPSR. To make an instruction conditionally executed, the desired condition code is added to the opcode as the postfix. The conditional branch instructions are commonly used. Table 2-6 shows some of the conditional branch instructions. Chapter 4 discusses the conditional branch instructions and how they are used.

Instruction	Flags Affecting the branch
BCS	Branch if C = 1
BCC	Branch if C = 0
BEQ	Branch if Z = 1
BNE	Branch if Z = 0
BMI	Branch if N = 1
BPL	Branch if N = 0
BVS	Branch if V = 1
BVC	Branch if V = 0

Table 2- 6: ARM Branch (Jump) Instructions Using Flag Bits

Review Questions

1. The register holding the status flags in the ARM CPU is called the ________.

2. What is the size of the status register in the ARM?

3. Find the C and Z flag bits for the following code:

```
; assume R2 = 0xFFFFFF9F
; assume R1 = 0x00000061
ADDS  R2, R1, R2
```

4. Find the Z flag bit for the following code:

```
; assume R7 = 0x22
; assume R3 = 0x22
ADDS  R7, R3, R7
```

5. Find the C and Z flag bits for the following code:

```
; assume R2 = 0x67
; assume R1 = 0x99
ADDS  R2, R1, R2
```

Section 2.5: ARM Data Format, Pseudo-instructions and Directives

In this section we look at some commonly used data formats, pseudo-instructions, and directives supported by the ARM assembler.

ARM data type

ARM has four data types. They are bit, byte (8-bit), half-word (16-bit) and word (32 bit). Due to the fact that ARM registers are 32-bit it is the job of programmer/compiler to break down data larger than 32 bits to be processed by the CPU. The data types used by the ARM can be signed or unsigned. A discussion of signed numbers is given in Chapter 5.

Data format representation

There are several ways to represent literal data in the ARM assembly source code. The numbers can be in hex, binary, decimal, ASCII or other formats. The following are examples of how each works using Keil ARM Assembler.

Hexadecimal numbers

To represent Hex numbers in Keil ARM assembler we put 0x (or 0X) in front of the number like this:

```
MOV   R1, #0x99
```

Here are a few lines of code that use the hex format:

```
MOV   R2, #0x75        ; R2 = 0x75
ADD   R1, R2, #0x11    ; R2 = R2 + 0x11
```

Decimal numbers

To indicate decimal numbers in some ARM assemblers such as Keil we simply use the decimal (e.g., 12) and nothing before or after it. Here are some examples of how to use it:

```
MOV   R7, #12      ; R7 = 00001100 or 0C in hex
MOV   R1, #32      ; R1 = 32 = 0x20
```

Binary numbers

To represent binary numbers in Keil ARM Assembler we put 2_ in front of the number. It is as follows:

```
MOV    R6, #2_10011001   ; R6 = 10011001 in binary or 99 in hex
```

Numbers in any base between 2 and 9

To indicate a number in any base n between 2 and 9 in Keil ARM Assembler we simply use the n_ in front of it. Here are some examples of how to use it:

```
MOV    R7, #8_33    ; R7 = 33 in base 8 or 011011 in binary format
MOV    R6, #2_10011001   ; R6 = 10011001 in base 2 or 99 in hex
```

ASCII characters

To represent ASCII data in Keil ARM Assembler we use single quotes as follows:

```
LDR    R3, #'2'    ; R3 = 00110010 or 32 in hex (See Appendix F)
```

This is the same as other assemblers such as the 8051 and x86. Here is another example:

```
LDR    R2, #'9'    ; R2 = 0x39, which is hex number for ASCII '9'
```

To represent a string, double quotes are used; and for defining ASCII strings (more than one character), we use the DCB directive which will be discussed next.

Pseudo-instructions

We saw earlier in this chapter the limitation of loading a literal value into a register using MOV instruction with immediate value. Yet, loading a 32-bit literal value in a register is used often in the program. There are ways that allow the loading of 32-bit literal values but writing the code is tedious. The ARM assembler provides two pseudo-instructions to help ease the task. Although these are called pseudo-instructions, they are converted to real ARM instructions by the assembler. We will mention the formats and the usages here and defer the discussion of the details later.

LDR pseudo-instruction

We stated loading a register with MOV immediate value is limited to an 8-bit value or an even-bit rotation of an 8-bit value. So the valid immediate values are limited. What do we do if we need to load a value that is not a legal immediate value of the MOV instruction? The ARM assembler provides us a pseudo-instruction of "LDR Rd, *=32-bit_immediate_value*" to load any 32-bit value into a register. We will examine how this pseudo-instruction works in Chapter 6. For now, just notice the '=' sign used in the syntax. The following pseudo-instruction loads R7 with 0x11223344.

```
LDR    R7, =0x11223344
```

We will use this pseudo-instruction to load 32-bit value into register extensively throughout the book. Some assembler such as Keil ARM Assembler, will replace the LDR pseudo-instruction with a MOV instruction if the immediate value fits a MOV instruction.

ADR pseudo-instruction

To load registers with the addresses of memory locations we can also use the ADR pseudo-instruction. ADR has the following syntax:

```
ADR     Rn, label
```

Assembler directives

While instructions tell the CPU what to do, directives give directions to the assembler. For example, the MOV and ADD instructions are commands to the CPU, but EQU, END, and ENTRY are directives to the assembler. The following section presents some often used directives of the ARM and how they are used. The directives help us develop our program easier and make our program legible (more readable). Table 2-7 shows some assembler directives.

Directive	Description
AREA	Instructs the assembler to assemble a new code or data section
END	Informs the assembler that it has reached the end of a source code.
EQU	Associate a symbolic name to a numeric constant.
INCLUDE	It adds the contents of a file to the current program.

Table 2- 7: Some Widely Used ARM Directive

> **Note**
>
> Traditionally, pseudo-instruction and directive are treated as synonyms. But with ARM, the pseudo-instructions are translated to real instructions for CPU while directives are not.

AREA

The AREA directive tells the assembler to define a new section of memory. The memory can be code (instructions) or data and can have attributes such as READONLY, READWRITE, and so on. This is used to define one or more blocks of indivisible memory for code or data to be used by the linker. Every assembly language program has at least one AREA. The following is the format:

```
AREA        sectionname, attribute, attribute, ...
```

The following line defines a new area named MY_ASM_PROG1 which has CODE and READONLY attributes:

```
AREA  MY_ASM_PROG1, CODE, READONLY
```

Among commonly used attributes are CODE, DATA, READONLY, READWRITE, and ALIGN. The following paragraphs describe them in more details.

READONLY is an attribute given to an area of memory which can only be read from. Since it is READONLY section of the program it is by default for CODE. In ARM assembly language we use this area to write our instructions for machine code execution. All the READONLY sections of the same program are put next to each other in the flash memory by the linker.

READWRITE is an attribute given to an area of memory which can be read from and written to. Since it is READWRITE section of the program it is by default for DATA. In ARM assembly language we use this area to set aside SRAM memory for variables and stack. The linker puts all the READWRITE sections of the same program next to each other in the SRAM memory.

> **Note**
>
> In Keil, the memory space of **READONLY** and **READWRITE** are defined in the ***Target*** tabs of the **Project-Options**. Keil project wizard sets the default values according to the memory map of the chosen device.

CODE is an attribute given to an area of memory used for executable machine instructions. Since it is used for code section of the program it is by default READONLY memory. In ARM assembly language we use this area to write our instructions. The following line defines a new area for writing programs:

```
AREA  OUR_ASM_PROG, CODE, READONLY
```

DATA is an attribute given to an area of memory used for data and no instructions (machine instructions) can be placed in this area. Since it is used for data section of the program it is by default a

READWRITE memory. In ARM assembly language we use this area to set aside SRAM memory for variables and stack. The following line defines a new area for defining variables:

```
AREA   OUR_VARIABLES, DATA, READWRITE
```

To define constant values in the flash memory we write the following:

```
AREA   OUR_CONSTS, DATA, READONLY
```

ALIGN is another attribute given to an area of memory to indicate how memory should be allocated according to the addresses. When the ALIGN is used for CODE and READONLY, it is aligned in 4-bytes address boundary by default since the ARM instructions are all 32-bit (4-bytes) word. The ALIGN attribute of AREA has a number after like ALIGN=3 which indicates the information should be placed in memory with addresses of 2^3, that is 0x50000, 0x50008, 0x50010, 0x50018, and so on. The usage and importance of ALIGN attribute is discussed in Chapter 6.

END

Another important pseudocode is the END directive. This indicates to the assembler the end of the source code (not the file). The END directive is the last line of the ARM assembly program, meaning that anything after the END directive in the source file is ignored by the assembler. Program 2-1 shows how the AREA and END directives are used.

Program 2-1

```
; ARM Assembly Language Program to Add Some Data and Store the SUM in R3.

       AREA    PROG_2_1, CODE, READONLY
       MOV    R1, #0x25     ; R1 = 0x25
       MOV    R2, #0x34     ; R2 = 0x34
       ADD    R3, R2, R1    ; R3 = R2 + R1
HERE   B      HERE          ; stay here forever
       END
```

EQU (equate)

This is used to define a constant value or a fixed address by a name to make the program easier to read. The EQU directive does not set aside storage for a data item in the program, it merely associates an identifier with the constant value. The following code uses EQU for the counter constant, and then the constant is used to load the R2 register:

```
COUNT         EQU    0x25
       ...    ...    ....
       MOV    R2, #COUNT   ; R2 = 0x25
```

The assembler remembers the association between the word "COUNT" and the value 0x25 when it encounters the line with EQU. When it assembles the line with #COUNT, it replaces COUNT by the value

0x25. So the instruction "MOV R2, #COUNT" is converted to "MOV R2, #0x25". When executing the above instruction "MOV R2, #COUNT", the register R2 will be loaded with the value 0x25.

What are the advantages of using EQU? First, as we mentioned earlier, it enhances the readability. The meaning is more obvious in the word "COUNT" than the value "0x25." Furthermore, if a constant is used multiple times throughout the program, and the programmer wants to change its value everywhere. By the use of EQU, the programmer can change it once and the assembler will change all of its occurrences in the program. This allows the programmer to avoid searching the entire program trying to find and change every occurrence which is tedious and error prong.

Using EQU for fixed data assignment

To get more practice using EQU to assign constant values, examine the following:

```
DATA1 EQU   0x39          ; the way to define hex value
DATA2 EQU   2_00110101    ; the way to define binary value (35 in hex)
DATA3 EQU   39            ; decimal numbers (27 in hex)
DATA4 EQU   '2'           ; ASCII characters
```

Using EQU for special register address assignment

EQU is also used to assign special function register (including peripheral registers) addresses to more readable names. This is so widely used, many manufacturers supply files with all the registers defined for the devices they make.

Examine the following code:

```
FIO2SET0    EQU    0x3FFFC058   ; PORT2 output set register 0 address
      MOV   R6, #0x01           ; R6 = 0x01
      LDR   R2, =FIO2SET0       ; R2 = 0x3FFFC058
      STRB  R6, [R2]            ; Write 0x01 to FIO2SET0
```

Each identifier may only be used by EQU once. If you try to use EQU to assign a name with a new value, an assembler error occurs.

Using EQU for RAM address assignment

Another usage of EQU is for the address assignment of the internal SRAM. It is exactly like using EQU for special function register address assignment. Examine the following code:

```
SUM   EQU   0x40000120          ; assign RAM location to SUM
      MOV   R2, #5              ; load R2 with 5
      MOV   R1, #2              ; load R1 with 2
      ADD   R2, R2, R1          ; R2 = R2 + R1
      LDR   R3, =SUM            ; load R3 with 0x40000120
      STRB  R2, [R3]            ; store the result SUM
```

With the new software development toolchains that usually use linker to assign memory location in RAM, this is rarely used because of possible assignment conflicts. To define RAM location, SPACE directive is preferred. We will discuss SPACE directive shortly in this section.

RN (equate)

"RN" is used to give a CPU register a name. We have seen the built-in naming of the registers such as naming R13 SP, R14 LR and R15 PC. The RN directive allows the programmer to associate a register with a name. It improves the readability of the code. Program 2-2 shows how we RN to name register R1, R2, and R3. Unlike EQU, each register may be renamed by RN as many times as needed.

Program 2-2: An ARM Assembly Language Program Using RN Directive

```
        ; ARM Assembly Language Program to Add Some Data
        ; and store the SUM in R3.

VAL1    RN      R1      ; define VAL1 as a name for R1
VAL2    RN      R2      ; define VAL2 as a name for R2
SUM     RN      R3      ; define SUM as a name for R3

        AREA            PROG_2_2, CODE, READONLY

        MOV     VAL1, #0x25         ; R1 = 0x25
        MOV     VAL2, #0x34         ; R2 = 0x34
        ADD     SUM, VAL1, VAL2     ; R3 = R2 + R1
HERE    B       HERE
        END
```

INCLUDE directive

The INCLUDE directive tells the ARM assembler to read in the content of a file to the current program file (like the #include directive in C language).

Assembler data allocation directives

In most assembly languages there are some directives to allocate memory and initialize its value. In ARM assembly language DCB, DCD, and DCW allocate memory and initialize them. The SPACE directive allocates memory without initializing it.

DCB directive (define constant byte)

The DCB directive allocates a byte size memory and initializes their values.

```
MYVALUE     DCB    5                   ; MYVALUE = 5
MYMSAGE     DCB    "HELLO WORLD"       ; ASCII string
```

Each alphanumeric letter in a string is converted to its ASCII encoding value.

DCW directive (define constant half-word)

The DCW directive allocates a half-word size memory and initializes the values.

```
MYDATA      DCW    0x20, 0xF230, 5000, 0x9CD7
```

DCD directive (define constant word)

The DCD directive allocates a word size memory and initializes the values.

```
MYDATA      DCD   0x200000, 0x30F5, 5000000, 0xFFFF9CD7
```

See Tables 2-8 and 2-9.

Directive	Description
DCB	Allocates one or more bytes of memory, and defines the initial runtime contents of the memory
DCW	Allocates one or more halfwords of memory, aligned on two-byte boundaries, and defines the initial runtime contents of the memory.
DCWU	Allocates one or more halfwords of memory, and defines the initial runtime contents of the memory. The data is not aligned.
DCD	Allocates one or more words of memory, aligned on four-byte boundaries, and defines the initial runtime contents of the memory.
DCDU	Allocates one or more words of memory and defines the initial runtime contents of the memory. The data is not aligned.

Table 2- 8: Some Widely Used ARM Memory Allocation Directives

Data Size	Bits	Decimal	Hexadecimal	Directive	Instruction
Byte	8	0 – 255	0 - 0xFF	DCB	STRB/LDRB
Half-word	16	0 – 65535	0 - 0xFFFF	DCW	STRH/LDRH
Word	32	$0 - 2^{32}-1$	0 - 0xFFFFFFFF	DCD	STR/LDR

Table 2- 9: Unsigned Data Range in ARM and associated Instructions

In Program 2-3A you see an example of storing constant values in the program memory using the directives. Figure 2-12 shows how the data is stored in memory. In the example, the program goes from location 0x00 to 0x0F. The DCB directive stores data in addresses 0x10–0x17. As you see one byte is allocated for each data. The DCD allocates 4 bytes for each data. As a result, the lowest byte of 0x23222120 (which is 0x20) is stored in location 0x18 and the next bytes are stored in the next locations. In this order, the least significant byte of the word is stored at the lowest address and the most significant byte of the word is stored at the highest address. The ordering of bytes in a word is called "endian" and we will discuss it in more details in Section 2.8.

Program 2-3A: Sample of Storing Fixed Data in Program Memory

```
; storing data in program memory.
AREA   LOOKUP_EXAMPLE, READONLY, CODE

LDR    R2, =OUR_FIXED_DATA      ; point to OUR_FIXED_DATA

LDRB   R0, [R2]     ; load R0 with the contents
                    ; of memory pointed to by R2
ADD    R1, R1, R0   ; add R0 to R1
```

```
HERE   B      HERE          ; stay here forever

OUR_FIXED_DATA
       DCB   0x55, 0x33, 1, 2, 3, 4, 5, 6
       DCD   0x23222120, 0x30
       DCW   0x4540, 0x50
       END
```

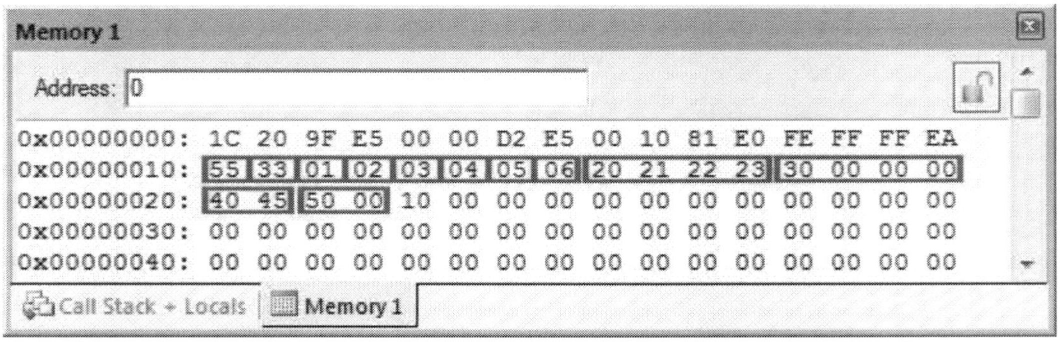

Figure 2- 12: Memory Dump for Program 2-3A

The DCW directive allocates 2 bytes for each data. For example, the low byte of 0x4540 is located in address 0x20 and the high byte of it goes to address 0x21. Similarly, the low byte of 0x50 is located in address 0x22 and the high byte of it in address 0x23.

In the program, to access the data, first the R2 register is loaded with the address of OUR_FIXED_DATA. In this example, OUR_FIXED_DATA has address 0x10. So, R2 is loaded with 0x10. Then, the contents of location 0x10 is loaded into register R0, using the LDRB instruction.

Notice that the ADR pseudo-instruction can also be used to load addresses into registers. For example, in Program 2-3A we can load R2 with the address of OUR_FIXED_DATA using the following pseudo-instruction:

```
       ADR   R2, OUR_FIXED_DATA        ;point to OUR_FIXED_DATA
```

SPACE directive

Using the SPACE directive, we can allocate memory for variables without initial values. The following lines allocate 4 and 2 bytes of memory and name them as LONG_VAR and OUR_ALFA:

```
LONG_VAR     SPACE        4      ; Allocate 4 bytes
OUR_ALFA     SPACE        2      ; Allocate 2 bytes
```

In the following program, three variables are defined: A, B, and C. A and B are initialized with values 5 and 4, respectively. In the next step A and B are added together and the result is stored in C:

Program 2-3B

```
        AREA OUR_PROG, CODE, READONLY

; A = 5
LDR    R0, =A        ; R0 = Addr. of A
MOV    R1, #5        ; R1 = 5
STR    R1, [R0]      ; init. A with 5

; B = 4
LDR    R0, =B        ; R0 = Addr. of B
MOV    R1, #4        ; R1 = 4
STR    R1, [R0]      ; init. B with 4

; R1 = A
LDR    R0, =A        ; R0 = Addr. of A
LDR    R1, [R0]      ; R1 = value of A

; R2 = B
LDR    R0, =B        ; R0 = Addr. of A
LDR    R2, [R0]      ; R2 = value of A

; C = R1 + R2 (C = A + B)
ADD    R3, R1, R2  ; R3 = A + B
LDR    R0, =C        ; R0 = Addr. of C
STR    R3, [R0]      ; C = R3

loop  B   loop

AREA   OUR_DATA, DATA, READWRITE
; Allocates the followings in SRAM memory
A      SPACE 4
B      SPACE 4
C      SPACE 4
END
```

ALIGN

This is used to make sure data is aligned on the 32-bit word or 16-bit half word address boundary. The following uses ALIGN to make the data 32-bit word aligned:

```
        ALIGN 4      ; the next instruction is word (4 bytes) aligned
        ...
        ALIGN 2      ; the next instruction is half-word (2 bytes) aligned
        ...
```

Example 2-7 shows the result of using the ALIGN directive.

Example 2-7

Compare the result of using ALIGN in the following programs:

a)

```
        AREA   E2_7A, READONLY, CODE

        ADR    R2, DTA
        LDRB   R0, [R2]
        ADD    R1, R1, R0
H1      B      H1

DTA     DCB    0x55
        DCB    0x22
        END
```

b)

```
        AREA   E2_7B, READONLY, CODE

        ADR    R2, DTA
        LDRB   R0, [R2]
        ADD    R1, R1, R0
H1      B      H1

DTA     DCB    0x55
        ALIGN 2
        DCB    0x22
        END
```

c)

```
        AREA   E2_7C, READONLY, CODE
        ENTRY
        ADR    R2, DTA
        LDRB   R0, [R2]
        ADD    R1, R1, R0
H1      B      H1

DTA     DCB    0x55
        ALIGN 4
        DCB    0x22
        END
```

Solution:

a) When there is no ALIGN directive the DCB directive allocates the first empty location for its data. In this example, address 0x10 is allocated for 0x55. So 0x22 goes to address 0x11.

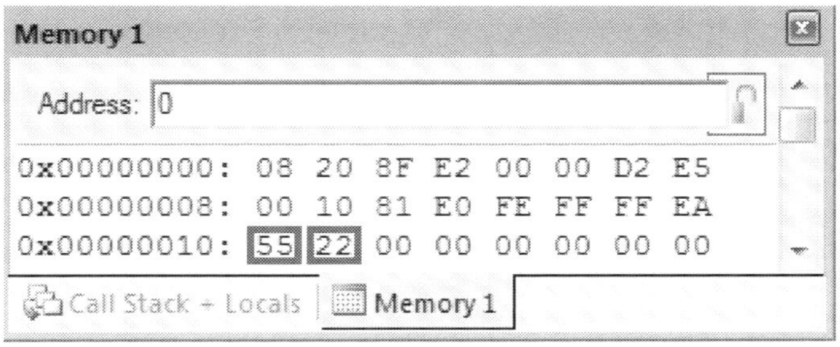

b) In the example the ALIGN is set to 2 which means the data should be put in a location with even address. The 0x55 goes to the first empty location which is 0x10. The next empty location is 0x11 which is not a multiple of 2. So, it is filled with 0 and the next data goes to location 0x12.

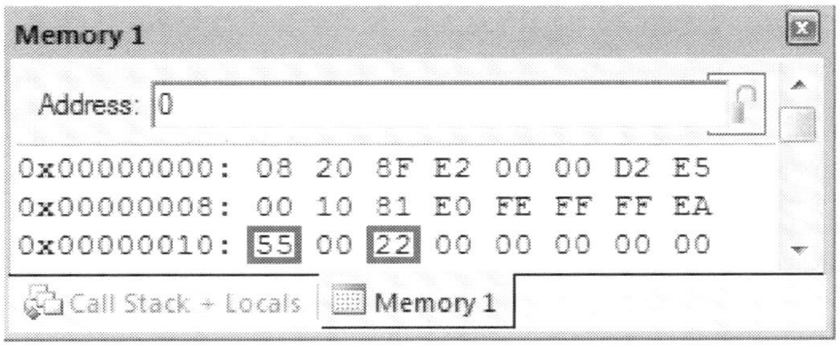

c) In the example the ALIGN is set to 4 which means the data should go to locations whose address is multiple of 4. The 0x55 goes to the first empty location which is 0x10. The next empty locations are 0x11, 0x12, and 0x13 which are not a multiple of 4. So, they are filled with 0s and the next data goes to location 0x14.

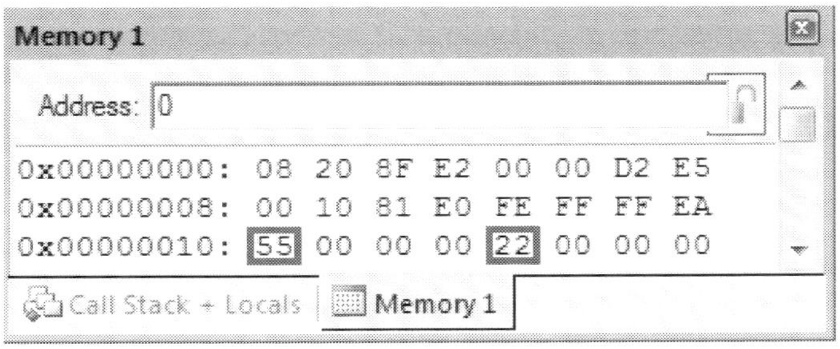

Rules for labels in assembly language

By choosing label names that are meaningful, a programmer can make a program much easier to read and maintain. There are several rules that label names must follow. First, each label name must be unique in the file. The names used for labels in assembly language programming consist of alphabetic letters in both uppercase and lowercase, the digits 0 through 9, and the special characters underscore '_'. The first character of the label must be an alphabetical letter or underscore and cannot be a numeral. Every assembler has some reserved words that must not be used as labels in the program. Foremost among the reserved words are the mnemonics for the instruction opcodes and the directives. For example, "MOV" and "ADD" are reserved because they are instruction mnemonics. Check your assembler manual for the list of reserved words.

Review Questions

1. Give an example of hex data representation in the ARM assembler.

2. Show how to represent decimal 20 in formats of (a) hex, (b) decimal, and (c) binary in the ARM assembler.

3. What is the advantage in using the EQU directive to define a constant value?

4. Show the hexadecimal value of the numbers used by the following directives:

   (a) ASC_DATA EQU '4'   (b) MY_DATA EQU 2_00011111

5. Give the value in R2 after the execution of the following instruction:

```
MYCOUNT      EQU   15
       MOV   R2, #MYCOUNT
```

6. Give the value in memory location 0x200000 after the execution of the following instructions:

```
MYCOUNT      EQU   0x95
MYMEM EQU    0x200000
       MOV   R0, #MYCOUNT
       LDR   R2, =MYMEM
       STRB  R0, [R2]
```

7. Give the value in data memory 0x630000 after the execution of the following instructions:

```
MYDATA       EQU   12
MYMEM        EQU   0x00630000
FACTOR       EQU   0x10
       MOV   R1, #MYDATA
       MOV   R2, #FACTOR
       LDR   R3, =MYMEM
       ADD   R1 R2, R1
       STRB  R1, [R3]
```

Section 2.6: Introduction to ARM Assembly Programming

In this section we discuss assembly language format and define some widely used terminology associated with assembly language programming.

While the CPU can work only in binary, it can do so at a very high speed. It is quite tedious and slow for humans, however, to deal with 0s and 1s in order to program the computer. A program that consists of 0s and 1s is called machine language. In the early days of the computer, programmers coded programs in machine language. Although the octal or hexadecimal system was used as a more efficient way to represent binary numbers, the process of working in machine code was still cumbersome for humans. Eventually, assembly languages were developed, which provided mnemonics for the machine code instructions, plus other features that made programming easier and less prone to error. The term mnemonic is frequently used in computer science and engineering literature to refer to codes and abbreviations that are relatively easy to remember. Assembly language programs must be translated into machine code by a program called assembler. Assembly language is referred to as a low-level language because it deals directly with the internal structure of the CPU. To program in assembly language, the programmer must know all the registers of the CPU and the size of each, as well as other details.

Today, one can use many different programming languages, such as C, C++, Java, Python, and numerous others. These languages are called *high-level* languages because the programmer does not have to be concerned with the internal details of the CPU. Whereas an assembler is used to translate an assembly language program into machine code, high-level languages are translated into machine code by a program called a compiler. For instance, to write a program in C, one must use a C compiler to translate the program into machine language.

Next, we look at the ARM assembly language format.

Structure of assembly language

An assembly language program consists of, among other things, a series of lines of assembly language instructions. An assembly language instruction consists of a mnemonic of opcode, optionally followed by one, two or three operands. The operands are the data items being manipulated, and the opcodes are the commands to the CPU, telling it what to do with the operands. See Program 2-4.

Program 2-4: Sample of an ARM Assembly Language Program

```
	; ARM Assembly language program to add some data and store the SUM in
R3.

	AREA	PROG_2_4, CODE, READONLY
	MOV	R1, #0x25	; R1 = 0x25
	MOV	R2, #0x34	; R2 = 0x34
	ADD	R3, R2, R1	; R3 = R2 + R1
HERE	B	HERE
	END
```

In addition to the instructions, an assembly language program contains directives. While instructions tell the CPU what to do, directives give directions to the assembler. For example, in Program 2-4, the MOV and ADD instructions are commands to the CPU, AREA and END are directives to the assembler.

An assembly language instruction consists of four fields:

```
[label]   opcode   [operands]   [; comment]
```

Brackets indicate that a field is optional and not all lines have them. Brackets should not be typed in. Regarding the above format, the following points should be noted:

1. The label field allows the program to refer to the address of a line of code by name.

2. The assembly language opcode and operand(s) fields together perform the real work of the program and accomplish the tasks for which the program was written for. In assembly language statements such as

```
MOV     R3, #0x55
MOV     R2, #0x67
ADD     R2, R2, R3    ; R2 = R2 + R3
```

   ADD and MOV are the mnemonics of the opcodes; the "0x55" and "0x67" are the operands.

3. Instead of instructions, the program may contain directives. The following line is an assembly directive that tells the assembler that the following lines are for program instructions.

```
AREA        PROG_2_4, CODE, READONLY
```

4. The comment field begins with a semicolon comment indicator "; ". Comments may be at the end of a line or on a line by themselves. The assembler ignores comments, but they are indispensable to programmers. Although comments are optional, it is recommended that they be used to describe the program in a way that makes it easier for someone else to read and understand.

5. Notice the label "HERE" in the label field in Program 2-4. In the B (Branch) statement the ARM is told to stay in this loop indefinitely.

Note!

The first column of each line is always considered as label. Thus, be careful to press a Tab at the beginning of each line that does not have a label; otherwise, your instruction is considered as a label and an error message will appear when compiling.

Review Questions

1. What is the purpose of assembler directives?
2. ______________ are translated by the assembler into machine code, whereas ___________________ are not.
3. True or false. Assembly language is a high-level language.
4. Which of the following instructions produces machine code? List all that do.
   (a) MOV R6, #0x25 (b) ADD R2, R1, R3 (c) END (d) HERE B HERE
5. True or false. Assembler directives are not used by the CPU itself. They are simply a guide to the assembler.
6. In Question 4, which one is an assembler directive?

Section 2.7: Creating an ARM Assembly Program

Now that the basic form of an Assembly language program has been given, the next question is: How it is created, assembled, and made ready to run? The steps to create an executable assembly language program (Figure 2-13) are outlined as follows:

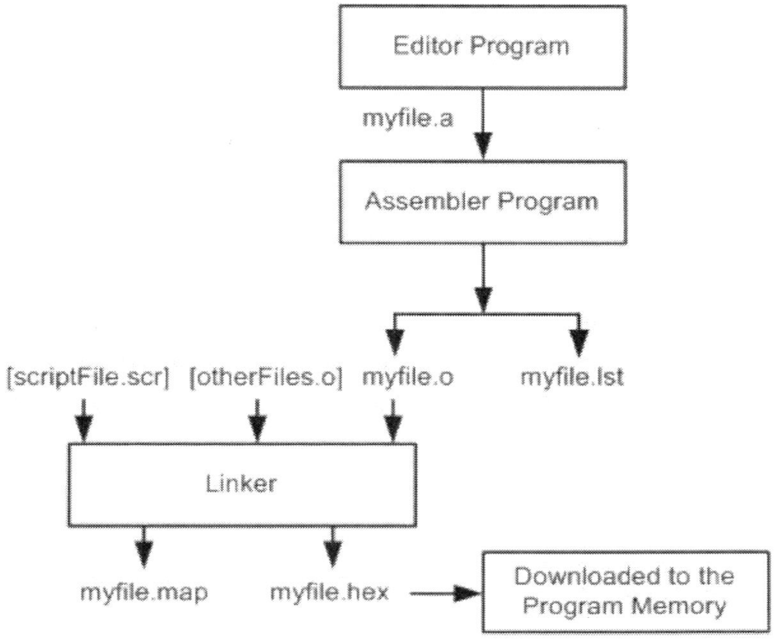

Figure 2- 13: Steps to Create a Program

1. First we use a text editor to type in a program similar to Program 2-4. In the case of ARM, we can use the Keil MDK-ARM IDE, which has a text editor, assembler, simulator, debugger, and much more all in one software package. It is an excellent development software that supports all the ARM chips. A free version with 32k byte limit is available at www.keil.com. Many editors or word processors also can be used to create or edit the program. A widely used editor is the Notepad in Windows, which comes with all Microsoft operating systems. Notice that the editor must be able to produce an ASCII file. For assemblers, the file names follow the usual DOS conventions, but the source file should have the extension ".s", ".a" or ".asm". The ".asm" extension for the source file is used by an assembler in the next step.

2. The ".asm" source file containing the program code created in step 1 is fed to the ARM assembler. The assembler produces an object file, and a listing file. The object file has the extension ".o", and the listing file has ".lst" extension.

3. The object file plus a linker script file are used by the linker to produce the map file and the memory image files. The map file has the extension ".map"

4. The memory image file contains the binary code that can be downloaded to the target device or the simulator for execution. By default, Keil IDE produces a ".axf" file that contains the binary code and the symbols for debugger. Optionally, an Intel hex format file may be

produced. The hex file has ".hex" extension. The linker script file (or scatter file in Keil) is optional and can be replaced by some command line options. After a successful link, the hex file is ready to be burned into the ARM processor's program FLASH memory and is downloaded into the ARM chip.

More about asm and object files

The assembler converts the assembler source file's assembly language instructions into machine code and provides the ".o" (object) file. The object file, as mentioned earlier, has a ".o" as its extension. The object file is used as input to the linker.

Before we can assemble a program to create a ready-to-run program, we must make sure that it is free of syntax errors. The Keil uVision IDE provides us error messages and we examine them to see the location and nature of the syntax error. The assembler will not assemble the program until all the syntax errors are fixed. A sample of an error message is shown in Figure 2-14.

```
Build target 'Target 1'
assembling a1.asm...a1.asm(7): error: A1163E: Unknown opcode MOVE, expecting opcode or Macro
Target not created
```

Figure 2- 14: Sample of an Error Message

"lst" and "map" files

The map file shows the labels defined in the program together with their values. Examine Figure 2-15. It shows the Map file of Program 2-4.

```
Memory Map of the image

  Image Entry point : 0x00000000

  Load Region LR_1 (Base: 0x00000000, Size: 0x00000010, Max: 0xffffffff, ABSOLUTE)

  Execution Region ER_RO (Base: 0x00000000, Size: 0x00000010, Max: 0xffffffff, ABSOLUTE)

    Base Addr    Size         Type   Attr      Idx    E Section Name        Object
    0x00000000   0x00000010   Code   RO           1   * PROG_2_1            a2.o

    Execution Region ER_RW (Base: 0x40000000, Size: 0x00000000, Max: 0xffffffff, ABSOLUTE)
    **** No section assigned to this execution region ****


    Execution Region ER_ZI (Base: 0x40000000, Size: 0x00000000, Max: 0xffffffff, ABSOLUTE)
    **** No section assigned to this execution region ****
```

Figure 2- 15: Sample of a Map File

The lst (listing) file is very useful to the programmer. The listing shows the binary and source code; it also shows which instructions are used in the source code, and the amount of memory the program uses. See Figure 2-16.

```
ARM Macro Assembler      Page 1
1 00000000               ; ARM Assembly Language Program To Add Some Data and Store the SUM in
                         R3.
2 00000000

3 00000000                       AREA    PROG_2_4, CODE, READONLY
```

```
4 00000000                          ENTRY
5 00000000   E3A01025               MOV     R1, #0x25       ; R1 = 0x25
6 00000004   E3A02034               MOV     R2, #0x34       ; R2 = 0x34
7 00000008   E0823001               ADD     R3, R2,R1       ; R3 = R2 + R1
8 0000000C   EAFFFFFE    HERE       B       HERE
9 00000010                          END
```

Figure 2- 16: Sample of a List File for ARM

These files can be accessed by a text editor such as Notepad and displayed on the monitor, or sent to the printer to get a hard copy. The programmer uses the listing and map files to help debugging the program.

There are many different ARM assemblers available for evaluation nowadays. If you use the Windows operating system, IAR IDE and Keil uVision can be used. They have great features and nice environments. GNU assembler is popular because it if free and open source. It is also generic and can be used for most of the processors in the market. The drawbacks of GNU assembler are that its syntax is slightly different from the other ARM assembler and it takes some effort to set up the toolchain.

Review Questions

1. True or false. The editor of ARM uVision IDE and Windows Notepad text editor both produce an ASCII file.
2. True or false. The extension for the assembly program source file may be ".a".
3. Which of the following files is usually produced by a text editor?

   (a) myprog.asm (b) myprog.obj (c) myprog.hex (d) myprog.lst

4. Which of the following files is produced by an assembler?

   (a) myprog.asm (b) myprog.obj (c) myprog.hex (d) myprog.lst

Section 2.8: The Program Counter and Program Memory Space in the ARM

In this section we discuss the role of the program counter (PC) in executing a program and show how the code is fetched from ROM and executed. We will also discuss the program (code) memory space for various ARM family members. Finally, we examine the Harvard architecture of the ARM.

Program counter in the ARM

The most important register in ARM is the PC (program counter). As we mentioned earlier, register R15 is the program counter in ARM CPU. The program counter is used by the CPU to point to the address of the next instruction to be executed. As the CPU fetches the opcode from the program memory, the program counter is incremented automatically to point to the next instruction.

The program counter in the ARM family is 32 bits wide. This means that the ARM family can access addresses 00000000 to 0xFFFFFFFF, a total of 4 gigabytes of memory space locations. The 4 gigabytes of memory space locations are allocated among the I/O peripherals, RAM, and Flash ROM. However, at the time of this writing, none of the members of the ARM family have the entire 4 gigabytes of memory space populated with on-chip peripherals, SRAM, and Flash.

Power up location for ARM

One question that we must ask about any microcontroller (or microprocessor) is: "at what address does the CPU wake up to when power is applied or when the CPU is reset?" Each microprocessor is different. In the case of the ARM7 microcontrollers, the CPU wakes up at memory address 0x00000000. In other words, when the ARM7 CPU is powered up or reset, the PC (program counter) has the value of 0x00000000 in it. This means that it expects the first instruction to be stored at memory address 0x00000000. For this reason, in the ARM system, the first instruction must be burned into memory location 0x00000000 of program ROM. Next, we discuss the step-by-step action of the program counter in fetching and executing a sample program.

Power up reset of ARM Cortex-M

ARM Cortex-M has a very different start up sequence. When a Cortex-M CPU is power up or coming out of reset, it reads four bytes from the memory location 0x00000004-0x00000007 and put them into the program counter. The CPU then fetch the first instruction using the content of PC as the address. So the programmer (working with the software tools) shall put the starting address of the program at memory location 0x00000004.

Placing code in program ROM

To get a better understanding of the role of the program counter in fetching and executing a program, we examine the action of the program counter as each instruction is fetched and executed. First, we examine once more the listing file of the sample program and show how the code is placed into the Flash ROM of the ARM chip. As we can see in Figure 2-16, the machine code for each instruction is listed on the left side of the listing file.

After the program is burned into ROM of an ARM chip, the machine code is placed in ROM memory locations starting at 0x00000000 as shown in the Program 2-4 listing file.

The listing shows that address 0x00000000 contains 0xE3A01025, which is the machine code for moving an immediate value (in this case 0x25) into a register (in this case R1). Therefore, the instruction "MOV R1, #0x25" has a machine code of "E3A01025", where E3A is the opcode and 01025 is the operands. See Figure 2-16. Similarly, the machine code "E3A02034" is located in ROM memory location 0x00000004 and represents the opcode and the operands for the instruction "MOV R2, #0x34". In the same way, machine code "E0813002" is located in memory location 0x00000008 and represents the opcode and the operand for the instruction "ADD R3, R1, R2". The opcode for "B HERE" and its target address offset are located in location 0x0000000C. Notice that all the instructions in this program are 4-byte long.

Executing a program instruction by instruction

Assuming that the above program is burned into the ROM of an ARM chip, the following is a step-by-step description of the action of the ARM upon applying power to it:

1. When the ARM is powered up, the PC (program counter) has 0x00000000 and starts to fetch the first instruction from location 0x00000000 of the program ROM. In the case of the above program the first code is 0xE3A01025, which is the code for moving operand 0x25 to R1. Upon

executing the code, the CPU places the value of 25 in R1. Now one instruction is finished. The program counter is already incremented to point to 0x00000004 (PC = 0x00000004), which contains code 0xE3A02034, the machine code for the instruction "MOV R2, #0x34".

2. Upon executing the machine code E3A02034, the value 0x34 is loaded to R2. The program counter is incremented to 0x00000008.

3. ROM location 0x00000008 has the machine code for instruction "ADD R3, R2, R1". This instruction is executed and now PC = 0x0000000C.

4. PC = 0x0000000C points to the next instruction, which is "HERE B HERE". After the execution of this instruction, PC = 0x0000000C (Although the PC is incremented to 0x00000010, the execution of the instruction loads 0x0000000C into PC. More on branch instructions will be in Chapter 4.). This keeps the program in an infinite loop.

The fact that the program counter points at the next instruction to be executed explains why some microprocessors (notably the x86) call the program counter the instruction pointer.

The actual steps of running a code in ARM is slightly different from what mentioned above because of the use of pipeline in ARM architecture. We will examine pipelines later in Chapter 7.

Instruction formation of the ARM

Next we explore the instruction formation for a few of the instructions we have used in this chapter. This should give you some insight into the encoding of instructions of the ARM.

ADD instruction formation

The encoding of the ADD instruction is shown in Figure 2-17. Of the 32 bits, the first 4 bits are set aside for the condition field which will be discussed more in Chapter 4. Bits 26 and 27 are always 0 in ADD instruction. Bit 25 which is indicated by I defines the type of second operand. As we mentioned before, the second operand can be either a register or an immediate value. If I = 1, the second operand is an immediate value otherwise it is a register. Bits 24 to 21 are the opcode of the ADD instruction. When these bits are 0100 it tells the CPU to perform an addition operation. Bit 20 which is indicated by S defines either the instruction should update the flag bits in the PSCR register or not. In ADD instruction this bit is zero while in ADDS instruction it is one. Bits 19 to 16 define the first operand (Rn). It can be a register number between R0 to R15. Likewise, bits 15 to 12 define the destination register (Rd). Finally, bits 11 to 0 define the second operand. As we mentioned before, bit 25 (I) defines that either the second operand should be a register or an immediate value. We will discuss the bits of Operand 2 in more detail in Chapter 3.

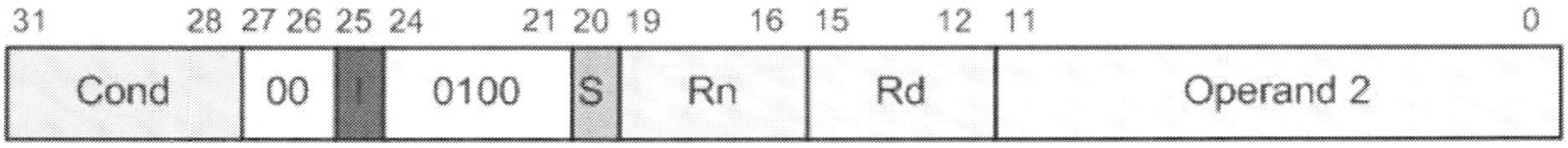

Figure 2- 17: ADD Instruction Formation

SUB instruction formation

Compare the SUB instruction format in Figure 2-18 to the ADD instruction format in Figure 2-17, you will see the only difference is the bits 24-21. In an ADD instruction, these bits are 0100 but they are 0010 in a SUB instruction.

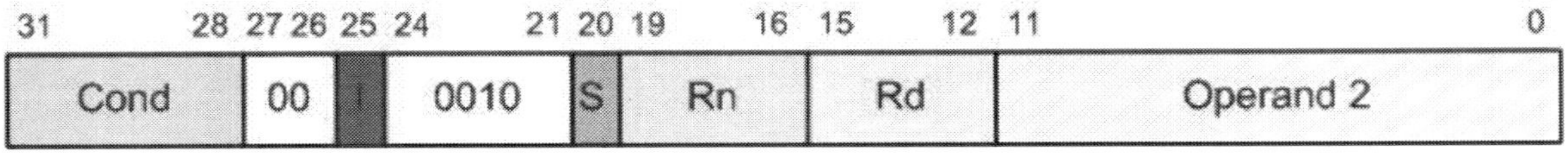

Figure 2- 18: SUB Instruction Formation

General formation of data processing instructions

As you may have noticed, the formation of ADD and SUB instructions are the same except bits 24 to 21 which are called the op code and it tells the CPU what operation to execute. In ARM, all of the data processing instructions have the same format. Figure 2-19 shows the general formation of data processing instructions. Each of the data processing instruction has a unique opcode.

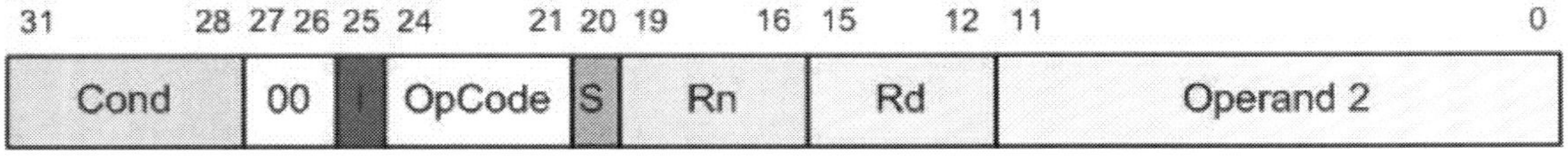

Figure 2- 19: General Formation of Data Processing Instructions

Branch instruction formation

Of the 32 bits of a branch instruction, the first 4 bits are set aside for the condition field which will be discussed more in Chapter 4. Bits 27 to 25 are always 101 in B instruction. Bit 24 which is indicated by L is zero in B instruction and one in BL instruction. Bits 23 to 0 give us the branch target offset, which is the difference between the branch target address and the current value of program counter. These will be discussed further in Chapter 4.

Figure 2- 20: Branch Instruction Formation

ROM width in the ARM

To bring in more information (code or data) into the CPU in each bus cycle, ARM CPU uses 32 bits for the width of the data bus. In an analogy, the data bus is like traffic lanes on the highway. The more lanes the highway is, the more traffic throughput it can accommodate. The widening of the data path between the program ROM and the CPU is another way in which the ARM designers increased the processing power of the ARM family. Another reason to make the code memory 32 bits wide is to match it with the instruction width of the ARM because all of the instructions are 4-byte wide. This way, the CPU brings in an instruction from memory every time it makes a trip to the program memory. That will make instruction fetch a single cycle, as we will see in the Chapter 4 when instruction timing is discussed.

The ARM designers have made all instructions fixed at 4-byte; there are no 1-byte, 2-byte, or 3-byte instructions, as is the case with the x86 and many other microprocessors. This is part of the RISC architectural philosophy, which will be discussed later in this chapter. It must also be noted that the data memory SRAM bus in the ARM microcontroller are also 4-byte wide.

Although the memory bus of the CPU is 32-bit wide, in some low-cost devices 16-bit memory is used. This certainly will degrade the performance. A 16-bit instruction set named "Thumb" was created for ARM processors. The Thumb code performance with 16-bit memory bus is better than 32-bit bus if everything else is the same. We will discuss the Thumb instruction set in Chapter 8.

Harvard and von Neumann architectures in the ARM

In Chapter 0, we discussed Harvard and Von Neumann architecture. ARM9 and newer architectures use Harvard architecture, which means that there are separate buses for the code and the data memory. See Figure 2-21. The program bus provides access to the program memory whereas the data bus is used for bringing data to the CPU.

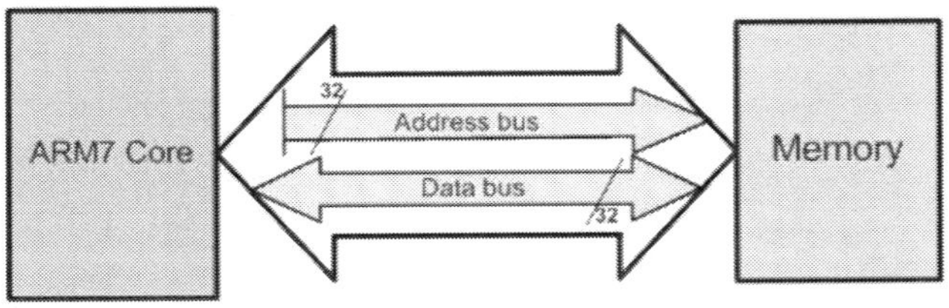

(a) Von Neumann

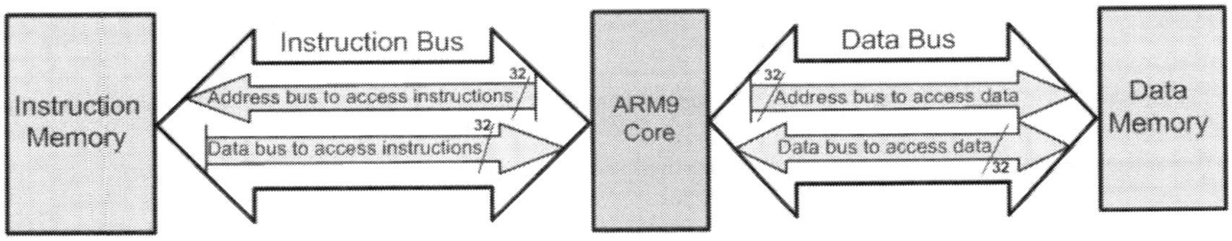

(b) Harvard

Figure 2- 21: Harvard vs. Von Neumann Architecture

In Sections 2-2 and 2-3, we learned about data memory space and how to use the STR and LDR instructions. When the CPU wants to execute the "LDR Rd, [Rx]" instruction, it puts Rx on the address bus of the data bus, and receives data through the data bus. For example, to execute "LDR R2, [R5]", assuming that R5 = 0x40000200, the CPU puts the value of 0x40000200 on the address bus. The location 0x40000200 is in the SRAM (see Figure 2-4). Thus, the SRAM puts the contents of location 0x40000200 on the data bus. The CPU gets the contents of location 0x40000200 through the data bus and brings into CPU and puts it in R2.

The "STR Rx, [Rd]" instruction is executed similarly. The CPU puts Rd on the address bus and the contents of Rx on the data bus. The memory location whose address is on the address bus receives the contents of data bus.

Little endian vs. big endian war

Examine the placing of the code in the ARM program memory, shown in Figure 2-22. The low byte goes to the low memory location, and the high byte goes to the high memory address. This convention is called "little endian" to contrast it with "big endian". Figure 2-23 shows storing the same data using big endian convention. The origin of the terms big endian and little endian was from an argument in a Gulliver's Travels story over how an egg should be opened: from the big end or the little end. In the big endian method, the high byte goes to the low address, whereas in the little endian method, the high byte goes to the high address. All Intel microprocessors and many microcontrollers use the little endian convention. Freescale (formerly Motorola and now NXP) microprocessors, use big endian. The difference might seem as trivial as whether to break an egg from the big end or the little end, but it is a nuisance in converting software and data from one camp to be run on a computer of the other camp. Some microprocessors, including the ARM, has a hardware switch that is controlled by software to run on little endian or big endian and let the software designer choose the convention.

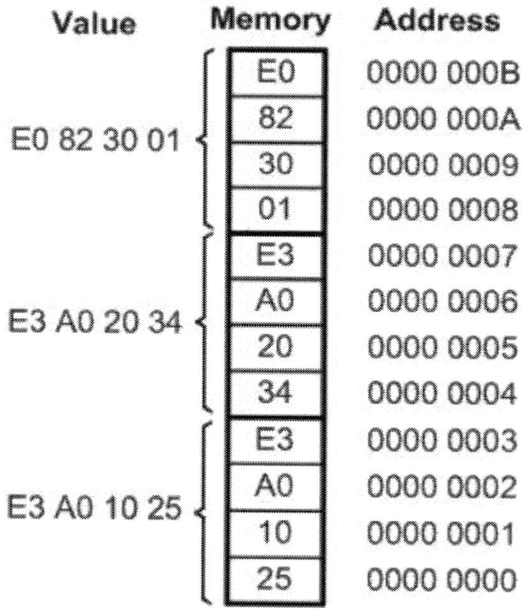

Figure 2- 22: ARM Program Memory Contents for Program 2-4 List File (Little Endian)

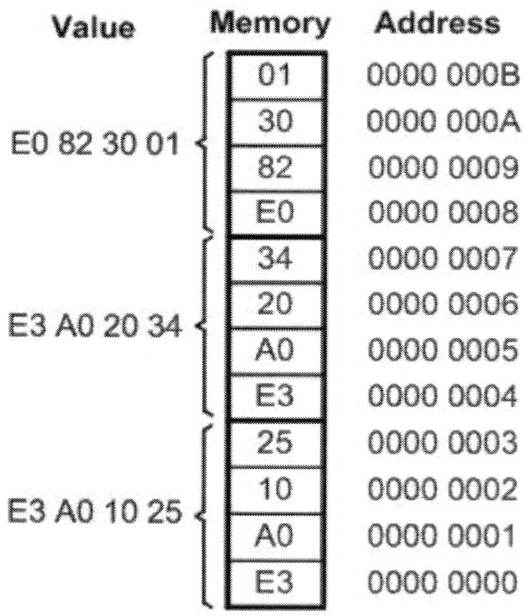

Figure 2- 23: Big Endian Convention

Review Questions

1. In the ARM, the program counter is ______ bits wide.
2. True or false. Every member of the ARM family wakes up at memory 0x00000000 when it is powered up.
3. At what ROM location do we store the first opcode of an ARM7 program?
4. True or false. All the instructions in the ARM are 4-byte instructions.
5. True or false. ARM9 and newer architectures use von Neumann architecture.
6. True or false. ARM7 and older architectures use von Neumann architecture.

Section 2.9: Some ARM Addressing Modes

The various ways operands are specified in the instruction are called addressing modes. In the narrower definition, it is the way CPU generates address from instruction to read/write the operands in the memory. But the term addressing mode is used to cover a broader definition including the operands that are not in the memory. With the RISC architecture, the destinations of all ARM instructions are always a register except the "store" instructions, which is a mirror of "load."

Using advanced addressing modes to access different data types and data structures (e.g. arrays, pointers) are discussed in Chapter 6. Some of the simple ARM addressing modes are:

1. register
2. immediate
3. register indirect (indexed addressing mode)

Register addressing mode

The register addressing mode involves the use of registers to hold the data to be manipulated. Memory is not accessed when this addressing mode is executed; therefore, it is relatively fast. See Figure 2-24.

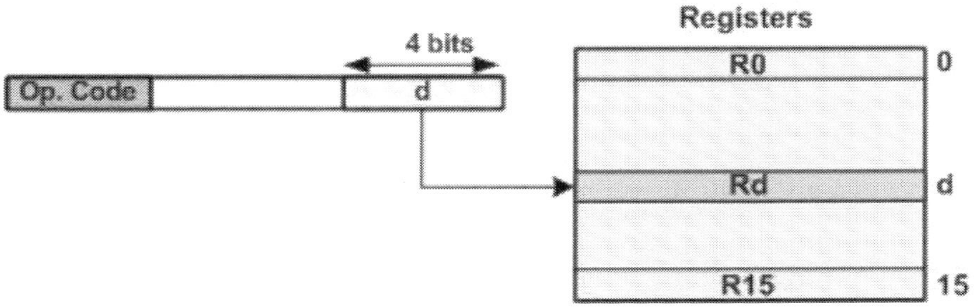

Figure 2- 24: Register Addressing Mode

Examples of register addressing mode are as follow:

```
MOV   R6, R2       ; copy the contents of R2 into R6
ADD   R1, R1, R3   ; add the contents of R3 to contents of R1
SUB   R7, R7, R2   ; subtract R2 from R7
```

Immediate addressing mode

In the immediate addressing mode, the source operand is a literal constant. In immediate addressing mode, as the name implies, when the instruction is assembled, the operand comes immediately after the opcode in the encoding of the instruction. For this reason, this addressing mode executes quickly. See Figure 2-25. Examples:

```
MOV    R9, #0x25          ; move 0x25 into R9
MOV    R3, #62            ; load the decimal value 62 into R3
ADD    R6, R6, #0x40      ; add 0x40 to R6
```

Figure 2- 25: Immediate Addressing Mode

In the first two addressing modes, the operands are either inside the CPU or tagged along with the instruction, which is fetched into the CPU before the instruction is executed. In most programs, the data to be processed are originally in some memory location outside the CPU. There are many ways of accessing the data in the memory space. The following describes one of the methods. We will discuss more ways of accessing data memory in Chapter 6.

Register Indirect Addressing Mode (Indexed addressing mode)

In the register indirect addressing mode, the address of the memory location where the operand resides is held by a register. See Figure 2-26. For example:

```
STR    R5, [R6]     ; write the content of R5 into the memory location
                    ; pointed to by R6
LDR    R10, [R3]    ; load into R10 the content of the
                    ; memory location pointed to by R3.
```

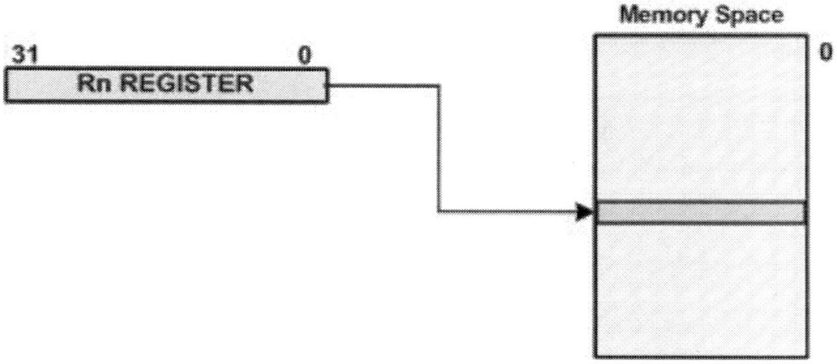

Figure 2- 26: Register Indirect Addressing Mode

Sample Usage: Register indirect addressing mode

Using register indirect addressing mode, we can implement the different pointers. Since the registers are 32-bit they can address the entire memory space. Here you see a simple code in C and its equivalent in Assembly:

C Language:

```
char *ourPointer;
ourPointer = (char*) 0x12456; //Point to location 12456
*ourPointer = 25;  //store 25 in location 0x12456
ourPointer ++;     //point to next location
```

Assembly Language:

```
LDR     R2, =0x12456  ; point to location 0x12456
MOV     R0, #25       ; R0 = 25
STRB    R0, [R2]      ; store R0 in location 0x12456
ADD     R2, R2, #1    ; increment R2 to point to next location
```

Depending on the data type that the pointer points to, STR/LDR, STRH/LDRH, or STRB/LDRB might be used. In the above example, since it points to char (which is 8-bit) STRB is used.

Review Questions

1. Can the ARM programmer make up new addressing modes?
2. Which registers can be used for the register indirect addressing mode?
3. Where is the data located in immediate addressing mode?

Section 2.10: RISC Architecture in ARM

There are three ways available to microprocessor designers to increase the processing power of the CPU:

1. Increase the clock frequency of the chip. Some drawbacks of this method are that the higher the frequency, the more power consumption and more heat dissipation. Power consumption is especially a problem for portable devices.

2. Use Harvard architecture by increasing the number of buses to bring more information (code and data) into the CPU to be processed concurrently. As we saw in Section 2.8, some of the ARM chips have Harvard architecture.

3. Change the internal architecture of the CPU and use what is called the RISC architecture.

ARM has used all three methods to increase the processing power of the ARM microcontrollers. In this section we discuss the merits of RISC architecture.

In the early 1980s, a controversy broke out in the computer design community, but unlike most controversies, it did not go away. Since the 1960s, in all mainframes and minicomputers, designers put as many instructions as they could think of into the CPU. Some of these instructions performed complex tasks like string operations. Naturally, microprocessor designers followed the lead of minicomputer and mainframe designers. Because these processors used such a large number of instructions, many of which performed highly complex activities, they came to be known as CISC (complex instruction set computer) processors. According to several studies in the 1970s, many of these complex instructions etched into CPUs were never used by programmers and compilers. The huge cost of implementing a large number of instructions (some of them complex) into the microprocessor, plus the fact that a good portion of the transistors on the chip are used by the instruction decoder, made some designers think of simplifying and reducing the number of instructions. As this concept developed, the resulting processors came to be known as RISC (reduced instruction set computer).

Features of RISC

The following are some of the features of RISC as implemented by the ARM microcontroller.

Feature 1

RISC processors have a fixed instruction size. In a CISC microprocessors such as the x86, instructions can be 1, 2, 3, or even 5 bytes. For example, look at the following instructions in the x86:

```
CLR    C                        ; clear Carry flag, a 1-byte instruction
ADD    Accumulator, #mybyte     ; a 2-byte instruction
LJMP   target_address           ; a 5-byte instruction
```

This variable instruction size makes the task of the instruction decoder very difficult because the size of the incoming instruction is never known. In a RISC architecture, the size of all instructions is fixed. Therefore, the CPU can decode the instructions quickly. This is like a bricklayer working with bricks of the same size as opposed to using bricks of variable sizes. Of course, it is much more efficient to use bricks of the same size. In the last section we saw how the ARM uses 4-byte instructions and if not all the 32 bits are needed to form the instruction it fills with zeros.

Feature 2

One of the major characteristics of RISC architecture is a large number of registers. All RISC architectures have at least 8 or 16 registers. Of these 16 registers, only a few are assigned to dedicated functions. One advantage of a large number of registers is that it avoids the need for a large stack to store temporary data. Accessing data on the stack is a memory read/write and is much slower than CPU register access. Although a stack is implemented on a RISC processor, it is not as essential as in CISC because so many registers are available. In ARM the use of a large number of general-purpose registers satisfies this RISC feature. The stack for the ARM is covered in Chapter 6.

Feature 3

RISC processors have a smaller instruction set. RISC processors have only basic instructions such as ADD, SUB, MUL, LOAD, STORE, AND, ORR, EOR, CALL, B, and so on. The limited number of instructions is one of the criticisms leveled at the RISC processor because it makes the task of assembly language programmers much more tedious and difficult compared to CISC assembly language programming. It is interesting to note that some defenders of CISC have called it "complete instruction set computer" instead of "complex instruction set computer" because it has a complete set of every kind of instruction. How many of these instructions are used and how often is another matter. In the recent years, almost all the new programs are written in high level languages such as C or Java. The advantage of CISC in this regard is no longer valid. The limited number of instructions in RISC leads to programs that are larger. Although these programs can use more memory, this is not a problem because memory is cheaper. Before the advent of semiconductor memory in the 1960s, however, CISC designers had to pack as much action as possible into a single instruction to get the maximum bang for their buck. In the ARM we have around 50 instructions. We will examine more of the instruction set for the ARM in future chapters.

Feature 4

At this point, one might ask, with all the difficulties associated with RISC programming, what is the gain? The most important characteristic of the RISC processor is that more than 99% of instructions are executed with only one clock cycle because the instructions are much simpler, in contrast to CISC instructions which take various number of clock cycles to execute. Even some of the 1% of the RISC instructions that are executed with two clock cycles can be executed with one clock cycle by juggling instructions around (code scheduling). Code scheduling is discussed in Chapter 7. We will examine the instruction cycle time and pipelining of the ARM in Chapter 7.

Feature 5

Because CISC has such a large number of instructions, each with so many different addressing modes, microinstructions (microcode) are used to implement them. The implementation of microinstructions inside the CPU employs more than 40–60% of transistors in many CISC processors. RISC instructions, however, due to the small set of instructions, are implemented using the hardwire method. Hardwiring of RISC instructions takes no more than 10% of the transistors. With much smaller circuit, the RISC processor consumes much less power. This is a major reason ARM processor is used in majority of the portable devices like cellphone or tablet.

Feature 6

RISC uses load/store architecture. In CISC microprocessors, data can be manipulated while it is still in memory. For example, in instructions such as "ADD Reg, Memory", the microprocessor must bring the contents of the external memory location into the CPU, add it to the contents of the register, then move the result back to the external memory location. The problem is there might be a delay in accessing the data from external memory then the whole process would be stalled, preventing other instructions from proceeding in the pipeline. In RISC, designers did away with these kinds of instructions. In RISC, instructions can only load from external memory into registers or store registers into external memory locations. There is no direct way of doing arithmetic and logic operations between a register and the contents of external memory locations. All these instructions must be performed by first bringing both operands into the registers inside the CPU, then performing the arithmetic or logic operation, and then sending the result back to memory. This idea was first implemented by the Cray 1 supercomputer in 1976 and is commonly referred to as load/store architecture. In the last section, we saw that the arithmetic and logic operations are between the

GPRs registers, but none involves a memory location. For example, there is no "ADD R1, RAM-Loc" instruction in ARM. Operating only on the CPU registers guarantees that the memory bus contention will not slow down the instruction execution.

In concluding this discussion of RISC processors, it is interesting to note that RISC technology was explored by the scientists at IBM in the mid-1970s, but it was David Patterson of the University of California at Berkeley who in 1980 brought the merits of RISC concepts to the attention of computer scientists. It must also be noted that in recent years CISC processors such as the Pentium have used some RISC features in their design. This was the only way they could enhance the processing power of the x86 processors and stay competitive. Of course, they had to add circuits in the CPU to translate the x86 instructions into an internal RISC instruction set, because they had to deal with all the CISC instructions of the x86 processors and the legacy software of DOS/Windows.

Review Questions

1. What do RISC and CISC stand for?
2. True or false. The CISC architecture executes the vast majority of its instructions in 2, 3, or more clock cycles, while RISC executes them in one clock.
3. RISC processors normally have a _____ (large, small) number of general-purpose registers.
4. True or false. Instructions such as "ADD R16, ROMmemory" do not exist in RISC microprocessors such as the ARM.
5. How many instructions of ARM are 32-bit wide?
6. True or false. While CISC instructions are of variable sizes, RISC instructions are all the same size.
7. Which of the following operations do not exist for the ADD instruction in RISC?
   (a) register to register (b) immediate to register (c) memory to memory
8. True or false. Harvard architecture uses the same address and data buses to fetch both code and data.

Section 2.11: Viewing Registers and Memory with ARM Keil IDE

The ARM microprocessor has great tools and support systems, many of them free or inexpensive. ARM Keil uVision has an assembler and simulator provided by Keil Corporation and can be downloaded from the www.keil.com website. The Keil IDE is free for the evaluation version with limited code size. See https://nicerland.com/ for tutorials on how to use the Keil ARM uVision assembler and simulator.

Many assemblers and C compilers come with a simulator. Simulators allow us to view the contents of registers and memory after executing each instruction (single-stepping). It is strongly recommended to use a simulator to single-step some of the programs in this chapter and future chapters. Single-stepping a program with a simulator gives us a deeper understanding of microcontroller architecture, in addition to the fact that we can use it to find the errors in our programs.

Figures 2-27 and 2-28 show screenshots for ARM simulators from ARM Keil uVision.

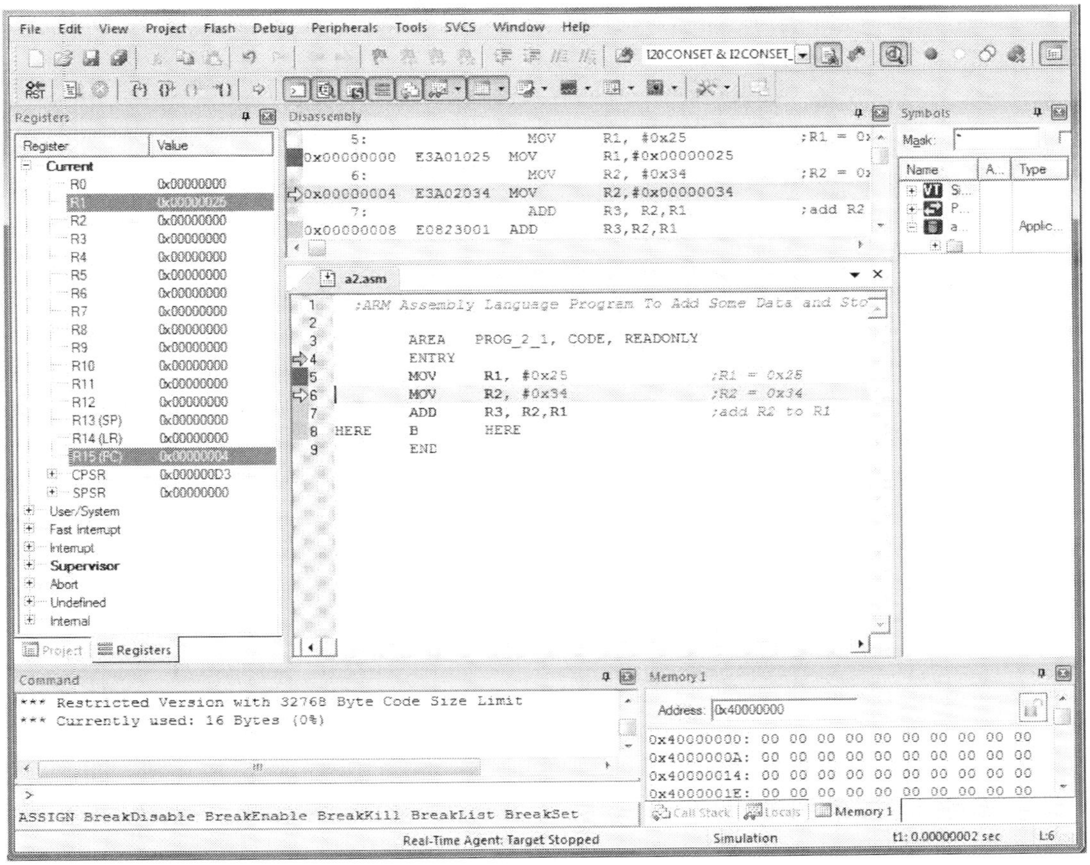

Figure 2- 27: Keil uVision Screenshot

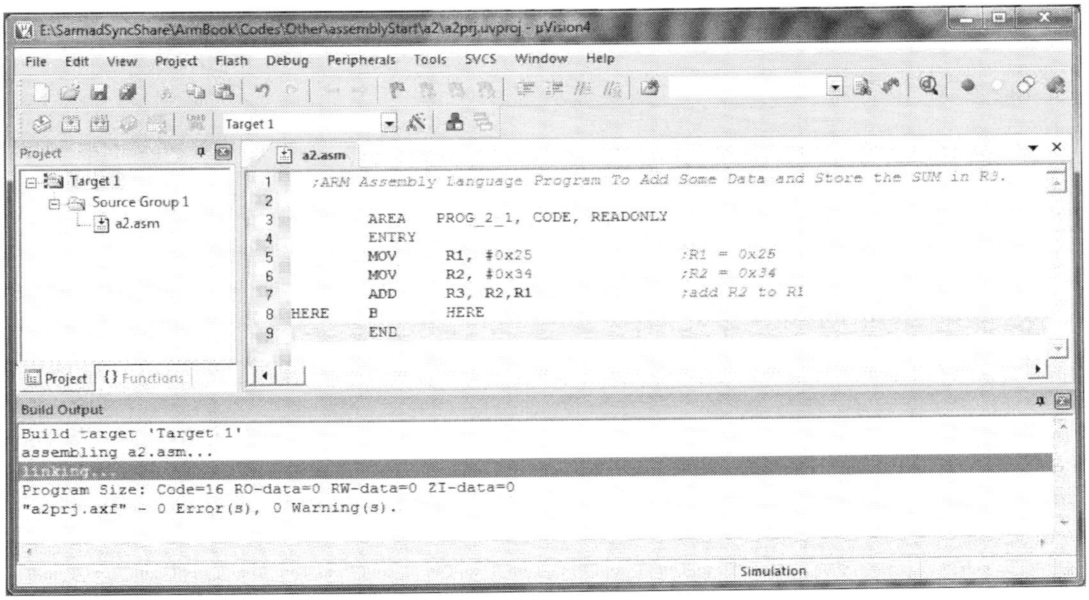

Figure 2- 28: Keil uVision Screenshot

Problems

Section 2.1: The General Purpose Registers in the ARM

1. ARM is a(n) _____-bit microprocessor.
2. The general-purpose registers are _____ bits wide.
3. The value in MOV R2, #value is _____ bits wide.
4. The largest number that an ARM GPR register can have is _____ in hex.
5. What is the result of the following code and where is it kept?
```
MOV   R2, #0x15
MOV   R1, #0x13
ADD   R2, R1, R2
```
6. Which of the followings is (are) illegal?
   (a) MOV R2, #0x50000 (b) MOV R2, #0x50 (c) MOV R1, #0x00
   (d) MOV R1, 255 (e) MOV R17, #25 (f) MOV R23, #0xF5
   (g) MOV 123, 0x50
7. Which of the following is (are) illegal?
   (a) ADD R2, #20, R1 (b) ADD R1, R1, R2 (c) ADD R5, R16, R3
8. What is the result of the following code and where is it kept?
```
MOV  R9, #0x25
ADD  R8, R9, #0x1F
```
9. What is the result of the following code and where is it kept?
```
MOV  R1, #0x15
ADD  R6, R1, #0xEA
```
10. True or false. We have 32 general purpose registers in the ARM.

Section 2.2: The ARM Memory Map

11. True or false. R13 and R14 are special function registers.
12. True or false. The peripheral registers are mapped to memory space.
13. True or false. The On-chip Flash is the same size in all members of ARM.
14. True or false. The On-chip data SRAM is the same size in all members of ARM.
15. What is the difference between the EEPROM and data SRAM space in the ARM?
16. Can we have an ARM chip with no EEPROM?
17. Can we have an ARM chip with no data RAM?
18. What is the maximum number of bytes that the ARM can access?
19. Find the address of the last location of on-chip Flash for each of the following, assuming the first location is 0:
    (a) ARM with 32 KB (b) ARM with 8 KB
    (c) ARM with 64 KB (d) ARM with 16 KB
    (e) ARM with 128 KB (f) ARM with 256 KB
20. Show the lowest and highest values (in hex) that the ARM program counter can take.

21. A given ARM has 0x7FFF as the address of the last location of its on-chip ROM. What is the size of on-chip Flash for this ARM?
22. Repeat Question 21 for 0x3FFF.
23. Find the on-chip program memory size in K for the ARM chip with the following address ranges:
    (a) 0x0000–0x1FFF (b) 0x0000–0x3FFF
    (c) 0x0000–0x7FFF (d) 0x0000–0xFFFF
    (e) 0x0000–0x1FFFF (f) 0x00000–0x3FFFF
24. Find the on-chip program memory size in K for the ARM chips with the following address ranges:
    (a) 0x00000–0xFFFFFF (b) 0x00000–0x7FFFF
    (c) 0x00000–0x7FFFFF (d) 0x00000–0xFFFFF
    (e) 0x00000–0x1FFFFF (f) 0x00000–0x3FFFFF

Section 2.3: Load and Store Instructions in ARM

25. Show a simple code to store values 0x30 and 0x97 into locations 0x20000015 and 0x20000016, respectively.
26. Show a simple code to load the value 0x55 into locations 0x20000030–0x20000038.
27. True or false. We cannot load immediate values into the data SRAM directly.
28. Show a simple code to load the value 0x11 into locations 0x20000010–0x20000015.
29. Repeat Problem 28, except load the value into locations 0x20000034–0x2000003C.

Section 2.4: ARM CPSR (Current Program Status Register)

30. The status register is a(n) ______ -bit register.
31. Which bits of the status register are used for the C and Z flag bits, respectively?
32. Which bits of the status register are used for the V and N flag bits, respectively?
33. In the ADD instruction, when is C raised?
34. In the ADD instruction, when is Z raised?
35. What is the status of the C and Z flags after the following code?

```
LDR     R0, =0xFFFFFFFF
LDR     R1, =0xFFFFFFF1
ADDS    R1, R0, R1
```

36. Find the C flag value after each of the following codes:

(a)
```
LDR R0, =0xFFFFFF54
LDR R5, =0xFFFFFFC4
ADDS R2, R5, R0
```

(b)
```
MOV R3, #0
LDR R6, =0xFFFFFFFF
ADDS R3, R3, R6
```

(c)
```
LDR R3, =0xFFFFFFFF
LDR R8, =0xFFFFFF05
ADDS R2, R3, R8
```

37. Write a simple program in which the value 0x55 is added 5 times.

Section 2.5: ARM Data Format and Directives

38. State the value (in hex) used for each of the following data:

    MYDAT_1 EQU 55
    MYDAT_2 EQU 98
    MYDAT_3 EQU 'G'
    MYDAT_4 EQU 0x50
    MYDAT_5 EQU 200
    MYDAT_6 EQU 'A'
    MYDAT_7 EQU 0xAA
    MYDAT_8 EQU 255
    MYDAT_9 EQU 2_10010000
    MYDAT_10 EQU 2_01111110
    MYDAT_11 EQU 10
    MYDAT_12 EQU 15

39. State the value (in hex) for each of the following data:

    DAT_1 EQU 22
    DAT_2 EQU 0x56
    DAT_3 EQU 2_10011001
    DAT_4 EQU 32
    DAT_5 EQU 0xF6
    DAT_6 EQU 2_11111011

40. Show a simple code to load the value 0x10102265 into locations 0x40000030–0x4000003F.
41. Show a simple code to (a) load the value 0x23456789 into locations 0x40000060–0x4000006F, and (b) add them together and place the result in R9 as the values are added. Use EQU to assign the names TEMP0–TEMP3 to locations 0x40000060–0x4000006F.

Section 2.6: Introduction to ARM Assembly Programming

Section 2.7: Assembling an ARM Program

42. Assembly language is a ________ (low, high)-level language while C is a ________ (low, high)-level language.
43. Of C and assembly language, which is more efficient in terms of code generation (i.e., the amount of program memory space it uses)?
44. Which program produces the .obj file?
45. True or false. The assembly source file may have the extension ".asm".
46. True or false. The source code file can be a non-ASCII file.
47. True or false. Every source file must have EQU directive.
48. Do the EQU and END directives produce opcodes?
49. The file with the _______ extension is downloaded into ARM Flash ROM.

50. Give three file extensions produced by ARM Keil.

Section 2.8: The Program Counter and Program ROM Space in the ARM

51. Every ARM7 family member wakes up at address _________ when it is powered up.
52. A programmer puts the first opcode at address 0x100. What happens when the microcontroller is powered up?
53. ARM instructions are _______ bytes.
54. Write a program to add each of your 5-digit ID to a register and place the result into memory location 0x4000100. Use the program listing to show the Flash memory addresses and their contents.
55. Show the placement of data in following code:

```
LDR R1, =0x22334455
LDR R2, =0x20000000
STR R1, [R2]
```

    Use a) little endian and b) big endian.
56. Show the placement of data in following code:

```
LDR R1, =0xFFEEDDCC
LDR R2, =0x2000002C
STR R1, [R2]
```

    Use a) little endian and b) big endian.
57. How wide is the memory in the ARM chip?
58. How wide is the data bus between the CPU and the program memory in the ARM7 chip?
59. In "ADD Rd, Rn, operand2", explain how many bits are set aside for Rd and how it covers the entire GPRs in the ARM chip.

Section 2.9: Some ARM Addressing Modes

60. Give the addressing mode for each of the following:

(a) MOV R5, R3 (b) MOV R0, #56

(c) LDR R5, [R3] (d) ADD R9, R1, R2

(e) LDR R7, [R2] (f) LDRB R1, [R4]

61. Show the contents of the memory locations after the execution of each instruction.

(a)
```
LDR R2, =0x129F
LDR R1, =0x1450
LDR R2, [R1]
```

0x1450 = (.......)

0x1451 = (.......)

(b)
```
LDR R4, =0x8C63
LDR R1, =0x2400
LDRH R4, [R1]
```

0x2400 = (.......)

0x2401 = (.......)

Section 2.10: RISC Architecture in ARM

62. What do RISC and CISC stand for?
63. In _______ (RISC, CISC) architecture we can have 1-, 2-, 3-, or 4-byte instructions.
64. In _______ (RISC, CISC) architecture instructions are fixed in size.
65. In _______ (RISC, CISC) architecture instructions are mostly executed in one or two cycles.
66. In _______ (RISC, CISC) architecture we can have an instruction to ADD a register to external memory.
67. True or false. Most instructions in CISC are executed in one or two cycles.

Answers to Review Questions

Section 2.1

1. `MOV R2, #0x34`
2.

```
MOV   R1, #0x16
MOV   R2, #0xCD
ADD   R1, R1, R2
```

or

```
MOV   R1, #0x16
ADD   R1, R1, #0xCD
```

3. False
4. 32

Section 2.2

1. True
2. general-purpose registers
3. 32
4. Special function registers (SFRs)
5. 32

Section 2.3

1. True
2.

```
MOV   R1, #0x20
MOV   R2, #0x95
STRB  R2, [R1]
```

3. `STR R2, [R8]`
4.

```
MOV   R1, #0x20
LDR   R4, [R1]
```

5. 0xFF in hex or 255 in decimal
6. R6
7. It copies the lower 8 bits of R1 into location pointed to by R2.
8. 0xFFFFFFFF in hex or 4,294,967,295 in decimal (2^{32}-1)

Section 2.4

1. CPSR (current program status register)
2. 32 bits
3.

Hex	Binary
FFFFFF9F	1111 1111 1111 1111 1111 1111 1001 1111
+00000061	+ 0000 0000 0000 0000 0000 0000 0110 0001
1 00000000	1 0000 0000 0000 0000 0000 0000 0000 0000

This leads to C = 1 and Z = 1.

4.

Hex	Binary
00000022	0000 0000 0000 0000 0000 0000 0010 0010
+00000022	+ 0000 0000 0000 0000 0000 0000 0010 0010
0 00000000	0000 0000 0000 0000 0000 0000 0100 0100

This leads to Z = 0.

5.

Hex	Binary
0000 0067	0000 0000 0000 0000 0000 0000 0110 0111
+ 0000 0099	+ 0000 0000 0000 0000 0000 0000 1001 1001
0000 0100	0000 0000 0000 0000 0000 0001 0000 0000

This leads to C = 0 and Z = 0.

Section 2.5

1. MOV R1, #0x20
2. (a) MOV R2, #0x14 (b) MOV R2, #20 (c) MOV R2, #2_00010100
3. If the value is to be changed later, it can be done once in one place instead of at every occurrence in the file and the code becomes more readable, as well.
4. (a) 0x34 (b) 0x1F
5. 15 in decimal (0x0F in hex)
6. Value of location 0x00000200 = 0x95
7. 0x0C + 0x10 = 0x1C will be in data memory location 0x00000630.

Section 2.6

1. Assembly directives direct the assembler in doing its job.
2. The instructions, assembler directives

3. False
4. All except (c)
5. True
6. (c)

Section 2.7
1. True
2. True
3. (a)
4. (b), (c) and (d)

Section 2.8
1. 32
2. False
3. 0x00000000
4. True
5. False
6. True

Section 2.9
1. No
2. The general-purpose registers (R0 to R15)
3. It is a part of the instruction

Section 2.10
1. RISC is Reduced Instruction Set Computer; CISC stands for Complex Instruction Set Computer.
2. True
3. Large
4. True
5. All of them
6. True
7. (c)
8. False

Chapter 3: Arithmetic and Logic Instructions and Programs

In this chapter, most of the arithmetic and logic instructions are discussed and program examples are given to illustrate the application of these instructions. Unsigned numbers are used in this discussion of arithmetic and logic instructions. In Section 3.1 we examine the arithmetic instructions for unsigned numbers. The logic instructions and programs are covered in Section 3.2. Section 3.3 is dedicated to rotate and shift operations. We examine loading literal (constant) values into registers using rotate options, as well. In Section 3.4 we discuss the ARM instructions for rotate and shift. Section 3.5 is dedicated to BCD and ASCII data conversion.

Section 3.1: Arithmetic Instructions

Unsigned numbers are numbers that represent only zero or positive numbers. All the bits are used to represent data and no bits are set aside for the positive or negative sign. This means that the operand can be between 00 and 0xFF (0 to 255 decimal) for 8-bit data and between 0x0000 and 0xFFFF (0 to 65535 decimal) for 16-bit data. For the 32-bit operand it can be between 0 and 0xFFFFFFFF (0 to 2^{32} -1). See Table 3-1. This section covers the ADD, SUB, and multiply instructions for unsigned number.

Data Size	Bits	Decimal	Hexadecimal	Load instruction used
Byte	8	0 – 255	0 – 0xFF	STRB
Half-word	16	0 – 65535	0 – 0xFFFF	STRH
Word	32	0 – 2^{32}-1	0 – 0xFFFFFFFF	STR

Table 3-1: Unsigned Data Range Summary in ARM

Affecting flags in ARM instructions

A unique feature of the execution of ARM arithmetic instructions is that it does not affect (updates) the flags in the CPSR register unless we explicitly request it. This is different from most of other microprocessors and microcontrollers. In other processors the arithmetic/logic instructions (and sometimes other instructions) automatically change the N, Z, C, and V flags according to the result of the operation. To update the flags in CPSR register in ARM CPU by the data processing instructions, the S flag in the instruction must be set. This is done by appending the 'S' suffix to the opcode of the instruction. With the S suffix, the ARM assembler will set the S flag in the instruction. For example, we use SUBS instead of SUB if we want the instruction to update the flags in CPSR. The SUBS means subtract and set the flags, while the SUB simply subtracts without having any effect on the flags. See Table 3-2 and Figure 3-1.

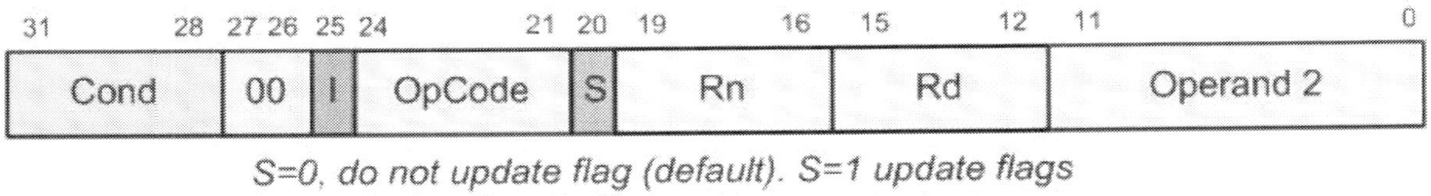

Figure 3- 1: General Formation of Data Processing Instruction

Instruction (Flags unchanged)		Instruction (Flags updated)	
ADD	Add	**ADDS**	Add and set flags
ADC	Add with carry	**ADCS**	Add with carry and set flags
SUB	SUBS	**SUBS**	Subtract and set flags
SBC	Subtract with carry	**SBCS**	Subtract with carry and set flags
MUL	Multiply	**MULS**	Multiply and set flags
UMULL	Multiply long	**UMULLS**	Multiply Long and set flags
RSB	Reverse subtract	**RSBS**	Reverse subtract and set flags
RSC	Reverse subtract with carry	**RSCS**	Reverse subtract with carry and set flags
Note: The above instruction affect all the N, Z, C, and V flag bits of CPSR (current program status register) but the N and V flags are for signed data and are discussed in Chapter 5.			

Table 3-2: Arithmetic Instructions and Flag Bits for Unsigned Data

Addition of unsigned numbers

The form of the ADD instruction is

```
ADD    Rd, Rn, Op2          ; Rd = Rn + Op2
```

The instructions ADD and ADC are used to add two operands. The destination operand must be a register. The Op2 (or operand 2) can be a register or an immediate value. Remember that memory-to-register or memory-to-memory arithmetic and logic operations are never allowed in ARM processor since it is a RISC processor. The instruction could change any of the N, Z, C, or V bits of the program status register, as long as we use the ADDS instead of ADD. The effects of the ADDS instruction on the V (overflow) and N (negative) flags are discussed in Chapter 5 since they are used in signed number operations. Look at Examples 3-1 and 3-2 for the effect of ADDS instruction on Z and C flags.

Example 3-1

Show the flag bits of status register for the following cases:

a)

```
LDR    R2, =0xFFFFFFF5     ; R2 = 0xFFFFFFF5 (notice the = sign)
MOV    R3, #0x0B
ADDS   R1, R2, R3          ; R1 = R2 + R3 and update the flags
```

b)

```
LDR    R2, =0xFFFFFFFF
ADDS   R1, R2, #0x95       ; R1 = R2 + 95 and update the flags
```

Solution:

a)

```
   0xFFFFFFF5     1111 1111 1111 1111 1111 1111 1111 0101
 + 0x0000000B   + 0000 0000 0000 0000 0000 0000 0000 1011
  0x100000000   1 0000 0000 0000 0000 0000 0000 0000 0000
```

First, notice how the "LDR R2, =0xFFFFFFF5" pseudo-instruction loads the 32-bit value into R2 register. Also notice the use of ADDS instruction instead of ADD since the ADD instruction does not update the flags. Now, after the addition, the R1 register (destination) contains 0 and the flags are as follows:
C = 1, since there is a carry out from D31
Z = 1, the result of the action is zero (for all 32 bits)

b)

```
   0xFFFFFFFF       1111 1111 1111 1111 1111 1111 1111 1111
 + 0x00000095     + 0000 0000 0000 0000 0000 0000 1001 0101
  0x100000094     1 0000 0000 0000 0000 0000 0000 1001 0100
```

After the addition, the R1 register (destination) contains 0x94 and the flags are as follows:
C = 1, since there is a carry out from D31
Z = 0, the result of the action is not zero (for the 32 bits)

Example 3-2

Show the flag bits of status register for the following case:

```
LDR   R2, =0xFFFFFFF1    ; R2 = 0xFFFFFFF1
MOV   R3, #0x0F
ADDS  R3, R3, R2         ; R3 = R3 + R2 and update the flags
ADD   R3, R3, #0x7       ; R3 = R3 + 0x7 and flags unchanged
MOV   R1, R3
```

Solution:

```
   0xFFFFFFF1       1111 1111 1111 1111 1111 1111 1111 0001
 + 0x0000000F     + 0000 0000 0000 0000 0000 0000 0000 1111
  0x100000000     1 0000 0000 0000 0000 0000 0000 0000 0000
```

After the ADDS addition, the R3 register (destination) contains 0 and the flags are as follows:
C = 1, since there is a carry out from D31
Z = 1, the result of the action is zero (for the 32 bits)

After the "ADD R3, R3, #0x7" addition, the R3 register (destination) contains 0x7 (0 + 07 = 07) and the flags are unchanged from previous instruction since we used ADD instead of ADDS. Therefore, the Z = 1 and C = 1. If we used "ADDS R3, R3, #0x7" instruction instead of "ADD R3, R3, #0x7", we would have Z = 0 and C = 0. Use the Keil ARM simulator to verify this.

Comment

Microsoft Windows comes with a calculator. Use the Programmer mode to verify the calculations in this and future chapters. The calculator supports data size of up to 64-bit

No increment instruction in ARM

There is no increment instruction in the ARM processor. Instead, we use ADD 1 to perform this action. The instruction "ADD R4, R4, #1" will increment the R4 and places the result in R4 register. The RISC processors eliminate the unnecessary instructions and use an existing instruction to perform the operation.

ADC (add with carry)

This instruction is used for adding multiword (data larger than 32-bit) numbers. The form of the ADC instruction is

```
ADC   Rd, Rn, Op2 ; Rd = Rn + Op2 + Carry
```

In discussing addition, the following two cases will be examined:

- Addition of single word data
- Addition of multiword data

CASE 1: Addition of single word data

In previous addition program examples, the sum was purposely kept less than 0xFFFFFFFF, the maximum value a 32-bit register can hold. In real world to calculate the sum of any number of operands, the carry flag should be checked after the addition of each operand to see if the sum is greater than 0xFFFFFFFF. See Example 3-3 and Program 3-1.

Example 3-3

Show the flag bits of status register for the following case:

```
LDR    R2, =0xFFFFFFF1    ; R2 = 0xFFFFFFF1
MOV    R3, #0x0F
ADDS   R3, R3, R2         ; R3 = R3 + R2 and update the flags
ADD    R3, R3, #0x7       ; R3 = R3 + 0x7 and flags unchanged
MOV    R1, R3
```

Solution:

```
   0xFFFFFFF1      1111 1111 1111 1111 1111 1111 1111 0001
+  0x0000000F    + 0000 0000 0000 0000 0000 0000 0000 1111
  0x100000000    1 0000 0000 0000 0000 0000 0000 0000 0000
```

After the ADDS addition, the R3 register (destination) contains 0 and the flags are as follows:
C = 1, since there is a carry out from D31
Z = 1, the result of the action is zero (for the 32 bits)

After the "ADD R3, R3, #0x7" addition, the R3 register (destination) contains 0x7 (0x0 + 0x7 = 0x7) and the flags are unchanged from previous instruction since we used ADD instead of ADDS. Therefore, the Z = 1 and C = 1. If we use "ADDS R3, R3, #0x7" instruction instead of "ADD R3, R3, #0x7", we will have Z = 0 and C = 0. Use the Keil ARM simulator to verify this.

Program 3-1

Write a program to calculate the total sum of five words of data. Each data value represents the mass of a planet in integer. The decimal data are as follow: 1000000000, 2000000000, 3000000000, 4000000000, and 4100000000.

```
        AREA    PROG3_1, CODE, READONLY

        LDR    R1, =1000000000
        LDR    R2, =2000000000
        LDR    R3, =3000000000
        LDR    R4, =4000000000
        LDR    R5, =4100000000

        MOV    R8, #0         ; R8 = 0 for saving the lower word
        MOV    R9, #0         ; R9 = 0 for accumulating the carries

        ADDS   R8, R8, R1     ; R8 = R8 + R1
        ADC    R9, R9, #0     ; R9 = R9 + 0 + Carry
                              ; (increment R9 if there is carry)
        ADDS   R8, R8, R2     ; R8 = R8 + R2
        ADC    R9, R9, #0     ; R9 = R9 + 0 + Carry
        ADDS   R8, R8, R3     ; R8 = R8 + R3
        ADC    R9, R9, #0     ; R9 = R9 + 0 + Carry
        ADDS   R8, R8, R4     ; R8 = R8 + R4
        ADC    R9, R9, #0     ; R9 = R9 + 0 + Carry
        ADDS   R8, R8, R5     ; R8 = R8 + R5
        ADC    R9, R9, #0     ; R9 = R9 + 0 + Carry
HERE    B      HERE
        END                   ; mark end of program
```

CASE 2: Addition of multi-word numbers

Assume a program is needed that will add the total U.S. budget for the last 100 years or the mass of all the planets in the solar system. In cases like this, the numbers being added could be up to 8 bytes wide or more. Since ARM registers are only 32 bits wide (4 bytes), it is the job of the programmer to write the code to break down these large numbers into smaller chunks to be processed by the CPU. If a 32-bit register is used and the operand is 8 bytes wide, that would take a total of two iterations. See Example 3-4. However, if a 16-bit register is used, the same operands would require four iterations. This obviously takes more time for the CPU, one reason to have wide registers in the design of the CPU.

Example 3-4

Analyze the following program which adds 0x35F62562FA to 0x21F412963B:

```
LDR     R0, =0xF62562FA     ; R0 = 0xF62562FA
LDR     R1, =0xF412963B     ; R1 = 0xF412963B
MOV     R2, #0x35           ; R2 = 0x35
MOV     R3, #0x21           ; R3 = 0x21
ADDS    R5, R1, R0          ; R5 = 0xF62562FA + 0xF412963B
                            ; now C = 1
ADC     R6, R2, R3          ; R6 = R2 + R3 + C
                            ;    = 0x35 + 21 + 1 = 0x57
```

Solution:

After the R5 = R0 + R1 the carry flag is one. Since C = 1, when ADC is executed, R6 = R2 + R3 + C = 0x35 + 0x21 + 1 = 0x57.

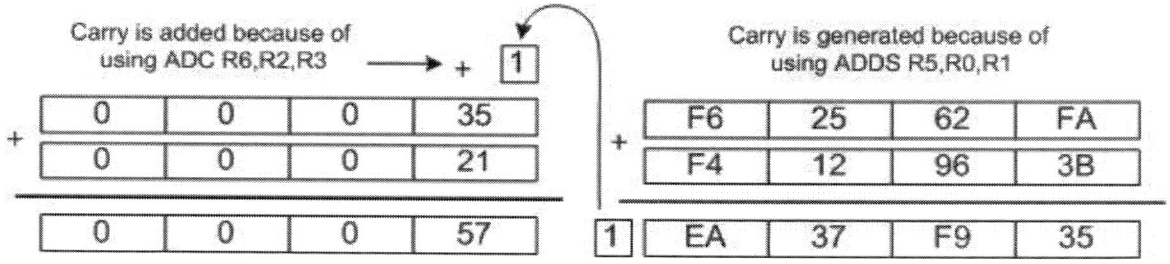

Microsoft Windows calculator support data size of up 64-bit (double word). Use it to verify the above calculations.

Subtraction of unsigned numbers

```
SUB    Rd, Rn, Op2 ; Rd = Rn - Op2
```

In subtraction, the ARM microprocessors (and almost all modern CPUs) use the 2's complement method. All CPUs contain adder circuitry. It would be redundant to design a separate subtractor circuitry if subtraction can be performed with adder. Assuming that the ARM is executing simple subtract instructions, one can summarize the steps of the hardware of the CPU in executing the SUB instruction for unsigned numbers as follows:

1. Take the 2's complement of the subtrahend (Operand 2).

2. Add it to the minuend (Rn operand).

3. Place the result in destination Rd.

4. Update the flags in CPSR if the S flag is set in the instruction.

These four steps are performed for every SUBS instruction by the internal hardware of the ARM CPU. It is after these four steps that the result is obtained and the flags are set. Examples 3-5 through 3-7 illustrates the four steps.

Example 3-5

Show the steps involved for the following cases:

a)

```
MOV   R2, #0x4F         ; R2 = 0x4F
MOV   R3, #0x39         ; R3 = 0x39
SUBS  R4, R2, R3        ; R4 = R2 - R3
```

b)

```
MOV   R2, #0x4F         ; R2 = 0x4F
SUBS  R4, R2, #0x05     ; R4 = R2 - 0x05
```

Solution:

a)

```
  0x4F          0000004F
- 0x39        + FFFFFFC7   2's complement of 0x39
    16        1 00000016   (C = 1 step 4)
```

The flags would be set as follows: C = 1, and Z = 0.

b)

```
  0x4F           0000004F
- 0x05        +  FFFFFFFB   2's complement of 0x05
  0x4A         1 0000004A   (C=1 step 4)
```

Example 3-6

Analyze the following instructions:

```
LDR   R2, =0x88888888    ; R2 = 0x88888888
LDR   R3, =0x33333333    ; R3 = 0x33333333
SUBS  R4, R2, R3         ; R4 = R2 - R3
```

Solution:

Following are the steps for "SUB R4, R2, R3":

```
  88888888       88888888
- 33333333     + CCCCCCCD   (2's complement of 0x33333333)
  55555555     1 55555555   (C = 1 step 4)
```

After the execution of SUBS, if C=1, there was no borrow; if C = 0, borrow occurred at the most significant bit. Since we are only dealing with unsigned numbers in this chapter, the result is incorrect with a borrow.

Example 3-7

Analyze the following instructions:

```
MOV   R1, #0x4C    ; R1 = 0x4C
MOV   R2, #0x6E    ; R2 = 0x6E
SUBS  R0, R1, R2   ; R0 = R1 - R2
```

Solution:

Following are the steps for "SUB R0, R1, R2":

```
  4C     0000004C
- 6E   + FFFFFF92   (2's complement of 0x6E)
- 22   0 FFFFFFDE   (C = 0 step 4) result is incorrect
```

SBC (subtract with borrow)

```
SBC   Rd, Rn, Op2 ; Rd = Rn - Op2 - 1 + C
```

This instruction is used for subtraction of multiword (data larger than 32-bit) numbers. Notice that in some other architectures, the CPU inverts the C flag after subtraction so the content of carry flag is the borrow bit of subtract operation. But in ARM the carry flag is not inverted after subtraction and the carry flag after the subtraction is the invert of the borrow. This difference does not affect the use of SBC instruction because in those architectures the subtract with borrow is implemented as "Rd = Rn – Op2 – C" but in ARM, it is implemented as "Rd = Rn – Op2 – 1 + C". So the polarity of the carry bin in subtraction is compensated by SBC instruction. See Example 3-8.

Example 3-8

Analyze the following program which subtracts 0x21F62562FA from 0x35F412963B:

```
LDR   R0, =0xF62562FA   ; R0 = 0xF62562FA,
                        ; notice the syntax for LDR
LDR   R1, =0xF412963B   ; R1 = 0xF412963B
MOV   R2, #0x21         ; R2 = 0x21
MOV   R3, #0x35         ; R3 = 0x35
SUBS  R5, R1, R0        ; R5 = R1 - R0
                        ;    = 0xF412963B - 0xF62562FA, and C = 0
SBC   R6, R3, R2        ; R6 = R3 - R2 - 1 + C
                        ;    = 0x35 - 0x21 - 1 + 0 = 0x13
```

Solution:

After the R5 = R1 – R0 there is a borrow so the carry flag is cleared. Since C = 0, when SBC is executed, R6 = R3 – R2 – 1 + C = 0x35 – 0x21 – 1 + 0 = 0x35 – 0x21 – 1= 0x13.

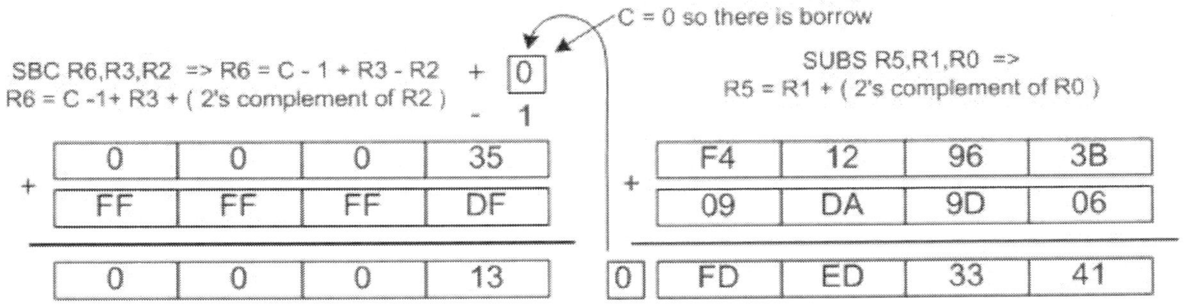

No decrement instruction in ARM

There is no decrement instruction in the ARM processor. Instead we use SUB to perform the action. The instruction “SUB R4, R4, #1” will decrement one from R4 and places the result in R4 register. The RISC processors eliminate the unnecessary instructions and use an existing instruction to perform the desired operation.

RSB (reverse subtract)

The format for the RSB instruction is

```
RSB   Rd, Rn, Op2        ; Rd = Op2 - Rn
```

Notice the difference between the RSB and SUB instruction. They are essentially the same except the way the source operands are subtracted is reversed. See Example 3-9.

Example 3-9

Find the result of R0 for the followings:

a)

```
MOV    R1, #0x6E    ; R1 = 0x6E
RSB    R0, R1, #0   ; R0 = 0 - R1
```

b)

```
MOV    R1, #0x1     ; R1 = 1
RSB    R0, R1, #0   ; R0 = 0 - R1 = 0 - 1
```

Solution:

a) Following are the steps for "RSB R0, R1, #0":

```
   0     00000000
- 6E   + FFFFFF92   (2's complement)
- 6E     FFFFFF92   (C = 0) result is negative
```

RSC (reverse subtract with carry)

The form of the RSC instruction is

```
RSC    Rd, Rn, Op2 ; Rd = Op2 - Rn - 1 + C
```

Notice the difference between the RSB and SBC instructions. They are essentially the same except the way the source operands are subtracted is reversed. This instruction can be used to get the 2's complement of the 64-bit operand. See Example 3-10.

Example 3-10

Show how to create 2's complement of a 64-bit data in R0 and R1 register. The R0 hold the lower 32-bit.

Solution:

```
LDR    R0, =0xF62562FA    ; R0 = 0xF62562FA
LDR    R1, =0xF812963B    ; R1 = 0xF812963B
RSB    R5, R0, #0   ; R5 = 0 - R0
                    ;    = 0 - 0xF62562FA = 9DA9D06 and C=0
RSC    R6, R1, #0   ; R6 = 0 - R1 - 1 + C
                    ;    = 0 - 0xF812963B-1+0 = 7ED69C4
```

Use Microsoft Windows calculator to verify the above calculations.

Multiplication and division of unsigned numbers

Because multiplication and division circuits are complex, not all processors have instructions for multiplication and division. All the ARM processors have multiplication instructions but not all have the division. Some family members such as ARM Cortex-M3 and M4 have both the division and multiplication instructions. In this section we examine the multiplication of unsigned numbers. Signed numbers multiplication is treated in Chapter 5.

Multiplication of unsigned numbers in ARM

The ARM gives you two choices of unsigned multiplication: regular multiply and long multiply. The regular multiply instruction (MUL) is used when the result is less than 32-bit, while the long multiply (MULL) must be used when the result is greater than 32-bit. See Table 3-3. In this section we examine both of them.

Instruction	Source 1	Source 2	Destination	Result
MUL	Rn	Op2	Rd (32 bits)	Rd=Rn×Op2
UMULL	Rn	Op2	RdLo, RdHi (64 bits)	RdLo:RdHi=Rn×Op2
Note 1: *Using MUL for word × word multiplication preserves only the lower 32-bit result in Rd and the rest are dropped. If the result is greater than 0xFFFFFFFF, then we must use UMULL (unsigned Multiply Long) instruction.* ***Note 2:*** *In some CPUs the C flag is used to indicate the result is greater than 32-bit but this is not the case with ARM MUL instruction.*				

Table 3- 3: Unsigned Multiplication (UMUL Rd, Rn, Op2) Summary

MUL (multiply)

```
MUL    Rd, Rn, Op2  ; Rd = Rn × Op2
```

In multiplication, all the operands must be in register. Immediate value is not allowed as an operand. After the multiplication, the destination register will contain the result. See the following example:

```
MOV    R1, #0x25    ; R1=0x25
MOV    R2, #0x65    ; R2=0x65
MUL    R3, R1, R2   ; R3 = R1 × R2 = 0x65 × 0x25
```

Note that in the case of half-word times half-word or smaller sources since the destination register is 32-bit there is no problem in keeping the result of 65,535 × 65,535, the highest possible unsigned 16-bit data. That is not the case in word times word multiplication because 32-bit × 32-bit can produce a result greater than 32-bit. If the MUL instruction is used, the destination register will only hold the lower word (32-bit) and the portion beyond 32-bit is dropped. So, it is not safe to use MUL for multiplication of numbers greater than 65,536. In ARM, the flags do not reflect the fact that the multiplication result exceeds the size of the destination register. See the following example:

```
LDR    R1, =100000 ; R1=100,000
LDR    R2, =150000 ; R2=150,000
MUL    R3, R2, R1  ; R3 is not 15,000,000,000 because
                   ; it cannot fit in 32 bits.
```

For this reason, we must use UMULL (unsigned multiply long) instruction if the result is going to be greater than 0xFFFFFFFF.

UMULL (unsigned multiply long)

```
UMULL  RdLo, RdHi, Rn, Op2     ; RdHi:RdLoRd = Rn × Op2
```

In unsigned long multiplication, all the operands must be in register and no immediate value is allowed. After the multiplication, the destination registers will contain the result. Notice that the left most register in the instruction, RdLo in our case, will hold the lower word and the higher portion beyond 32-bit is saved in the second register, RdHi. See the following example:

```
LDR   R1, =0x54000000    ; R1 = 0x54000000
LDR   R2, =0x10000002    ; R2 = 0x10000002
UMULL R3, R4, R2, R1     ; 0x54000000 × 0x10000002 = 0x054000000A8000000
                         ; R3 = 0xA8000000, the lower 32 bits
                         ; R4 = 0x05400000, the higher 32 bits
```

Notice that it is the job of programmer to choose the best type of multiplication depending on the size of operands and the result. See Example 3-11.

Example 3-11

Write a short program to multiply 0xFFFFFFFF by itself.

Solution:

```
MOV R1, #0xFFFFFFFF      ; R1 = 0xFFFFFFFF
UMULL R3, R4, R1, R1
```

Since 0xFFFFFFFF × 0xFFFFFFFF = 0xFFFFFFFE00000001, then R4=0xFFFFFFFE and R3=0x00000001. If we had used MUL instruction, then the 0xFFFFFFFF would have been dropped and only 0x00000001 would have been kept by the destination register.

Multiply and Accumulate Instructions in ARM

In some applications such as digital signal processing (DSP) we need to multiply two variables and add the result to another variable. The ARM has an instruction to do both in a single instruction. The format of MLA (multiply and accumulate) instruction is as follows:

```
MLA   Rd, Rm, Rs, Rn     ; Rd = Rm × Rs + Rn
```

In multiplication and accumulate, all the operands must be in register. After the multiplication and add, the destination register will contain the result. See the following example:

```
MOV   R1, #100           ; R1 = 100
MOV   R2, #5             ; R2 = 5
MOV   R3, #40            ; R3 = 40
MLA   R4, R1, R2, R3     ; R4 = R1 × R2 + R3 = 100 × 5 + 40 = 540
```

To accumulate the products of the multiplication, just use the same register for Rd and Rn:

```
MLA    R3, R1, R2, R3      ; R3 = R1 × R2 + R3 or R3 += R1 × R2
```

Notice that multiply and accumulate can produce a result greater than 32-bit, if the MLA instruction is used, the destination register will only hold the lower word (32 bits) of the sum and the portion beyond 32-bit is dropped. For this reason, we must use UMLAL (unsigned multiply and accumulate long) instruction if the result is going to be greater than 0xFFFFFFFF. The format of UMLAL instruction is as follows:

```
UMLAL RdLo, RdHi, Rn, Op2      ; RdHi:RdLo = Rn × Op2 + RdHi:RdLo
```

In UMALL instruction, all the operands must be in register. Notice that the addend and the destination use the same registers, the two left most registers in the instruction. It means that the contents of the registers which have the addend will be changed after execution of UMLAL instruction. See the following example:

```
LDR    R1, =0x34000000     ; R1 = 0x34000000
LDR    R2, =0x2000000      ; R2 = 0x2000000
MOV    R3, #0              ; R3 = 0x00
LDR    R4, =0x00000BBB     ; R4 = 0x00000BBB
UMLAL  R4, R3, R2, R1      ; 0x34000000×0x2000000+0xBBB
                           ;  = 0x0680000000000BBB
```

Division of unsigned numbers in ARM

Some ARM families do not have instructions for division of unsigned numbers since it takes many gates to implement it. We can use SUB instructions to perform the division. In the next chapter, after explaining conditional branches, we will show an example of unsigned division using subtract operation.

Review Questions

1. Explain the difference between ADDS and ADD instructions.
2. The ADC instruction that has the syntax "ADC Rd, Rn, Op2" means _____________.
3. Explain why the Z=0 for the following:

```
MOV          R2, #0x4F
MOV          R4, #0xB1
ADDS         R2, R4, R2
```

4. Explain why the Z=1 for the following:

```
MOV          R2, #0x4F
LDR          R4, =0xFFFFFFB1
ADDS         R2, R4, R2
```

5. Show how the CPU would subtract 0x05 from 0x43.
6. If C = 1, R2 = 0x95, and R3 = 0x4F prior to the execution of "SBC R2, R2, R3", what will be the contents of R2 after the subtraction?

7. In unsigned multiplication of "MUL R2, R3, R4", the product will be placed in register __________.
8. In unsigned multiplication of "MUL R1, R2, R4", the R2 can be maximum of __________ if R4 = 0xFFFFFFFF so that there are no bits lost by the operation.

Section 3.2: Logic Instructions

In this section we discuss the logic instructions AND, OR, and Ex-OR in the context of many examples. Just like arithmetic instruction, we must use the S suffix in the instruction if we want to update the flags. If the S suffix is used the Z flag will be set if and only if the result is all zeros, and the N flag will be set to the logical value of bit 31 of the result. The V flag in the CPSR will be unaffected, and the C flag will be updated according to the calculation of the Operand 2. See Table 3-4.

Instruction (Flags Unchanged)	Action	Instruction (Flags Changed)	Hexadecimal
AND	ANDing	**ANDS**	Anding and set flags
ORR	ORRing	**ORS**	Oring and set flags
EOR	Exclusive-ORing	**EORS**	Exclusive Oring and set flags
BIC	Bit Clearing	**BICS**	Bit clearing and set flags

Table 3-4: Logic Instructions and Flag Bits

The instruction format of logic instructions in ARM is similar to the format of other data processing instructions. See Figure 3-2.

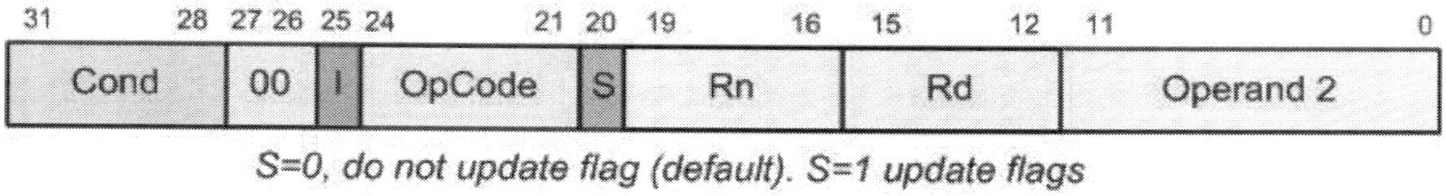

Figure 3-2: General Formation of Data Processing Instruction

AND

```
AND   Rd, Rn, Op2          ; Rd = Rn ANDed Op2
```

Inputs		Output	Symbol
X	Y	X AND Y	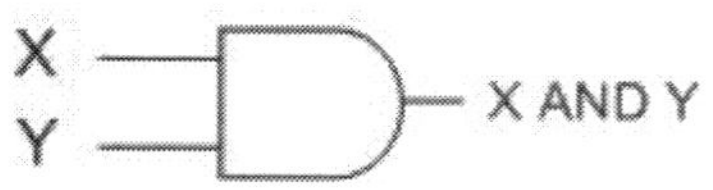
0	0	0	
0	1	0	
1	0	0	
1	1	1	

This instruction will perform a bitwise logical AND on the operands and place the result in the destination. The destination and the first source operand are registers. The second source operand can be a register or an immediate value of less than 0xFF with even bits of rotate.

If we use ANDS instead of AND it will change the N and Z flags according to the result (and C flag during the calculation of operand 2). As seen in Example 3-12, AND can be used to mask certain bits of the operand.

Example 3-12

Show the results of the following cases

a)

```
MOV    R1, #0x35
AND    R2, R1, #0x0F        ; R2 = R1 ANDed with 0x0F
```

b)

```
MOV    R0, #0x97
MOV    R1, #0xF0
AND    R2, R0, R1           ; R2 = R0 ANDed with R1
```

Solution:

a)

	0x35	0 0 1 1 0 1 0 1
AND	0x0F	0 0 0 0 1 1 1 1
	0x05	0 0 0 0 0 1 0 1

b)

	0x97	1 0 0 1 0 1 1 1
AND	0xF0	1 1 1 1 0 0 0 0
	0x90	1 0 0 1 0 0 0 0

ORR

```
ORR    Rd, Rn, Op2  ; Rd = Rn ORed Op2
```

Inputs		Output	Symbol
X	Y	X OR Y	
0	0	0	
0	1	1	
1	0	1	
1	1	1	

The operands are ORed and the result is placed in the destination. ORR can be used to set certain bits of an operand to one. The destination and the first source operand are registers. The second source operand can be either a register or an immediate value of less than 0xFF with even bits of rotate.

If we use ORRS instead of ORR, the flags will be updated, just the same as for the ANDS instruction. See Example 3-13.

Example 3-13

Show the results of the following cases:

a)

```
MOV   R1, #0x04          ; R1 = 0x04
ORRS  R2, R1, #0x68      ; R2= R1 ORed 0x68
```

b)

```
MOV   R0, #0x97
MOV   R1, #0xF0
ORR   R2, R0, R1         ; R2= R0 ORed with R1
```

Solution:

a)

	0x04	0000 0100	
OR	0x68	0110 1000	Flag will be: Z = 0
	0x6C	0110 1100	

b)

	0x97	1001 0111	
OR	0xF0	1111 0000	Flag will be unchanged
	0xF7	1111 0111	

The ORR instruction can also be used to test for a zero operand. For example, "ORRS R2, R2, #0" will OR the register R2 with zero and make Z = 1 if R2 is zero.

EOR

```
EOR   Rd, Rn, Op2 ; Rd = Rn Ex-ORed with Op2
```

Inputs		Output	Symbol
X	Y	X EOR Y	
0	0	0	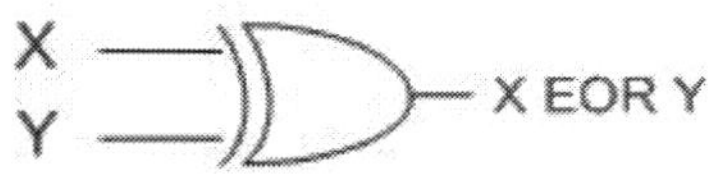
0	1	1	
1	0	1	
1	1	0	

The EOR instruction will perform an Exclusive-OR of the two operands and place the result in the destination register. EOR sets the result bits to 1 if the corresponding source bits are not equal; otherwise, they are clear to 0. The flags are updated if we use EORS instead of EOR. The rules for the operands are the same as in the AND and OR instructions. See Examples 3-14 and 3-15.

Example 3-14

Show the results of the following:

```
MOV     R1, #0x54
EOR     R2, R1, #0x78     ; R2 = R1 ExOred with 0x78
```

Solution:

	0x54	0 1 0 1 0 1 0 0
EOR	0x78	0 1 1 1 1 0 0 0
	0x2C	0 0 1 0 1 1 0 0

Example 3-15

The EOR instruction can be used to clear the contents of a register by Ex-ORing it with itself. Show how "EOR R1, R1, R1" clears R1, assuming that R1 = 0x45.

Solution:

	0x45	0 1 0 0 0 1 0 1
EOR	0x45	0 1 0 0 0 1 0 1
	0x00	0 0 0 0 0 0 0 0

Another application of EOR is to toggle bits of an operand. For example, to toggle bit 2 of register R2:

```
EOR    R2, R2, #0x04      ; EOR R2 with 0000 0100
```

This would cause bit 2 of R2 to change to the complement value; all other bits would remain unchanged.

BIC (bit clear)

```
BIC    Rd, Rn, Op2        ; clear certain bits of Rn specified by
                          ; the Op2 and place the result in Rd
```

Inputs		Output
X	Y	X AND (NOT Y)
0	0	0
0	1	0
1	0	1
1	1	0

The BIC (bit clear) instruction is used to clear the selected bits of the Rn register. The selected bits are held by Op2. The bits that are HIGH in Op2 will be cleared and bits with LOW will be left unchanged. For example, assuming that R3 = 0000000000001000 binary, the instruction "BIC R2, R2, R3" will clear bit 3 of R2 and leaves the rest of the bits unchanged. In reality, the BIC instruction performs AND operation on Rn register with the complement of Op2 and places the result in destination register. Look at the following example:

```
MOV    R2, #0xAA
BIC    R3, R2, #0x0F        ; now R3 = 0xAA AND 0xF0 = 0xA0
```

We can use the AND operation with complement to achieve the same result:

```
MOV R2, #0xAA
AND R3, R2, #~0x0F          ; AND R2 with the complement of #0x0F
                            ; and store the result in R3
```

If we want the flags to be updated, then we must use BICS instead of BIC.

MVN (move not)

```
MVN    Rd, Rn           ; move the complement of Rn to Rd
```

The MVN (move not) instruction is used to generate one's complement of an operand. For example, the instruction "MVN R2, #0" will make R2=0xFFFFFFFF. Look at the following example:

```
LDR    R2, =0xAAAAAAAA              ; R2 = 0xAAAAAAAA
MVN    R2, R2                       ; R2 = 0x55555555
```

We can also use Ex-OR instruction to generate one's complement of an operand. Ex-ORing an operand with 0xFFFFFFFF will generate the 1's complement. See the following code:

```
LDR    R2, =0xAAAAAAAA              ; R2 = 0xAAAAAAAA
MVN    R0, #0                       ; R0 = 0xFFFFFFFF
EOR    R2, R2, R0                   ; R2 = R2 ExORed with 0xFFFFFFFF
                                    ;    = 0x55555555
```

It must be noted that the instruction "MVN Rd, #0" is used to load the literal value of 0xFFFFFFFF into destination register. We can use the "LDR Rd, =0xFFFFFFFF" pseudo-instruction to achieve the same thing, but the ARM assembler will substitute it with eight bytes of code therefore it takes more code space.

Review Questions

1. Use operands 0x4FCA and 0xC237 to perform:

   (a) AND (b) OR (c) XOR

2. ANDing a word operand with 0xFFFFFFFF will result in what value for the word operand? To set all bits of an operand to 0, it should be ANDed with ______.

3. To set all bits of an operand to 1, it could be ORed with _______.

4. XORing an operand with itself results in what value for the operand?

5. Write an instruction that sets bit 4 of R7.

6. Write an instruction that clears bit 3 of R5.

Section 3.3: Rotate and Barrel Shifter

Although ARM has shift and rotate instructions that we will discuss in the following section, we can also perform the shift and rotate operations as part of the other data processing instructions (arithmetic and logic instructions) such as MOV, ADD, or SUB. In previous sections, we discussed that as the second operand of data process instructions we can use register or immediate values. The data processing instructions can be used in one of the following forms:

opcode Rd, Rn, Rs (e.g. ADD R1, R2, R3)

opcode Rd, Rn, immediate_value (e.g. ADD R2, R3, #5)

ARM is able to shift or rotate the second operand before using it in the data processing. In this section we first discuss shifting and rotating on register operand and then we cover rotating of the immediate value.

Barrel Shifter and Shifts

There are two kinds of shifts: logical and arithmetic. The logical shift is used for unsigned operations and the arithmetic shift is for signed operations. Logical shift will be discussed in this section and the discussion of arithmetic shift will be covered in Chapter 5.

Logical shift right – LSR

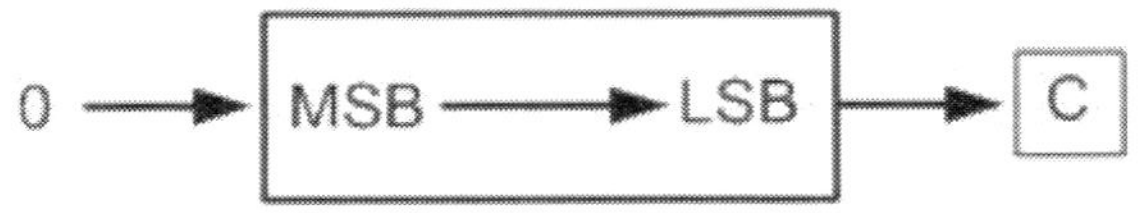

The operand is shifted right bit by bit, and for every shift the LSB (least significant bit) will go to the carry flag (C) in CPSR if the 'S' suffix is used in the instruction and the MSB (most significant bit) is filled with 0. At the end of the execution of the instruction, the carry flag will hold the last bit shifted out if the 'S' suffix is used in the instruction. One can use an immediate value or a register to hold the number of times it is to be shifted. Examples 3-16 and 3-17 should help to clarify LSR.

Example 3-16

Show the result of the MOVS instruction with LSR in the following:

```
MOV   R0, #0x9A         ; R0 = 0x9A
MOVS  R1, R0, LSR #3    ; shift R0 to right 3 times
                        ; then store the result in R1
```

Solution:

0x9A = 00000000 00000000 0000000 00000000 10011010
first shift: 00000000 00000000 0000000 00000000 01001101 C = 0
second shift: 00000000 00000000 0000000 00000000 00100110 C = 1
third shift: 00000000 00000000 0000000 00000000 00010011 C = 0

After shifting right three times, R1 = 0x00000013 and C = 0. Another way to write the above code is:

```
MOV   R0, #0x9A
MOV   R2, #0x03
MOVS  R1, R0, LSR R2    ; shift R0 to right R2 times
                        ; and move the result to R1
```

Example 3-17

Show the results of the ADDS with LSR in the following:

```
LDR   R1, =0x777            ; R1=0x777
LDR   R2, =0xA6D            ; R2=0xA6D
ADDS  R3, R1, R2, LSR #4    ; shift R2 right 4 times then add it to
                            ; R1 and place the result in R3
                            ; R3 = 0x777 + 0xA6 = 0x81D
```

Solution:

After four shifts, the R2 will contain 0xA6. The four LSBs are lost through the carry, one by one, and 0s fill the four MSBs. 0xA6 is added to 0x777 in R1 and the sum 0x81D is placed in R3. Unlike MOVS operation, which does not affect the C flag itself, the ADDS operation generates C flag depending on the carry out of the MSB by the ADD, which will overwrite the C flag generated from the shift of operand 2. In this example, "R2, LSR #4" generates C = 1 but the add results in C = 0. So, at the end of the ADDS instruction, C = 0.

One can use the LSR to divide a number by 2. See Example 3-18.

Example 3-18

Show the results of LSR in the following:

```
LDR   R0, =0x88         ; R0=0x88
MOVS  R1, R0, LSR #3    ; shift R0 right three times (R1 = 0x11)
```

Solution:

After the three shifts, the R1 will contain 0x11. This divides the number by 8 since 2 to the power of 3 is 8.

Logical shift left – LSL

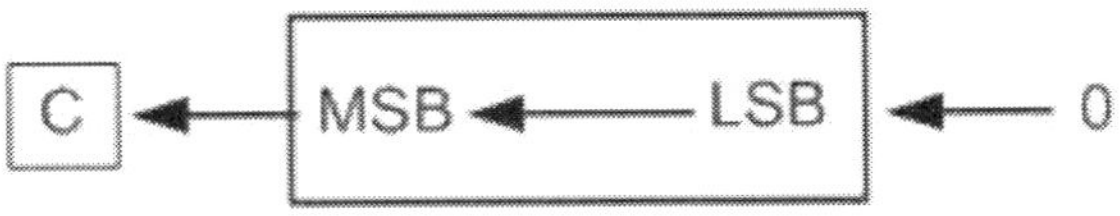

Shift left is also a logical shift. It is the reverse of LSR. After every shift, the LSB is filled with 0 and the MSB goes to C flag in CPSR if the 'S' suffix is used in the instruction. All the rules are the same as for LSR. One can use an immediate value or a register to hold the number of times it is to be shifted left. See Example 3-19. One can use the LSL to multiply a number by 2. See Example 3-20.

Example 3-19

Show the effects of LSL in the following:

```
LDR   R1, =0x0F000006
MOVS  R2, R1, LSL #8
```

Solution:

	00001111 00000000 00000000 00000110
C=0	00011110 00000000 00000000 00001100 (shifted left once)
C=0	00111100 00000000 00000000 00011000
C=0	01111000 00000000 00000000 00110000
C=0	11110000 00000000 00000000 01100000
C=1	11100000 00000000 00000000 11000000
C=1	11000000 00000000 00000001 10000000
C=1	10000000 00000000 00000011 00000000
C=1	00000000 00000000 00000110 00000000 (shifted eight times)

After eight shifts left, the R2 register has 0x00000600 and C = 1. The eight MSBs are lost through the carry, one by one, and 0s fill the eight LSBs. Another way to write the above code is:

```
LDR   R1, =0x0F000006
MOV   R0, #0x08
MOV   R2, R1, LSL R0
```

Example 3-20

Show the results of LSL in the following:

```
TIMES EQU   0x5
      LDR   R1, #0x7          ; R1=0x7
      MOV   R2, #TIMES        ; R2=0x05
      MOV   R1, R1, LSL R2    ; shift R1 left R2 number of times
                              ; and place the result in R1
```

Solution:

After the five shifts, the R1 will contain 0x000000E0. 0xE0 is 224 in decimal. Notice that it multiplies number by power of 2. That means 7 × 32 = 224 = 0xE0 since 2 to the power of 5 is 32.

Table 3-5 lists the logical shift operations in ARM.

Operation	Destination	Source	Number of shifts
LSR (Shift Right)	Rd	Rn	Immediate value
LSR (Shift Right)	Rd	Rn	register Rm
LSL (Shift Left)	Rd	Rn	Immediate value
LSL (Shift Left)	Rd	Rn	register Rm
Note: Number of shift cannot be more than 32.			

Table 3-5: Logic Shift operations for unsigned numbers in ARM

Arithmetic shift right – ASR

The arithmetic shift ASR is used for signed numbers and will be discussed in Chapter 5.

Rotating the bits of an operand right and left

There are two types of rotations. One is a simple rotation of the bits of the operand, and the other is a rotation through the carry. Each is explained below.

Rotate right – ROR

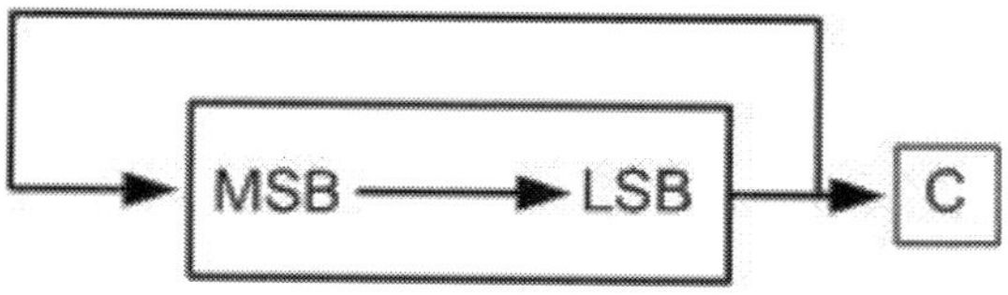

In rotate right, as bits are shifted from left to right, they exit from the right end (LSB) and enter the left end (MSB). In addition, as each bit exits the LSB, a copy of it is given to the carry flag in CPSR if the 'S' suffix is used in the instruction. One can use an immediate value or a register to hold the number of times it is to be rotated.

```
MOV   R1, #0x36
; R1 = 0000 0000 0000 0000 0000 0000 0011 0110
MOVS  R1, R1, ROR #1
; R1 = 0000 0000 0000 0000 0000 0000 0001 1011  C=0
MOVS  R1, R1, ROR #1
; R1 = 1000 0000 0000 0000 0000 0000 0000 1101  C=1
MOVS  R1, R1, ROR #1
; R1 = 1100 0000 0000 0000 0000 0000 0000 0110  C=1
```

or:

```
MOV   R1, #0x36
; R1 = 0000 0000 0000 0000 0000 0000 0011 0110
MOV   R0, #3
; R0 = 3 number of times to rotate
MOVS  R1, R1, ROR R0
; R1 = 1100 0000 0000 0000 0000 0000 0000 0110 C=1
```

also look at the following case:

```
LDR   R2, =0xC7E5
; R2 = 0000 0000 0000 0000 1100 0111 1110 0101
MOV   R4, #0x06
; R4 = 6 number of times to rotate
MOVS  R3, R2, ROR R4
; R3 = 1001 0100 0000 0000 0000 0011 0001 1111 C=1
```

Rotate left using ROR

There is no rotate left option in ARM since one can always use the rotate right instruction (ROR) to get the job done. That means instead of rotating left n bits we can use rotate right (32–n) bits to do the job of rotate left. Using this method does not give us the proper carry if actual instruction of ROL was available. Look at the following examples:

```
LDR   R0, =0x00000072
; R0 = 0000 0000 0000 0000 0000 0000 0111 0010
MOVS  R0, R0, ROR #31
; R0 = 0000 0000 0000 0000 0000 0000 1110 0100  C=0
MOVS  R0, R0, ROR #31
; R0 = 0000 0000 0000 0000 0000 0001 1100 1000  C=0
MOVS  R0, R0, ROR #31
; R0 = 0000 0000 0000 0000 0000 0011 1001 0000  C=0
MOVS  R0, R0, ROR #31
; R0 = 0000 0000 0000 0000 0000 0111 0010 0000  C=0
```

or:

```
MOV   R0, #0x72         ; R0 = 0111 0010
MOV   R1, #28           ; R1 = 32 - 4 = 28
MOVS  R0, R0, ROR R1    ; R0 = 0111 0010 0000  C=0
```

```
LDR    R2, =0x671A
; R2 = 0000 0000 0000 0000 0110 0111 0010 1010
MOVS   R2, R2, ROR #27
; R2 = 0000 0000 0000 1100 1110 0101 0100 0000
; C = 0
```

Rotate right through carry RRX

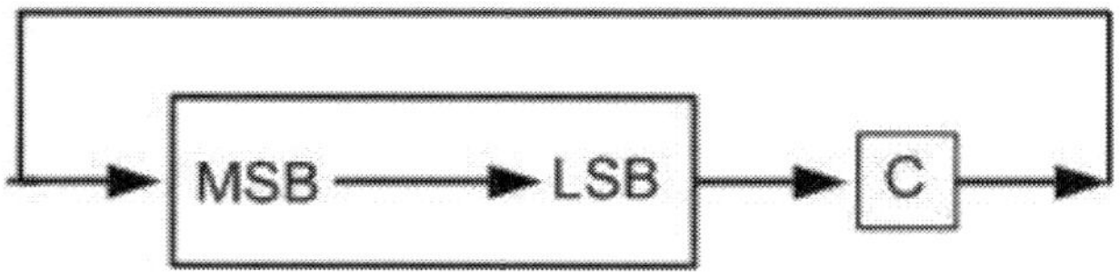

In RRX, as bits are shifted from left to right, they exit from the right end (LSB) to the carry flag if the 'S' suffix is used in the instruction. If the 'S' suffix is not used in the instruction, the bits rotated out just get lost. On the other end, the carry flag always rotates into the MSB. So if the 'S' suffix is set, the C flag acts as if it is part of the operand and the RRX is like rotating a 33-bit register. When the 'S' suffix is not set, the RRX works similar to a right shift but the bit shifted in depends on the current value of the C flag in CPSR and the C flag does not change.

The RRX takes no arguments and the number of times the operand to be rotated is always one.

```
; assume C=0
MOV    R2, #0x26
; R2 = 0000 0000 0000 0000 0000 0000 0010 0110
MOVS   R2, R2, RRX
; R2 = 0000 0000 0000 0000 0000 0000 0001 0011 C=0
MOVS   R2, R2, RRX
; R2 = 0000 0000 0000 0000 0000 0000 0000 1001 C=1
MOVS   R2, R2, RRX
; R2 = 1000 0000 0000 0000 0000 0000 0000 0100 C=1
MOV    R2, #0x0F
; R2 = 0000 0000 0000 0000 0000 0000 0000 1111
MOVS   R2, R2, RRX
; R2 = 0000 0000 0000 0000 0000 0000 0000 0111 C=1
MOVS   R2, R2, RRX
; R2 = 1000 0000 0000 0000 0000 0000 0000 0011 C=1
MOVS   R2, R2, RRX
; R2 = 1100 0000 0000 0000 0000 0000 0000 0001 C=1
```

Table 3-6 lists the rotate instructions of the ARM.

Operation	Destination	Source	Number of Rotates
ROR (Rotate Right)	Rd	Rn	Immediate value
ROR (Rotate Right)	Rd	Rn	register Rm
RRX (Rotate Right Through Carry)	Rd	Rn	1 bit

Table 3- 6: Rotate operations for unsigned numbers in ARM

Rotating Immediate Arguments

We just examined the rotate and shift operations of the second operand that is a register. One can use the rotate operation to load literal (constant) values into ARM registers as well. Examine the MOV instruction bit assignment in Figure 3-3. Of the 32-bit opcode, the upper 12 bits (D31–D20) are used for the opcode itself. The lowest 8 (D7–D0) bits are used for literal values and 4 bits (D11–D8) are used for the number of times rotate right operation is performed before loading the value into the register. The 8 bits for the literal value give us 0 to 255 (0x00 to 0xFF in hex) range and the 4 bits of the rotate number give us 0 to 15 (0 to 0xF in hex) range. The number of times the literal value is rotated right is always twice the number in the rotate portion in the instruction. Since rotate value can be 0–15 that gives number of rotations between 0–30. This means that whenever the second operand is an immediate value the number of rotations is always an even number.

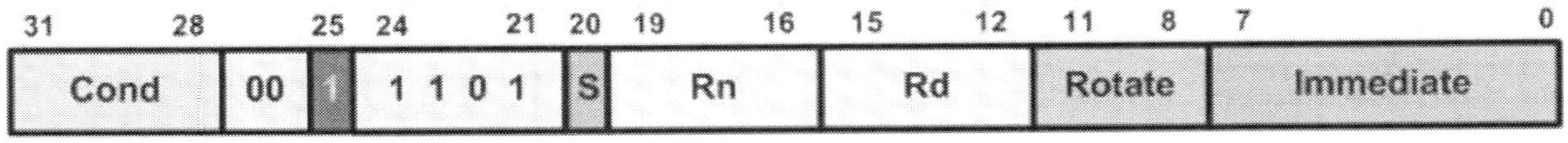

Figure 3- 3: MOV Instruction

When writing the immediate value with rotate as operand 2, the immediate value is written first preceded by a "#" sign. The number of rotate is written after the immediate value also preceded by a "#" sign. The immediate value and the number of rotate are separated by a comma. As we mentioned earlier, the ARM supports only rotate right and there is no rotate left option. So, to do rotate left we must use 32-n for the number of rotations right. Therefore, "MOV R0, #0xFF, #30" is the same as rotating left 2 times and "MOV R0, #0xFF, #28" is the same as rotating left 4 times. Remember the number of rotate must be an even number, otherwise a syntax error occurs.

You may also choose to write the result of the rotated literal values in the source file and the ARM assembler will separate the 8-bit literal and the number of rotate for you. For example, if you write the instruction "MOV R2, #0x00FF0000" in the program, ARM assembler will treat it as "MOV R2, #0xFF, #16". Of course, the immediate value you write must be a valid literal value that can be expressed by an 8-bit value with even number of rotate.

See Examples 3-21 through 3-23.

Example 3-21

Show all the possible cases of using MOV instruction for 0xFF value and rotate options.

Solution:

```
MOV   R0, #0xFF, #0
; R0 = 0xFF is rotated right 0 times. R0 = 0x000000FF
MOV   R0, #0xFF, #2
; R0 = 0xFF is rotated right 2 times. R0 = 0xC000003F
MOV   R0, #0xFF, #4
; R0 = 0xFF is rotated right 4 times. R0 = 0xF000000F
```

```
MOV   R0, #0xFF, #6
; R0 = 0xFF is rotated right 6 times. R0 = 0xFC000003
MOV   R0, #0xFF, #8
; R0 = 0xFF is rotated right 8 times. R0 = 0xFF000000
MOV   R0, #0xFF, #10
; R0 = 0xFF is rotated right 10 times. R0 = 0x3FC00000
MOV   R0, #0xFF, #12
; R0 = 0xFF is rotated right 12 times. R0 = 0x0FF00000
MOV   R0, #0xFF, #14
; R0 = 0xFF is rotated right 14 times. R0 = 0x03FC0000
MOV   R0, #0xFF, #16
; R0 = 0xFF is rotated right 16 times. R0 = 0x00FF0000
MOV   R0, #0xFF, #18
; R0 = 0xFF is rotated right 18 times. R0 = 0x003FC000
MOV   R0, #0xFF, #20
; R0 = 0xFF is rotated right 20 times. R0 = 0x000FF000
MOV   R0, #0xFF, #22
; R0 = 0xFF is rotated right 22 times. R0 = 0x0003FC00
MOV   R0, #0xFF, #24
; R0 = 0xFF is rotated right 24 times. R0 = 0x0000FF00
MOV   R0, #0xFF, #26
; R0 = 0xFF is rotated right 26 times. R0 = 0x00003FC0
MOV   R0, #0xFF, #28
; R0 = 0xFF is rotated right 28 times. R0 = 0x00000FF0
MOV   R0, #0xFF, #30
; R0 = 0xFF is rotated right 30 times. R0 = 0x000003FC
```

Example 3-22

Using MOV instruction, show how to rotate left the literal value of 0x99 total of (a) 4, (b) 8, and (c) 16 times. Also give the value in the register after the rotation.

Solution:

Since we do not have rotate left operation, we must use rotate right 32–n times.

```
MOV   R1, #0x99, #28
; rotating right 28 times is the same as rotate left 4 times
MOV   R2, #0x99, #24
; rotating right 24 times is the same as rotate left 8 times
MOV   R3, #0x99, #16
; rotating right 16 times is the same as rotate left 16 times
```

Now, we have (a) R1 = 0x00000990, (b) R2 = 0x00009900, and (c) R3=0x00990000

Example 3-23

Using the Keil IDE, assemble the program in Example 3-21 and examine the list file. Compare and contrast the count value in the instruction with count value of the opcodes.

Solution:

```
Disassembly
        3:          MOV     R0,#0xFF,#0      ;R0 = 0xF
0x00000000  E3A000FF  MOV         R0,#0x000000FF
        4:          MOV     R0,#0xFF,#2      ;R0 = 0xF
0x00000004  E3A001FF  MOV         R0,#0xC000003F
        5:          MOV     R0,#0xFF,#4      ;R0 = 0xF
0x00000008  E3A002FF  MOV         R0,#0xF000000F
        6:          MOV     R0,#0xFF,#6      ;R0 = 0xF
0x0000000C  E3A003FF  MOV         R0,#0xFC000003
        7:          MOV     R0,#0xFF,#8      ;R0 = 0xF
0x00000010  E3A004FF  MOV         R0,#0xFF000000
        8:          MOV     R0,#0xFF,#10 ;R0 = 0xFF
0x00000014  E3A005FF  MOV         R0,#0x3FC00000
        9:          MOV     R0,#0xFF,#12 ;R0 = 0xFF
0x00000018  E3A006FF  MOV         R0,#0x0FF00000
       10:          MOV     R0,#0xFF,#14 ;R0 = 0xFF
0x0000001C  E3A007FF  MOV         R0,#0x03FC0000
       11:          MOV     R0,#0xFF,#16 ;R0 = 0xFF
0x00000020  E3A008FF  MOV         R0,#0x00FF0000
       12:          MOV     R0,#0xFF,#18 ;R0 = 0xFF
0x00000024  E3A009FF  MOV         R0,#0x003FC000
       13:          MOV     R0,#0xFF,#20 ;R0 = 0xFF
0x00000028  E3A00AFF  MOV         R0,#0x000FF000
       14:          MOV     R0,#0xFF,#22 ;R0 = 0xFF
```

	31 – 16	15 – 12	11 – 8	7 – 0
MOV R0, #0xFF, #0	E3A0	3	**0**	FF
	Opcode	Rd	Rotate	Immediate

	31 – 16	15 – 12	11 – 8	7 – 0
MOV R0, #0xFF, #2	E3A0	3	**1**	FF
	Opcode	Rd	Rotate	Immediate

	31 – 16	15 – 12	11 – 8	7 – 0
MOV R0, #0xFF, #4	E3A0	3	**2**	FF
	Opcode	Rd	Rotate	Immediate

	31 – 16	15 – 12	11 – 8	7 – 0
MOV R0, #0xFF, #6	E3A0	3	**3**	FF
	Opcode	Rd	Rotate	Immediate

	31 – 16	15 – 12	11 – 8	7 – 0
MOV R0, #0xFF, #8	E3A0	3	**4**	FF
	Opcode	Rd	Rotate	Immediate

As expected, the number of times rotated right is twice the number of rotate field.

Also see Example 3-24 for further examples of rotate operation.

Example 3-24

Give the register value for each of the following instructions after it is executed.

```
MOV   R0, #0xAA, #2
MOV   R1, #0x20, #28
MOV   R4, #0x99, #6
MOV   R2, #0x55, #24
MOV   R3, #0x01, #20
MOV   R7, #0x80, #12
MOV   R10, #0x0F, #14
MOV   R5, #0x66, #2
```

Solution:

```
MOV   R0, #0xAA, #2
; R0 = 0xAA is rotated right 2 times. R0 = 0x8000002A
MOV   R1, #0x20, #28
; R1 = 0x20 is rotated right 28 times. R0 = 0x00000200
MOV   R4, #0x99, #6
; R4 = 0x99 is rotated right 6 times. R0 = 0x64000002
MOV   R2, #0x55, #24
; R2 = 0x55 is rotated right 24 times. R0 = 0x00005500
MOV   R3, #0x01, #20
; R3 = 0x01 is rotated right 20 times. R0 = 0x00001000
MOV   R7, #0x80, #12
; R7 = 0x80 is rotated right 12 times. R0 = 0x08000000
MOV   R10, #0x0F, #14
; R10 = 0x0F is rotated right 14 times. R0 = 0x003C0000
MOV   R5, #0x66, #2
; R5 = 0x66 is rotated right 2 times. R0 = 0x80000019
```

Like MOV instruction, MVN can have an 8-bit literal operand with even number of rotate. For example, "MVN R1, #0xAE, #18" will leave 0xFFD47FFF in R1. That is if you rotate 0xAE by 18 bits to the right, you end up with 0x002B8000. Take the 1's complement of 0x002B8000 and you have 0xFFD47FFF. This allows you to have many more choices of immediate value to be loaded into the registers. And like MOV instruction, you may also write "MVN R1, #0xFFD47FFF" in the program and the ARM assembler will format the instruction for you. Even better, you can write "MOV R1, #0xFFD47FFF" in the program and the ARM assembler will replace the MOV by MVN.

See Example 3-25.

Example 3-25

Give the register value for each of the following instructions after it is executed.

```
MVN   R0, #0xAA, #2
MVN   R1, #0x20, #28
MVN   R4, #0x99, #6
MVN   R2, #0x55, #24
MVN   R3, #0x01, #20
MVN   R7, #0x80, #12
MVN   R10, #0x0F, #14
MVN   R5, #0x66, #2
```

Solution:

```
MVN   R0, #0xAA, #2
; 0xAA rotated right 2 times = 0x8000002A; R0 = 0x7FFFFFD5
MVN   R1, #0x20, #28
; 0x20 is rotated right 28 times = 0x00000200; R1 = 0xFFFFFDFF
MVN   R4, #0x99, #6
; 0x99 is rotated right 6  times = 0x64000002; R4 = 0x9BFFFFFD
MVN   R2, #0x55, #24
; 0x55 is rotated right 24 times = 0x00001A40; R2 = 0xFFFFAAFF
MVN   R3, #0x01, #20
; 0x01 is rotated right 20 times = 0x00001000; R3 = 0xFFFFEFFF
MVN   R7, #0x80, #12
; 0x8C is rotated right 12 times = 0x08000000; R7 = 0xF7FFFFFF
MVN   R10, #0x0F, #14
; 0x0F is rotated right 14 times = 0x003C0000; R10= 0xFFC3FFFF
MVN   R5, #0x66, #2
; 0x66 is rotated right 2  times = 0x80000019; R5 = 0x7FFFFFE6
```

General Formation of Data Processing Instruction

Next we will show how the different operands are supported by ARM. In Figure 3-4 you see the general formation of process instructions.

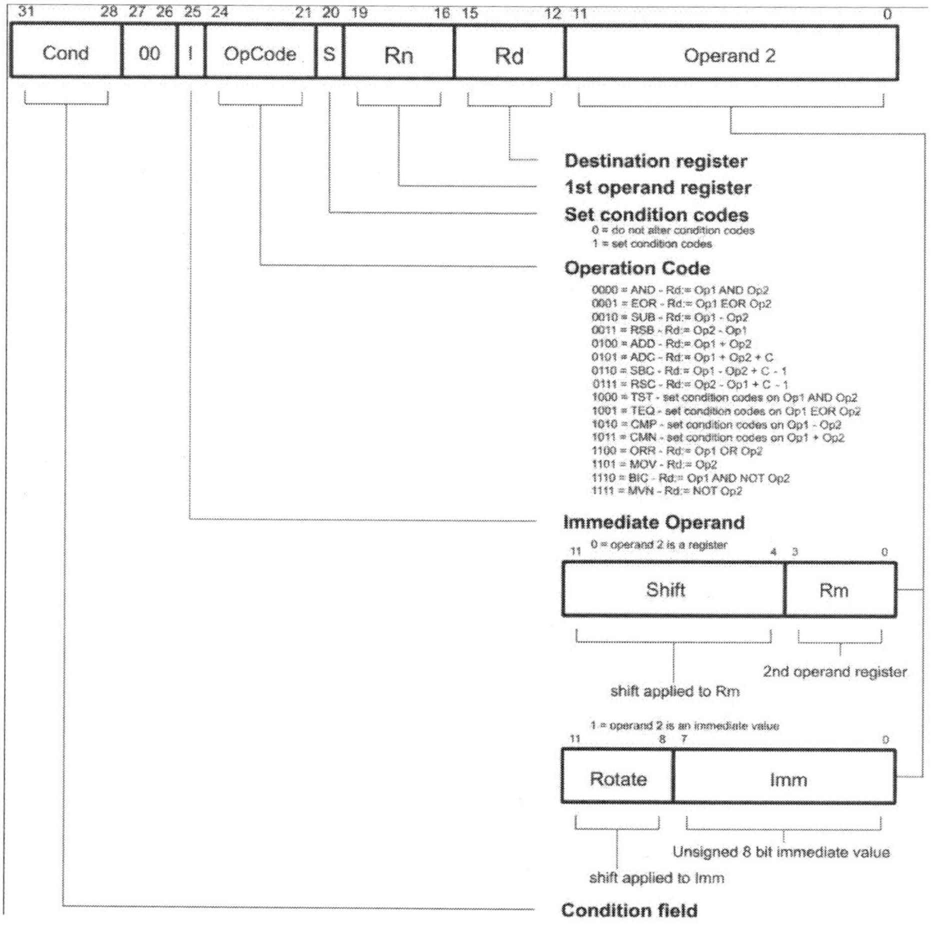

Figure 3- 4: Data Process Instructions

In all ARM instructions, bits 28–31 are put aside for condition field which is covered in Chapter 4.

Bits 26 and 27 are 0 in process instructions showing that the instruction is a process instruction and the opcode is represented by bits 24–21. Using 4 bits 16 different instructions are provided as shown in Figure 3-4.

The S bit (bit 20) shows if the flags should be updated. When we add an S (e.g. MOVS) the bit will be set which shows that the flags should be updated by the CPU.

Bits 12–15 contain the destination register. Using 4 bits we can select registers R0–R15.

Bits 16–19 represent the first operand register.

Bit 25 (I) shows the type of second operand. The bit is 1 when the second operand is an immediate value. Whenever the second operand is a register, this bit is zero.

Immediate values: In the case that I is 1, bits 0–7, contain an immediate value which can be a number between 0–0xFF.

Second register: In the case that I is 0, bits 0–11 represent the second operand register, together with the amount of shift/rotate and type of shift/rotate. As mentioned earlier the shift amount can be provided either by a register or an immediate value. Whenever the I bit is cleared, bit 4 shows the way shift amount is provided. See Figure 3-5.

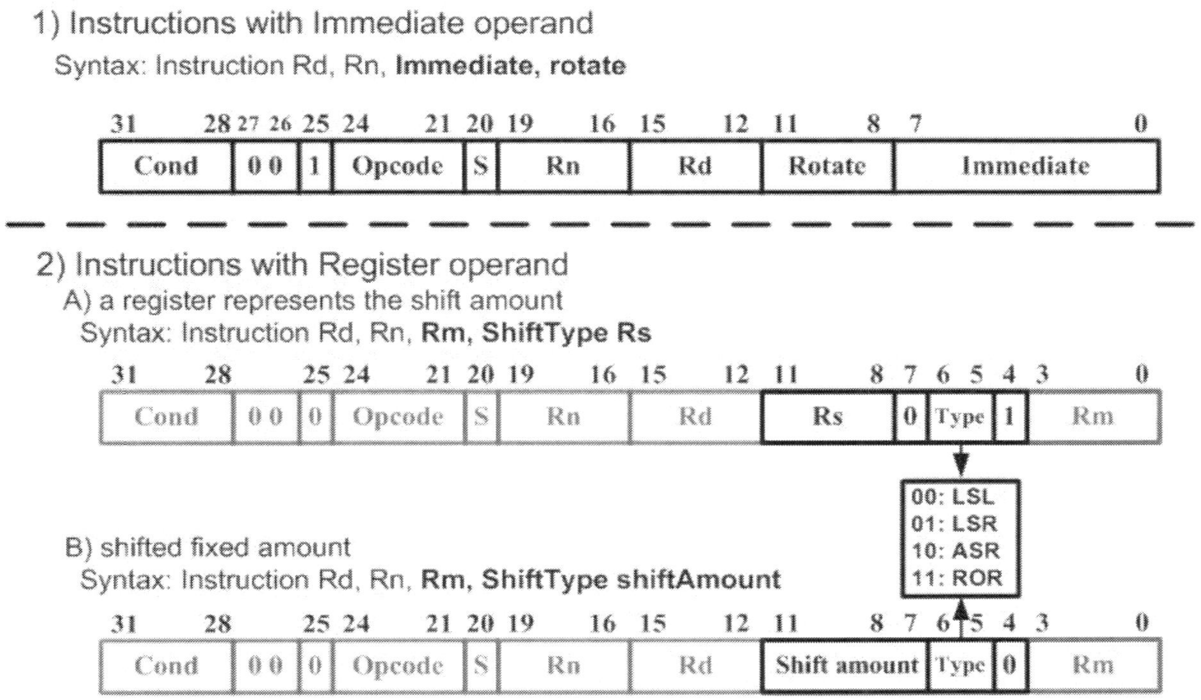

Figure 3- 5: Data Process Instructions

Example 3-26 should help to clarify this.

Example 3-26

Using the Keil IDE, assemble the following program and compare the instruction with the process instruction format.

```
        AREA EX3_26, CODE, READONLY

        ADD   R0, R1, R5, LSR #2
        ADD   R0, R1, R5, LSR R2
        ADD   R0, R1, R5, LSL R2
        ADD   R0, R1, R5
        ADD   R0, R1, #5, #2
        ADD   R0, R1, #5
H1      B     H1
        END
```

Solution:

```
Disassembly
      3:          ADD      R0,R1,R5,LSR #2
0x00000000  E0810125  ADD          R0,R1,R5,LSR #2
      4:          ADD      R0,R1,R5,LSR R2
0x00000004  E0810235  ADD          R0,R1,R5,LSR R2
      5:          ADD      R0,R1,R5,LSL R2
0x00000008  E0810215  ADD          R0,R1,R5,LSL R2
      6:          ADD      R0,R1,R5
0x0000000C  E0810005  ADD          R0,R1,R5
      7:          ADD      R0,R1,#5,#2
0x00000010  E2810105  ADD          R0,R1,#0x40000001
      8:          ADD      R0,R1,#5
0x00000014  E2810005  ADD          R0,R1,#0x00000005
```

Condition		I	Opcode	S	Rn	Rd	Shift amount	Shift Type	Arg. Type	Rm
1 1 1 0	0 0	0	0 1 0 0	0	0 0 0 1	0 0 0 0	0 0 0 1 0	0 1	0	0 1 0 1
			ADD		R1	R0	2 bits	LSR		R5

In "ADD R0, R1, R5, LSR #2" the second operand is a register. Therefore, the I bit is cleared. Since the shift amount is an immediate value, the bit 4 is cleared, as well. The shift type is set to 01 representing LSR.

Condition		I	Opcode	S	Rn	Rd	Rs		Shift Type	Arg. Type	Rm
1 1 1 0	0 0	0	0 1 0 0	0	0 0 0 1	0 0 0 0	0 0 1 0	0	0 1	1	0 1 0 1
			ADD		R1	R0	R2		LSR		R5

In "ADD R0, R1, R5, LSR R2" the second operand is a register. Therefore, the I bit is cleared. As a register provides the shift amount, the bit 4 is set.

Condition		I	Opcode	S	Rn	Rd	Rs		Shift Type	Arg. Type	Rm
1 1 1 0	0 0	0	0 1 0 0	0	0 0 0 1	0 0 0 0	0 0 1 0	0	0 0	1	0 1 0 1
			ADD		R1	R0	R2		LSL		R5

The "ADD R0, R1, R5, LSL R2" instruction is the same as "ADD R0, R1, R5, LSR R2" except that the shift type is set to 00 to represent LSL.

Condition		I	Opcode	S	Rn	Rd	Shift amount	Shift Type	Arg. Type	Rm
1 1 1 0	0 0	0	0 1 0 0	0	0 0 0 1	0 0 0 0	0 0 0 0 0	0 0	0	0 1 0 1
			ADD		R1	R0	0 bits	LSL		R5

The machine code represents in fact the instruction "ADD R0, R1, R5, LSL #0". But, if we shift a number 0 bits to left, the number remains unchanged. As a result, it represents "ADD R0, R1, R5".

Condition		I	Opcode	S	Rn	Rd	Rotate	Immediate
1 1 1 0	0 0	1	0 1 0 0	0	0 0 0 1	0 0 0 0	0 0 0 1	0 0 0 0 0 1 0 1
			ADD		R1	R0	2 bits	#5

In "ADDR0, R1, #5, #2" the second operand is immediate. Therefore, the I bit is set. In immediate operands the value is shifted twice the rotate field. That is why the rotate field is 1.

Condition		I	Opcode	S	Rn	Rd	Rotate	Immediate
1 1 1 0	0 0	1	0 1 0 0	0	0 0 0 1	0 0 0 0	0 0 0 0	0 0 0 0 0 1 0 1
			ADD		R1	R0	0 bits	#5

In "ADD R0, R1, #5", the immediate value is rotated 0 bits. Therefore, the immediate value remains unchanged.

Review Questions

1. Find the contents of R3 after executing the following code:

```
MOV   R0, #0x04
MOV   R3, R0, LSR #2
```

2. Find the contents of R4 after executing the following code:

```
LDR   R1, =0xA0F2
MOV   R2, #0x3
MOV   R4, R1, LSR R2
```

3. Find the contents of R3 after executing the following code:

```
LDR   R1, =0xA0F2
MOV   R2, #0x3
MOV   R3, R1, LSL R2
```

4. Find the contents of R5 after executing the following code:

```
SUBS  R0, R0, R0
MOV   R0, #0xAA
MOV   R5, R0, ROR #4
```

5. Find the contents of R0 after executing the following code:

```
LDR   R2, =0xA0F2
MOV   R1, #0x1
MOV   R0, R2, ROR R1
```

6. Give the result in R1 for the following:

```
MVN   R1, #0x01, #2
```

7. Give the result in R2 for the following:

```
MVN    R2, #0x02, #28
```

Section 3.4: Shift and Rotate Instructions

As we have seen in the previous section, the barrel shifter may be engaged during a data processing instruction. If no other data processing besides shift or rotate is needed, the MOV opcode in conjunction with the shift/rotate operation is used. To make the assembly code more readable, the ARM assembler provides the shift and rotate instructions that we will describe below. The programmers write the shift/rotate instructions in the source code and the ARM assembler will assemble them if it is a MOV instruction with shift/rotate. For example, if you write the logic shift left instruction as:

```
LSL    R0, R2, #8
```

the ARM assembler will assemble it as

```
MOV    R0, R2, LSL #8
```

Since the shift/rotate instructions are more readable than a MOV instruction with shift/rotate operand 2, it is recommended that the shift/rotate instructions be used where they are appropriate. For full instruction set see Appendix A. For the purpose of comparison, we have copied this section from Appendix A.

ASR – Arithmetic Shift right

```
ASR Rd, Rm, Rn
```

Function: As each bit of Rm register is shifted right, the LSB is removed and the empty bits filled with the sign bit (MSB). The number of bits to be shifted right is given by Rn and the result is placed in Rd register. The flags are unchanged. To update the flags, use ASRS instruction.

Example 1:

```
LDR    R2, =0xFFFFFF82
ASR    R0, R2, #6   ;R0=R2 is shifted right 6 times
                    ;now, R0 = 0xFFFFFFFE
```

Example 2:

```
LDR    R0, =0x2000FF18
MOV    R1, #12
ASR    R2, R0, R1   ;R2=R0 is shifted right R1 number of times.
                    ;now, R2 = 0x0002000F
```

Example 3:

```
LDR    R0, =0x0000FF18
MOV    R1, #16
ASR    R2, R0, R1   ;R2=R0 is shifted right R1 number of times
                    ;now, R2 = 0x00000000
```

ASR arithmetic shift is used for signed number shifting. ASR essentially divides Rm by a power of 2 for each bit shift.

LSL – Logical Shift Left

```
        LSL    Rd, Rm, Rn
```

Function: As each bit of Rm register is shifted left, the MSB is removed and the empty bits are filled with zeros. The number of bits to be shifted left is given by Rn and the result is placed in Rd register. To update the flags, use LSLS instruction.

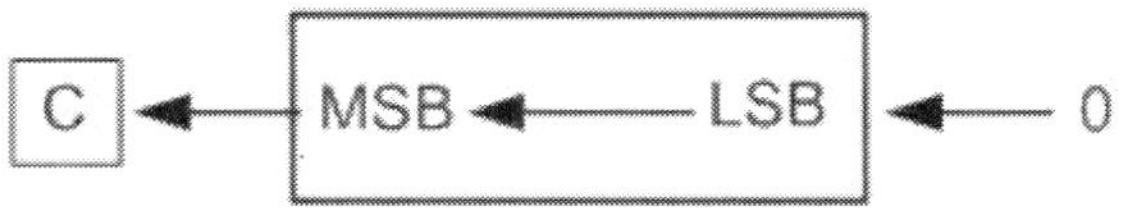

Example 1:

```
        LDR    R2, =0x00000010
LSL    R0, R2, #8   ; R0=R2 is shifted left 8 times
                    ; now, R0= 0x00001000, flags not updated
```

Example 2:

```
        LDR    R0, =0x00000018
        MOV    R1, #12
        LSL    R2, R0, R1   ; R2=R0 is shifted left R1 number of times
                            ; now, R2= 0x000018000, flags not updated
```

Example 3:

```
        LDR    R0, =0x0000FF18
        MOV    R1, #16
        LSL    R2, R0, R1   ; R2=R0 is shifted left R1 number of times
                            ; now, R2= 0xFF180000, flags not updated
```

LSR – Logical Shift Right

```
        LSR    Rd, Rm, Rn
```

Function: As each bit of Rm register is shifted right, the LSB is removed and the empty bits are filled with zeros. The number of bits to be shifted left is given by Rn and the result is placed in Rd register. To update the flags, use LSRS instruction.

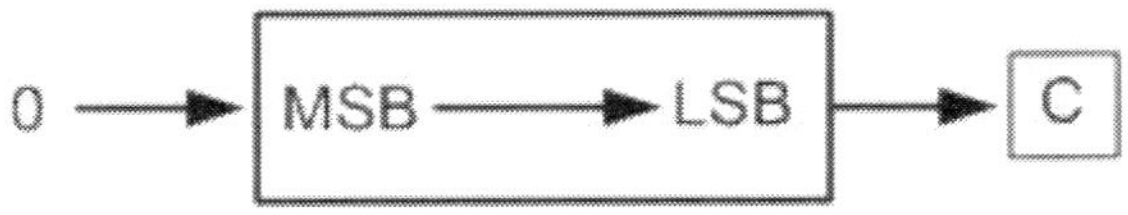

Example 1:

```
        LDR    R2, =0x00001000
        LSR    R0, R2, #8         ; R0=R2 is shifted right 8 times
                                  ; now, R0= 0x00000010, C=0
```

Example 2:

```
LDR   R0, =0x000018000
MOV   R1, #12
LSR   R2, R0, R1        ; R2=R0 is shifted right R1 number of times
                        ; now, R2= 0x00000018, C=0
```

Example 3:

```
LDR   R0, =0x7F180000
MOV   R1, #16
LSR   R2, R0, R1        ; R2=R0 is shifted right R1 number of times
                        ; now, R2=0x00007F18, C=0
```

The logical shift right is used for shifting unsigned numbers. LSR essentially divides Rm by a power of 2 after each bit is shifted.

ROR – Rotate Right

```
ROR   Rd, Rm, Rn   ; Rd=rotate Rm right Rn bit positions
```

Function: As each bit of Rm register is shifted from left to right, they exit from the end (LSB) and entered from left end (MSB). The number of bits to be rotated right is given by Rn and the result is placed in Rd register. To update the flags use RORS instruction.

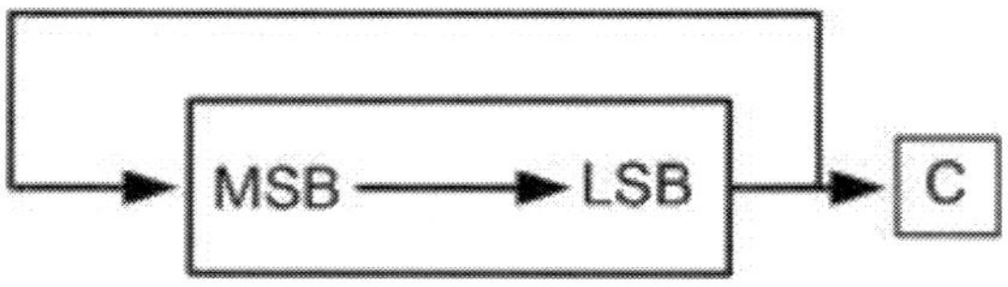

Example 1:

```
LDR   R2, =0x00000010
ROR   R0, R2, #8   ; R0=R2 is rotated right 8 times
                   ; now, R0 = 0x10000000, C=0
```

Example 2:

```
LDR   R0, =0x00000018
MOV   R1, #12
ROR   R2, R0, R1   ; R2=R0 is rotated right R1 number of times
                   ; now, R2 = 0x01800000, C=0
```

Example 3:

```
LDR   R0, =0x0000FF18
MOV   R1, #16
ROR   R2, R0, R1   ; R2=R0 is rotated right R1 number of times
                   ; now, R2 = 0xFF180000, C=0
```

RRX – Rotate Right with extend

```
RRXS  Rd, Rm       ; Rd=rotate Rm right 1 bit through C flag
```

Function: Each bit of Rm register is rotated from left to right one bit through C flag when RRXS instruction is used. If the 'S' suffix is not used, the LSB is lost and the current C flag is shifted into MSB.

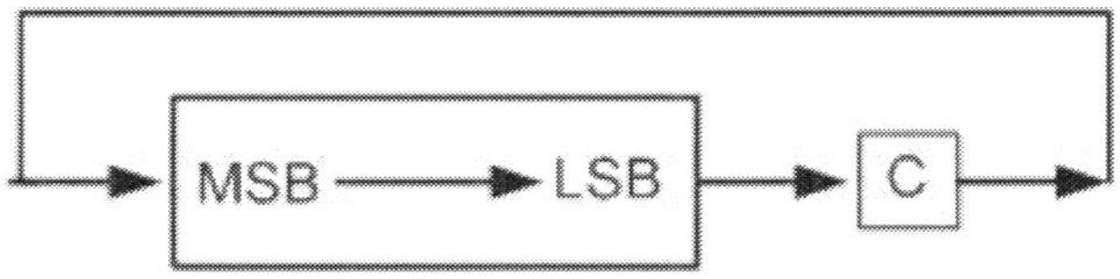

Example:

```
LDR   R2, =0x00000002
RRX   R0, R2        ; R0=R2 is shifted right one bit
                    ; now, R0=0x00000001
```

Review Quest ons

1. Find the contents of R2 after executing the following code:

```
MOV   R1, #0x08
ROR   R2, R1, #2
```

2. Find the contents of R4 after executing the following code:

```
MOV   R3, #0x3
LSL   R4, R3, #2
```

Section 3.5: BCD and ASCII Conversion

This section covers binary, BCD, and ASCII conversions with some examples.

BCD number system

BCD stands for Binary Coded Decimal. Most of the computers these days perform arithmetic in binary because binary arithmetic is easier and faster to implement in electronic circuit. But most of the numbers used in real lift are decimal, so it requires to convert the decimal numbers to binary before the computations can be done. Earlier computers did arithmetic in decimal because it does not require the decimal to binary and binary to decimal conversions.

Digit	BCD
0	0000
1	0001
2	0010
3	0011
4	0100
5	0101
6	0110
7	0111
8	1000
9	1001

Table 3-7: BCD Codes

To perform arithmetic in decimal, data need to be encoded in decimal format but using binary system of the computer so binary coded decimal (BCD) is often used. See Table 3-9. In the modern computing, you may still encounter the usage of BCD in some applications. For example, BCD is used in many real-time clock (RTC) of the embedded systems.

There are two formats for BCD numbers: (1) unpacked BCD, and (2) packed BCD.

Unpacked BCD

In unpacked BCD, each decimal digit is represented by a byte (8-bit). The lower 4 bits of the byte represent the BCD number and the rest of the bits are 0. For example, "0000 1001" and "0000 0101" are unpacked BCD for 9 and 5, respectively.

Packed BCD

In the case of packed BCD, two decimal digits are packed in one byte, one in the lower 4 bits and one in the upper 4 bits. For example, "0101 1001" is packed BCD for 59. Obviously, packed BCD is more efficient in memory usage but to perform arithmetic with packed BCD, the circuit has to be able to detect the decimal carry from the lower digit to the upper digit in the same byte. ARM CPU does not do that.

ASCII encoding

The American Standard Code for Information Interchange was established in the early 1960's as a character encoding standard for telegraph in United States. It was adopted by computer developers to be used as the encoding for transmitting text between computer and peripherals, text file storage, and communication between computers. The ASCII code has the advantage over other encode of the earlier time as the code within the three groups of code (numerals, uppercase alphabets, and alphabets) are all in consecutive order. That makes conversion between ASCII and BCD or between uppercase and lowercase easier.

ASCII codes are 7-bit long. The ASCII encoding of numerals starts from "011 0000" (0x30) for "0". Since all the numeral codes are consecutive, "1" is encoded as "011 0001" (0x31) "2" is encoded as "011 0010" (0x32) and so on.

For example, in an ASCII keyboard when a key is pressed, the ASCII encoding of that key is transmitted to the computer. So, when key "0" is pressed, "011 0000" (0x30) is sent to the computer. In the same way, when key "5" is pressed, "011 0101" (0x35) is sent. The ASCII codes of numerals are shown in the following table together with the corresponding BCD code:

Key	ASCII	Binary(hex)	BCD (unpacked)
0	30	011 0000	0000 0000
1	31	011 0001	0000 0001
2	32	011 0010	0000 0010
3	33	011 0011	0000 0011
4	34	011 0100	0000 0100
5	45	011 0101	0000 0101
6	36	011 0110	0000 0110
7	37	011 0111	0000 0111
8	38	011 1000	0000 1000
9	39	011 1001	0000 1001

Though we mentioned earlier that processing decimal data in BCD does not require to convert the data to binary. But often the input/output data and the data stored in the files are in ASCII code for ease of human reading. Input/output devices like keyboard and LCD display are usually using ASCII encoding. These ASCII data need to be converted to BCD before performing decimal data processing and be converted back to ASCII afterward. These are the subjects covered next.

ASCII to unpacked BCD conversion

The lower nibble (least significant four bits) of the ASCII codes for numeral contain the binary value of that digit. To convert ASCII data to unpacked BCD, the programmer must get rid of the "011" in the upper 3 bits of the 7-bit ASCII. To do that, each ASCII number is ANDed with "0000 1111" (0x0F).

ASCII to packed BCD conversion

To convert ASCII numbers to packed BCD, they are first converted to unpacked BCD (remove the upper 3 bits) and then combined every two digits to make a packed BCD. For example, if the user typed digit 2 and 7 on an ASCII keyboard, the keyboard transmits ASCII codes 0x32 and 0x37 to the computer. The goal is to produce 0x27 or "0010 0111", which is called packed BCD. This process is illustrated in detail in the program snippet below.

Key	ASCII	Unpacked BCD	Packed BCD
2	32	00000010	
7	37	00000111	00100111 (0x27)

```
MOV   R1, #0x37          ; R1 = 0x37
MOV   R2, #0x32          ; R2 = 0x32
AND   R1, R1, #0x0F      ; mask 3 to get unpacked BCD
AND   R2, R2, #0x0F      ; mask 3 to get unpacked BCD
ORR   R3, R1, R2, LSL #4 ; shift R2 4 bits to the left and combine
                         ; with R1 to get packed BCD in R3 = 0x27
```

Packed BCD to ASCII conversion

For data to be displayed or printed on a device that accepts only ASCII format, they need to be converted to ASCII first. Conversion from packed BCD to ASCII is discussed next. To convert packed BCD to ASCII, it must first be unpacked and then tagged with 011 0000 (0x30) to encode in ASCII. The following code snippet shows the process of converting from packed BCD to ASCII.

Packed BCD	Unpacked BCD	ASCII
0x29	0x02 & 0x09	0x32 & 0x39
0010 1001	0000 0010 & 0000 1001	011 0010 & 011 1001

```
MOV   R0, #0x29
AND   R1, R0, #0x0F     ; mask upper four bits
ORR   R1, R1, #0x30     ; combine with 30 to get ASCII
MOV   R2, R0, LSR #04   ; shift right 4 bits to get unpacked BCD
ORR   R2, R2, #0x30     ; combine with 30 to get ASCII
```

Review Questions

1. For the following decimal numbers, give the packed BCD and unpacked BCD representations in binary
   (a) 15   (b) 99
2. For the following packed BCD numbers, give the decimal and unpacked BCD representations.
   (a) 0x41   (b) 0x09
3. Repeat question 2 for ASCII.

Problems

Section 3.1: Arithmetic Instructions

1. Find C and Z flags for each of the following. Also indicate the result of the addition and where the result is saved.

(a)

```
MOV   R1, #0x3F
MOV   R2, #0x45
ADDS  R3, R1, R2
```

(b)

```
LDR   R0, =0x95999999
LDR   R1, =0x94FFFF58
ADDS  R1, R1, R0
```

(c)

```
LDR    R0, =0xFFFFFFFF
ADDS   R0, R0, #1
```

(d)

```
LDR   R2, =0x00000001
LDR   R1, =0xFFFFFFFF
ADDS  R0, R1, R2
ADCS  R0, R0, #0
```

(e)

```
LDR   R0, =0xFFFFFFFE
ADDS  R0, R0, #2
ADC   R1, R0, #0x0
```

2. State the three steps involved in a SUB and show the steps for the following data.

   (a) 0x23 – 0x12 (b) 0x43 – 0x51 (c) 0x99 – 0x99

Section 3.2: Logic Instructions

3. Assume that the following registers contain these hex contents: R0 = 0xF000, R1 = 0x3456, and R2 = 0xE390. Perform the following operations. Indicate the result and the register where it is stored.

   Note: the operations are independent of each other.

(a) AND R3, R2, R0

(b) ORR R3, R2, R1

(c) EOR R0, R0, #0x76

(d) AND R3, R2, R2

(e) EOR R0, R0, R0

(f) ORR R3, R0, R2

(g) AND R3, R0, #0xFF

(h) ORR R3, R0, #0x99

(i) EOR R3, R1, R0

(j) EOR R3, R1, R1

4. Give the value in R2 after the following code is executed:

```
MOV   R0, #0xF0
MOV   R1, #0x55
BIC   R2, R1, R0
```

5. Give the value in R2 after the following code is executed:

```
LDR   R1, =0x55555555
MVN   R0, #0
EOR   R2, R1, R0
```

Section 3.3: Rotate and Barrel Shifter

6. Assuming C = 0, what is the value of R1 after the following?

```
MOV   R1, #0x25
MOVS  R1, R1, ROR #4
```

7. Assuming C = 0, what are the values of R0 and C after the following?

```
LDR   R0, =0x3FA2
MOV   R2, #8
MOVS  R0, R0, ROR R2
```

8. Assuming C = 0 what is the value of R2 and C after the following?

```
MOV   R2, #0x55
MOVS  R2, R2, RRX
```

9. Assuming C = 0 what is the value of R1 after the following?

```
MOV   R1, #0xFF
MOV   R3, #5
MOVS  R1, R1, ROR R3
```

10. Give the register value for each of the following instructions after it is executed.

a) `MOV R1, #0x88, #4`

b) `MOV R0, #0x22, #22`

c) `MOV R2, #0x77, #8`

d) `MOV R4, #0x5F, #28`

e) `MOV R6, #0x88, #22` f) `MOV R5, #0x8F, #16`

g) `MOV R7, #0xF0, #20` h) `MOV R1, #0x33, #28`

11. Give the register value for each of the following instructions after it is executed.

a) `MVN R2, #0x1` b) `MVN R2, #0xAA, #20`

c) `MVN R1, 0x55, #4` d) `MVN R0, #0x66, #28`

e) `MVN R1, #0x80, #24` f) `MVN R6, #0x10, #20`

g) `MVN R7, #0xF0, #24` h) `MVN R4, #0x99, #4`

12. Find the contents of registers and C flag after executing each of the following codes:

a)

```
MOV  R0, #0x04
MOVS R1, R0, LSR #2
MOVS R3, R0, LSR R1
```

b)

```
LDR  R1, =0xA0F2
MOV  R2, #0x3
MOVS R3, R1, LSL R2
```

c)

```
LDR  R1, =0xB085
MOV  R2, #3
MOVS R4, R1, LSR R2
```

13. Find the contents of registers and C flag after executing each of the following codes:

a)

```
SUBS R2, R2, R2
MOV  R0, #0xAA
MOVS R1, R0, ROR #4
```

b)

```
MOV  R2, #0xAA, #4
MOV  R0, #1
MOVS R1, R2, ROR R0
```

c)

```
LDR  R1, =0x1234
MOV  R2, #0x010, #2
MOVS R1, R0, ROR R2
```

d)

```
MOV  R0, #0xAA
MOVS R1, R0, RRX
```

14. Using MOV instruction, show how you rotate left the literal value of 0x33 total of a) 4, b) 8, and c) 12 times. Also give the value in the register after the rotation.

Section 3.5: BCD and ASCII Conversion

15. Write a program to convert 0x76 from packed BCD number to ASCII. Place the ASCII codes into R1 and R2.
16. For "3" and "2" the keyboard gives 0x33 and 0x32, respectively. Write a program to convert 0x33 and 0x32 to packed BCD and store the result in R2.

Answers to Review Questions

Section 3.1: Arithmetic Instructions

1. The ADDS instruction updates the flag bits in CPSR register while ADD does not do that.
2. Rd = Rn + Op2 + C
3. 0x4F + 0xB1 = 0x100, since the result is less than 32-bit the C = 0 and Z = 0.
4. 0x4F + 0xFFFFFFB1 = 0x00000000, since the result is greater than 32-bit, there is a carry out from the MSB and the remaining 32 bits are all 0, the C = 1 and Z = 1.
5.

0x43	0100 0011		00000000000000000000000001000011
–0x05	0000 0101	2's complement =	+ 11111111111111111111111111111011
0x3E			1 00000000000000000000000000111110

C = 1; therefore, the result is positive

6. R2 = R2 – R3 – C + 1 = 0x95 – 0x4F – 1 + 1 = 0x46
7. R2
8. R2 = 1

Section 3.2: Logic Instructions

1. (a) 0x4202 (b) 0xCFFF (c) 0x8DFD
2. The operand will remain unchanged; all zeros
3. All ones
4. All zeros
5. ORR R7, R7, #0x10 ; R7 = R7 ORed 0001 0000
6. BIC R5, R5, #0x8 ; R5 = R5 ANDed 1111 1111 1111 0111

Section 3.3: Rotate and Barrel Shifter Operation

1. R3 = 1
2. R4 = 0x0000141E
3. R3 = 0x00050790
4. R5 = 0xA000000A
5. R0 = 0x00005079
6. 0xBFFFFFFF
7. 0xFFFFFFDF

Section 3.4: Shift and Rotate Instructions

1. 0x02
2. 0x0C

Section 3.5: BCD and ASCII Conversion

1. (a) 15 = 0001 0101 packed BCD = 0000 0001 0000 0101 unpacked BCD

   (b) 99 = 1001 1001 packed BCD = 0000 1001 0000 1001 unpacked BCD

2. (a) 0x41 = 0000 0100 0000 0001 unpacked BCD = 41 in decimal

   (b) 0x09 = 0000 0000 0000 1001 unpacked BCD = 9 in decimal

3. (a) 0x34, 0x31

   (b) 0x30, 0x39

Chapter 4: Branch, Call, and Looping in ARM

In the sequence of instructions to be executed, it is often necessary to transfer program control to a different location (e.g. when a function is called, execution of a loop is repeated, or an instruction executes conditionally). There are many instructions in ARM to achieve this. This chapter covers the control transfer instructions available in ARM assembly language. In Section 4.1, we discuss instructions used for looping, as well as instructions for conditional and unconditional branches (jumps). In Section 4.2, we examine the instructions associated with calling subroutine. In Section 4.3, instruction pipelining of the ARM is examined. Instruction timing and time delay subroutines are also discussed in Section 4.3. In Section 4.4, we examine the conditional execution of the ARM instructions which is a unique feature of ARM.

Section 4.1: Looping and Branch Instructions

In this section we first discuss how to perform a looping action in ARM and then the branch (jump) instructions, both conditional and unconditional.

Looping in ARM

Repeating a sequence of instructions or an operation for a certain number of times is called a *loop*. The loop is one of the most widely used programming techniques. In the ARM, there are several ways to repeat an operation many times. One way is to repeat the operation over and over until it is finished, as shown below:

```
MOV   R0, #0      ; R0 = 0
MOV   R1, #9      ; R1 = 9
ADD   R0, R0, R1  ; R0 = R0 + R1, add 9 to R0 (Now R0 is 0x09)
ADD   R0, R0, R1  ; R0 = R0 + R1, add 9 to R0 (Now R0 is 0x12)
ADD   R0, R0, R1  ; R0 = R0 + R1, add 9 to R0 (Now R0 is 0x1B)
ADD   R0, R0, R1  ; R0 = R0 + R1, add 9 to R0 (Now R0 is 0x24)
ADD   R0, R0, R1  ; R0 = R0 + R1, add 9 to R0 (Now R0 is 0x2D)
ADD   R0, R0, R1  ; R0 = R0 + R1, add 9 to R0 (Now R0 is 0x36)
```

In the above program, we add 9 to R0 six times. That makes 6 × 9 = 54 = 0x36. One problem with the above technique is that too much code space would be needed for a large number of repetitions like 50 or 1000. A much better way is to use a loop. Next, we describe the method to do a loop in ARM.

Using instruction BNE for looping

The BNE (branch if not equal) instruction uses the zero flag in the status register (CPSR). The BNE instruction is used as follows:

```
BACK  .........           ; start of the loop
      .........           ; body of the loop
      .........           ; body of the loop
      SUBS  Rn, Rn, #1    ; Rn = Rn - 1, set the flag Z = 1 if Rn = 0
      BNE   BACK          ; branch if Z = 0
```

In the last two instructions, the Rn (e.g. R2 or R3) is decremented; if it is not zero, it branches (jumps) back to the target address referred to by the label. Prior to the start of the loop, the Rn is loaded with the counter value for the number of repetitions (loop count). Notice that the BNE instruction refers to the Z flag of the status register affected by the previous instruction, SUBS. This is shown in Example 4-1.

Example 4-1

Write a program to (a) clear R0, (b) add 9 to R0 a thousand times, then (c) place the sum in R4. Use the zero flag and BNE instruction.

Solution:

```
            ; --- this program adds value 9 to the R0 a 1000 times ---
            AREA   EXAMPLE4_1, CODE, READONLY

            LDR    R2, =1000    ; R2 = 1000 (decimal) for counter
            MOV    R0, #0       ; R0 = 0 (sum)
AGAIN       ADD    R0, R0, #9   ; R0 = R0 + 9 (add 09 to R1, R1 = sum)
            SUBS   R2, R2, #1   ; Decrement counter and set the flags.
            BNE    AGAIN        ; repeat until COUNT = 0 (when Z = 1)
            MOV    R4, R0       ; store the sum in R4
HERE        B      HERE         ; stay here
            END
```

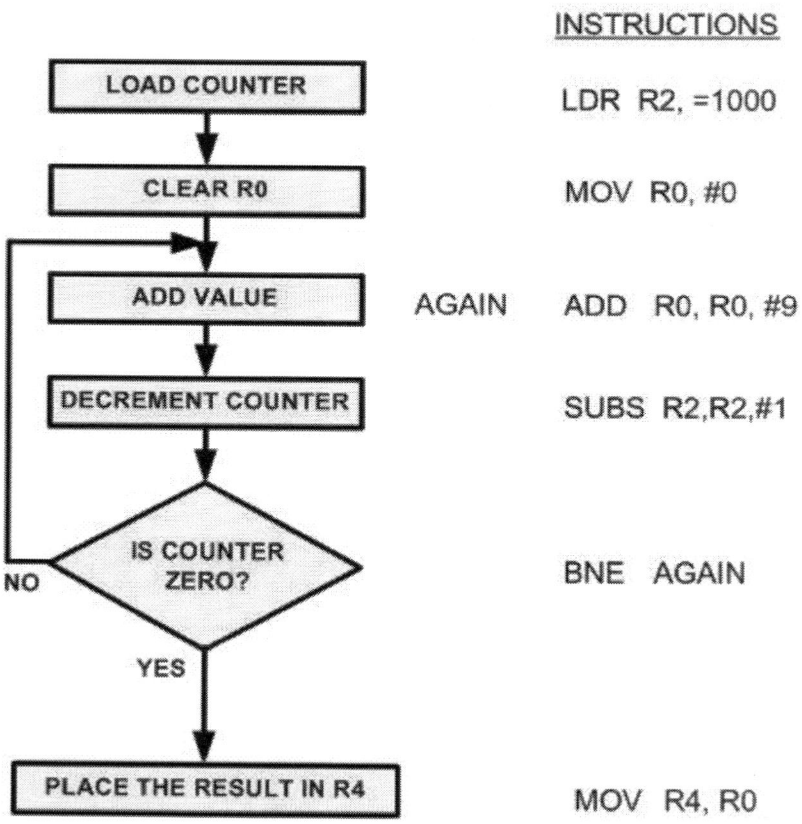

In the program in Example 4-1, register R2 is used as a counter. The counter is first set to 1000. In each iteration, the SUBS instruction decrements the R2 and sets the flag bits accordingly. If R2 is not zero (Z = 0), it jumps to the target address associated with the label "AGAIN". This looping action continues until R2 becomes zero. After R2 becomes zero (Z = 1), it falls through the loop and executes the instruction immediately below it, in this case "MOV R4, R0".

It must be emphasized again that we must use SUBS instead of SUB since the SUB instruction will not change (update) the flags in CPSR. As we mentioned in Chapter 3, many of the ARM instructions have the option of affecting the flags. In these instructions the default is not to affect the flags. Therefore, to update the flag we must add 'S' suffix to the instruction. That means SUBS and ADDS instructions are different from SUB and ADD, as far as the flags are concerned. As another example see Example 4-2.

Example 4-2

Write a program to place value 0x55 into 100 consecutive bytes of RAM locations.

Solution:

```
      AREA   EXAMPLE4_2, CODE, READONLY

RAM_ADDR EQU 0x40000000         ; change the address for your ARM

      MOV    R2, #25            ; counter (25 x 4 = 100 byte block size)
      LDR    R1, =RAM_ADDR      ; R1 = RAM Address
      LDR    R0, =0x55555555    ; R0 = 0x55555555

OVER  STR    R0, [R1]           ; send it to RAM
      ADD    R1, R1, #4         ; R1 = R1 + 4 to increment pointer
      SUBS   R2, R2, #1         ; R2 = R2 - 1 for decrement counter
      BNE    OVER               ; keep doing it

HERE  B      HERE
      END
```

Looping a trillion times with loop inside a loop

As shown in Example 4-3, the maximum count is 2^{32}-1. What happens if we want to repeat an action more times than that? To do that, we use a loop inside a loop, which is called a nested loop. In a nested loop, we use two registers to hold the loop counts. See Example 4-3.

Example 4-3

Explain what is the maximum number of times that the loop in Example 4-1 can be repeated? Now, write a program to (a) load the R0 register with the value 0x55, and (b) complement it 16,000,000,000 (16 billion) times.

Solution:

Because ARM registers are 32-bit long, they can hold a maximum of 0xFFFFFFFF ($2^{32} - 1$ decimal); therefore, the loop can be repeated a maximum of $2^{32} - 1$ times. This example shows how to create a nesting loop to go beyond 4 billion times. Because 16,000,000,000 is larger than 0xFFFFFFFF (the maximum capacity of any R0–R12 registers), we use two registers to hold the counts. The following code shows how to use R2 and R1 as a register for counters in a nesting loop.

```
        AREA   EXAMPLE4_3, CODE, READONLY

        MOV    R0, #0x55          ; R0 = 0x55
        MOV    R2, #16            ; load 16 into R2 (outer loop count)
L1      LDR    R1, =1000000000    ; R1 = 1,000,000,000 (inner loop count)
L2      EOR    R0, R0, #0xFF      ; complement R0 (R0 = R0 Ex-OR 0xFF)
        SUBS   R1, R1, #1         ; R1 = R1 - 1, decrement R1 (inner loop)
        BNE    L2                 ; repeat it until R1 = 0
        SUBS   R2, R2, #1         ; R2 = R2 - 1, decrement R2 (outer loop)
        BNE    L1                 ; repeat it until R2 = 0
HERE    B      HERE               ; stay here
        END
```

In this program, R1 is used to keep the inner loop count. In the instruction "BNE L2", whenever R1 becomes 0 it falls through and "SUBS R2, R2, #1" is executed. The next instructions force the CPU to load the inner count with 1,000,000,000 if R2 is not zero, and the inner loop starts again. This process will continue until R2 becomes zero and the outer loop is finished. If you use the Keil IDE to verify the operation of the above program, use smaller values for counter to go through the iterations. See Figure 4-1.

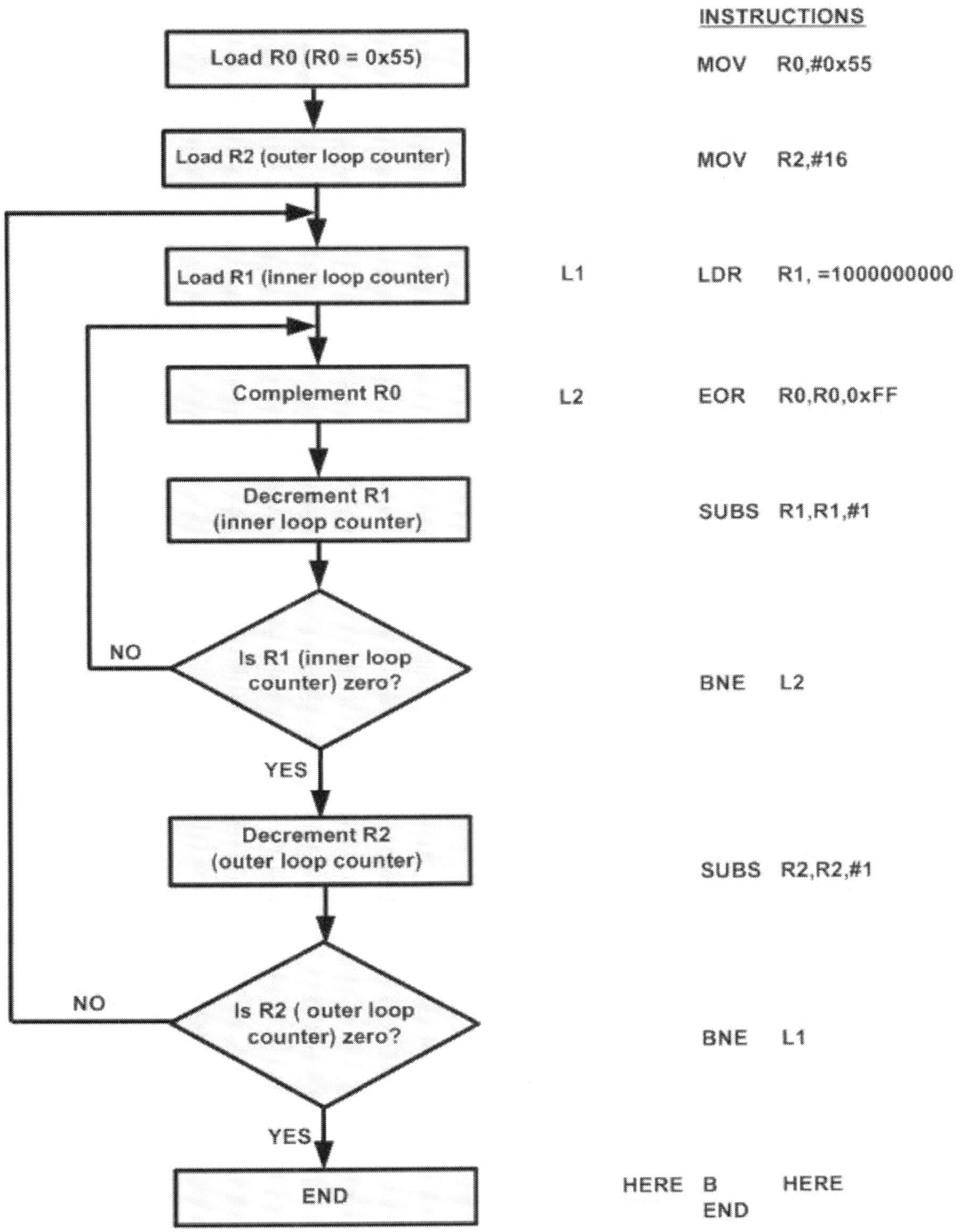

Figure 4- 1: Flowchart for Example 4-3

Other conditional Branches

As we mentioned in Chapter 3, C and Z flags reflect the result of calculation on unsigned numbers. Table 4-1 lists available conditional branches for unsigned numbers that use C and Z flags. More details of each instruction are provided in Appendix A. In Table 4-1 notice that the instructions, such as BEQ (Branch if Z = 1) and BCS (Branch if carry set, C = 1), jump only if a certain condition is met. Next, we examine some conditional branch instructions with examples. The other conditional branch instructions associated with the signed numbers are discussed in Chapter 5 when arithmetic operations for signed numbers are discussed.

Instruction		Action
BCS/BHS	branch if carry set/branch if higher or same	Branch if C = 1
BCC/BLO	branch if carry clear/branch if lower	Branch if C = 0
BEQ	branch if equal	Branch if Z = 1
BNE	branch if not equal	Branch if Z = 0
BLS	branch if lower or same	Branch if Z = 1 or C = 0
BHI	branch if higher	Branch if Z = 0 and C = 1

Table 4-1: ARM Conditional Branch Instructions for Unsigned Data

BCC (branch if carry is clear, branch if C = 0)

In this instruction, the carry flag bit in program status registers (CPSR) is used to make the decision whether to branch or not. In executing "BCC label", the processor looks at the carry flag to see if it is cleared (C = 0). If it is, the CPU starts to fetch and execute instructions from the address of the label. If C = 1, it will not jump but will execute the next instruction below BCC. See Example 4-4.

Example 4-4

Examine the following code and give the result in registers R0, R1, and R2.

```
        MOV     R1, #0              ; clear high word (R1 = 0)
        MOV     R0, #0              ; clear low word (R0 = 0)
        LDR     R2, =0x99999999     ; R2 = 0x99999999
        ADDS    R0, R0, R2          ; R0 = R0 + R2 and set the flags
        BCC     L1                  ; if C = 0, jump to L1 and add next number
        ADDS    R1, R1, #1          ; ELSE, increment (R1 = R1 + 1)
L1      ADDS    R0, R0, R2          ; R0 = R0 + R2 and set the flags
        BCC     L2                  ; if C = 0, add next number
        ADDS    R1, R1, #1          ; if C = 1, increment
L2      ADDS    R0, R2              ; R0 = R0 + R2 and set the flags
        BCC     L3                  ; if C = 0, add next number
        ADDS    R1, R1, #1          ; C = 1, increment
L3      ADDS    R0, R2              ; R0 = R0 + R2 and set the flags
        BCC     L4                  ; if C = 0, add next number
        ADDS    R1, R1, #1          ; if C = 1, and set the flags
L4
```

Solution:

This program adds 0x99999999 together four times.

	R1 (high word)	R0 (low word)
At first	0	0
Just before L1	0	0x99999999
Just before L2	1	0x33333332
Just before L3	1	0xCCCCCCCB
Just before L4	2	0x66666664

Here is the loop version of the above program that runs 10 times.

```
        AREA    EXAMPLE4_4, CODE, READONLY

        MOV     R1, #0              ; clear high word (R1 = 0)
        MOV     R0, #0              ; clear low word (R0 = 0)
        LDR     R2, =0x99999999     ; R2 = 0x99999999
        MOV     R3, #10             ; counter
L1      ADDS    R0, R2              ; R0 = R0 + R2 and set the flags
        BCC     NEXT                ; if C = 0, add next number
        ADD     R1, R1, #1          ; if C = 1, increment the upper word
NEXT    SUBS    R3, R3, #1          ; R3 = R3 - 1 and set the flags
                                    ; (Decrement counter)
        BNE     L1                  ; next round if Z = 0
HERE    B       HERE                ; stay here
        END
```

Note that there is also a "BCS label" instruction. In the BCS instruction, if C = 1 it jumps to the target address. We will give more examples of these instructions in the context of applications.

Comparison of unsigned numbers

```
        CMP     Rn, Op2       ; compare Rn with Op2 and set the flags
```

The CMP instruction compares two operands and set or clear the flags according to the result of the comparison. The operands themselves remain unchanged. There is no destination register and the second source operands can be a register or an immediate value (an 8-bit value with even number or rotate). It must be emphasized that "CMP Rn, Op2" instruction is really a subtract operation (SUBS) without a destination. Op2 is subtracted from Rn (Rn – Op2), the result is discarded and flags are set accordingly. Although all the C, S, Z, and V flags reflect the result of the comparison, only C and Z are used for unsigned numbers, as outlined in Table 4-2.

Instruction	C	Z
Rn > Op2	1	0
Rn = Op2	1	1
Rn < Op2	0	0

Table 4- 2: Flag Settings for Compare (CMP Rn, Op2) of Unsigned Data

Look at the following case:

```
      LDR   R1, =0x35F  ; R1 = 0x35F
      LDR   R2, =0xCCC  ; R2 = 0xCCC
      CMP   R1, R2      ; compare 0x35F with 0xCCC
      BCC   OVER        ; branch if C = 0
      MOV   R1, #0      ; if C = 1, then clear R1
OVER  ADD   R2, R2, #1  ; R2 = R2 + 1 = 0xCCC + 1 = 0xCCD
```

Figure 4-2 shows the diagram and the C language version of the code.

Pseudo code:	**In C:**	

R1 = 0x35F
R2 = 0xCCC
 	
IF (R1 >= R2) THEN
R1 = 0
ENDIF
 	
R2 = R2 + 1
	R1 = 0x35F;
	R2 = 0xCCC;
	
	if (R1 >= R2)
	{
	R1 = 0;
	}
	
	R2 = R2 + 1;
		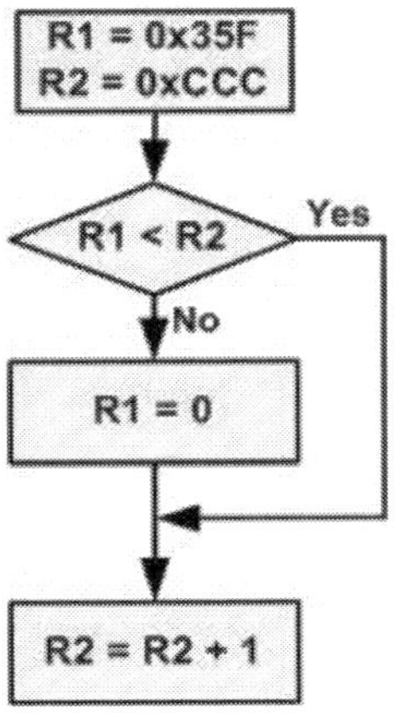

Figure 4- 2: Flowchart of if Instruction

In the above program, R1 is less than the R2 (0x35F < 0xCCC); therefore, C = 0 and BCC (branch if carry clear) will go to target OVER. In contrast, look at the following:

```
      LDR   R1, =0xFFF
      LDR   R2, =0x888
      CMP   R1, R2           ; compare 0xFFF with 0x888
      BCC   NEXT
      ADD   R1, R1, #0x40
NEXT  ADD   R1, R1, #0x25
```

In the above, R1 is greater than R2 (0xFFF > 0x888), which sets C = 1, the branch, "BCC NEXT," is not taken and the execution falls through so that "ADD R1, R1, 0x40" is executed.

Again, it must be emphasized that in CMP instructions, the operands are unaffected regardless of the result of the comparison. Only the flags are affected. It also may be noted that, unlike other arithmetic and logic instructions, there is no need to put the ‘S’ suffix in the CMP instruction to update the flags. In other words, the CMP instruction always updates the flags.

Program 4-1 uses the CMP instruction to search for the highest byte in a series of 5 data bytes. To search for the highest value, the instruction "CMP R1, R3" works as follows where R1 is the contents of the memory location brought into R1 register by the [R2] pointer.

a) If R1 < R3, then C = 0 and R3 becomes the basis of the new comparison.

b) If R1 ≥ R3, then C = 1 and R1 is the larger of the two values and remains the basis of comparison.

Program 4-1
Assume that there is a class of five people with the following grades: 69, 87, 96, 45, and 75. Find the highest grade.

```
; searching for highest value in a list
COUNT       RN    R0             ; COUNT is the new name of R0
MAX         RN    R1             ; MAX is the new name of R1
                                 ; (MAX has the highest value)
POINTER     RN    R2             ; POINTER is the new name of R2
NEXT        RN    R3             ; NEXT is the new name of R3

            AREA   PROG_4_1D, DATA, READONLY
MYDATA      DCD   69, 87, 96, 45, 75

            AREA   PROG_4_1, CODE, READONLY
            MOV   COUNT, #5            ; COUNT = 5
            MOV   MAX, #0              ; MAX = 0
            LDR   POINTER, =MYDATA     ; POINTER has the address of first data
AGAIN       LDR   NEXT, [POINTER]      ; load NEXT with contents at address
                                       ; in POINTER
            CMP   MAX, NEXT            ; compare MAX and NEXT
            BHS   CTNU                 ; if MAX > NEXT branch to CTNU
            MOV   MAX, NEXT            ; MAX = NEXT
CTNU        ADD   POINTER, POINTER, #4      ; increment POINTER for next word
            SUBS  COUNT, COUNT, #1     ; decrement counter
            BNE   AGAIN                ; branch AGAIN if counter is not zero

HERE        B     HERE
            END
```

Program 4-1 searches through five data items to find the highest value. The program has a variable called "MAX" that holds the highest grade found so far. One by one, the grades are brought into the register and compared to MAX. If any of them is higher, that value is placed in MAX. This continues until all data items are checked. A REPEAT-UNTIL structure was chosen in the program design. Figure 4-3 shows the flowchart for Program 4-1. This design could be used to code the program in many different languages.

Program 4-1 also demonstrates using aliasing for registers. This practice improves the readability of the small programs.

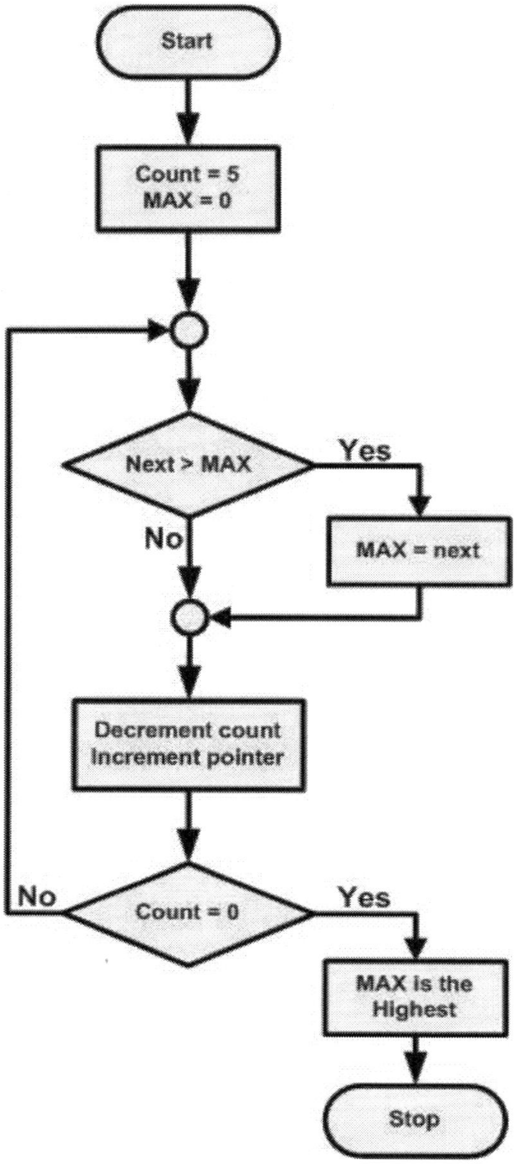

Pseudo code:

Count = 5
Highest = 0

REPEAT
IF (Next > MAX)
THEN
MAX = Next
ENDIF
Increment pointer
Decrement Count
UNTIL Count = 0

now MAX is the Highest

In C:

```
//In Keil, int is 32-bit wide
unsigned int myData[5]= {69, 87, 96,
45, 75};
unsigned int count = 5;
unsigned int max = 0;
unsigned int next;
unsigned int *pointer = myData;

do
{
  next = *pointer;

  if (max < next)
    max = next;

  pointer ++;
  count --;
} while(count != 0);
```

Figure 4- 3: Flowchart and Pseudocode for Program 4-1

Using CMP instruction followed by conditional branches we can make comparison on numbers, as shown in Table 4-3. Although BCS (branch carry set) and BCC (branch carry clear) check the carry flag and can be used after a compare instruction, it is recommended that BHS (branch higher or same) and BLO (branch lower) be used because "branch higher" and "branch lower" are easier to understand than "branch carry set" and "branch carry clear, " since it is more immediately apparent that one number is larger than another than whether a carry would be generated if the two numbers were subtracted.

Instruction		Action
BCS/BHS	branch if carry set/branch if higher or same	Branch if Rn ≥ Op2
BCC/BLO	branch if carry clear/branch lower	Branch if Rn < Op2
BEQ	branch if equal	Branch if Rn = Op2
BNE	branch if not equal	Branch if Rn ≠ Op2
BLS	branch if less or same	Branch if Rn ≤ Op2
BHI	branch if higher	Branch if Rn > Op2

Table 4- 3: ARM Conditional Branch Instructions for Unsigned Data

Division of unsigned numbers in ARM

Some of the older ARM family members do not have instructions for division since it took too many gates to implement it. In ARMs with no divide instructions, we can use SUB instruction to perform the division. Program 4-2 shows an example of an unsigned division using simple subtract operation. In the program the numerator is placed in a register and the denominator is subtracted from it repeatedly. The quotient is the number of times we subtracted and the remainder is in the register upon completion. This program is to demonstrate the used of conditional branch in a loop. The program is not efficient in calculating the quotient. There are much more efficient algorithms to perform division but they are beyond the scope here. See Figure 4-4 for the flowchart of the simple division program.

Program 4-2: Division by Repeated Subtractions

```
      AREA   PROG_4_2, CODE, READONLY     ; Division by subtractions

      LDR    R0, =2012     ; R0 = 2012 (numerator)
                           ; it will contain remainder
      MOV    R1, #10       ; R1 = 10 (denominator)
      MOV    R2, #0        ; R2 = 0 (quotient)
L1    CMP    R0, R1        ; Compare R0 with R1 to see if less than 10
      BLO    FINISH        ; if R0 < R1 jump to finish
      SUB    R0, R0, R1    ; R0 = R0 - R1 (division by subtraction)
      ADD    R2, R2, #1    ; R2 = R2 + 1 (quotient is incremented)
      B      L1            ; goto L1 (B is discussed in the next section)
FINISH B     FINISH
```

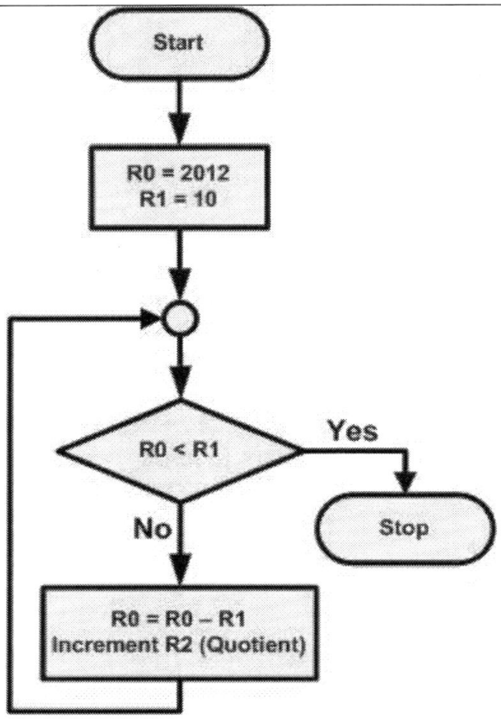

Pseudo code:

NUM = 2012
DENOM = 10

WHILE NUM >= DENOM
  Subtract DENOM from NUM
  Increment QUOTIENT
END WHILE

In C:

```
R0 = 2012;
R1 = 10;

while (R0 >= R1)
{
        R0 = R0 - R1;
        R2 = R2 + 1;
}
```

Figure 4- 4: Flowchart and Pseudo-code for Program 4-2

TST (Test)

```
        TST     Rn, Op2            ; Rn AND with Op2 and flag bits are updated
```

The TST instruction is used to test the contents of register to see if one or multiple bits are HIGH. Similar to CMP instruction, TST is an ANDS instruction without a destination. After the operands are ANDed together the flags are updated. If the result is zero, then Z flag is raised and one can use BEQ (branch equal) to make decision. In the following example below, the program execution stays in the loop between OVER and BEQ OVER until bit 2 (0x04) of the content at "myport" becomes high.

```
        MOV     R0, #0x04          ; R0=00000100 in binary
        LDR     R1, =myport        ; port address
OVER    LDRB    R2, [R1]           ; load R2 from myport
        TST     R2, R0             ; is bit 2 HIGH?
        BEQ     OVER               ; keep checking
```

In TST, like other data processing instructions, the Op2 can be an immediate value (an 8-bit value with even number of rotate). Look at the following example, which does the same as the program snippet above.

```
        LDR     R1, =myport        ; port address
OVER    LDRB    R2, [R1]           ; load R2 from myport
        TST     R2, #0x04          ; is bit 2 HIGH?
        BEQ     OVER               ; keep checking
```

See Example 4-5.

Example 4-5

Assume address location 0x00200000 is assigned to an input port address and connected to 8 DIP switches. Write a short program to check the input port and whenever both pins 4 or 6 are LOW, R4 register is incremented.

Solution:

```
MYPORT EQU 0x00200000
       MOV   R0, #2_01010000     ; R0=0x50 (01010000 in binary)
       LDR   R1, =MYPORT         ; R1 = port address
OVER   LDRB  R2, [R1]            ; get a byte from PORT and place it in R2
       TST   R2, R0              ; are bits 4 and 6 LOW?
       BNE   OVER                ; keep checking
       ADD   R4, R4, #1
```

TEQ (test equal)

```
       TEQ   Rn, Op2             ; Rn EX-ORed with Op2 and flag bits are set
```

The TEQ instruction is used to test to see if the contents of two registers or one register and the immediate value are equal. Like CMP and TST, TEQ is an EORS instruction without a destination. After the source operands are Ex-ORed together the flag bits are set according to the result. If result is 0, then Z flag is raised and one can use BEQ (branch zero) to make decision. Recall that if we Exclusive-OR a value with itself, the result is zero. Look at the following example for checking to see whether the temperature on a given port is equal to 100 or not:

```
TEMP   EQU   100
       MOV   R0, #TEMP           ; R0 = Temp
       LDR   R1, =myport         ; port address
OVER   LDRB  R2, [R1]            ; load R2 from myport
       TEQ   R2, R0              ; is it 100?
       BNE   OVER                ; keep checking
```

Unconditional branch (jump) instruction

The unconditional branch is a jump in which control is transferred unconditionally to the target location. In the ARM there are two unconditional branches: B (branch) and BX (branch and exchange). This is discussed next.

B (Branch)

B (branch) is an unconditional jump that can go to any memory location within the $\pm$32M byte address range. Another syntax for B instruction is BAL (branch always).

B has different usages like implementing if/else, while, and for instructions. In the following code you see an example of implementing the if/else instruction:

```
        CMP     R1, R2
        BHS     L1
        MOV     R3, #2
        B       OVER
L1      MOV     R3, #5
OVER
```

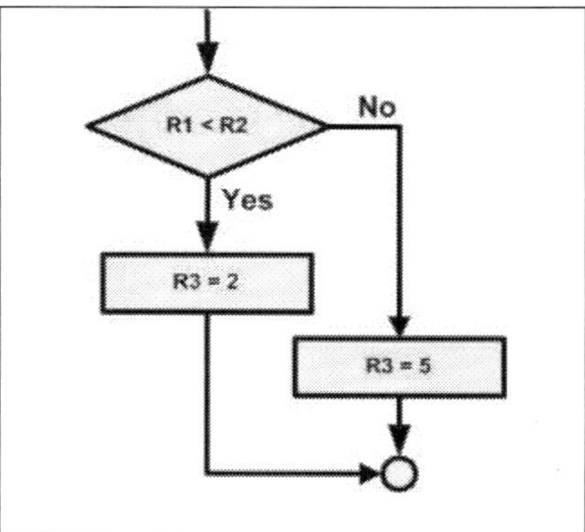


```
//in C
if(R1 < R2)
{
        R3 = 2;
}
else
{
        R3 = 5;
}
```

In the above code, R3 is initialized with 2 when R1 is lower than R2. Otherwise, it is initialized with 5.

As an example of implementing the while instruction see the following program. It calculates the sum of numbers between 1 and 5:

```
        MOV     R1, #1
        MOV     R2, #0
L1      CMP     R1, #5
        BHI     L2
        ADD     R2, R2, R1
        ADD     R1, R1, #1
        B       L1
L2      MOV     R3, #5
```

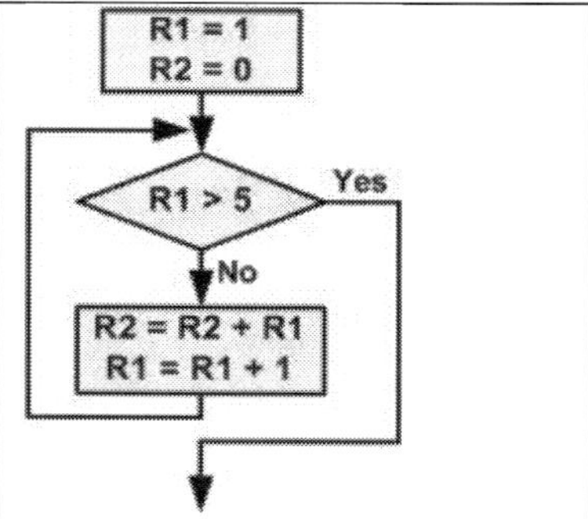


```
//in C
unsigned int R1 = 1;
unsigned int R2 = 0;
while (R1 <= 5)
{
  R2 = R2 + R1;
  R1 = R1 + 1;
}
```

The *for* instruction can be implemented the same way as the *while* instruction. For example, the above assembly program can be considered as a *for* loop.

In cases where there is no operating system or monitor program, we use the "branch to itself" in order to keep the program from running away. In a stand-alone program, if we allow it to continue beyond the end of program, there is no telling what it is going to happen. A simple way of keeping the program from running away is shown below:

```
HERE   B      HERE   ; stay here
```

Another syntax for the B instruction is BAL (branch always) as shown below:

```
HERE   BAL    HERE   ; stay here
```

Since ARM instruction is 32-bit, 8 bits are used for the opcode, and the other 24 bits represent the address of the target location. The 24-bit target address is shifted left twice and that allows a jump to –32M to +32M bytes of memory locations from the address of current instruction. Next, we explain the reason for this.

All branches are short branches (jumps)

It must be noted that all branch instructions (conditional and unconditional) are short jumps, meaning the address of the target must be within ±32M bytes of the program counter (PC). That means the short jumps cannot cover the entire address space of 4G bytes (0x00000000 to 0xFFFFFFFF).

Calculating the short branch address

In the branch instruction the opcode is 8 bits and the relative address is 24 bits. See Figure 4-5. The target address is relative to the value in the program counter. If the relative address is positive, the jump is forward. If the relative address is negative, then the jump is backward. Because all the ARM instructions are 4-byte long, the lowest two bits of the addresses for instructions are always 0. There is no need to keep the lowest two bits in the relative address and the offset in the instruction holds bits 25-2. When the instruction is decoded, the offset is shifted left for two bits to form a 26 bit offset. Since one bit is used for positive or negative sign, we have 25 left bits for magnitude. The 25-bit magnitude gives us 32Mbytes (2^{25} = 32M) in each direction. That is –32Mbytes if it is backward and +32MB if it is forward jump. It must be noted that the next instruction to be fetched is two instructions below the current branch instruction. See Figure 4-5.

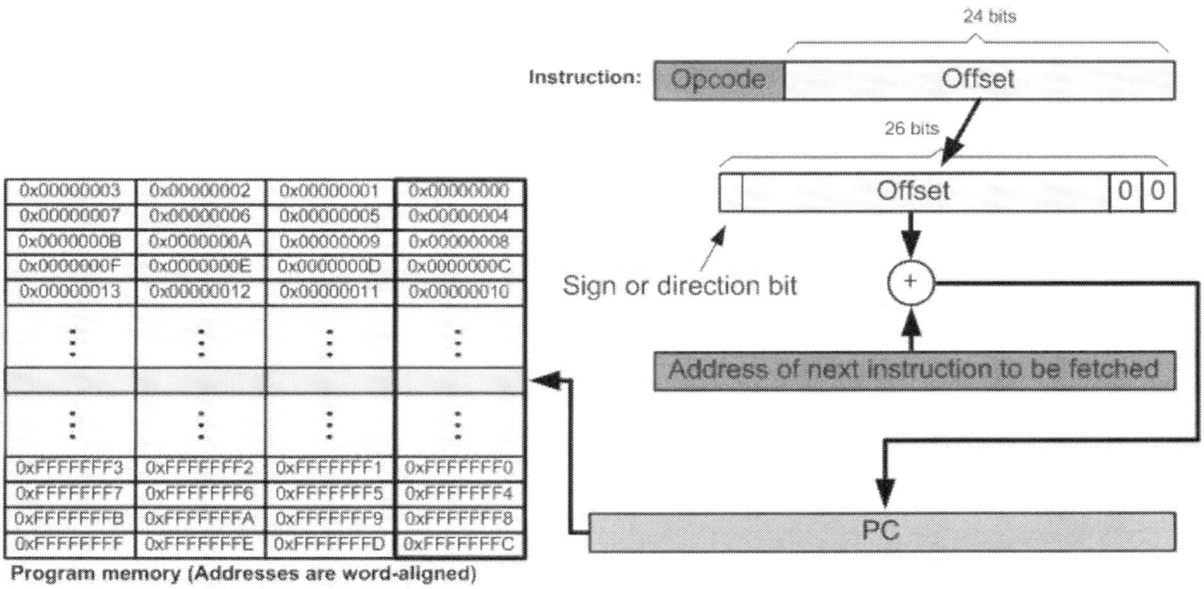

Figure 4- 5: B (Branch) Instruction

You might ask why we add the relative address to the address of two instructions below the current instruction. (why don't we add the relative address to the address of the instruction right below the current instruction as it is in other CPUs). This is due to the working of the pipeline. When the branch instruction is executed, the next instruction is already fetched into the pipeline and the program counter is pointing to two instructions below. We will discuss pipeline in Chapter 7.

Although branch instruction does not cover the whole 4 GB memory space of ARM, it is more than adequate for most of the applications. In rare cases that there is need to branch beyond 32MB, there are other mechanisms to handle it as we will see later in this chapter.

Example 4-6

In ARM7, the next instruction to be fetched is 2 instructions below the current executing instruction. Using the following list file verify the jump forward address calculation.

LINE	*ADDRESS*	*Machine*	*Mnemonic*		*Operand*	
1	00000000			AREA	EXAMPLE_4_6, CODE, READONLY	
2						
3	00000000	E3A01015		MOV	R1, #0x15	; R1 = 0x15
4	00000004	EA000002		B	THERE	
5	00000008	E3A01025		MOV	R1, #0x25	; R1 = 0x25
6	0000000C	E3A02035		MOV	R2, #0x35	; R2 = 0x35
7	00000010	E3A03045		MOV	R3, #0x45	; R3 = 0x45
8	**00000014**	E3A04055	THERE	MOV	R4, #0x55	; R4 = 0x55
9	00000018	EAFFFFFE	HERE	B	HERE	
10				END		

Solution:

First notice that the B instruction in line 4 jumps forward. To calculate the target address, the relative address (offset) is shifted left twice and added to the PC of the next instruction to be fetched. The position of the next instruction to be fetched is 2 instructions below the current instruction. Each instruction of ARM takes 4 bytes. So, the next instruction to be fetched is 2 × 4 bytes = 8 bytes below the current instruction address (00000004). So, the address of the next instruction to be fetched is 0000004 + 8 = 000000C (the position of MOV instruction in line 6).

In line 4 the instruction "B THERE" has the machine code of EA000002. If we compare it with the B instruction format, we see that the opcode is EA and the operand is 000002. The 000002 is the offset, relative to the address of the next instruction. Recall that to calculate the target address, the relative address (offset) is shifted left twice and added to the current value of the PC (Program Counter). Shifting the offset (000002) left twice results in 000008 and then adding it to the address of the next instruction to be fetched (0000000C) we have 000008 + 0000000C = 00000014 which is exactly the address of THERE label. All the jump instructions, whose mnemonics begin with B, have the same instruction format with different opcode. So, we can calculate the short branch address for any of them, as we just did in this example.

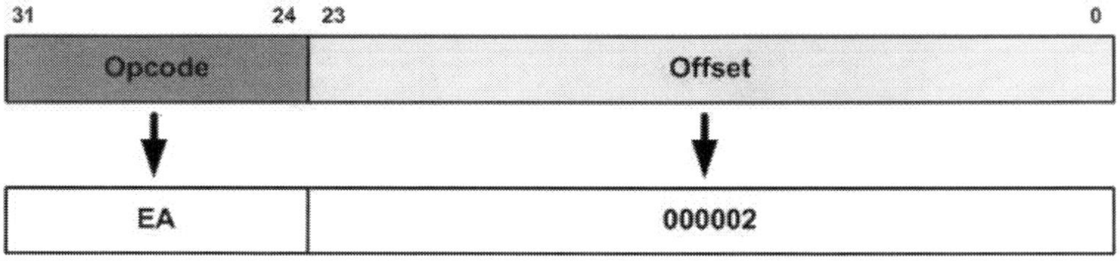

It must also be noted that for the backward branch the relative value is negative (2's complement). That is shown in Example 4-7.

Example 4-7

Verify the calculation of backward jumps for the listing of Example 4-1, shown below.

LINE	ADDRESS	Machine	Mnemonic		Operand	
5	00000000	E3A02FFA		LDR	R2, =1000	; R2 = 1000
6	00000004	E3A00000		MOV	R0, #0	; R0 = 0, sum
7	00000008	E2800009	AGAIN	ADD	R0, R0, #9	; R0 = R0 + 9
8	0000000C	E2522001		SUBS	R2, R2, #1	; R2 = R2 - 1
9	00000010	1AFFFFFC		BNE	AGAIN	; repeat
10	00000014	E1A04000		MOV	R4, R0	; store the sum in R4
11	00000018	EAFFFFFE	HERE	B	HERE	; stay here
12	0000001C			END		

Solution:

In the program list, "BNE AGAIN" in line 9 has machine code 1AFFFFFC. To separate the operand and opcode, we compare the instruction with the branch instruction format, which you saw in the previous example. The opcode is 1A and the operand (relative offset address) is FFFFFC. The FFFFFC gives us –4, which means the displacement is (–4 × 4 = –16 = **–0x10**).

The branch is located in address 0x0010. The address of the next instruction to be fetched is two instructions ahead of current branch instruction, and each instruction is 4-byte wide. Therefore, address of the next instruction to be fetched = 0x0010 + (2 × 4) = **0x0018**.

When the relative address of –0x10 is added to 00000018, we have –0x0010 + 0x0018 = 0x08

Notice that 00000008 is the address of the label AGAIN.

FFFFFC is a negative number and that means it will branch backward. For further discussion of the addition of negative numbers, see Chapter 5.

Branching beyond 32MB byte limit

To branch beyond the address range of $\pm$32M bytes, we use BX (branch and exchange) instruction. The "BX Rn" instruction uses register Rn to hold target address. Since Rn can be any of the R0–R14 registers and they are 32-bit registers, the "BX Rn" instruction can land anywhere in the 4G bytes address space of the ARM. In the instruction "BX R2" the content of R2 is loaded into the program counter (R15) and CPU starts to fetch instructions from the target address pointed to by the program counter. See Figure 4-6. Since the instructions are word aligned, we must make sure that the lower two bits of the Rn are 0s.

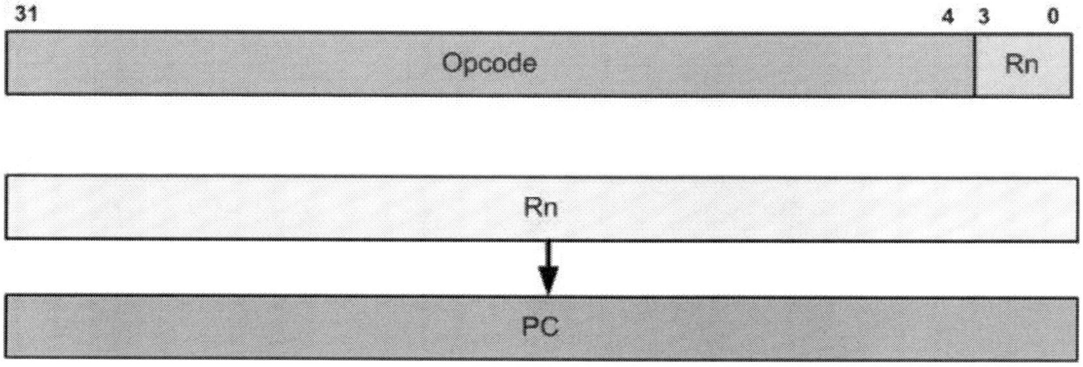

Figure 4- 6: BX (Branch and exchange) Instruction Target Address

The BX instruction is also used to switch between ARM and THUMB modes using bit 0 of the register operand. We will discuss in more details in Chapter 8.

Review Questions

1. The mnemonic BNE stands for _______.
2. True or false. "BNE BACK" makes its decision based on the last instruction affecting the Z flag.
3. "BNE HERE" is a ___ -byte instruction.
4. In "BEQ NEXT", which flag bit is checked to see if it is high?
5. B(ranch) is a(n) ___ -byte instruction.
6. Compare B and BX instructions.

Section 4.2: Calling Subroutine with BL

Another control transfer instruction is the BL (branch with link) instruction, which is used to call a subroutine. Subroutines are often used to perform tasks that need to be performed frequently. This makes a program more structured in addition to saving memory space.

BL (Branch and Link) instruction and calling subroutine

In the 32-bit instruction BL, 8 bits are used for the opcode and the other 24 bits are used for the offset to the address of the target subroutine just like in the Branch instruction. Therefore, BL can be used to call subroutines located anywhere within the $\pm$32M address range, as shown in Figure 4-7.

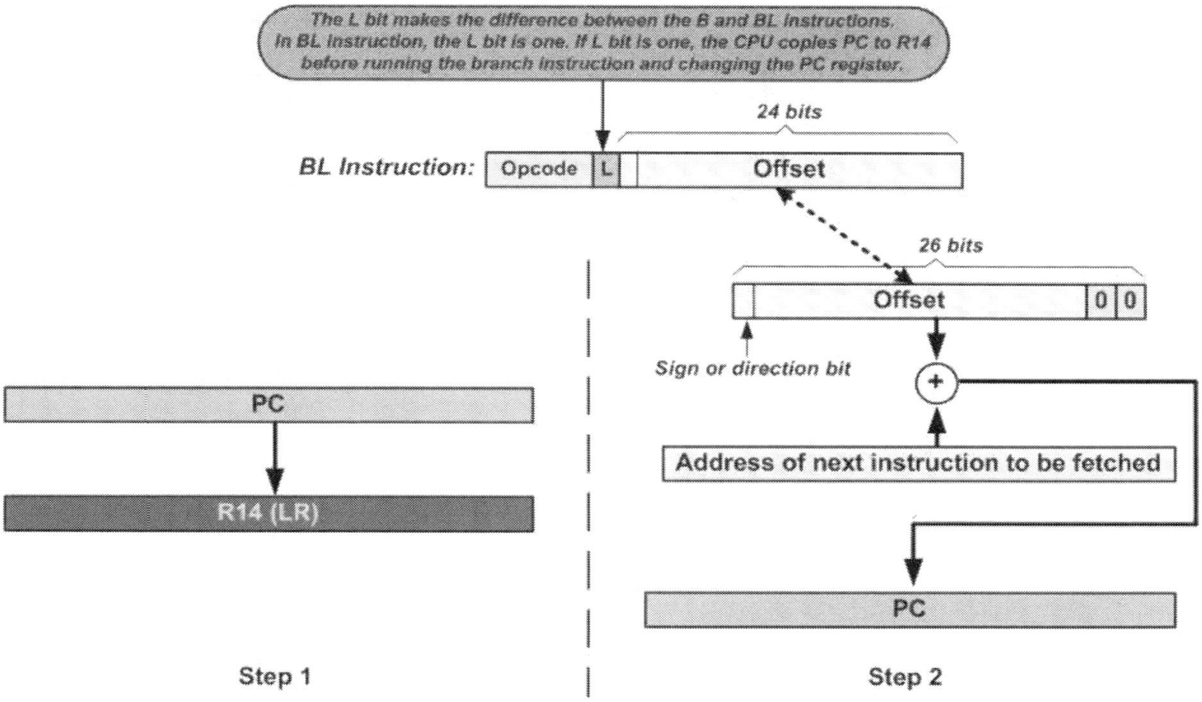

Figure 4- 7: BL (Branch and Link) Instruction

The link register and returning from subroutine

To make sure that the ARM knows where to return to after execution of the called subroutine, the BL instruction automatically saves the address of the instruction immediately below the BL (the return address) in the link register (LR), the R14. After finishing the subroutine, the program execution should return to where the caller is left off. This is done by putting the return address into the program counter. To return, we may use "BX LR" instruction, which copies the content of LR to PC, to transfer control back to the caller.

To further understand the role of the R14 register in BL instruction and the return, examine the Examples 4-8. The following points should be noted for the Example 4-8:

1. Notice the DELAY subroutine. Upon executing the first "BL DELAY", the address of the instruction right below it, "MOV R0, #0xAA", is saved onto the R14 register, and the CPU starts to execute instructions at DELAY subroutine.

2. In the DELAY subroutine, first the counter R3 is set to 5 (R3 = 5); therefore, the inner loop is repeated 5 times. When R3 becomes 0, control falls to the "BX LR" instruction, which restores the address into the program counter and returns to main program to resume executing the instructions after the BL.

Example 4-8

Write a program to toggle all the bits of address 0x40000000 by sending to it the values 0x55 and 0xAA continuously. Put a time delay between each issuing of data to address 0x40000000 location.

Solution:

```
        AREA    EXAMPLE4_8, CODE, READONLY

RAM_ADDR        EQU     0x40000000   ; change the address for your ARM
        LDR     R1, =RAM_ADDR        ; R1 = RAM address
AGAIN MOV     R0, #0x55     ; R0 = 0x55
        STRB    R0, [R1]      ; send it to RAM
        BL      DELAY         ; call delay (R14 = PC of next instruction)
        MOV     R0, #0xAA     ; R0 = 0xAA
        STRB    R0, [R1]      ; send it to RAM
        BL      DELAY         ; call delay
        B       AGAIN         ; keep doing it

        ; --------------------DELAY SUBROUTINE
DELAY LDR     R3, =5        ; R3=5, modify this value for different delay
L1      SUBS    R3, R3, #1    ; R3 = R3 - 1
        BNE     L1
        BX      LR            ; return to caller
        ; --------------------end of DELAY subroutine

        END           ; notice the place for END directive
```

Use Keil IDE simulator for ARM to simulate the above program and examine the registers and memory location 0x40000000. You might have to change the address 0x40000000 to some other value depending on the RAM address of the ARM chip you use.

In above program, in place of "BX LR" for return, we could have used "BX R14", "MOV R15, R14", or "MOV PC, LR" instructions. All of them will copy the content of LR to PC; but it is recommended to use the "BX LR" instruction.

The amount of time delay in Example 4-8 depends on the frequency of the ARM chip. The time calculation will be explained in the last section of this chapter.

Main Program and Calling Subroutines

In real world projects we divide the programs into small subroutines (also called functions) and the subroutines are called from the main program. Figure 4-8 shows the format.

```
      ; MAIN program calling subroutines
      AREA   PogramName, CODE, READONLY

MAIN  BL     SUBR_1             ; Call Subroutine 1
      BL     SUBR_2             ; Call Subroutine 1
      BL     SUBR_3             ; Call Subroutine 1
HERE  BAL    HERE         ; stay here. BAL is the same as B
      ; -------end of MAIN

      ; --------------------SUBROUTINE 1
SUBR_1             ....
             ....
      BX     LR     ; return to main
      ; ------    end of subroutine 1

      ; --------------------SUBROUTINE 2
SUBR_2       ....
      ....
      BX     LR     ; return to main
      ; ------    end of subroutine 2

      ; --------------------SUBROUTINE 3
SUBR_3       ....
      ....
      BX     LR     ; return to main
      ; ------    end of subroutine 3
      END           ; notice the END of file
```

Figure 4- 8: ARM Assembly Main Program That Calls Subroutines

Program 4-3 shows an example of the main program calling subroutine.

Program 4-3

```
      ; This program fills a block of memory with a fixed value and
      ; then transfers (copies) the block to new area of memory
      AREA   PROGRAM4_3, CODE, READONLY

RAM1_ADDR   EQU   0x40000000   ; Change the address for your ARM
RAM2_ADDR   EQU   0x40000100   ; Change the address for your ARM
      BL     FILL              ; call block fill subroutine
      BL     COPY              ; call block transfer subroutine
HERE  BAL    HERE              ; BAL(branch always) is the same as B
      ; ----------------BLOCK FILL SUBROUTINE
FILL  LDR    R1, =RAM1_ADDR    ; R1 = RAM Address pointer
      MOV    R0, #10           ; counter
      LDR    R2, =0x55555555
L1    STR    R2, [R1]          ; send it to RAM
      ADD    R1, R1, #4        ; R1 = R1 + 4 to increment pointer
      SUBS   R0, R0, #1        ; R0 = R0 - 1 to decrement counter
      BNE    L1                ; keep doing it until R0 is 0
      BX     LR                ; return to caller
```

```
      ; -----------------BLOCK COPY SUBROUTINE
COPY  LDR   R1, =RAM1_ADDR     ; R1 = RAM Address pointer (source)
      LDR   R2, =RAM2_ADDR     ; R2 = RAM Address pointer (destination)
      MOV   R0, #10            ; counter
L2    LDR   R3, [R1]           ; get from RAM1
      STR   R3, [R2]           ; send it to RAM2
      ADD   R1, R1, #4         ; R1 = R1 + 4 to increment pointer for RAM1
      ADD   R2, R2, #4         ; R2 = R2 + 4 to increment pointer for RAM2
      SUBS  R0, R0, #1         ; R0 = R0 - 1 for decrementing counter
      BNE   L2                 ; keep doing it
      BX    LR                 ; return to caller
      ; ----------
      END                      ; notice the place of END directive
```

Register usage and preservation in a subroutine

Link register holds the return address during a subroutine call so that at the end of the subroutine, the program knows where to return to. What happens when we need to call a subroutine within a subroutine (nested call)? If we use a BL instruction in a subroutine, the content of the link register will be overwritten and we will lose the return address. One solution often used is to save the content of the link register before making another subroutine call and restore the content of the link register afterward. Stack is a convenient place to store data temporarily. We will discuss the use of stack in Chapter 6.

Link register is not the only register that we need to preserve its content in a subroutine. In general, you should save the registers you are going to use in the subroutine when entering the subroutine and restore their contents before return.

The other function of the registers is to pass data between the caller and the subroutine. When calling a subroutine, the parameters may be stored in the registers. When exiting the subroutine, the return value may also be left in the register. To improve the compatibility of the reusable software modules, ARM published ARM Architecture Procedure Call Standard (AAPCS), which defines the register usages among other things. According to AAPCS, the first four registers (R0-R3) are used to pass data between caller and subroutine. Caller should not expect the data in these four registers to be preserved. The rest of the registers except PC (program counter, R15) and SP (stack pointer, R13) should be preserved across a subroutine call.

Review Questions

1. The mnemonic BL stands for ________.
2. True or false. "BL DELAY" saves the address of the instruction below BL in LR register.
3. "BL DELAY" is a ___ -byte instruction.
4. LR is an ___ -bit register.
5. LR is the same as _______register.
6. Explain the difference between B and BL instructions.

Section 4.3: ARM Time Delay and Instruction Pipeline

In this section we discuss how to generate various time delays and calculate time delays for the ARM. We will also discuss instruction pipelining and its impact on execution time.

Delay calculation for the ARM

In creating a time delay using assembly language instructions, one must be mindful of two factors that can affect the accuracy of the delay:

1. **The core clock frequency:** The frequency of the core clock connected to the CPU is one factor in the time delay calculation. The duration of the clock period for the instruction cycle is a function of this core clock frequency.

2. **The ARM design:** Since the 1970s, both the field of IC technology and the architectural design of microprocessors have seen great advancements. Due to the limitations of IC technology and limited CPU design experience for many years, the instruction cycle duration was longer. Advances in both IC technology and CPU design in the 1980s and 1990s have made the single instruction cycle a common feature of many microprocessors. Indeed, one way to increase performance without losing code compatibility with the older generation of a given family is to reduce the number of instruction cycles it takes to execute an instruction. One might wonder how microprocessors such as ARM are able to execute an instruction in one cycle. There are three ways to do that: (a) Use Harvard architecture to get the maximum amount of code and data into the CPU, (b) use RISC architecture features such as fixed-size instructions, and finally (c) use pipelining to overlap fetching and execution of instructions. We have examined the Harvard and RISC architectures in Chapter 2. Next, we give a brief discussion of pipelining. Chapter 7 covers the ARM pipeline in much more detail.

Pipelining

In early microprocessors such as the 8085 or 6800, the CPU could either fetch or execute at a given time. In other words, the CPU had to fetch an instruction from memory, decode, and then execute it, and then fetch the next instruction, decode and execute it, and so on as shown in Figure 4-9. All steps of running a program occur serially. The idea of pipelining in its simplest form is to allow the CPU to fetch and execute at the same time. That is an instruction is being fetched while the previous instruction is being executed.

T1	T2	T3	T4	T5	T6
Fetch inst. 1	Execute inst. 1	Fetch inst. 2	Execute inst. 2	Fetch inst. 3	Execute inst. 3

Figure 4- 9: Non-pipeline execution

We can use a pipeline to speed up execution of instructions. In pipelining, the process of executing instructions is split into small steps that are executed in parallel. In this way, the executions of many instructions are overlapped. One limitation of pipelining is that the speed of execution is limited to the slowest stage of the pipeline. Compare this to making pizza. You can split the process of making pizza into many stages, such as flattening the dough, putting on the toppings, and baking, but the process is limited to the slowest stage, baking, no matter how fast the rest of the stages are performed.

ARM multistage execution pipeline

As shown in Figure 4-10, in the ARM, each instruction is executed in 3 stages: Fetch, Decode, and Execute.

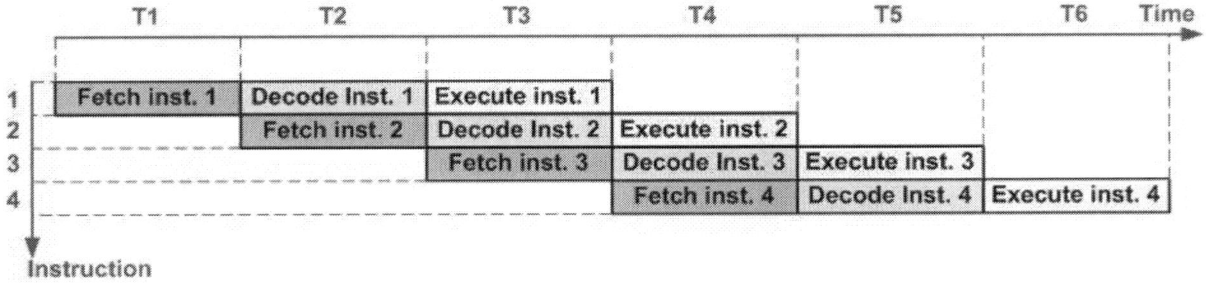

Figure 4- 10: Pipeline in ARM

In step 1, the opcode is fetched. In step 2, the opcode is decoded. In step 3, the instruction is executed and result is written into the destination register. This 3-stage pipeline was used in the original ARM. The newer version of ARM may have more stages of pipeline. See Chapter 7 and your ARM manual.

Instruction cycle time for the ARM

It takes certain amount of time for the CPU to execute an instruction. The unit of time is referred to as *machine cycles*. Thanks to the RISC architecture, ARM executes most instructions in one machine cycle. The length of the machine cycle depends on the frequency of the oscillator connected to the core clock of the CPU. The oscillator circuitry with external crystal or on-chip clock reference, provides the clock source for the ARM CPU. To calculate the machine cycle for the CPU, we take the inverse of the oscillator frequency, as shown in Example 4-9.

Example 4-9

The following shows the oscillator frequency for four different ARM-based systems. Find the period of the instruction cycle in each case.

(a) 80 MHz (b) 160 MHz (c) 100 MHz (d) 50 MHz

Solution:

(a) instruction cycle is 1/80 MHz = 0.0125 ms (microsecond) = 12.5 ns (nanosecond)
(b) instruction cycle = 1/160 MHz = 0.00625 ms = 6.25 ns
(c) instruction cycle = 1/100 MHz = 0.01 ms = 10 ns
(d) instruction cycle = 1/50 MHz = 0.02 ms = 20 ns

Branch penalty

The overlapping of fetch and execution of the instruction is widely used in today's microprocessors such as ARM. For the concept of pipelining to work, we need a buffer or queue in which instructions are pre-fetched and ready to be executed. In some circumstances, the CPU must flush out the queue. For example, when a branch is taken and the CPU starts to fetch code from a new memory location, the code in the queue that was previously fetched becomes useless. In this case, the execution unit must wait until the new instruction is fetched. This is called a branch penalty. The penalty is an extra instruction cycle time to fetch the instruction from the new location instead of executing the instruction already in the queue. This means that while the vast majority of ARM instructions take only one machine cycle, some instructions take three machine cycles. These are Branch, BL (call), and all the conditional branch instructions such as BNE, BLO, and so on. The conditional branch instruction can take only one machine cycle if the condition is not met and the branch is not taken. For example, the BNE will jump if Z = 0 and that takes three machine cycles. If Z = 1, then it falls through and it takes only one machine cycle. See Examples 4-10 and 4-11.

Example 4-10

For an ARM system with the core clock running at 100 MHz, find how long it takes to execute each of the following instructions:

(a) MOV	(b) SUB	(c) B
(d) ADD	(e) NOP	(f) BHI
(g) BLO	(h) BNE	(i) EQU

Solution:

The machine cycle for a system of 100 MHz clock is 10 ns, as shown in Example 4-9. Therefore, we have:

Instruction	*Instruction cycles*	*Time to execute*
(a) MOV	1	1 × 10 ns = 10 ns
(b) SUB	1	1 × 10 ns = 10 ns
(c) B	3	3 × 10 ns = 30 ns
(d) ADD	1	1 × 10 ns = 10 ns
(e) NOP	1	1 × 10 ns = 10 ns

For the following, due to branch penalty, 3 clock cycles if taken and 1 if it falls through:

(f) BHI	3/1	3 × 10 ns = 30 ns
(g) BLO	3/1	3 × 10 ns = 30 ns
(h) BNE	3/1	3 × 10 ns = 30 ns
(i) EQU	0	(directives do not produce machine instructions)

Delay calculation for ARM

A delay subroutine consists of two parts: (1) setting a counter, and (2) a loop. Most of the time delay is performed by the body of the loop, as shown in Example 4-11.

Example 4-11

Find the size of the delay of the code snippet below if the system clock frequency is 100 MHz:

```
DELAY MOV   R0, #255
AGAIN NOP
      NOP
      SUBS  R0, R0, #1
      BNE   AGAIN
      MOV   PC, LR              ; return
```

Solution:

We have the following machine cycles for each instruction of the DELAY subroutine:

	Instruction			Machine Cycle
DELAY	MOV	R0, #255	;	1
AGAIN	NOP		;	1
	NOP		;	1
	SUBS	R0, R0, #1	;	1
	BNE	AGAIN	;	3/1
	MOV	PC, LR	;	1

Therefore, we have a time delay of [1 + ((1+1+1+3) × 255) + 1] × 10 ns = 15, 320 ns.
Notice that BNE takes three instruction cycles if it jumps back, and takes only one cycle when falling through the loop. That means the above number should be 153.0 ns. Because the last time, when R0 is zero, the BNE takes only one cycle because it falls through the loop

Often, we calculate the time delay based on the instructions inside the loop and ignore the clock cycles associated with the instructions outside the loop.

In Example 4-11, the largest value the R0 register can take is 2^{32} = 4G. One way to increase the delay is to use many NOP instructions within the loop. NOP, which stands for "no operation, " simply wastes time, but takes 4 bytes of program memory and that is too heavy a price to pay for just one instruction cycle. A better way is to use a nested loop.

Loop inside a loop delay

Another way to get a large delay is to use a loop inside a loop, which is also called a *nested loop*. See Example 4-12.

Example 4-12

In a given ARM trainer an I/O port is connected to 8 LEDs. The following program toggles the LEDs by sending to it 0x55 and 0xAA values continuously. Calculate the time delay for toggling of LEDs. Assume the system clock frequency of 100 MHz.

Solution:

```
      AREA  Example4_12, CODE, READONLY

PORT_ADDR   EQU   0x40000000  ; change the address for your ARM
      LDR   R1, =PORT_ADDR    ; R1 = port address
AGAIN MOV   R0, #0x55   ; R0 = 0x55
      STRB  R0, [R1]          ; send it to LEDs
      BL    DELAY       ; call delay
      MOV   R0, #0xAA   ; R0 = 0xAA
      STRB  R0, [R1]          ; send it to LEDs
      BL    DELAY       ; call delay
      BAL   AGAIN       ; keep doing it forever (BAL is the same as B)

      ; --------------------DELAY SUBROUTINE
DELAY
      MOV   R3, #100  ; R3 = 100, modify this value for different size delay
L1    LDR   R4, =250000 ; R4 = 250, 000 (inner loop count)
L2    SUBS  R4, R4, #1  ; 1 clock
      BNE   L2          ; 3 clock
      SUBS  R3, R3, #1  ; R3 = R3 - 1
      BNE   L1
      MOV   PC, LR            ; return to caller
      END
```

Ignoring the delay associated with the outer loop, we have the following time delay:
$[(1 + 3) \times 250,000 \times 100] \times 10$ ns = 1 second since 1/100 MHz = 10 ns.

Examine the working frequency for your ARM trainer, change the above address 0x40000000 to your ARM trainer port address and verify the time delay using oscilloscope.

From these discussions we conclude that the use of instructions in generating time delay is not the most reliable method. To complicate the matter, newer performance enhancements of the CPU hardware or the compiler software may affect the loop timing.

To get more accurate time delay Timers are used. All ARM microcontrollers come with on-chip Timers. We can use Keil uVision's simulator to verify delay time and number of cycles used. Meanwhile, to get an accurate time delay for a given ARM microcontroller, we must use an oscilloscope to verify the exact time delay.

Review Questions

1. True or false. In the ARM, the machine cycle lasts 1 clock period of the core clock frequency.
2. The minimum number of machine cycles needed to execute an ARM instruction is _____.
3. Find the machine cycle for a core clock frequency of 66 MHz.
4. Assuming a core clock frequency of 100 MHz, find the time delay associated with the loop section of the following DELAY subroutine:

```
DELAY   LDR   R2, =50000000
HERE    NOP
        NOP
        NOP
        NOP
        NOP
        SUBS  R2, R2, #1
        BNE   HERE
        MOV   PC, LR
```

5. Find the machine cycle for an ARM if the core clock frequency is 50 MHz.
6. True or false. In the ARM, the instruction fetching and execution are done at the same time.
7. True or false. B and BL will always take 2 machine cycles.
8. True or false. The BNE instruction will always take 3 machine cycles.

Section 4.4: Conditional Execution

Every microprocessor has the conditional branch (jump) instruction based on the status of flag bits such as Z and C. Instructions such as BEQ (branch equal, Z = 1) or BNC (branch if no carry, C = 0) are common in all CPUs. The ARM CPU has a unique feature that we do not see in other microprocessors. In ARM, the concept of conditional execution is implemented for all instruction and not just for branch which makes you able to decide to run or ignore each single instruction depending on the status of flag bits in CPSR (current program status register). In other words, not only the branch instruction but all of the ARM instructions can be conditional. As we discussed in Chapters 2 and 3, the ADD, SUB, and other arithmetic instruction do not affect the flag bits in CPSR register unless they have suffix 'S' in the syntax. The default is not to update the flags. We override the default by having suffix 'S' in the instruction. The same thing is true about conditional field of each instruction. If we do not add a condition after an instruction, it will be executed unconditionally because the default is not to check the flags and execute unconditionally. If we want an instruction to be executed only when a condition is met, we put the condition suffix right after the instruction.

The ARM instructions have set aside the most significant 4 bits of the instruction field for the conditions. See Figure 4-11. The 4 bits gives us 16 possible conditions. Table 4-4 shows the list of all the 16 possible conditions.

Figure 4- 11: Condition Field in ARM Instructions

Bits	Mnemonic Extension	Meaning	Flag
0000	EQ	Equal	Z = 1
0001	NE	Not equal	Z = 0
0010	CS/HS	Carry Set/Higher or Same	C = 1
0011	CC/LO	Carry Clear/Lower	C = 0
0100	MI	Minus/Negative	N = 1
0101	PL	Plus	N = 0
0110	VS	V Set (Overflow)	V = 1
0111	VC	V Clear (No Overflow)	V = 0
1000	HI	Higher	C = 1 and Z = 0
1001	HS	Lower or Same	C = 1 and Z = 1
1010	GE	Greater than or Equal	N = V
1011	LT	Less than	N ≠ V
1100	GT	Greater than	Z = 0 and N = V
1101	LE	Less than or Equal	Z = 0 or N ≠ V
1110	AL	Always (unconditional)	
1111	---	Not Valid	

Table 4- 4: ARM Condition codes for the Opcode bits [31-28]

Note!

By default, all the instructions are executed unconditionally. As a result, the AL (Always) suffix has no effect on the instruction. For example, BAL (Branch Always) is exactly the same as B (Branch). The same is true for all instructions.

To make an instruction conditional, simply put the condition suffix from Table 4-4 after the opcode. See the following examples:

```
MOV   R1, #10     ; R1 = 10
MOV   R2, #12     ; R2 = 12
CMP   R2, R1      ; compare 12 with 10, Z=0 because they are not equal
MOVEQ R4, #20     ; this line is not executed because
                  ; the condition EQ is not met
```

The following code adds 10 to R1 if it is not zero:

```
MOV   R1, #10     ; R1 = 10
CMP   R1, #0      ; compare R1 with 0
ADDNE R1, R1, #10 ; this line is executed if Z = 0
                  ; (if in the last CMP operands were not equal)
```

Note that the 'S' suffix and the condition suffix are independent of each other. We can add both 'S' and condition suffix to the opcode of an instruction. It is common to put 'S' after the condition. See the following examples:

```
ADDNES  R1, R1, #10 ; this line is executed and set the flags if Z = 0
```

One advantage of using conditional execution is it saves the execution time of an instruction by avoiding branch penalty. As we discussed earlier, when a conditional branch is taken, the pre-fetched instructions are flushed from the queue and the new instructions have to be fetched from the memory while the CPU is waiting. Using conditional execution, if the condition is met, the instruction is executed. If the condition is not met, the instruction execution is skipped and the next instruction in the queue is executed. There is no need to flush the queue because of the condition.

Example 4-13 shows two versions of the Example 4-4 we covered earlier. In the new version, we use the conditional execution instructions. Simulate and compare both versions to see how the conditional instructions are executed.

Example 4-13

The following program adds 0x99999999 together 10 times. Compare the code syntax to see how the conditional execution of the code is used.

Code 1: (Example 4-4 using conditional branch instruction BCC)

```
        AREA  EXAMPLE4_4, CODE, READONLY

        MOV   R1, #0            ; clear high word (R1 = 0)
        MOV   R0, #0            ; clear low word (R0 = 0)
        LDR   R2, =0x99999999   ; R2 = 0x99999999
        MOV   R3, #10           ; counter
L1      ADDS  R0, R0, R2        ; R0 = R0 + R2 and update the flags
        BCC   NEXT              ; if C = 0, go to next number
        ADD   R1, R1, #1        ; if C = 1, increment the upper word
NEXT    SUBS  R3, R3, #1        ; R3 = R3 - 1 and update the flags
        BNE   L1                ; next round if z = 0
HERE    B     HERE              ; stay here
        END
```

Code 2: (Example 4-4 with conditional execution of instruction ADDCS)

```
        AREA  EXAMPLE4_13,      CODE, READONLY

        MOV   R1, #0            ; clear high word (R1 = 0)
        MOV   R0, #0            ; clear low word (R0 = 0)
        LDR   R2, =0x99999999   ; R2 = 0x99999999
        MOV   R3, #10           ; counter
L1      ADDS  R0, R0, R2        ; R0 = R0 + R2 and update the flags
```

```
        ADDCS R1, R1, #1          ; if C set (C = 1), increment the upper word
NEXT    SUBS  R3, R3, #1          ; R3 = R3 - 1 and update the flags
        BNE   L1                  ; next round if z = 0
HERE    B     HERE                ; stay here
        END
```

See also Examples 4-14 and 4-15.

Example 4-14

Rewrite the main part of Program 4-1 using conditional execution of ARM instructions

Solution:

```
        MOV   COUNT, #5           ; COUNT = 5
        MOV   MAX, #0             ; MAX = 0
        LDR   POINTER, =MYDATA    ; POINTER = MYDATA (address of first data)
AGAIN
        LDR   NEXT, [POINTER]     ; load contents of POINTER location to NEXT
        CMP   MAX, NEXT           ; compare MAX and NEXT
        MOVLO MAX, NEXT           ; if MAX is lower than NEXT then MAX=NEXT
        ADD   POINTER, POINTER, #4     ; POINTER = POINTER + 4 to point to next
        SUBS  COUNT, COUNT, #1    ; decrement counter
        BNE   AGAIN               ; branch AGAIN if counter is not zero
```

Example 4-15

Using rotation, write a program that counts the number of 1s in R0.

Solution:

```
        AREA  EXAMPLE4_15, CODE, READONLY

        LDR   R0, =0x34F37D36
        MOV   R1, #0       ; number of 1s
        MOV   R2, #32      ; counter
BEGIN   MOV   R0, R0, RRX  ; Rotate right with carry the R0 register
        ADDCS R1, R1, #1   ; if C = 1 then increment R1
        SUBS  R2, R2, #1   ; decrement counter
        BNE   BEGIN        ; if counter is not equal to zero branch BEGIN
        END
```

Review Questions

1. True or false. All the ARM instructions have the conditional execution feature.
2. How many bits of the ARM instruction are set aside for the condition codes?
3. The ADDAL stands for __________.
4. True or false. MOVVC is a valid instruction in ARM
5. True or false. SUBEQS is a valid instruction in ARM

Problems

Section 4.1: Looping and Branch Instructions

1. In the ARM, looping action using a single register is limited to _______ iterations.
2. If a conditional branch is not taken, what is the next instruction to be executed?
3. In calculating the target address for a branch, a displacement is added to the contents of register _______.
4. The mnemonic BNE stands for __________.
5. What is the advantage of using BX over B?
6. True or false. The target of a BNE can be anywhere in the 4G word address space.
7. True or false. All ARM branch instructions can branch to anywhere in the 4G byte address space.
8. Dissect the B instruction, indicating how many bits are used for the operand and the opcode, and indicate how far it can branch.
9. True or false. All conditional branches are 2-byte instructions.
10. Show code for a nested loop to perform an action 10, 000, 000, 000 times.
11. Show code for a nested loop to perform an action 200, 000, 000, 000 times.
12. Find the number of times the following loop is performed:

```
        MOV   R0, #0x55
        MOV   R2, #40
L1      LDR   R1, =10000000
L2      EOR   R0, R0, #0xFF
        SUB   R1, R1, #1
        BNE   L2
        SUB   R2, R2, #1
        BNE   L1
```

13. Indicate the status of Z and C after CMP is executed in each of the following cases.

(a)
```
MOV   R0, #50
MOV   R1, #40
CMP   R0, R1
```

(b)
```
MOV   R1, #0xFF
MOV   R2, #0x6F
CMP   R1, R2
```

(c)
```
MOV   R2, #34
MOV   R3, #88
CMP   R2, R3
```

(d)
```
SUB   R1, R1, R1
MOV   R2, #0
CMP   R1, R2
```

(e)
```
EOR   R2, R2, R2
MOV   R3, #0xFF
CMP   R2, R3
```

(f)
```
EOR   R0, R0, R0
EOR   R1, R1, R1
CMP   R0, R1
```

(g)

```
MOV     R4, #0x78
MOV     R2, #0x40
CMP     R4, R2
```

(h)

```
MOV     R0, #0xAA
AND     R0, R0, #0x55
CMP     R0, #0
```

14. Rewrite Program 4-1 to find the lowest grade in that class.
15. The target address of a BNE is backward if the relative address portion of opcode is _______ (negative, positive).
16. The target address of a BNE is forward if the relative address portion of opcode is _______ (negative, positive).

Section 4.2: Calling Subroutine with BL

17. BL is a(n) ___-byte instruction.
18. In ARM, which register is the linker register?
19. True or false. The BL target address can be anywhere in the 4G byte address space.
20. Describe how we can return from a subroutine in ARM.
21. In ARM, which address is saved when BL instruction is executed.

Section 4.3: ARM Time Delay and Instruction Pipeline

22. Find the core clock frequency if the machine cycle = 1.25 ns.
23. Find the machine cycle if the core clock frequency is 200 MHz.
24. Find the machine cycle if the core clock frequency is 100 MHz.
25. Find the machine cycle if the core clock frequency is 160 MHz.
26. Find the time delay for the delay subroutine shown below if the system has an ARM with a core clock frequency of 80 MHz:

```
        MOV     R8, #200
BACK    LDR     R1, =400000000
HERE    NOP
        SUBS    R1, R1, #1
        BNE     HERE
        SUBS    R8, R8, #1
        BNE     BACK
```

27. Find the time delay for the delay subroutine shown below if the system has an ARM with a core clock frequency of 50 MHz:

```
        MOV     R2, #100
BACK    LDR     R0, =50000000
HERE    NOP
        NOP
```

```
        SUBS   R0, R0, #1
        BNE    HERE
        SUBS   R2, R2, #1
        BNE    BACK
```

28. Find the time delay for the delay subroutine shown below if the system has an ARM with a core clock frequency of 40 MHz:

```
        MOV    R1, #200
BACK    LDR    R0, #20000000
HERE    NOP
        NOP
        NOP
        SUBS   R0, R0, #1
        BNE    HERE
        SUBS   R1, R1, #1
        BNE    BACK
```

29. Find the time delay for the delay subroutine shown below if the system has an ARM with a core clock frequency of 100 MHz:

```
        MOV    R8, #500
BACK    LDR    R1, =20000
HERE    NOP
        NOP
        NOP
        SUBS   R1, R1, #1
        BNE    HERE
        SUBS   R8, R8, #1
        BNE    BACK
```

Section 4.4: Conditional Execution

30. Which bits of the ARM instruction are set aside for condition execution?
31. True or false. Only ADD and MOV instructions have conditional execution feature.
32. True or false. In ARM, the conditional execution is default.
33. Which flag bit is examined before the MOVEQ instruction is executed?
34. State the difference between the ADDEQ and ADDNE instructions.
35. State the difference between the BAL and B instructions.
36. State the difference between the SUBCC and SUBCS instructions.
37. State the difference between the ANDEQ and ANDNE instructions.
38. True or false. The decision to execute the SUBCC is based on the status of Z flag.
39. True or false. The decision to execute the ADDEQ is based on the status of Z flag.

Answers to Review Questions

Section 4.1: Looping and Branch Instructions

1. Branch if not Equal
2. True
3. 4
4. Z flag of CPSR (status register)
5. 4
6. The B uses immediate value for offset and can only branch to an address location within ±32 MB address space, while the BX uses register operand to hold the branch target address and can go anywhere in the 4 GB address space of ARM.

Section 4.2: Calling Subroutine with BL

1. Branch and Link
2. True
3. 4
4. 32
5. R14
6. In both of them the target address is relative to the value of the program counter and the relative address can cover memory space of ±32MB from current location of program counter. The BL instruction saves the address of the next instruction in the LR register before jumping, while the B instruction just jumps without saving anything.

Section 4.3: ARM Time Delay and Instruction Pipeline

1. True
2. 1
3. MC = 1/66 MHz = 0.015 ms = 15 ns
4. [50, 000, 000 × (1 + 1 + 1 + 1 + 1 + 1 + 3)] × 10 ns = 4.5 seconds
5. Machine Cycle = 1 / 50 MHz = 0.02 ms = 20 ns
6. True
7. False
8. False. It takes 3 cycles, only if it branches to the target address.

Section 4.4: Conditional Execution

1. True
2. 4 bits
3. ADD ALways regardless of the status flag.
4. True
5. True

Chapter 5: Signed Integer Numbers Arithmetic

This chapter deals with signed integer number instructions and operations. In Section 5.1, we focus on the concept of signed numbers in software engineering. Signed number arithmetic operations and instructions are explained along with examples in Section 5.2.

Section 5.1: Signed Numbers Concept

All data items used so far have been unsigned integer numbers, meaning that the entire 8-bit, 16-bit or 32-bit operand was used for the magnitude and the numbers represented are all positive or zero. Many applications require the use of negative numbers or signed data. In this section the concept of signed integer numbers is discussed. The floating-point numbers are always signed and will be discussed in Chapter 9.

Concept of signed numbers in computers

In everyday life, numbers are used that could be positive or negative or zero. For example, a temperature of 5 degrees below zero can be represented as -5, and 20 degrees above zero as +20. Computers must be able to accommodate such numbers. To do that, computer scientists have devised the following arrangement for the representation of signed positive and negative numbers: The most significant bit (MSB) is set aside for the sign (+ or -) and the rest of the bits are used for the magnitude. The sign is represented by 0 for positive (+) numbers and 1 for negative (-) numbers. Signed byte and word representations are discussed below.

Sign-magnitude format

In sign-magnitude format the sign and magnitude of the number are represented independently. For a byte, D7 (MSB) is the sign and D0 to D6 are set aside for the magnitude of the number. If D7 = 0, the number is positive, and if D7 = 1, it is negative.

The range of magnitude that can be represented by the above format is 2^7 (0 to 127). And the range of the number that can be represented is -127 to +127.

Dec.	Binary
0	0000 0000
+1	0000 0001
...	....
+5	0000 0101
...	....
+127	0111 1111

Dec.	Binary
-0	1000 0000
-1	1000 0001
...	....
-5	1000 0101
...	....
-127	1111 1111

The sign-magnitude format is easier for human to understand but more complex for computer to process.

Negative numbers using 2's complement

To simplify ALU circuitry, we often use 2's complement for the negative number representation. Adding a negative number in 2’s complement has the same result as a subtraction. Using 2’s complement representation, the adder in the ALU will be able to perform both add and subtract. With 2’s complement, the most significant bit is still 0 for positive numbers and 1 for negative numbers like sign magnitude format.

In writing negative numbers in program source file, we usually use sign-magnitude format (e.g.: -75 for negative 75) and the assembler/compiler will convert the negative number to 2’s complement. We will demonstrate the following process used to convert a positive number to a negative number represented in 2's complement to help you understand the 2’s complement representation. Follow these steps:

1. Write the positive number in binary.
2. Invert bit.
3. Add 1 to it.

Unlike sign-magnitude format that has a positive zero and a negative zero, with 2’s complement representation, there is only one zero. And there is one more negative number than positive.

Dec.	Binary
0	0000 0000
+1	0000 0001
...	....
+5	0000 0101
...	....
+127	0111 1111

Dec.	Binary
0	0000 0000
-1	1111 1111
...	....
-5	1111 1011
...	....
-127	1000 0001
-128	1000 0000

Examples 5-1, 5-2, and 5-3 demonstrate these three steps.

Example 5-1

Show how the computer would represent -5 in 8-bit 2’s complement.

Solution:

1. 0000 0101 5 in 8-bit binary
2. 1111 1010 invert each bit
3. 1111 1011 add 1 (0xFB)

This is the signed number representation in 2's complement for -5.

Example 5-2

Show -34 hex as it is represented in 2's complement.

Solution:

1. 0011 0100 (0x34)
2. 1100 1011
3. 1100 1100 (which is 0xCC)

Example 5-3

Show the 2's complement representation for -128_{10}.

Solution:

1. 1000 0000 (128_{10})
2. 0111 1111
3. 1000 0000 Notice that this is not negative zero (–0).

From the examples above it is clear that the range of byte-sized negative numbers is -1 to -128. The following lists byte-sized signed number ranges:

Decimal	Binary	Hex
-128	1000 0000	80
-127	1000 0001	81
-126	1000 0010	82
...	....	..
-2	1111 1110	FE
-1	1111 1111	FF
0	0000 0000	00
+1	0000 0001	01
+2	0000 0010	02
...	....	..
+127	0111 1111	7F

Halfword-sized signed numbers

In ARM CPU a half-word is 16 bits in length. Using 2's complement representation, the MSB (D15) is used for the sign leaving a total of 15 bits (D14–D0) for the magnitude. This gives a range of –32,768 (–2^{15}) to +32,767 (2^{15}–1).

The following table shows the range of signed half-word numbers. To convert a half-word positive number to a negative half-word number in 2's complement representation, the same steps discussed above for byte size number are used.

Decimal	Binary	Hex
-32,768	1000 0000 0000 0000	8000
-32,767	1000 0000 0000 0001	8001
-32,766	1000 0000 0000 0010	8002
...	....	..
-2	1111 1111 1111 1110	FFFE
-1	1111 1111 1111 1111	FFFF
0	0000 0000 0000 0000	0000
+1	0000 0000 0000 0001	0001
+2	0000 0000 0000 0010	0002
...	....	...
+32,766	0111 1111 1111 1110	7FFE
+32,767	0111 1111 1111 1111	7FFF

Using Microsoft Windows calculator for signed numbers

All Microsoft Windows operating systems come with a handy calculator. Use it in programmer's mode to verify the signed number operations in this section.

Word-sized signed numbers

In ARM CPU a word is 32 bits in length. Using 2's complement representation, the MSB (D31) is used for the sign leaving a total of 31 bits (D30–D0) for the magnitude. This gives a range of -(2^{31}) to +(2^{31}-1).

To convert a word-size positive number to a negative word-size number in 2's complement representation, the same steps discussed above for byte size number are used. See Example 5-4.

Example 5-4

Show how the computer would represent -5 in 2's complement for (a) 8-bit, (b) 16-bit, and (c) 32-bit data sizes.

Solution:

(a) 8-bit

1. 0000 0101   5 in 8-bit binary
2. 1111 1010   invert each bit
3. 1111 1011   add 1   (0xFB)

(b) 16-bit

1. 0000 0000 0000 0101   5 in 16-bit binary
2. 1111 1111 1111 1010   invert each bit
3. 1111 1111 1111 1011   add 1 (0xFFFB)

(c) 32-bit

1. 0000 0000 0000 0000 0000 0000 0000 0101 5 in 32-bit binary
2. 1111 1111 1111 1111 1111 1111 1111 1010 invert each bit
3. 1111 1111 1111 1111 1111 1111 1111 1011 add 1   (0xFFFFFFFB)

Use the Windows calculator to verify these examples.

If a number is larger than 32-bit, it must be treated as a 64-bit double-word number and be processed word by word the same way as unsigned numbers. The following shows the range of signed word-size numbers.

Decimal	Binary	Hex
-2,147,483,648	10000000000000000000000000000000	80000000
-2,147,483,647	10000000000000000000000000000001	80000001
-2,147,483,646	10000000000000000000000000000010	80000002
...	...	...
-2	11111111111111111111111111111110	FFFFFFFE
-1	11111111111111111111111111111111	FFFFFFFF
0	00000000000000000000000000000000	00000000
+1	00000000000000000000000000000001	00000001
+2	00000000000000000000000000000010	00000002
...	...	...
+2,147,483,646	01111111111111111111111111111110	7FFFFFFE
+2,147,483,647	01111111111111111111111111111111	7FFFFFFF

Table 5-1 shows a summary of signed data ranges.

Data Size	Bits	2^n	Decimal	Hexadecimal
Byte	8	-2^7 to $+2^7-1$	-128 to +127	0x80–0x7F
Half-word	16	-2^{15} to $+2^{15}-1$	-32,768 to +32,767	0x8000–0x7FFF
Word	32	-2^{31} to $+2^{31}-1$	-2,147,483,648 to +2,147,483,647	0x80000000–0x7FFFFFFF

Table 5-1: Signed Data Range Summary

Review Questions

1. In an 8-bit number, bit _____ is used for the sign bit, whereas in a 16-bit number, bit _____ is used for the sign bit. Repeat for 32-bit signed data.
2. Compute the byte-sized 2's complement of 0x16.
3. The range of byte-sized signed operands is -______ to +______. The range of half word-sized signed numbers is -__________ to +__________.
4. The range of word-sized signed numbers is -________________ to +________________.
5. Compute the 2's complement of 0x00500000.

Section 5.2: Signed Number Instructions and Operations

In this section we examine issues associated with signed number arithmetic operations. We will also discuss the ARM instructions for signed numbers and how to use them. It must be noted that in ARM the N flag bit in CSPR is the sign bit. N=0 is for positive and N=1 for negative numbers.

Overflow problem in signed number operations

When using signed numbers, a serious problem arises that must be dealt with. This is the overflow problem. The CPU indicates the existence of the problem by raising the V (oVerflow) flag, but it is up to the programmer to take care of it. Now what is an overflow? If the result of an operation on signed numbers is too large for the register and resulted in an error, an overflow occurs and the programmer is notified. Look at Example 5-5.

Example 5-5

Look at the following case for 8-bit data size:

```
  + 96    0110 0000
  + 70   +0100 0110
  +166    1010 0110
```

We are adding two positive numbers together and the result is -90 in 2's complement notation, which is wrong. (V = 1, N = 1, C = 0)

In the example above, +96 is added to +70 and the result according to 2's complement notation is -90. Why? The reason is that the result was more than 8 bits could handle. The largest positive number an 8-bit registers can hold is +127. The sum of +96 and +70 is +166, which is more than +127. The designers of the CPU created the overflow flag specifically for the purpose of informing the programmer that the result of the signed number operation is erroneous.

When the overflow flag is set in 8-bit operations

In 8-bit signed number operations, V is set to 1 if either of the following two conditions occurs:

1. There is a carry from D6 to D7 but no carry out of D7 (C = 0).
2. There is a carry from D7 out (C = 1) but no carry from D6 to D7.

In other words, the overflow flag is set to 1 if there is a carry into D7 or out of D7, but not both. In Example 5-5, there is only a carry from D6 to D7 and no carry from D7 out so V was set to 1. Examples 5-6, 5-7, and 5-8 give further illustrations of the overflow flag in signed number arithmetic.

Example 5-6

Examine the following case:

```
   - 128    1000 0000
+    -2    +1111 1110
   - 130    0111 1110   V=1, N=0 (positive), C=1
```

In this example, we add two negative numbers together and resulted in +126, which is wrong. The error is indicated by the fact that V = 1.

Example 5-7

Observe the results of the following:

```
; assume R3=+7 (R3=0x07)
; assume R2=+18 (R2=0x12)
ADD R2,R2,R3        ; (R2=0x19=+25, correct)
```

```
    +7     0000 0111
+ +18    +0001 0010
   +25     0001 1001
```

V = 0, C = 0, and N = 0 (positive). The result is correct.

Example 5-8

Observe the results of the following:

```
     -2   1111 1110
  +  -5   1111 1011
     -7   1111 1001
```

V = 0, C = 0, and N = 1 (negative); the result is correct since V = 0.

Overflow flag in 16-bit operations

In a 16-bit operation, V is set to 1 in either of two cases:

1. There is a carry from D14 to D15 but no carry out of D15 (C = 0).
2. There is a carry from D15 out (C = 1) but no carry from D14 to D15.

Again the overflow flag is set to 1 when there is a carry into the most significant bit (D15) or out of the most significant bit, but not both. See Examples 5-9 and 5-10.

Example 5-9

Observe the results in the following 16-bit hex numbers:

```
    +6E2F   0110 1110 0010 1111
  + +13D4   0001 0011 1101 0100
    +8203   1000 0010 0000 0011   = –0x7DFD = –32,253 incorrect!
                                   V = 1, C = 0, N = 1
```

Example 5-10

Observe the results in the following 16-bit hex numbers:

```
    +542F    0101 0100 0010 1111
  + +12E0   +0001 0010 1110 0000
    +670F    0110 0111 0000 1111   = +0x670F = +26,383 (correct answer);
                                    V = 0, C = 0, N = 0
```

Overflow flag in 32-bit operations

In a 32-bit operation, V is set to 1 in either of two cases:

1. There is a carry from D30 to D31 but no carry out of D31 (C = 0).

2. There is a carry from D31 out (C = 1) but no carry from D30 to D31.

Again, the overflow flag is set to 1 when there is a carry into the most significant bit (D31) or out of the most significant bit, but not both. See Examples 5-11 and 5-12.

Example 5-11

Observe the results in the following 32-bit hex numbers:

	+6E2F356F	0110 1110 0010 1111 0011 0101 0110 1111	
+	+13D49530	+0001 0011 1101 0100 1001 0101 0011 0000	
	+8203CA9F	1000 0010 0000 0011 1100 1010 1001 1111	= –0x7DFC3561

The result is incorrect! V = 1, C = 0, N = 1

Example 5-12

Observe the results in the following 32-bit hex numbers:

	+542F356F	0101 0100 0010 1111 0011 0101 0110 1111	
+	+12E09530	0001 0010 1110 0000 1001 0101 0011 0000	
	+670FCA9F	0110 0111 0000 1111 1100 1010 1001 1111	= +670FCA9F

The result is correct; V = 0, C = 0, N = 0

Sign extension and avoiding erroneous results in signed number operations

To avoid the overflow problems associated with signed number operations, one can sign-extend the operand to a larger size. For a byte-size data, sign extension copies the sign bit (D7) of the lowest byte of a register into the upper 24 bits of the 32-bit register. For a half-word-size data, copies the sign bit (D15) to the upper 16 bits of the 32-bit register. The LDRSB (load register signed byte) instruction and the LDRSH (load register signed half-word) do just that. They work as follows:

LDRSB loads into the destination register a byte from memory and sign extends (copy D7, the sign bit) to the remaining 24 bits. This is illustrated in Figure 5-1.

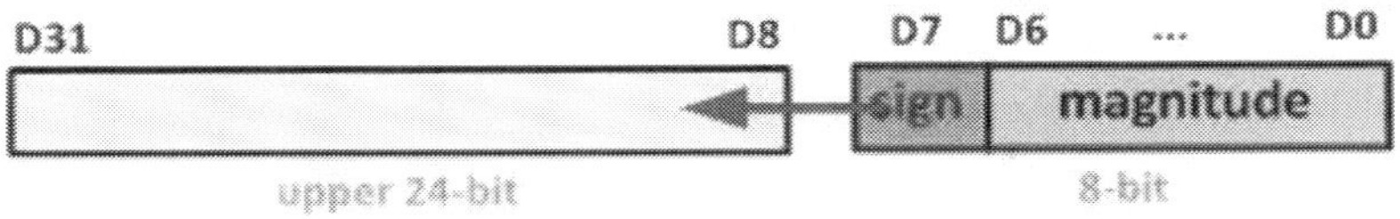

Figure 5-1: Sign Extending a Byte

Look at the following example:

```
; assume memory location 0x80000 has +96 = 0110 0000 and R1=0x80000
LDRSB R0, [R1]      ; now R0 =  00000000000000000000000001100000
; assume memory location 0x80000 contains -2 = 1111 1110 and R2=0x80000
LDRSB R4, [R2]   ; now R4 = 11111111111111111111111111111110
```

As can be seen in the above examples, LDRSB does not alter the lower 8 bits. The sign bit of the 8-bit data is copied to the rest of the 32-bit register.

LDRSH loads the destination register with a 16-bit signed number and sign-extends to the rest of the 16 bits of the 32-bit register. This is used for signed half-word operand and is illustrated in Figure 5-2.

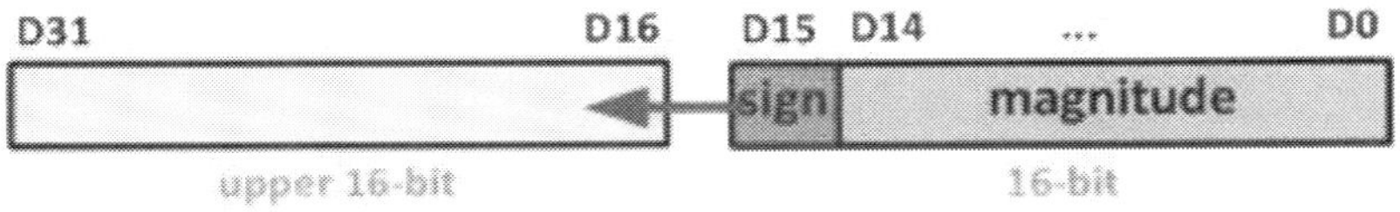

Figure 5- 2: Sign Extending a Half-word

Look at the following example:

```
; assume 0x80000 contains +260 = 0000 0001 0000 0100 and R1=0x80000
LDRSH R0, [R1]   ; R0=0000 0000 0000 0000 0000 0001 0000 0100
```

Another example:

```
; assume location 0x20000 has -327660=0x8002 and R2=0x20000
LDRSH R1, [R2]            ; R1=FFFF8002
```

As we see in the above examples, LDRSH does not alter the lower 16 bits. The sign bit of the 16-bit data is copied to the rest of the 32-bit register. How can these instructions help correct the overflow error? To answer that question, Example 5-13 shows Example 5-5 rewritten to correct the overflow problem.

Example 5-13

Write a program for Example 5-5 to handle the overflow problem.

Solution:

```
AREA   EXAMPLE5_13, CODE, READONLY

       LDR   R1, =DATA1
       LDR   R2, =DATA2
```

```
        LDR     R3, =RESULT

        LDRSB        R4, [R1]          ; R4 = +96
        LDRSB        R5, [R2]          ; R5 = +70
        ADD     R4, R4, R5  ; R4 = R4 + R5 = 96 + 70 = +166
        STR     R4, [R3]          ; Store +166 in location RESULT
HL      B       HL

DATA1           DCB    +96
DATA2           DCB    +70
        ALIGN
        AREA    VARIABLES, DATA, READWRITE    ; The following is stored in RAM
RESULT          DCW    0
        END
```

The following is an analysis of the values in Example 5-13. Each is sign-extended and then added as follows:

Sign	Binary numbers	Decimal
0	000 0000 0000 0000 0000 0000 0110 0000	+96 after sign ext.
0	000 0000 0000 0000 0000 0000 0100 0110	+70 after sign ext.
0	000 0000 0000 0000 0000 0000 1010 0110	+166

As a rule, if the possibility of overflow exists, all byte-sized signed numbers should be sign-extended into a word, and similarly, all halfword-sized signed operands should be sign-extended to a word before they are processed. This is shown in Program 5-1. Program 5-1 finds total sum of a group of signed number data.

Program 5-1

```
        ; This program calculates the sum of signed numbers

        AREA    PROG5_1, CODE, READONLY

        LDR     R0, =SIGN_DAT
        MOV     R3, #9
        MOV     R2, #0
LOOP    LDRSB        R1, [R0]
        ; Load into R1 and sign extend it.
        ADD     R2, R2, R1   ; R2 = R2 + R1
        ADD     R0, R0, #1   ; point to next
        SUBS    R3, R3, #1   ; decrement counter
        BNE     LOOP
        LDR     R0, =SUM
```

```
      STR   R2, [R0]     ; Store R2 in location SUM
HERE  B     HERE

SIGN_DAT DCB      +13, -10, +19, +14, -18, -9, +12, -19, +16

      AREA  VARIABLES, DATA, READWRITE
SUM   DCD   0
      END
```

Signed number multiplication

Signed number multiplication is similar in its operation to the unsigned multiplication described in Chapter 3. The only difference between them is that the operands including the result in signed number operations are treated as 2's complement representation of positive or negative numbers. In ARM we have SMULL (signed multiply long) that multiplies two 32-bit signed numbers and resulted in a 64-bit signed number. ARM also have 16-bit × 16-bit and 32-bit × 16-bit signed multiplication instructions but they are not available in all versions of the processors. Table 5-2 shows the 32-bit × 32-bit signed multiplication; it is similar to Table 3-3 in Chapter 3. See Examples 5-14 and 5-15.

Multiplication	Operand 1	Operand 2	Result
word×word	Rm	Rs	RdHi= upper 32-bit,RdLo=lower 32-bit
Note: *Using SMULL (signed multiply long) for word × words multiplication provides the 64-bit result in RdLo and RdHi register. This is used for 32-bit × 32-bit numbers in which result can go beyond 0xFFFFFFFF.*			

Table 5-2: Signed Multiplication (SMULL RdLo, RdHi, Rm, Rs) Summary

Example 5-14

Observe the results of the following multiplication of signed numbers:

```
      LDR   R1, =-3500   ; R1 = -3500 (0xFFFFF254)
      LDR   R0, =-100    ; R0 = -100 (0xFFFFFF9C)
      SMULL R2, R3, R0, R1
```

Solution:

-3500 × -100 = 350,000 = 0x55730 in hex. After executing the above program R2 and R3 will contain 0x55730 and 00000000, respectively.

Example 5-15

The following program is similar to Example 5-14. But, instead of SMULL, the UMULL instruction is used. Observe the results of the following multiplication:

```
LDR    R1, =-3500   ; R1 = -3500 (0xFFFFF254)
MOV    R0, #-100    ; R0 = -100 (0xFFFFFF9C)
UMULL  R2, R3, R0, R1
```

Solution:

0xFFFFF254 × 0xFFFFFF9C = 0xFFFFF1F000055730. Thus, R2 and R3 will contain 0x00055730 and 0xFFFFF1F0, respectively. As you can see, the results of the programs are completely different. In the previous program the SMULL instruction considers the operands signed numbers and the product of two negative numbers becomes positive. As a result, the sign bit becomes zero, but in this example the operands are considered as unsigned numbers.

Signed number comparison

In Chapter 4 we saw that the CMP instruction affects the Z and C flags; using the flags we compared unsigned numbers. This instruction affects the N and V flags as well. We can use flags Z, V, and N to compare signed numbers. The Z flag shows if the numbers are equal or not. When the numbers are equal the Z flag is set to one. N and V flags show if the left operand is bigger than the right operand or not. When N and V have the same value, the first operand has a greater value.

In summary, after executing the instruction *CMP Rn, Op2* the flags are changed as follows:

Op2 > Rn	V = N
Op2 = Rn	Z = 1
Op2 < Rn	N ≠ V

Instruction		Action
BEQ	Branch equal	Branch if Z = 1
BNE	Branch not equal	Branch if Z = 0
BMI	Branch minus (branch negative)	Branch if N = 1
BPL	Branch plus (branch positive)	Branch if N = 0
BVS	Branch if V set (branch overflow)	Branch if V = 1
BVC	Branch if V clear (branch if no overflow)	Branch if V = 0
BGE	Branch greater than or equal	Branch if N = V
BLT	Branch less than	Branch if N ≠ V
BGT	Branch greater than	Branch if Z = 0 and N = V
BLE	Branch less than or equal	Branch if Z = 1 or N ≠ V

Table 5- 3: ARM Conditional Branch (Jump) Instructions for Signed Data

Table 5-3 lists the branch instructions which check the Z, V, and N flags. The instructions can be used together with the CMP instruction to compare signed numbers.

Program 5-2 finds the lowest number among a list of numbers. The lowest number known so far is kept in R2. The numbers are brought into R1 and compared to R2. If a smaller one is found, it replaces the one in R2. The program starts by putting the first number in R2 since it is the lowest number known so far.

Program 5-2

```
        ; Finding the lowest of signed numbers
        AREA     PROG5_2, CODE, READONLY

        LDR R0, =SIGN_DAT
        MOV R3, #9
        LDRSB    R2, [R0]     ; bring first number into R2 and sign extend it
LOOP    ADD      R0, R0, #1   ; point to next
        SUBS     R3, R3, #1   ; decrement counter
        BEQ      DONE         ; if R3 is zero, done
        LDRSB    R1, [R0]     ; bring next number into R1 and sign extend it
        CMP      R1, R2       ; compare R1 and R2
        MOVLT    R2, R1       ; if R1 is smaller, keep it in R2
        B        LOOP
DONE    LDR      R0, =LOWEST  ; R0 = address of LOWEST
        STR      R2, [R0]     ; store R2 in location SUM
HERE    B        HERE

SIGN_DAT DCB       +13, -10, +19, +14, -18, -9, +12, -19, +16
        ALIGN
        AREA     VARIABLES, DATA, READWRITE
LOWEST      DCD      0
        END
```

CMN instruction

```
        CMN    Rn, Op2
```

In ARM we have two compare instructions: CMP and CMN. While the CMP instruction sets the flags by subtracting operand2 from operand1, the CMN sets the flags by adding operand2 from operand1. As the result CMN compares the destination operand with the negative of the source operand:

destination > (-1 × source)	V = N
destination = (-1 × source)	Z = 1
destination < (-1 × source)	N ≠ V

When the source operand is an immediate value, the instructions can be used interchangeably. Example 5-16 is an example of using the CMN instruction.

Example 5-16

Assuming R5 has a positive value, write a program that finds its negative match in an array of data (OUR_DATA).

Solution:

```
            AREA   EXAMPLE5_16, CODE, READONLY

            MOV    R5, #13
            LDR    R0, =OUR_DATA
            MOV    R3, #9
BEGIN
            LDRSB  R1, [R0]      ; R1 = contents of loc. pointed to by R0
                                 ; (sign extended)
            CMN    R1, R5        ; compare R1 and negative of R5
            BEQ    FOUND         ; branch if R1 is equal to negative of R5

            ADDS   R0, R0, #1    ; increment pointer
            SUBS   R3, R3, #1    ; decrement counter
            BNE    BEGIN         ; if R3 is not zero branch BEGIN

NOT_FOUND   B      NOT_FOUND
FOUND       B      FOUND

OUR_DATA    DCB    +13, -10, -13, +14, -18, -9, +12, -19, +16
            END
```

In the above program R5 is initialized with 13. Therefore, it finishes searching when it gets to −13.

Arithmetic shift

As was discussed in Chapter 3, there are two types of shifts: logical and arithmetic. Logical shift, which is used for unsigned numbers, was discussed in Chapter 3. The arithmetic shift is used for signed numbers. It is basically the same as the logical shift, except that the old sign bit is copied to the new sign bit so that the sign of the number does not change.

ASR (arithmetic shift right)

```
MOV    Rn, Op2, ASR count
or
ASR    Rn, Op2, count
```

The number of bits to shift can be a register or an immediate value. As the bits of the source are shifted to the right into C, the empty bits are filled with the original sign bit. One can use the ASR instruction to divide a signed number by 2, as shown below:

```
MOV   R0, #-10      ; R0 = -10 = 0xFFFFFFF6
MOV   R3, R0, ASR #1     ; R0 is arithmetic shifted right once
                    ; R3 = 0xFFFFFFFB = -5
```

Review Questions

1. Explain the difference between an overflow and a carry.
2. Explain the purpose of the LDRSB and LDRSH instructions. Demonstrate the effect of LDRSB on R0 = 0xF6. Demonstrate the effect of LDRSH on R1 = 0x124C.
3. The instruction for signed multiplication long is ________.
4. For each of the following instructions, indicate the flag condition necessary for each branch to occur: (a) BLE (b) BGT

Problems

Section 5.1: Signed Numbers Concept

1. Show how the 32-bit computers would represent the following numbers in 2's complement notation and verify each with a calculator.

(a) -23	(b) +12	(c) -0x28
(d) +0x6F	(e) -128	(f) +127
(g) +365	(h) -32,767	

2. Show how the 32-bit computers would represent the following numbers in 2's complement and verify each with a calculator.

(a) -230	(b) +1200	(c) - 0x28F
(d) +0x6FF		

Section 5.2: Signed Number Instructions and Operations

3. Find the overflow flag for each case and verify the result using an ARM IDE. Do byte-sized calculation on them.

(a) (+15) + (-12)	(b) (-123) + (-127)	(c) (+0x25) + (+34)
(d) (-127) + (+127)	(e) (+100) + (-100)	

4. Sign-extend the following values into 32 bits using ARM instructions in the Keil IDE.

(a) -122	(b) -0x999	(c) +0x17
(d) +127	(e) -129	

5. Modify Program 5-2 to find the highest number. Verify your program.

Answers to Review Questions

Section 5.1

1. D7, D15, and D31 for 32-bit signed data.
2. 0x16 = 0001 0110; its 2's complement is: 1110 1001 + 1 = 1110 1010
3. –128 to +127; –32,768 to +32,767 (decimal)
4. -2,147,483,648 to +2,147,483,647
5. 0x500000 = 0000 0000 0101 0000 0000 0000 0000 0000;
   Its 2's complement is: 1111 1111 1010 1111 1111 1111 1111 1111 + 1 =
   1111 1111 1011 0000 0000 0000 0000 0000 = 0xFFB00000

Section 5.2

1. C flag is raised when there is a carry out from the operation, but V flag is raised when there is a carry into the sign bit and no carry out of the sign bit or when there is no carry into the sign bit and there is a carry out of the sign bit. C flag is used to indicate overflow in unsigned arithmetic operations while V flag is involved in signed operations.
2. The LDRSB instruction sign extends the sign bit of a byte into a word; the LDRSH instruction sign extends the sign bit of a half-word into a word.
   In 0xF6 the sign bit is 1; thus, it is sign-extended into 0xFFFFFFF6
   0x124C sign-extended into R1 would be 0x0000124C.
3. SMULL
4. (a) BLE will jump if V is different from N, or if Z = 1.
   (b) BGT will jump if V equals N, and if Z = 0.

Chapter 6: ARM Memory Map, Memory Access, and Stack

This chapter discusses the issue of memory access and the stack. Section 6.1 is dedicated to ARM memory map and memory access. We will also explain the concepts of align, non-align, little endian, and big endian data access. Advanced indexed addressing mode is explained in Section 6.2. In Section 6.3, we examine the use of the stack in ARM. We discuss the bit-addressable (bit-banding) SRAM and peripherals in Section 6.4. In Section 6.5, we describe the PC relative addressing mode and its use in implementing ADR and LDR.

Section 6.1: ARM Memory Map and Memory Access

The ARM CPU uses 32-bit addresses to access memory and peripherals. This gives us a maximum of 4 GB (gigabytes) of memory space. This 4GB of directly accessible memory space has addresses 0x00000000 to 0xFFFFFFFF, meaning each byte is assigned a unique address (ARM is a byte-addressable CPU). See Figure 6-1.

D31 D24	D23 D16	D15 D8	D7 D0	
0x00000003	0x00000002	0x00000001	0x00000000	0x00000000
0x00000007	0x00000006	0x00000005	0x00000004	0x00000004
0x0000000B	0x0000000A	0x00000009	0x00000008	0x00000008
0x0000000F	0x0000000E	0x0000000D	0x0000000C	0x0000000C
⋮	⋮	⋮	⋮	
0xFFFFFFF3	0xFFFFFFF2	0xFFFFFFF1	0xFFFFFFF0	0xFFFFFFF0
0xFFFFFFF7	0xFFFFFFF6	0xFFFFFFF5	0xFFFFFFF4	0xFFFFFFF4
0xFFFFFFFB	0xFFFFFFFA	0xFFFFFFF9	0xFFFFFFF8	0xFFFFFFF8
0xFFFFFFFF	0xFFFFFFFE	0xFFFFFFFD	0xFFFFFFFC	0xFFFFFFFC

Figure 6-1: Memory Byte Addressing in ARM

The 4GB of memory space is divided into three regions: code, data, and peripheral devices. See Table 6-1.

Address range	Name	Description
0x00000000-0x1FFFFFFF	Code	ROM or Flash memory
0x20000000-0x3FFFFFFF	SRAM	SRAM region used for on-chip RAM
0x40000000-0x5FFFFFFF	Peripheral	On-chip peripheral address space
0x60000000-0x9FFFFFFF	RAM	Memory, cache support
0xA0000000-0xDFFFFFFF	Device	Shared and non-shared device space
0xE0000000-0xFFFFFFFF	System	PPB and vendor system peripherals

Table 6-1: Sample Memory Space Allocation in ARM

ARM uses the memory mapped I/O, which means the I/O control/data registers have memory addresses and are accessed using memory load/store instructions. For the ARM microcontrollers, generally the Flash ROM is used for program code, SRAM for scratch pad data, and memory-mapped I/O ports for peripherals. There are no mandatory address space allocations for memory and peripherals imposed by ARM, therefore the licensees can implement the memory and peripherals as they choose. For this reason, the amount and the address locations of memory used by Flash ROM, SRAM, and I/O peripherals varies among the family members and chip manufacturers. Make sure to examine the memory map of a given ARM chip in the datasheet before you start to program it. From the sample allocation in Table 6-1, you can see that some of the memory addresses are set aside for the external (off-chip) memory and peripherals. At the time of this writing, no ARM manufacturer has populated the entire 4 GB of memory space with on-chip ROM, RAM, and I/O peripherals.

ARM-based Motherboards

In ARM systems for Microsoft Windows, Unix, and Android operating systems the ARM motherboards use DRAM for the RAM memory, just like the x86 and Pentium PCs. As the ARM CPU is pushed into the laptop, desktop, and tablets PCs, and the high end of embedded systems products such as routers, we will see the use of DRAM as primary memory to store both the operating systems and the applications. In such systems, the Flash memory will be holding the POST (power on self-test), BIOS (basic Input/output systems) and boot programs. Just like x86 system, such systems have both on-chip and off-chip high speed SRAM for cache. Currently, there are ARM chips on the market with some on-chip Flash ROM, SRAM, and memory decoding circuitry for connection to external (off-chip) memory. This off-chip memory can be SRAM, Flash, or DRAM. The datasheet for such ARM chips provide the details of memory map for both on-chip and off-chip memories. Next, we examine the ARM buses and memory access.

The ARM buses and memory access

D31–D0 Data bus

See Figure 6-2. The 32-bit data bus of the ARM provides the 32-bit data path to the on-chip and off-chip memory and peripherals. They are grouped into 8-bit data bytes, D0–D7, D8–D15, D16–D23, and D24–D31.

A31–A0

These signals provide the 32-bit address path to the on-chip and off-chip memory and peripherals. Since the ARM supports data access of byte (8 bits), half word (16 bits), and word (32 bits), the buses must be able to access any of the 4 banks of memory connected to the 32-bit data bus. The A0 and A1 are used to select one of the 4 bytes of the D31-D0 data bus. See Figure 6-3.

AHB and APB buses

The ARM CPU is connected to the on-chip memory via an AHB (advanced high-performance bus). The AHB is used not only for connection to on-chip ROM and RAM, it is also used for connection to some of the high speed I/Os (input/output) such as GPIO (general purpose I/O). ARM chip also has the APB (advanced peripherals bus) bus dedicated for communication with the on-chip peripherals such as timers, ADC, UART, SPI, I2C, and other peripheral ports.

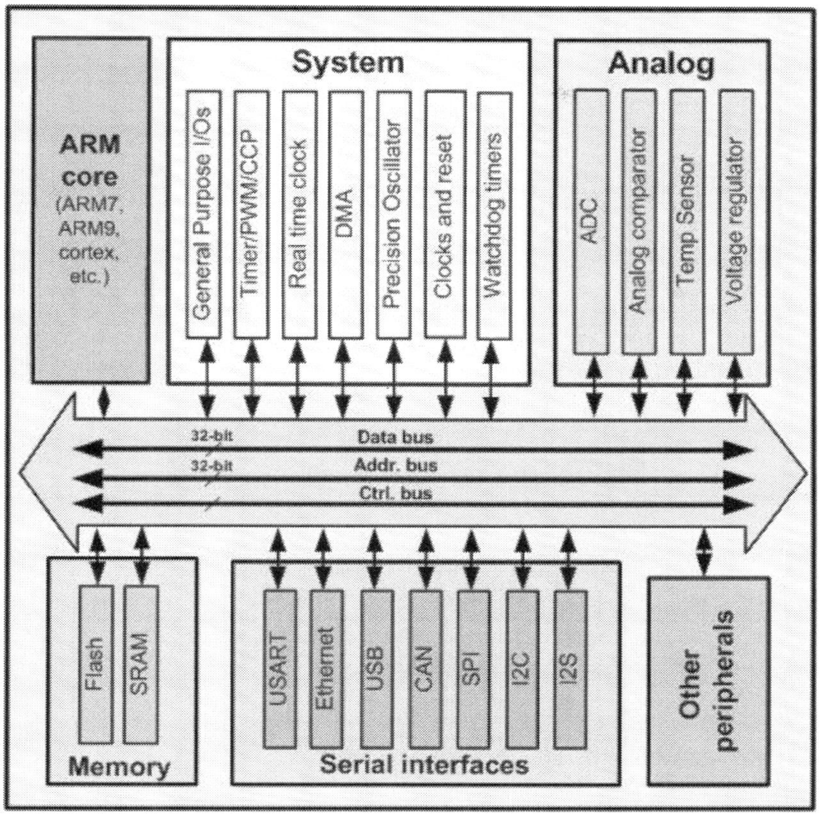

Figure 6-2: Memory Connection Block Diagram in ARM

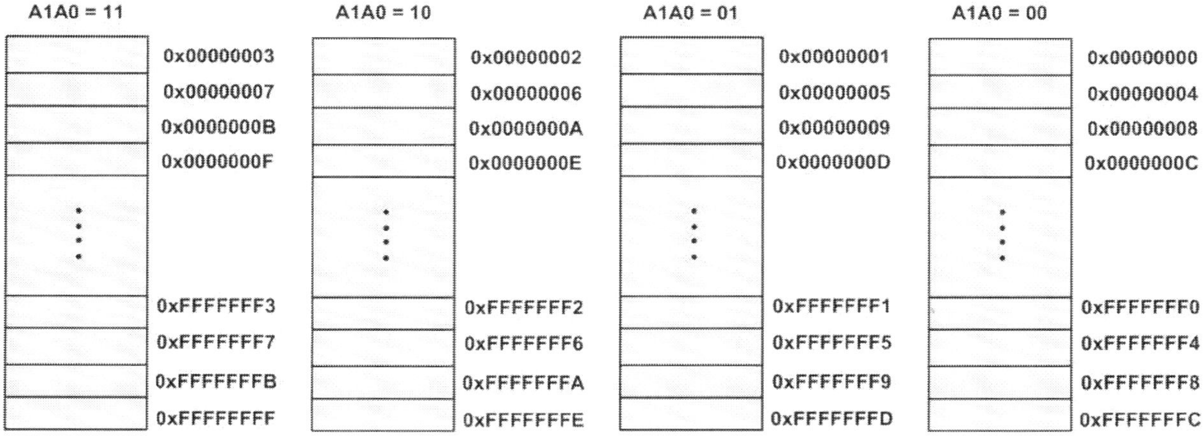

Figure 6-3: Memory Block Diagram in ARM

While we need the 32-bit data bus between CPU and the memory (RAM and ROM), many slower peripherals have no need for fast data bus pathway. For this reason, ARM uses the AHB-to-APB bridge to access the slower on-chip devices such as peripherals. Also, since peripherals do not need a high-speed bus, a bridge between AHB and APB allows going from the higher speed bus of AHB to lower speed bus of peripherals. The AHB bus allows a single-cycle access. See Figure 6-4 for AHB-to-APB bridge.

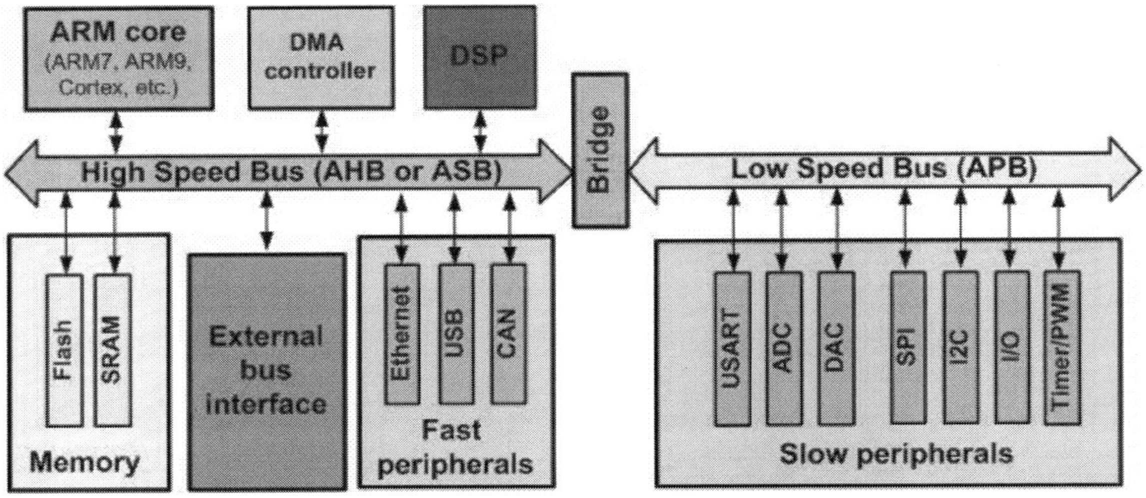

Figure 6-4: AHB and APB in ARM

Bus cycle time

To access a device such as memory or I/O, the CPU provides a fixed amount of time called a bus cycle time. During this bus cycle time, the read or write operation of memory or I/O must be completed. The bus cycle time used for accessing memory is often referred to as MC (memory cycle) time. The time from when the CPU provides the addresses at its address pins to when the data is expected at its data pins is called memory read cycle time. While for on-chip memory the cycle time can be 1 clock, in the off-chip memory the cycle time is often 2 clocks or more. If memory is slow and its access time does not match the MC time of the CPU, extra time can be requested from the CPU to extend the read cycle time. This extra time is called a wait state (WS). In the 1980s, the clock speed for memory cycle time was the same as the CPU's clock speed. For example, in the 20 MHz processors, the buses were working at the same speed of 20 MHz. This resulted in 2 × 50 ns = 100 ns for the memory cycle time (1/20 MHz = 50 ns). See Example 6-1.

Example 6-1

Calculate the memory cycle time of a 50-MHz bus system with
(a) 0 WS,
(b) 1 WS, and
(c) 2 WS.
Assume that the bus cycle time for off-chip memory access is 2 clocks.

Solution:

1/50 MHz = 20 ns is the bus clock period. Since the bus cycle time of zero wait states is 2 clocks, we have:

(a) Memory cycle time with 0 WS	$2 \times 20 = 40$ ns
(b) Memory cycle time with 1 WS	$40 + 20 = 60$ ns
(c) Memory cycle time with 2 WS	$40 + 2 \times 20 = 80$ ns

It is preferred that all bus activities be completed with 0 WS. However, if the read and write operations cannot be completed with 0 WS, we request an extension of the bus cycle time. This extension is in the form of an integer number of WS. That is, we can have 1, 2, 3, and so on WS, but not 1.25 WS.

When the CPU's speed was under 100 MHz, the bus speed was comparable to the CPU speed. In the 1990s the CPU speed exploded to 1 GHz (gigahertz) while the bus speed maxed out at around 200 MHz. The gap between the CPU speed and the bus speed is one of the biggest challenges in the design of high-performance systems. To avoid the use of too many wait states in interfacing memory to CPU, cache memory and other high-speed DRAMs are used.

Bus bandwidth

The rate of data transfer is generally called bus bandwidth. In other words, bus bandwidth is a measure of how fast buses transfer information between the CPU and memory or peripherals. The wider the data bus, the higher the bus bandwidth. However, the advantage of the wider external data bus comes at the cost of increasing the die size for system on-chip (SOC) or the printed circuit board size for off-chip memory. Now you might ask why we should care how fast buses transfer information between the CPU and outside, as long as the CPU is working as fast as it can. The problem is that the CPU cannot process information that it does not have. This is like driving a Porsche or Ferrari in first gear; it is a terrible under usage of CPU power. Bus bandwidth is measured in MB (megabytes) per second and is calculated as follows:

bus bandwidth = (1/bus cycle time) × bus width in bytes

In the above formula, bus cycle time can be for both memory and I/O since the ARM uses the memory mapped I/O. Example 6-2 clarifies the concept of bus bandwidth. As can be seen from Example 6-2, there are two ways to increase the bus bandwidth: Either use a wider data bus or shorten the bus cycle time (or do both). That is exactly what many processors have done. Again, it must be noted that although the processor's speed can go to 1 GHz or higher, the bus speed for off-chip memory is limited to around 200 MHz. The reason for this is that the signals become too noisy for the circuit board if they are above 200 MHz.

Example 6-2

Calculate memory bus bandwidth for the following CPU if the bus speed is 100 MHz.

(a) ARM Thumb with 0 WS and 1 WS (16-bit data bus)

(b) ARM with 0 WS and 1 WS (32-bit data bus)
Assume that the bus cycle time for off-chip memory access is 2 clocks.

Solution:

The memory cycle time for both is 2 clocks, with zero wait states. With the 100 MHz bus speed we have a bus clock of 1/100 MHz = 10 ns.

(a) Bus bandwidth = (1/(2 × 10 ns)) × 2 bytes = 100M bytes/second (MB/s)
With 1 wait state, the memory cycle becomes 3 clock cycles
3 × 10 = 30 ns and the memory bus bandwidth is = (1/30 ns) × 2 bytes = 66.6 MB/s

(b) Bus bandwidth = (1/(2 × 10 ns)) × 4 bytes = 200 MB/s
With 1 wait state, the memory cycle becomes 3 clock cycles
3 × 10 = 30 ns and the memory bus bandwidth is = (1/30 ns) × 4 bytes = 126.6 MB/s

From the above it can be seen that the two factors influencing bus bandwidth are:

1. The read/write cycle time of the CPU
2. The width of the data bus

Code memory region

The 4 GB of ARM memory space is organized as 1G × 32 bits since the ARM instructions are 32-bit. The internal data bus of the ARM is 32-bit, allowing the transfer of one instruction into the CPU every clock cycle. This is one of the benefits of the RISC fixed instruction size. The fetching of an instruction in every clock cycle can work only if the code is word aligned, meaning each instruction is placed at an address location ending with 0, 4, 8, or C. Example 6-3 shows the placement of code in ARM memory. Notice that the code addresses go up by 4 since the ARM instructions are fixed at 4 bytes each. While compilers ensure that codes are word aligned, it is job of the programmer to make sure the data in SRAM is word aligned too. We will examine this important topic soon.

Example 6-3

Compile and debug the following code in Keil and see the placement of instructions in memory locations.

```
AREA   ARMex, CODE, READONLY

MOV    R2, #0x00     ; R2=0x00
MOV    R3, #0x35     ; R3=0x35
ADD    R4, R3, R2
END                  ; Mark end of code
```

Solution

As you can see in the figure, the first MOV instruction starts from location 0x00000000, the second MOV instruction starts from location 0x00000004 and the ADD instruction starts from location 0x00000008.

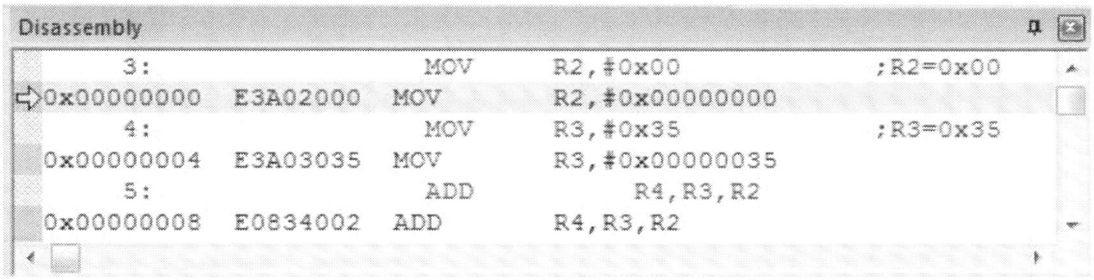

The following image displays the first locations of memory. The code of the first MOV instruction is located in the first word (four bytes) of memory which is word aligned. The same rule applies for the other instructions. Note that the code of MOV R2, #0x00 is E3 A0 20 00 but 00 20 A0 E3 is stored in the memory. We will discuss the reason in this chapter when we focus on the concept of big endian and little endian.

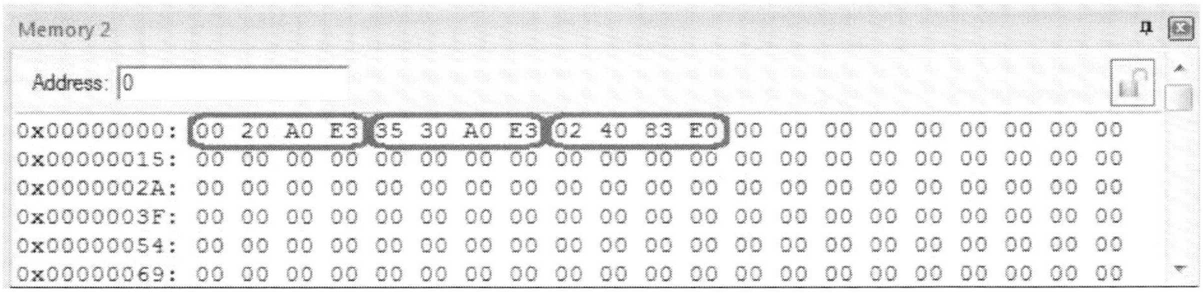

SRAM memory region

A section of the memory space is used by SRAM. The SRAM can be on-chip or off-chip (external). For small embedded systems, this on-chip SRAM is used by the CPU for scratch pad to store parameters and is also used by the CPU for the purpose of the stack. We will examine the stack usage by the ARM in the next section. For larger systems, the operating system and application programs may be run in Flash ROM or copied into the SRAM and run everything in the SRAM just like your laptop computer.

In using the SRAM memory for storing parameters, we must be careful when loading or storing data in the SRAM lest we use unaligned data access. Next, we discuss this important issue.

Data misalignment in SRAM

The case of misaligned data has a major effect on the ARM bus performance. If the data is aligned, for every memory read cycle, the ARM brings in 4 bytes of information (data or code) using the D31–D0 data bus. Such data alignment is referred to as word alignment. To make data word aligned, the least significant digits of the hex addresses must be 0, 4, 8, or C (in hex).

While the compilers make sure that program codes (instructions) are always aligned (Example 6-3), it is the placement of data in SRAM by the programmer that can be nonaligned and therefore subject to memory access penalty. In other words, the single cycle access of memory is also used by ARM to bring into registers 4 bytes of data every clock cycle assuming that the data is aligned. To make sure that data are also aligned we use the ALIGN directive. The use of ALIGN directive for RAM data makes sure that each word is located at an address location ending with address of 0, 4, 8, or C. If our data is word size (using DCDU directive) then the use of ALIGN directive at the start of the data section guaranties all the data placements will be word aligned. When a word size data is defined using the DCD directive, the assembler aligns it to be word aligned.

Accessing non-aligned data

As we have stated many times before, ARM defines 32-bit data as a word. The address of a word can start at any address location. For example, in the instruction "LDR R1, [R0]" if R0 = 0x20000004, the address of the word being fetched into R1 starts at an aligned address. In the case of "LDR R1, [R0]" if R0 = 0x20000001 the address starts at a non-aligned address. In systems with a 32-bit data bus, accessing a word from a non-aligned addressed location can be slower. This issue is important and applies to all 32-bit processors.

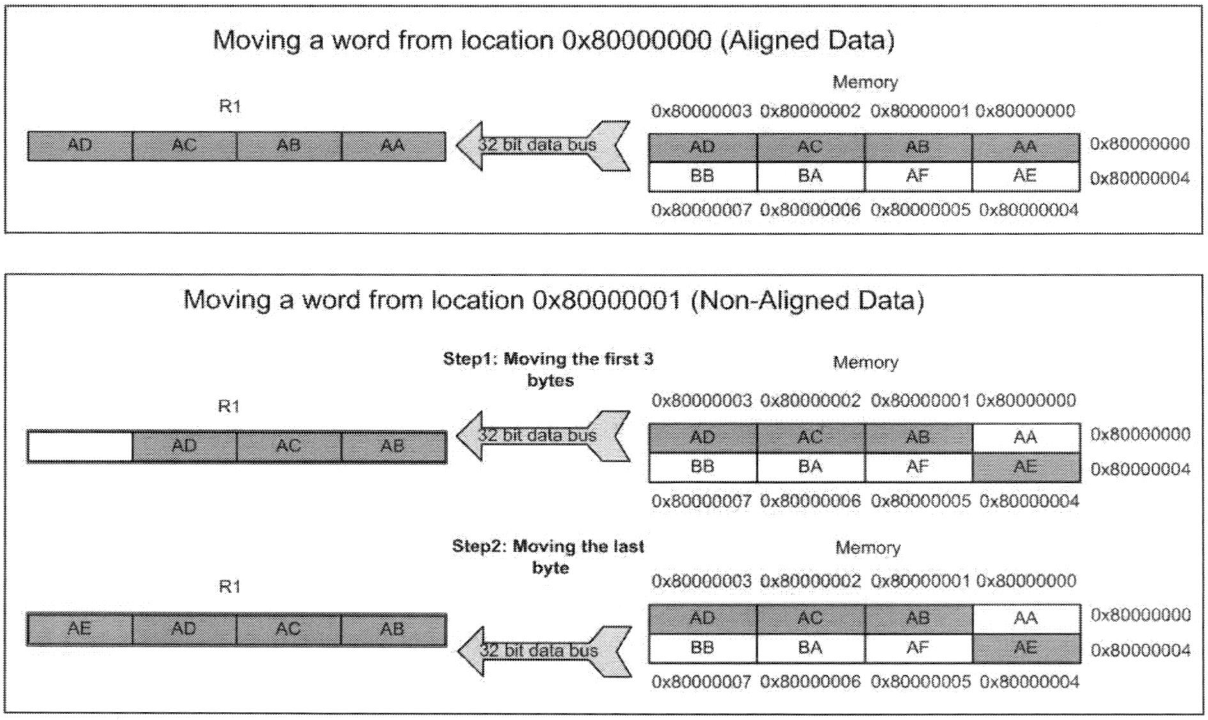

Figure 6-5: Memory Access for Aligned and Non-aligned Data

In the 8-bit system, accessing a word (4 bytes) is treated like accessing four consecutive bytes regardless of the address location. Since accessing a byte takes one memory cycle, accessing 4 bytes will take 4 memory cycles. In the 32-bit system, accessing a word with an aligned address takes one memory cycle. That is because each byte is carried on its own data path of D0–D7, D8–D15, D16–D23, and D24–D31 in the same memory cycle. However, accessing a word with a non-aligned address requires two memory cycles. For example, see how accessing the word in the instruction "LDR R1, [R0]" works as shown in Figure 6-5. As a case of aligned data, assume that R0 = 0x80000000. In this instruction, the contents of 4 bytes of memory (locations 0x80000000 through 0x80000003) are being fetched in one cycle. In only one cycle, the ARM CPU accesses locations 0x80000000 through 0x80000003 and puts them in R1.

Now assuming that R0 = 0x80000001 in this instruction, the contents of 8 bytes of memory (locations 0x80000000 through 0x80000007) are being fetched in two consecutive cycles but only 4 bytes of it are used. In the first cycle, the ARM CPU accesses locations 0x80000000 through 0x80000003 and puts them in R1 only the desired three bytes of locations 0x800000001 through 0x80000003. In the second cycle, the contents of memory locations 0x8000004 through 0x80000007 are accessed and only the desired byte of 0x80000004 is put into R1. See Example 6-4.

Example 6-4

Show the data transfer of the following cases and indicate the number of memory cycle times it takes for data transfer. Assume that R2 = 0x4598F31E.

```
LDR   R1, =0x40000000    ; R1=0x40000000
LDR   R2, =0x4598F31E    ; R2=0x4598F31E
STR   R2, [R1]           ; Store R2 to location 0x40000000
ADD   R1, R1, #1         ; R1 = R1 + 1 = 0x40000001
STR   R2, [R1]           ; Store R2 to location 0x40000001
ADD   R1, R1, #1         ; R1 = R1 + 1 = 0x40000002
STR   R2, [R1]           ; Store R2 to location 0x40000002
ADD   R1, R1, #1         ; R1 = R1 + 1 = 0x40000003
STR   R2, [R1]           ; Store R2 to location 0x40000003
```

Solution:

For the first STR R2, [R1] instruction, the entire 32 bits of R2 is stored into locations with addresses of 0x40000000, 0x40000001, 0x40000002, and 0x40000003. The 4-byte content of register R2 is stored into memory locations with starting address of 0x40000000 via the 32-bit data bus of D31–D0. This address is word aligned since address of the least significant digit is 0. Therefore, it takes only one memory cycle to transfer the 32-bit data.

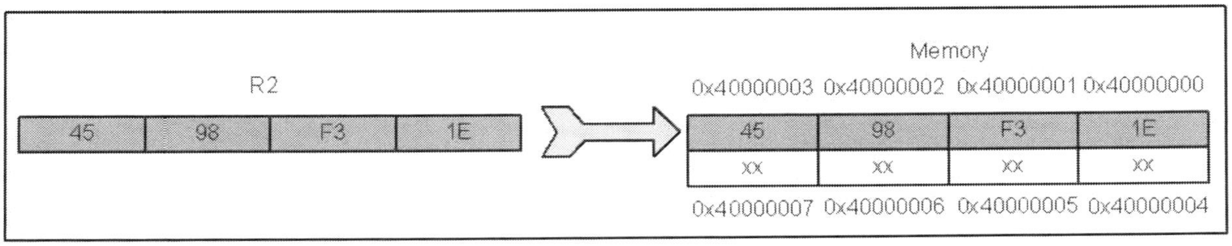

For the second STR R2, [R1] instruction, in the first memory cycle, the lower 24 bits of R2 is stored into locations 0x40000001, 0x40000002, and 0x40000003. In the second memory cycle, the upper 8 bits of R2 is stored into the 0x40000004 location.

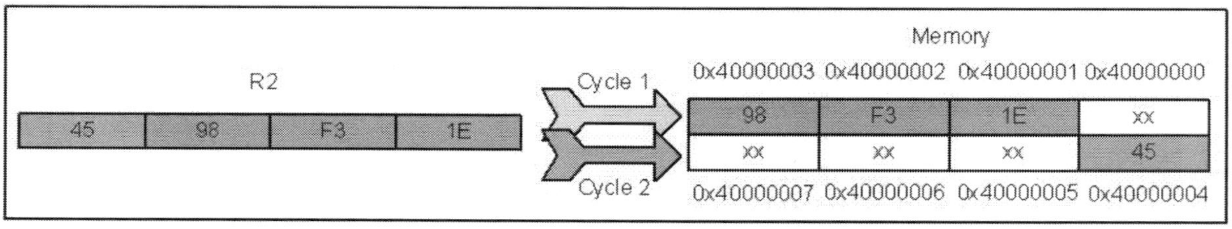

For the third STR R2, [R1] instruction, in the first memory cycle, the lower 16 bits of R2 is stored into locations 0x40000002 and 0x40000003. In the second memory cycle, the upper 16 bits of R2 is stored into locations 0x40000004 and 0x40000005.

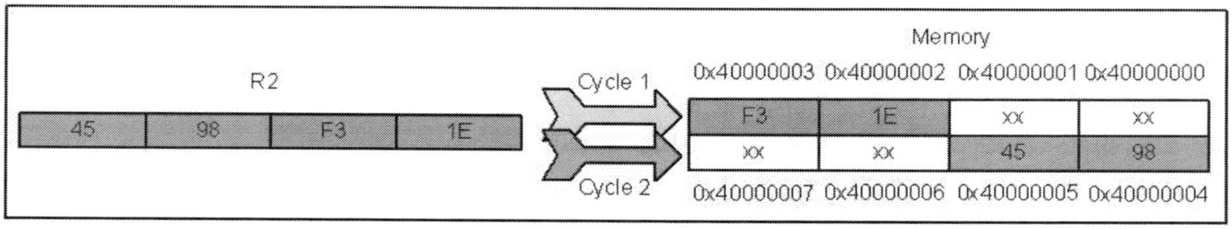

For the fourth STR R2, [R1] instruction, in the first memory cycle, the lower 8 bits of R2 is stored into locations 0x40000003. In the second memory cycle, the upper 24 bits of R2 is stored into the locations 0x40000004, 0x40000005, and 0x40000006.

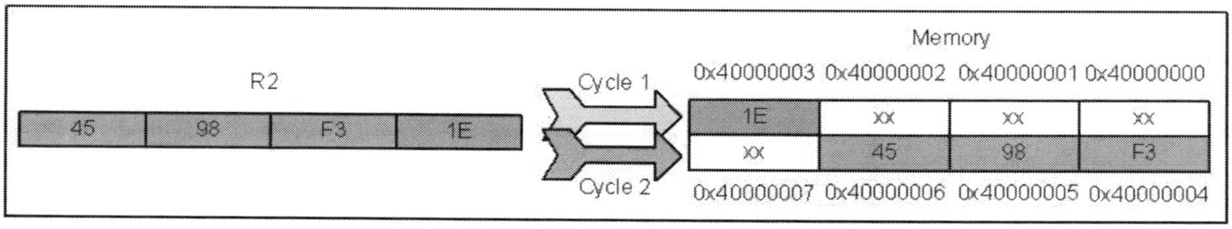

The lesson to be learned from this is to try not to put any words on a non-aligned address location in a 32-bit system. Indeed, this is so important that directive ALIGN is specifically designed for this purpose. Next, we discuss the issue of aligned data.

Using LDR instruction with DCD and ALIGN directives

The DCD and DCDU directives are used for 32-bit (word) data. The DCD directive ensures 32-bit data types are aligned, in contrast to DCDU which does not. DCD is used as follows:

```
VALUE1      DCD   0x99775533
```

This ensures that VALUE1, a word-sized operand, is located in a word aligned address location. Therefore, an instruction accessing it will take only a single memory cycle. Since performance of the CPU depends on how fast it can fetch the data we must ensure that any memory access reading 32-bit data is done in a single clock cycle. This means we must make sure all 32-bit data are word aligned. This is so important that ARM has an interrupt (exception) dedicated to misaligned data, meaning any time it accesses misaligned data, it lets us know that there is a problem. The one-time use of ALIGN directive at the beginning of data area using DCDU makes the data aligned for that group of data.

Different versions of ARM handle unaligned access differently. Some may allow unaligned access without generating interrupt. In this case, the programmer must be careful to allocate data on the word aligned boundary so that the system will perform at its optimal bus bandwidth.

Using LDRH with DCW and ALIGN directives

The problem of misaligned data is also an issue when the data size is in half-words (16-bit). In many cases using DCWU, we must use the ALIGN directive multiple times in the data area of a given program to ensure they are aligned. This is in contrast to the DCW directive which ensures data type to be half-word aligned. This is especially the case when we use the LDRH instruction. See Example 6-5. Aligned data is also an issue for the Thumb version of the ARM.

Example 6-5

Show the data transfer of the following LDRH instructions and indicate the number of memory cycle times it takes for data transfer.

```
LDR   R1, =0x80000000    ; R1=0x80000000
LDR   R3, =0xF31E4598    ; R3=0xF31E4598
LDR   R4, =0x1A2B3D4F    ; R4=0x1A2B3D4F
STR   R3, [R1]           ; (STR R3, [R1]) stores R3 to location 0x80000000
STR   R4, [R1, #4]       ; (STR R4, [R1+4]) stores R4 to location 0x80000004
LDRH  R2, [R1]           ; loads two bytes from location 0x80000000 to R2
LDRH  R2, [R1, #1]       ; loads two bytes from location 0x80000001 to R2
LDRH  R2, [R1, #2]       ; loads two bytes from location 0x80000002 to R2
LDRH  R2, [R1, #3]       ; loads two bytes from location 0x80000003 to R2
```

Solution:

In the LDRH R2, [R1] instruction, locations with addresses of 0x80000000, 0x80000001, 0x80000002, and 0x80000003 are accessed but only 0x80000000 and 0x80000001 are used to get the 16 bits to R2. This address is halfword aligned since the least significant digit is 0. Therefore, it takes only one memory cycle to transfer the data. Now, R2=0x00004598

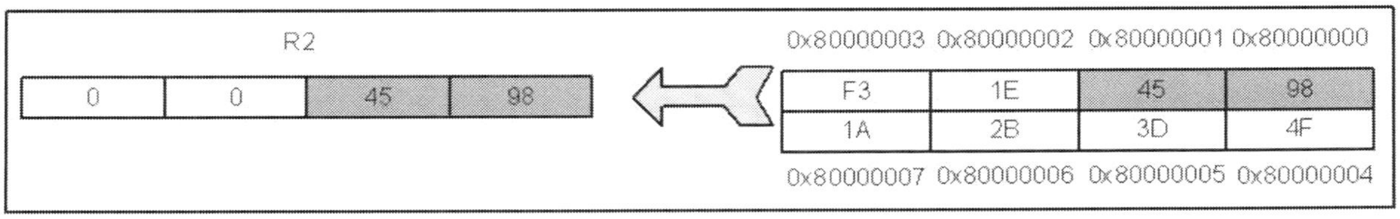

For the LDRH R2, [R1, #1], instruction, locations with addresses of 0x80000000, 0x80000001, 0x80000002, and 0x80000003 are accessed, but only 0x80000001 and 0x80000002 are used to get the 16 bits to R2. Therefore, it takes only one memory cycle to transfer the data. Now, R2=0x00001E45.

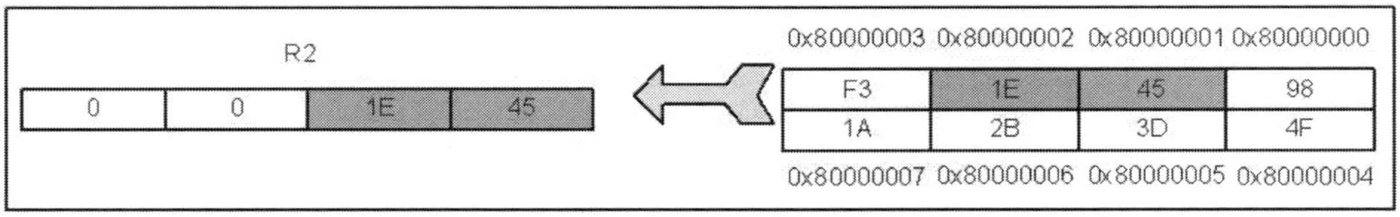

For the LDRH R2, [R1, #2], instruction, locations with addresses of 0x80000000, 0x80000001, 0x80000002, and 0x80000003 are accessed, but only 0x80000002 and 0x80000003 are used to get the 16 bits to R2. Therefore, it takes only one memory cycle to transfer the data. Now, R2=0x0000F31E.

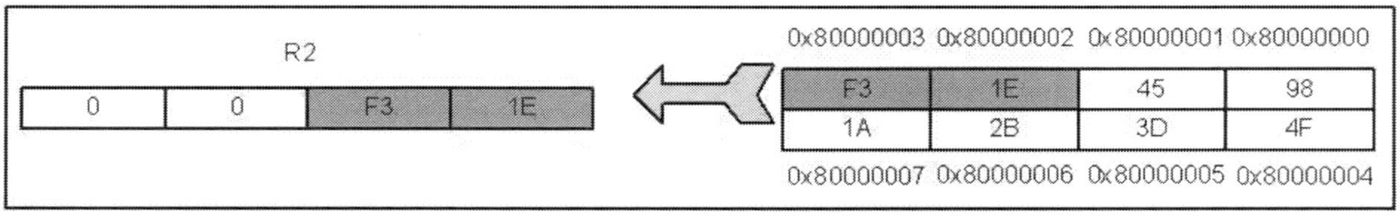

For the LDRH R2, [R1, #3] instruction, in the first memory cycle, locations with addresses of 0x80000000, 0x80000001, 0x80000002, and 0x80000003 are accessed, but only 0x80000003 is used to get the lower 8 bits to R2. In the second memory cycle, the address locations 0x80000004, 0x80000005, 0x80000006, and 0x80000007 are accessed where only the 0x80000004 location is used to get the upper 8 bits to R2. Now, R2=0x00004FF3.

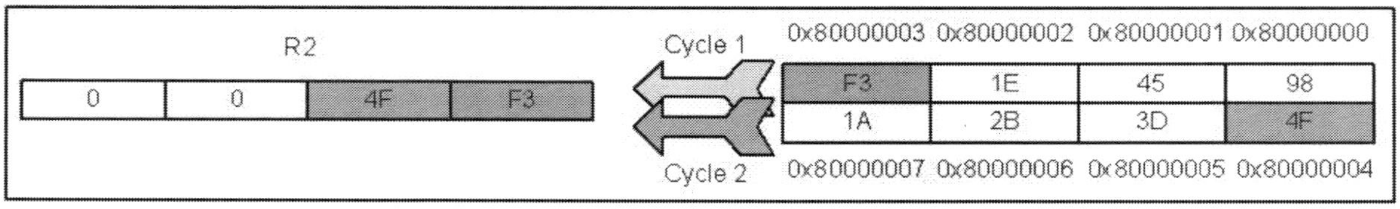

Using LDRB with DCB and ALIGN directives

The problem of misaligned data does not exist when the data size is bytes. A single byte of data will never straddle across a word boundary. In cases such as using the string of ASCII characters with the DCB directive, accessing a byte takes the same amount of time (one memory cycle) as an aligned word (4 bytes), regardless of the address location of the data. See Example 6-6.

Example 6-6

Show the data transfer of the following LDRB instructions and indicate the number of memory cycle times it takes for data transfer.

```
LDR    R1, =0x80000000    ; R1=0x80000000
LDR    R3, =0xF31E4598    ; R3=0xF31E4598
LDR    R4, =0x1A2B3D4F    ; R4=0x1A2B3D4F
```

```
STR    R3, [R1]      ; Store R3 to location 0x80000000
STR    R4, [R1, #4]  ; (STR R4, [R1+4]) Store R4 to location 0x80000004
LDRB   R2, [R1]      ; load one byte from location 0x80000000 to R2
LDRB   R2, [R1, #1]  ; (LDRB R2, [R1+1]) load one byte from location 0x80000001
LDRB   R2, [R1, #2]  ; (LDRB R2, [R1+2]) load one byte from location 0x80000002
LDRB   R2, [R1, #3]  ; (LDRB R2, [R1+3]) load one byte from location 0x80000003
```

Solution:

In the LDRB R2, [R1] instruction, locations with addresses of 0x80000000, 0x80000001, 0x80000002, and 0x80000003 are accessed but only 0x80000000 is used to get the 8 bits to R2. Therefore, it takes only one memory cycle to transfer the data. Now, R2=0x00000098.

In the LDRB R2, [R1, #1] instruction, locations with addresses of 0x80000000, 0x80000001, 0x80000002, and 0x80000003 are accessed but only 0x80000001 is used to get the 8 bits to R2. Therefore, it takes only one memory cycle to transfer the data. Now, R2=0x00000045.

In the LDRB R2, [R1, #2] instruction, locations with addresses of 0x80000000, 0x80000001, 0x80000002, and 0x80000003 are accessed but only 0x80000002 is used to get the 8 bits to R2. Therefore, it takes only one memory cycle to transfer the data. Now, R2=0x0000001E.

In the LDRB R2, [R1, #3] instruction, locations with addresses of 0x80000000, 0x80000001, 0x80000002, and 0x80000003 are accessed but only 0x80000003 is used to get the 8 bits to R2. Therefore, it takes only one memory cycle to transfer the data. Now, R2=0x000000F3.

Peripheral region

Table 6-1 showed a section of memory is set aside for peripherals. The type of peripherals and memory address locations used is unique to each device and determined by the manufacturer of the device. The ARM manufacturers provide the details of memory map for the peripherals in the datasheet and programmer's manual.

Little Endian vs. Big Endian war

In storing data in memory, there are two major byte orderings used. The little endian places the least significant byte (little end of the data) in the low address and the big endian places the most significant byte in the low address. The origin of the terms *big endian* and *little endian* was from a Gulliver's Travels story about how an egg should be opened: from the big end or the little end. ARM supports both little and big endian. In most of the ARM devices little endian is the default. Some ARM chip manufacturers provide an option for changing the endian by software. See Example 6-7 to understand little endian and big endian data storage.

Example 6-7

Show how data is placed after execution of the following code using

a) little endian and

b) big endian.

```
LDR    R2, =0x7698E39F    ; R2=0x7698E39F
LDR    R1, =0x80000000
STR    R2, [R1]
```

Solution:

a) For little endian we have:
Location 80000000 = (9F)
Location 80000001 = (E3)
Location 80000002 = (98)
Location 80000003 = (76)

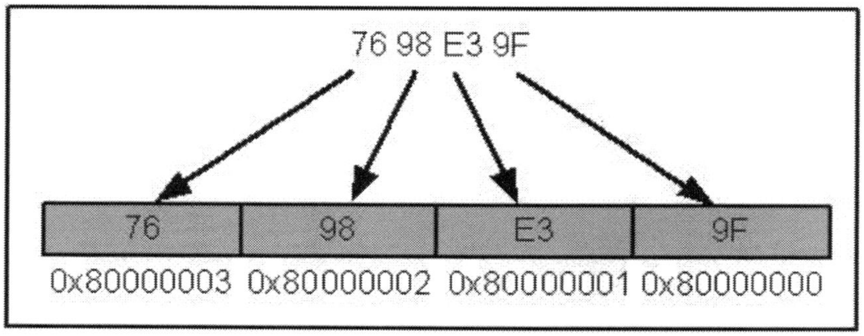

b) For big endian we have:
Location 80000000 = (76)
Location 80000001 = (98)
Location 80000002 = (E3)
Location 80000003 = (9F)

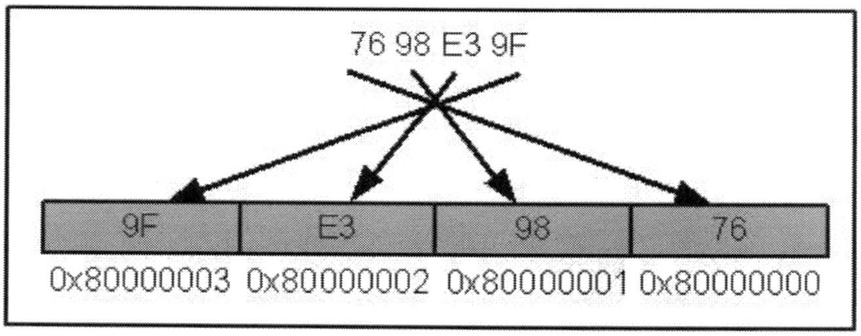

In Example 6-7, notice how the least significant byte (the little end of the data) 0x9F goes to the low address 0x80000000, and the most significant byte of the data 0x76 goes to the high address 0x80000003. This means that the little end of the data goes in first, hence the name little endian. In the ARM with big endian option enabled, data is stored the opposite way: The big end (most significant byte) goes into the low address first, and for this reason it is called big endian. Many of recent RISC processors allow selection of mode in software, big endian or little endian.

Harvard Architecture and ARM

In recent years many ARM manufacturers are using the Harvard architecture for ARM CPUs. Old ARM architectures up to ARM7 use Von Neumann architecture. The Harvard architecture feeds the CPU with both code and data at the same time via two sets of buses, one for code and one for data. This increases the processing power of the CPU since it can bring in more information.

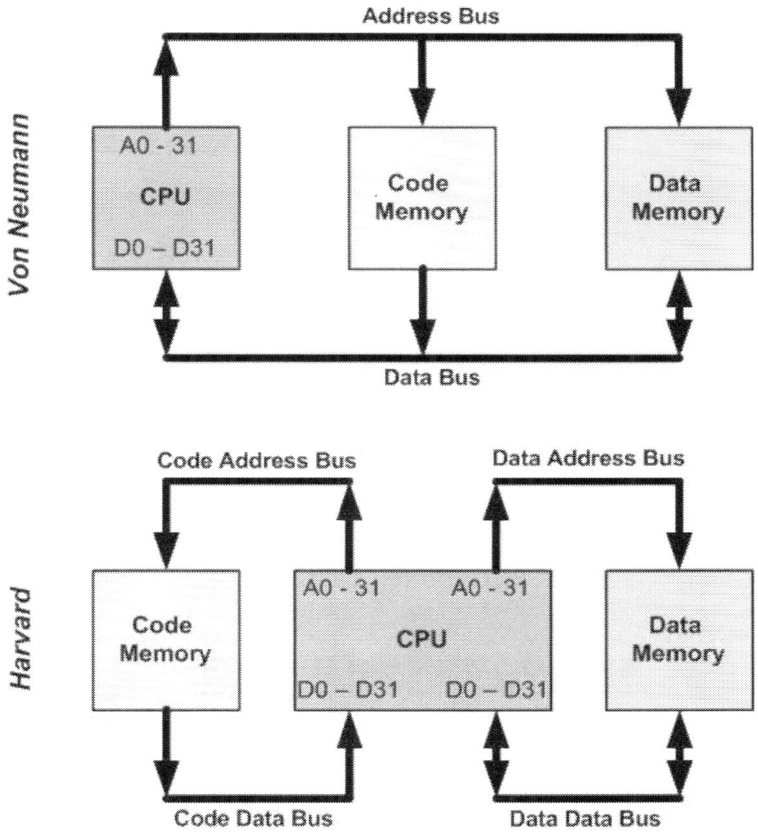

Figure 6-6: Von Neumann vs. Harvard Architecture

Review Questions

1. In ARM, all the instructions are ___bytes?
2. Who makes sure that instructions are aligned on word boundary?
3. In most of the ARM devices, the _____ endian is the default.
4. A 66 MHz system has a memory cycle time of _____ ns if it is used with a zero wait state.
5. To interface a 100 MHz processor to a 50 ns access time ROM, how many wait states are needed?
6. True or false. ARM uses big endian format when is powered up.

Section 6.2: Advanced Indexed Addressing Mode

In previous chapters we discussed the use of STR and LDR instructions in the form of "**`LDR Rd,[Rx]`**" and "**`STR Rx,[Rd]`**", where the registers within the brackets hold the pointer (the address where the data resides). These registers within the brackets are referred as the index register or base register. ARM provides three advanced indexed addressing mode that allow the modification of the value in the index register. We will discuss them in this section.

Base plus offset addressing modes

The ARM provides three advanced indexed addressing modes called base plus offset addressing modes. In addition to the base register specified within the bracket, an offset can be added to the value of the base register. These modes are: pre-index, pre-index with writeback, and post-index modes. Table 6-2 summarizes these modes. Each of these addressing modes can be used with offset of fixed value or offset of a shifted register. See Table 6-3. In this section we will discuss each mode in detail.

Addressing Mode	Syntax	Effective Address of Memory	Rm Value After Execution
Pre-index	LDR Rd, [Rm, #k]	Rm + #k	Rm
Pre-index with WB*	LDR Rd, [Rm, #k]!	Rm + #k	Rm + #k
Post-index	LDR Rd, [Rm], #k	Rm	Rm + #k
**WB means Writeback*			
*** Rd and Rm are any of registers and #k is a signed 12-bit immediate value between -4095 and +4095*			

Table 6-2: Indexed Addressing in ARM

Offset	Syntax	Pointing Location
Fixed value	LDR Rd, [Rm, #k]	Rm + #k
Shifted register	LDR Rd, [Rm, Rn, <shift>]	Rm + (Rn shifted <shift>)
** Rn and Rm are any registers and #k is a signed 12-bit immediate value between -4095 and +4095*		
*** <shift> is any of the shift operations studied in Chapter3 like LSL #2*		

Table 6-3: Offset of Fixed Value vs. Offset of Shifted Register

Pre-indexed addressing mode with fixed offset

In this addressing mode, a register and a positive or negative immediate value are used as a pointer to the data's memory location. The value of register does not change after instruction is executed. This addressing mode can be used with STR, STRB, STRH, LDR, LDRB, and LDRH. See Example 6-8.

Example 6-8

Write a program to store contents of R5 to the SRAM location 0x10000000 to 0x1000000F using pre-indexed addressing mode with fixed offset.

Solution:

```
LDR    R5, =0x55667788
LDR    R1, =0x10000000    ; load the address of first location
```

```
STR   R5, [R1]          ; store R5 to location 0x10000000
STR   R5, [R1, #4] ; store R5 to location 0x10000000 + 4 (0x10000004)
STR   R5, [R1, #8] ; store R5 to location 0x10000000 + 8 (0x10000008)
STR   R5, [R1, #0x0C]
            ; store R5 to location 0x10000000 + 0x0C (0x1000000C)
```

Notice that after running this code the content of R1 is still 0x10000000

It is a common practice to use a register to point to the first location of the memory space and access the different locations using proper offsets. For example, see the following program:

```
            ADR   R0, OUR_DATA             ; point to OUR_DATA
            LDRB  R2, [R0, #1]             ; load R2 with offset of BETA
            ...
OUR_DATA
ALFA        DCB   0x30
BETA        DCB   0x21
```

Pre-indexed addressing mode with writeback and fixed offset

This addressing mode is like pre-indexed addressing mode with fixed offset except that the calculated pointer is written back to the pointing register. We put '!' after the instruction to tell the assembler to enable writeback in the instruction. See Example 6-9.

Example 6-9

Rewrite Example 6-8 using pre-indexed addressing mode with writeback and fixed offset.

Solution:

```
LDR   R1, =0x10000000   ; load the address of first location
STR   R5, [R1]          ; store R5 to location 0x10000000
STR   R5, [R1, #4]!
            ; store R5 to location 0x10000000 + 4 (0x10000004)
            ; writeback makes R1 = 0x10000004
STR   R5, [R1, #4]!
            ; store R5 to location 0x10000004 + 4 (0x10000008)
            ; writeback makes R1 = 0x10000008
STR   R5, [R1, #4]!
            ; store R5 to location 0x10000008 + 4 (0x1000000C)
            ; writeback makes R1 = 0x1000000C
```

Notice that after running this code the content of R1 is 0x1000000C

Post-indexed addressing mode with fixed offset

This addressing mode is like pre-indexed addressing mode with fixed offset and writeback except that the instruction is executed on the location that Rn is pointing to regardless of offset value. The new value of the pointer is calculated after the load/store operation and written back to the index register. Examine the following instructions:

```
STR    R1, [R2], #4        ; store R1 into memory pointed to by
                           ; R2 and then write back R2 + 4 to R2
LDRB   R5, [R3], #1        ; load a byte from memory pointed to
                           ; by R3 and then write back R3 + 1 to R3
```

Notice that writeback is by default enabled in post-indexed addressing and there is no need to put '!' after instructions because in post-indexing without writeback the offset is neither used in the load/store operation nor written back to the index register. See Example 6-10.

Example 6-10

Rewrite Example 6-9 using post-indexed addressing mode with fixed offset.

Solution:

```
LDR    R1, =0x10000000     ; load the address of first location
STR    R5, [R1], #4        ; store R5 to location 0x10000000 and writeback
                           ; 0x10000000 + 4 (0x10000004) to R1
STR    R5, [R1], #4        ; store R5 to location 0x10000004 and writeback
                           ; 0x10000004 + 4 (0x10000008) to R1
STR    R5, [R1], #4        ; store R5 to location 0x10000008 and writeback
                           ; 0x10000008 + 4 (0x1000000C) to R1
STR    R5, [R1], #4        ; store R5 to location 0x1000000C and writeback
                           ; 0x1000000C + 4 (0x10000010) to R1
```

Notice that after running this code the content of R1 is 0x10000010.

Pre-indexed address mode with offset of a shifted register

This advanced addressing mode is a very important feature in the ARM. We start describing this mode from simple cases with no shift and then we will move on to more complex formats.

Simple format of pre-indexed address mode with offset register

The following is the simple syntax for LDR and STR.

```
LDR    Rd, [Rm, Rn]        ; Rd is loaded from location Rm + Rn of memory
STR    Rs, [Rm, Rn]        ; Rs is stored to location Rm + Rn of memory
```

This addressing mode is often used in implementing array access. Rm holds the base address of the array (the address of the first element of the array) and Rn holds the array index. Example 6-11 shows how we use this addressing mode in accessing different locations of an array with byte size elements in memory.

Example 6-11

Examine the value of R5 and R6 after the execution of the following program.

```
INDEX        RN     R2
ARRAY1       RN     R1
      AREA   EXAMPLE_6_11, CODE, READONLY

      LDR    ARRAY1, =MYDATA    ; use array address as base address
      LDRB   R4, [ARRAY1]
             ; load R4 with first element of ARRAY1 (R4=0x45)

      MOV    INDEX, #1    ; INDEX = 1 to point to location 1 of array
      LDRB   R5, [ARRAY1, INDEX]
                          ; Load R5 with second element of ARRAY1 (R5=0x24)
      MOV    INDEX, #2    ; INDEX = 2 to point to location 2 of array
      LDRB   R6, [ARRAY1, INDEX]
                          ; Load R5 with third element of ARRAY1 (R6=0x18)
HERE  B      HERE
MYDATA       DCB    0x45, 0x24, 0x18, 0x63
      END
```

Solution:

After running the LDRB R4, [ARRAY1] instruction, first element with offset 0 of MYDATA is loaded into R4. Now R4=0x45.
Next, after running the LDRB R5, [ARRAY1, INDEX] instruction, second element with offset 1 of MYDATA is loaded into R5. Now R5 = 0x24.
Next, after running the LDRB R6, [ARRAY1, INDEX] instruction, third element with offset 2 of MYDATA is loaded into R6. So the content of R6 = 0x18.

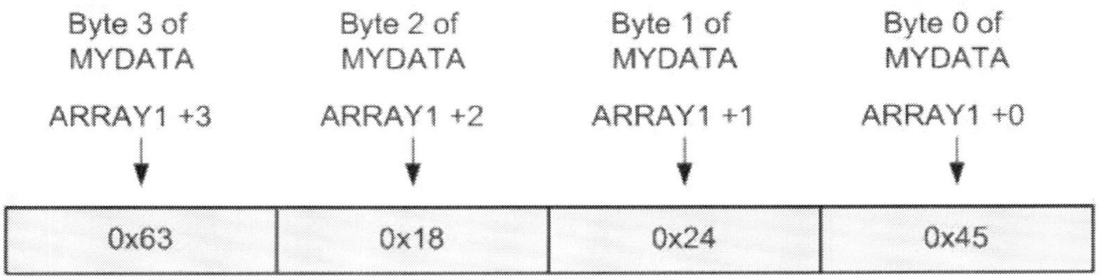

Notice that in Example 6-11, the array MYDATA contains byte size element so DCB and LDRB were used. It will not work if the data size of the array elements is different from a byte. In the next example, the array elements are word size (4 bytes each). We define the array using DCD, then we will not be able to use LDRB R5, [ARRAY1, INDEX] to load the INDEX location of ARRAY1. See Example 6-12 for clarification.

Example 6-12

In Example 6-11, change MYDATA DCB 0x45, 0x24, 0x18, 0x63 to MYDATA DCD 0x45, 0x2489ACF5 and examine the value of R5 and R6 after the execution of the following program.

```
INDEX        RN     R2
ARRAY1       RN     R1
      AREA   EXAMPLE_6_12, CODE, READONLY

      LDR    ARRAY1, =MYDATA    ; use array address as base address
      LDRB   R4, [ARRAY1]       ; load R4 with first element of ARRAY1
                                ; (R4=0x45)
      MOV    INDEX, #1          ; INDEX = 1 to point to location 1 of array
      LDRB   R5, [ARRAY1, INDEX]
                                ; Load INDEX location of ARRAY1 to R5
      MOV    INDEX, #2          ; INDEX = 2 to point to location 2 of array
      LDRB   R6, [ARRAY1, INDEX]
                                ; load INDEX location of ARRAY1 to R6
HERE  B      HERE
MYDATA       DCD    0x45, 0x2489ACF5
      END
```

Solution:

After running the LDRB R4, [ARRAY1] instruction, location 0 of MYDATA is loaded to R4. Now R4=0x45.
Next, after running the LDRB R5, [ARRAY1, INDEX] instruction, location 1 of MYDATA is loaded to R5. Now R5 = 0x00.
Next, after running the LDRB R6, [ARRAY1, INDEX] instruction, location 2 of MYDATA is loaded to R6. So the content of R6 = 0x00.

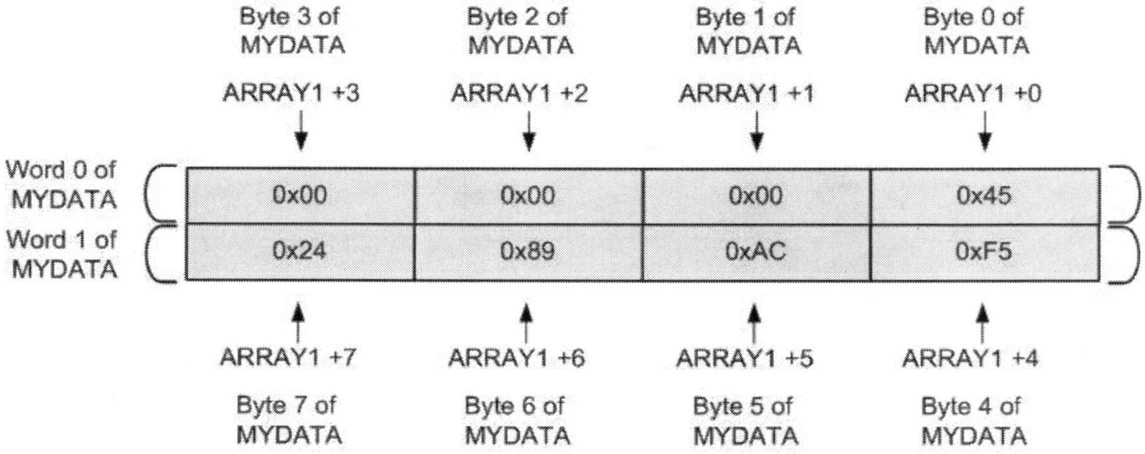

To access locations of a word size array we have to multiply the array index by four to yield the offset. Similarly, to access locations of a half-word size array we have to multiply the array index by two to get the offset. For example, we can correct program of Example 6-12 by replacing instruction

```
MOV    INDEX, #2    ; INDEX = 2 to point to location 2 of array
```

with following instructions:

```
MOV    INDEX, #2    ; INDEX = 2
MOV    INDEX, INDEX, LSL #2     ; INDEX is shifted left two bits (×4)
                                ; to point to word 2 of the array
```

Notice that by shifting left a value by two bits, we multiply it by four. Next, we will see how we can use indexed addressing with shifted registers to combine multiplication with the LDR and STR instructions.

General format of pre-indexed address mode with offset register

The general format of indexed addressing with shifted register for LDR and STR is as follows:

```
LDR Rd, [Rm, Rn, <shift>]   ; (Shifted Rn) + Rm is used as the address
STR Rd, [Rm, Rn, <shift>]   ; (Shifted Rn) + Rm is used as the address
```

In the above instructions <shift> can be any of shift instructions studied in Chapter 3 such as LSL, LSR, ASR and ROR. But for array indexing, LSL is most often used because it is the equivalent of signed multiply by power of two. Examine the following instructions:

```
LDR    R1, [R2, R3, LSL #2]     ; R2 + (R3 × 4) is used as the address
                    ; content at location R2 + (R3 × 4) is loaded into R1
STR    R1, [R2, R3, LSL #1]     ; R2 + (R3 × 2) is used as the address
                    ; R1 is stored at location R2+(R3 × 2)
STRB   R1, [R2, R3, LSL #2]     ; R2 + (R3 × 4) is used as the address
; least significant byte of R1 is stored at location R2 + (R3 × 4)
LDR    R1, [R2, R3, LSR #2]     ; R2 + (R3 / 4) is used as the address
                    ; content at location R2 + (R3 / 4) is loaded into R1
```

From the above code we can see that indexed addressing with shifted register is used to multiply the offset by a power of two and that is why it is also called indexed addressing with scaled register. Examine Example 6-13 to see how we can use scaled register indexing to access an array of words.

Notice that scaled register indexing is not supported for half-word load and store instructions.

Example 6-13

Examine the value of R5 and R6 after the execution of the following program.

```
INDEX       RN    R2
ARRAY1      RN    R1
      AREA   EXAMPLE_6_13, CODE, READONLY
```

```
        LDR    ARRAY1, = MYDATA
        MOV    INDEX, #0                ; INDEX = 0
        LDR    R4, [ARRAY1, INDEX, LSL #2]    ;

        MOV    INDEX, #1                ; INDEX = 1
        LDR    R5, [ARRAY1, INDEX, LSL #2]    ;

        MOV    INDEX, #2                ; INDEX = 2
        LDR    R6, [ARRAY1, INDEX, LSL #2]    ;

HERE    B      HERE
MYDATA         DCD    0x45, 0x2489ACF5, 0x2489AC23
        END
```

Solution:

After running the LDR R4, [ARRAY1, INDEX, LSL #2]] instruction, element 0 of array MYDATA is loaded to R4. Now R4=0x45.

Next, after running the LDR R5, [ARRAY1, INDEX, LSL #2] instruction, element 1 of array MYDATA is loaded to R5. Now R5 = 0x2489ACF5.

Next, after running the LDR R6, [ARRAY1, INDEX, LSL #2] instruction, element 2 of array of MYDATA is loaded to R6. So the content of R6 = 0x2489AC23.

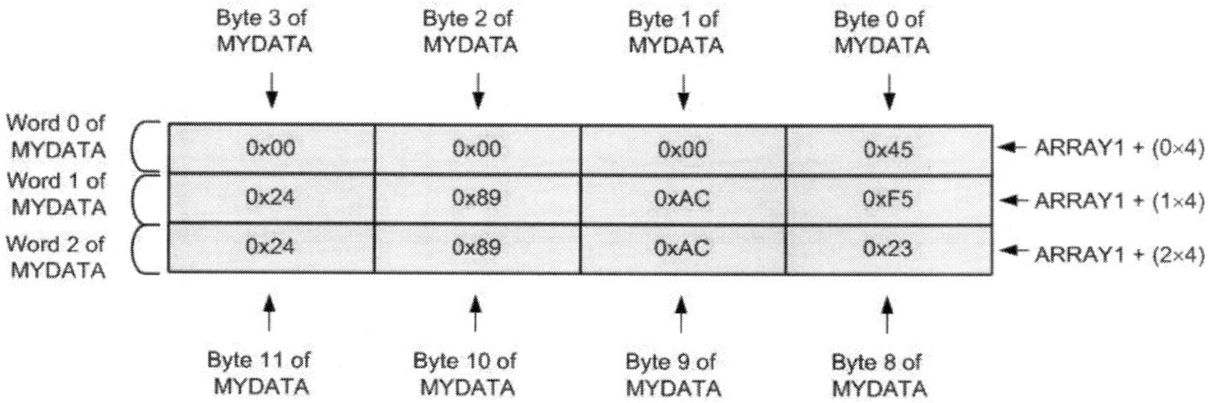

Writeback sign (!) in pre-indexed load and store with scaled register

We can force all scaled register load and store instructions to writeback the calculated pointer to the pointing register by putting '!' after each load and store instructions. Examine the following instructions:

```
        LDR    R1, [R2, R3, LSL #2]!
                  ; R2 + (R3 × 4) is used as the address,
                  ; content of location R2 + (R3 × 4) is loaded to R1
                  ; R2 = R2 + (R3 × 4) (R2 is updated.)
        STR    R1, [R2, R3, LSL #1]!
```

```
                ; R2 + (R3 × 2) is used as the address
                ; R1 is stored to location R2 + (R3 × 2)
                ; R2 = R2 + (R3 × 2) (R2 is updated.)
```

Scaled register post-indexed

The following instructions are some examples of scaled register post-indexed in load and store instructions:

```
STR   R1, [R2], R3, LSL #2
                ; store R1 at location R2 of memory
                ; and write back R2 + (R3 × 4) to R2.
LDR   R1, [R2], R3, LSL #2
                ; load location R2 of memory to R1
                ; and write back R2 + (R3 × 4) to R2.
```

Look-up table

One application of indexed addressing mode is for implementing look-up tables. The look-up table is an array of pre-calculated constants. It allows obtaining frequently used values with no complex arithmetic operations during run-time at the cost of the memory space for the table. This technique is often used in embedded systems with lower computing power and stringent real time demand. The constant data in the look-up table may be calculated when the program is written or they may be calculated during the initialization of the program. In the examples 6-14 through 6-16, the look-up tables are stored in program memory space and accessed as an array using indexed addressing mode.

Example 6-14

Write a program to use the x value in R9 and leave the value of $x^2 + 2x + 3$ in R10. Assume R9 has the x value range of 0–9. Use a look-up table instead of a multiply instructions.

Solution:

```
       AREA LOOKUP_EXAMP6_14, READONLY, CODE

       ADR  R2, LOOKUP        ; point to LOOKUP
       LDRB R10, [R2, R9]     ; R10 = entry of lookup table index by R9

HERE   B    HERE              ; stay here forever

LOOKUP DCB  3, 6, 11, 18, 27, 38, 51, 66, 83, 102
      END
```

Example 6-15

Write a program to use the x value in R9 and get the factorial of x in R10. Assume R9 has the x value range of 0–10. Use a look-up table instead of a multiply instruction.

Solution:

```
      AREA LOOKUP_EXAMP6_15, READONLY, CODE

      MOV   R9, #5
      ADR   R2, LOOKUP              ; point to LOOKUP
      LDR   R10, [R2, R9, LSL #2]   ; R10 = entry of lookup table index by R9

HERE  B     HERE                    ; stay here forever

LOOKUP DCD  1, 1, 2, 6, 24, 120, 720, 5040, 40320, 362880, 3628800
      END
```

Example 6-16

Write a program that calculates 10 to the power of R2 and stores the result in R3. Assume R2 has the x value range of 0–6. Use a look-up table instead of a multiply instruction.

Solution:

```
       AREA LOOKUP_EXAMP_6_16, READONLY, CODE

       ADR  R1, LOOKUP              ; point to LOOKUP
       LDR  R3, [R1, R2, LSL #2]    ; R3 = entry of lookup table index by R2

HERE   B    HERE                    ; stay here forever

LOOKUP DCD  1, 10, 100, 1000, 10000, 100000, 1000000
      END
```

Review Questions

1. Indexed addressing mode in ARM uses (register, memory) as pointer to data location.
2. List the three types of Indexed addressing mode in ARM
3. True or false. In the preindexed addressing mode the value of register does not change after the instruction is executed.
4. What is the difference between the preindexed and preindexed with write back?
5. What symbol do we use to indicate the preinexed with write back?

Section 6.3: Stack and Stack Usage in ARM

On the abstract level, stack is a data structure that allows easy access to the top of the stack. Data are pushed on the stack and popped off the stack in the order of last-in-first-out. Data in the stack have read/write access but are difficult to remove or insert. It is like a stack of pancakes that you usually put a new one on the top or take the one on the top off. The whole stack can be seen but it is difficult to take a pancake in the middle of the stack and it is difficult to insert a new one in the middle of the stack.

It is customary to pass the return address and parameters on the stack to the subroutines and allocate local variables on the stack. With the RISC architecture such as ARM, there are many CPU registers to use for the same purpose, a short subroutine call may use the registers for return address, parameters, and local variables to speed up the subroutine call. But when the needs for temporary storage exceeds the available registers or when the nested subroutine calls are made, the stack must be used.

Since stack is used extensively in handling subroutine call and interrupt, most of the processors have hardware support to facilitate the creation and maintenance of stacks in assembly language programming. At the assembly language level, a stack is a section of memory allocated to store information temporarily. The data is pushed onto the stack from a register and popped off the stack to a register. The top-of-stack (TOS) is the memory location where data is pushed onto or popped off. A register is used to point to the top-of-stack and is named stack pointer (SP). When data is pushed onto or popped off the stack, the value of the stack pointer is adjusted. In ARM CPU, all the general registers can be used as a stack pointer. So, you may have several stacks for the application.

Register R13 is a designated stack pointer used for instructions PUSH, POP and interrupt handling. During interrupt acknowledgement, some of the registers are pushed on to the stack using R13 as stack pointer. When return from interrupt handler, these registers are popped off the stack. Details of interrupt handling is beyond the scope of this book. We will discuss PUSH and POP instructions later in this section.

How stacks are accessed

As mentioned earlier, stack is allocated in a region of RAM. The location where the new item is added to the stack (push) or the old item is taken off the stack (pop) is pointed by a register named stack pointer. Stack is a last-in-first-out data structure therefore only one stack pointer is needed for each stack. There are three types of data access to the stack: pushing new data onto the stack, popping old data off the stack, and reading/writing data on the stack. We will discuss them in more details later.

When new data is pushed onto the stack, the stack pointer has to move to enlarge the stack. There are two directions the stack can grow: to the lower address or to the higher address. If the stack pointer is pointing to a lower address after a new data is pushed onto the stack, it is called a descending stack. If the stack pointer is pointing to a higher address after a new data is pushed onto the stack, it is called an ascending stack.

The stack pointer is pointing to the top-of-stack. There are two options for stack pointer: it may point to the address where the new data will be stored or it may point to the address where the old data will be taken off. If it is pointing to the address where the new data will be stored, it is called an empty stack (because where the stack pointer is pointing to does not have valid data in it). If the stack pointer is pointing to the address where the old data will be taken off, it is called a full stack.

The combinations of these two options for stack, we may have Full Ascending stack, Full Descending stack, Empty Ascending stack, or Empty Descending stack. ARM instructions support all four types of stack but the instructions PUSH, POP and interrupt handling assume the stack to be full descending. To simplify the rest of the section, we will limit our discussion to only the full descending stack because that will be the type of stack most likely to be used with the ARM processors.

Even though you could manage a stack using regular load/store instructions for various data sizes, the stacks are meant to store the content of the registers and the data size is a word (4-byte). The 4-byte increment stack size is enforced by multiple register load/store and PUSH/POP instructions that we will see soon.

Pushing onto the stack

The stack pointer (SP) points to the top of the stack (TOS). With a full descending stack, the stack pointer is pointing to the last word of data put onto the stack. If the stack is empty (no data stored in the stack yet), the SP is pointing to the word immediately below the stack. When new data is pushed onto the stack, the SP is decremented by 4 to point to the word above the top of stack then the content of a register is copied into that space. If multiple registers are pushed onto the stack, this process will repeat until all the registers are copied onto the stack.

We may use SUB and STR instructions to perform the task. For example, to push the value of R1 onto the stack using R10 as the stack pointer, we can write the following instructions:

```
SUB    R10, R10, #4        ; decrement R10 as stack pointer
STR    R1, [R10]           ; and push R1 onto the stack using R10
```

We may use the pre-index with writeback addressing mode to accomplish the same in one instruction. Notice negative offset -4 is used to perform decrement.

```
STR    R1, [R10, #-4]!     ; decrement R10 and store R1 using R10
```

Popping from the stack

Popping (loading) the top-of-stack back into a given register is the opposite process of pushing. When the POP is executed, the data in the top location of the stack is copied (loaded) back to the register and the SP is incremented.

For example, the following instructions pop from the top-of-stack and in to R2 using R11 as the stack pointer:

```
LDR    R2, [R11]           ; load (POP) the top of stack to R1
ADD    R11, R11, #4        ; increment SP
```

We may use the post-index addressing mode to accomplish the same in one instruction. Positive offset 4 is used to increment the stack pointer. Recall post-index always writes back so there is no need for the '!" sign.

```
        LDR   R2, [R11], #4       ; load R2 using R11 and increment R10 afterward
```

Initializing the stack pointer in ARM

When the ARM is powered up, the R13 (SP) register contains value 0. Therefore, we must initialize the SP at the beginning of the program so that it points to somewhere in the internal SRAM. In ARM, we can make the stack to grow from a higher memory location to a lower memory location. In this case when we push (store) onto the stack the SP is decremented. We can also make the stack to grow from a lower memory location to a higher memory location, therefore when we push (store) onto the stack, the SP is incremented. It is common to initialize the SP to the uppermost RAM memory region, which means as we push data onto the stack, the stack pointer must be decremented.

Different ARMs have different amounts of RAM. In some ARM assembler Stack_Top represents the address of top of the stack. So, if we want to initialize the SP, we can simply load Stack_Top into the SP. Notice that SP (R13) is a 32-bit register. So, we can use any 32-bit address of SRAM as a stack section.

Example 6-17 shows how to initialize the SP and use the store and load instructions for PUSH and POP operations.

Example 6-17

The following ARM program places some data into registers and calls a subroutine that uses the same registers. It shows how to use the stack. Examine the stack, stack pointer, and the registers used after the execution of each instruction.

```
Stack_Top equ 0x40008000

      AREA   EXAMPLE_6_17, CODE, READONLY
      ; initialize the SP to point to the last location of RAM
      LDR    R13, =Stack_Top   ; load SP
      LDR    R0, =0x125        ; R0 = 0x125
      LDR    R1, =0x144        ; R1 = 0x144
      MOV    R2, #0x56         ; R2 = 0x56
      BL     MY_SUB            ; call a subroutine
      ADD    R3, R0, R1        ; R3 = R0 + R1 = 0x125 + 0x144 = 0x269
      ADD    R3, R3, R2        ; R3 = R3 + R2 = 0x269 + 0x56 = 0x2BF
HERE  B      HERE              ; stay here

MY_SUB
      ; save R0, R1, and R2 on stack before they are used
      SUB    R13, R13, #4 ; R13 = R13 - 4, to decrement the stack pointer
      STR    R0, [R13]    ; save R0 on stack
      SUB    R13, R13, #4 ; R13 = R13 - 4, to decrement the stack pointer
      STR    R1, [R13]    ; save R1 on stack
      SUB    R13, R13, #4 ; R13 = R13 - 4, to decrement the stack pointer
```

```
STR   R2, [R13]     ; save R2 on stack

; -------- modify R0, R1, and R2
MOV   R0, #0       ; R0 = 0
MOV   R1, #0       ; R1 = 0
MOV   R2, #0       ; R2 = 0
; --------

; restore the original registers contents from stack
LDR   R2, [R13]     ; restore R2 from stack
ADD   R13, R13, #4 ; R13 = R13 + 4 to increment the stack pointer
LDR   R1, [R13]     ; restore R1 from stack
ADD   R13, R13, #4 ; R13 = R13 + 4 to increment the stack pointer
LDR   R0, [R13]     ; restore R0 from stack
ADD   R13, R13, #4 ; R13 = R13 + 4 to increment the stack pointer

BX    LR            ; return to caller

END
```

Solution:

After the execution of	Contents of some the registers (in Hex)				Stack
	R0	R1	R2	SP (R13)	
`LDR R13,= Stack_Top`	0	0	0	40008000	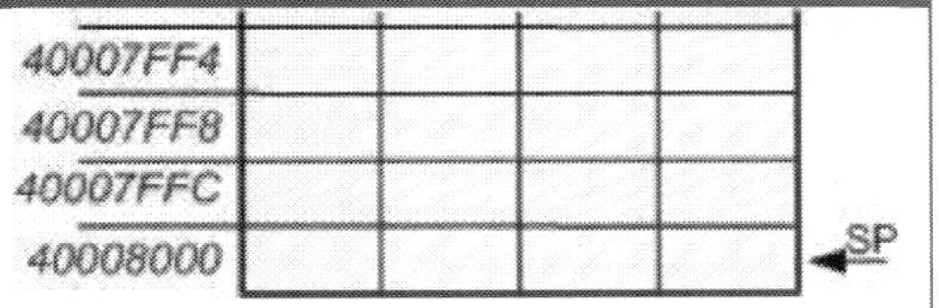

`LDR R0, =0x125`
`LDR R1, =0x144`
`LDR R2, =0x56`
	125	144	56	40008000	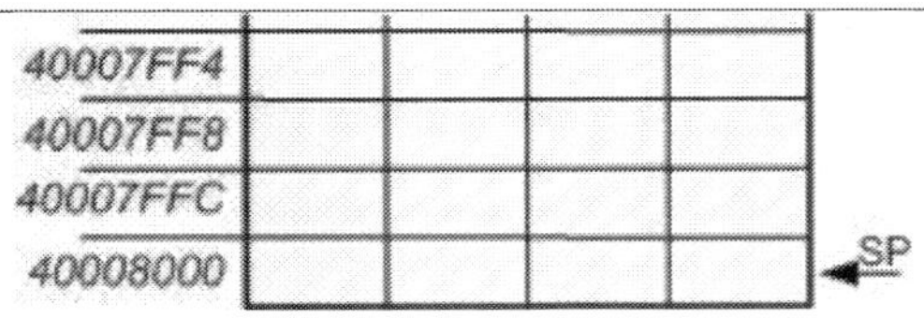

`SUB R13, R13, #4` `STR R0, [R13]`	125	144	56	40007FFC	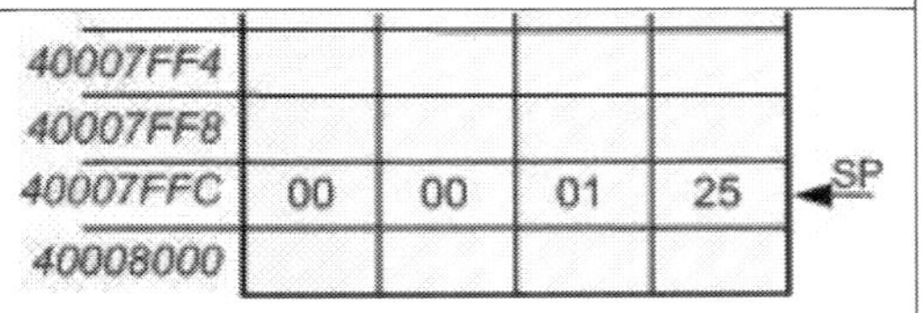

`SUB R13, R13, #4` `STR R1, [R13]`	125	144	56	40007FF8	40007FF4: 40007FF8: 00 00 01 44 ← SP 40007FFC: 00 00 01 25 40008000:
`SUB R13, R13, #4` `STR R2, [R13]`	125	144	56	40007FF4	40007FF4: 00 00 00 56 ← SP 40007FF8: 00 00 01 44 40007FFC: 00 00 01 25 40008000:

`MOV R0, #0`
`MOV R1, #0`
`MOV R2, #0`
	0	0	0	40007FF4	40007FF4: 00 00 00 56 ← SP
					40007FF8: 00 00 01 44
					40007FFC: 00 00 01 25
					40008000:

`LDR R2, [R13]` `ADD R13, R13, #4`	0	0	56	40007FF8	40007FF4: 40007FF8: 00 00 01 44 ← SP 40007FFC: 00 00 01 25 40008000:
`LDR R1, [R13]` `ADD R13, R13, #4`	0	144	56	40007FFC	40007FF4: 40007FF8: 40007FFC: 00 00 01 25 ← SP 40008000:
`LDR R0, [R13]` `ADD R13, R13, #4`	125	144	56	40008000	40007FF4: 40007FF8: 40007FFC: 40008000: ← SP

Example 6-18

Rewrite the program in Example 6-17 to use pre-index and post-index addressing modes.

Solution:

```
Stack_Top equ 0x40008000

      AREA   EXAMPLE_6_18, CODE, READONLY
      ; initialize the SP to point to the last location of RAM
      ; Assume Stack_Top = 0x40008000
      LDR    R13, =Stack_Top    ; load SP
      LDR    R0, =0x125         ; R0 = 0x125
```

```
        LDR     R1, =0x144          ; R1 = 0x144
        MOV     R2, #0x56           ; R2 = 0x56
        BL      MY_SUB              ; call a subroutine
        ADD     R3, R0, R1          ; R3 = R0 + R1 = 0x125 + 0x144 = 0x269
        ADD     R3, R3, R2          ; R3 = R3 + R2 = 0x269 + 0x56 = 0x2BF
HERE    B       HERE                ; stay here

MY_SUB
        ; save R0, R1, and R2 on stack before they are used
        STR     R0, [R13, #-4]!     ; save R0 on stack
        STR     R1, [R13, #-4]!     ; save R1 on stack
        STR     R2, [R13, #-4]!     ; save R2 on stack

        ; -------- modify R0, R1, and R2
        MOV     R0, #0          ; R0 = 0
        MOV     R1, #0          ; R1 = 0
        MOV     R2, #0          ; R2 = 0
        ; --------

        ; restore the original registers contents from stack
        LDR     R2, [R13], #4       ; restore R2 from stack
        LDR     R1, [R13], #4       ; restore R1 from stack
        LDR     R0, [R13], #4       ; restore R0 from stack

        BX      LR                  ; return to caller

        END
```

Writeback options of STM and LDM

The STM and LDM instructions allow you to store and load multiple registers with a single instruction. We can also specify the action to be taken for the pointer. The action can be increment or decrement before or after the pop is done. This is shown in Table 6-4.

IA stands for Increment After and adds four (the size of register in bytes) to the pointer after load or storing each register.

IB stands for Increment Before and adds four (the size of register in bytes) to the pointer before load or storing each register.

DA stands for Decrement After and subtracts four (the size of register in bytes) from the pointer after load or storing each register.

DB stands for Decrement Before and subtracts four (the size of register in bytes) from the pointer before load or storing each register.

Program 6-1: Using STMFA and LDMFA for Stack (Repeat of Example 6-17)

```
      ; Using Full Ascending Load and Store for stack
      AREA     PROG6_1, CODE, READONLY
      LDR    R13, =Stack_Top    ; load SP
      LDR    R0, =0x125   ; R0 = 0x125
      LDR    R1, =0x144   ; R1 = 0x144
      MOV    R2, #0x56    ; R2 = 0x56
      BL     MY_SUB       ; call a subroutine
      ADD    R3, R0, R1   ; R3 = R0 + R1 = 0x125 + 0x144 = 0x269
      ADD    R3, R3, R2   ; R3 = R3 + R2 = 0x269 + 0x56 = 0x2BF
HERE  B      HERE         ; stay here
      ; ---------------------------
MY_SUB
      ; --------save R0, R1, and R2 on stack before they are used by a loop
      STMFA  R13, {R0-R2}       ; save R0, R1, R2 on stack using Full Ascending
      ; --------R0, R1, and R2 are changed
      MOV    R0, #0             ; R0=0
      MOV    R1, #0             ; R1=0
      MOV    R2, #0             ; R2=0
      ; ---------restore the original registers contents from stack
      LDMFA R13, {R0-R2}
      ; restore R0, R1, and R2 from stack using F. Ascending
      BX     LR           ; return to caller
      END
```

It must be noted that ARM Cortex has PUSH and POP instructions. See Appendix A for more information.

Using LDM and STM instructions for the stack

As we can see in the previous examples, often multiple registers are pushed onto the stack of popped off the stack. ARM provides two sets of instructions STM (store multiple) and LDM (load multiple) to facilitate the tasks. With STM and LDM, one instruction may store or load several registers. These instructions make the program source code shorter and easier to read. They also reduce the instruction fetch and may increase the performance.

To support four types of the stack, STM and LDM instructions take four suffixes. This is shown in Table 6-4.

Option		Description
IA	Increment After	increment address after each transfer
IB	Increment Before	increment address before each transfer
DA	Decrement After	decrement address after each transfer
DB	Decrement Before	decrement address before each transfer

Table 6-4: Options for LDM and STM instructions

If no suffix is used, the default action is increment afterward (IA). In order to use them for stack, the final address needed to be written back to the register.

For further clarification, assume that R1 = 0x100. Figure 6-7 shows the memory after running STM R1!, {R2, R3} with each of IA, IB, DA and DB options.

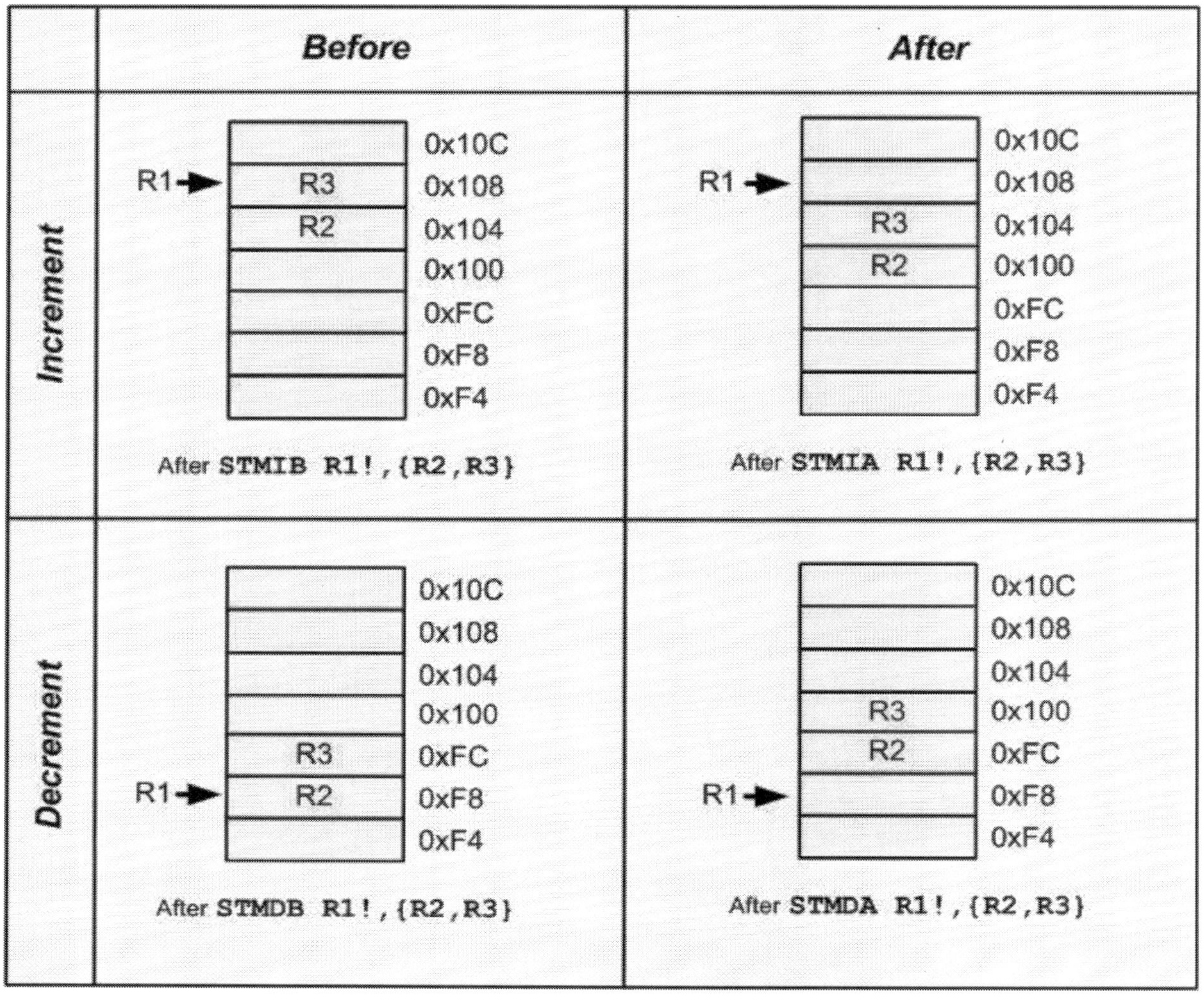

Figure 6-7: Four Options of STM and LDM in ARM

Notice that we have four stack structures, it is either ascending or descending. The stack is called ascending when it is incremented after each store (PUSH) instruction and decremented after each load (POP) instruction. It is called descending when it is decremented after each store (PUSH) instruction and incremented after each load (POP) instruction. The stack pointer can point to the last filled location; in this case the stack is called Full Stack. The stack pointer can point to the next available location as well; which is called an Empty Stack. See Figure 6-8 for more clarification.

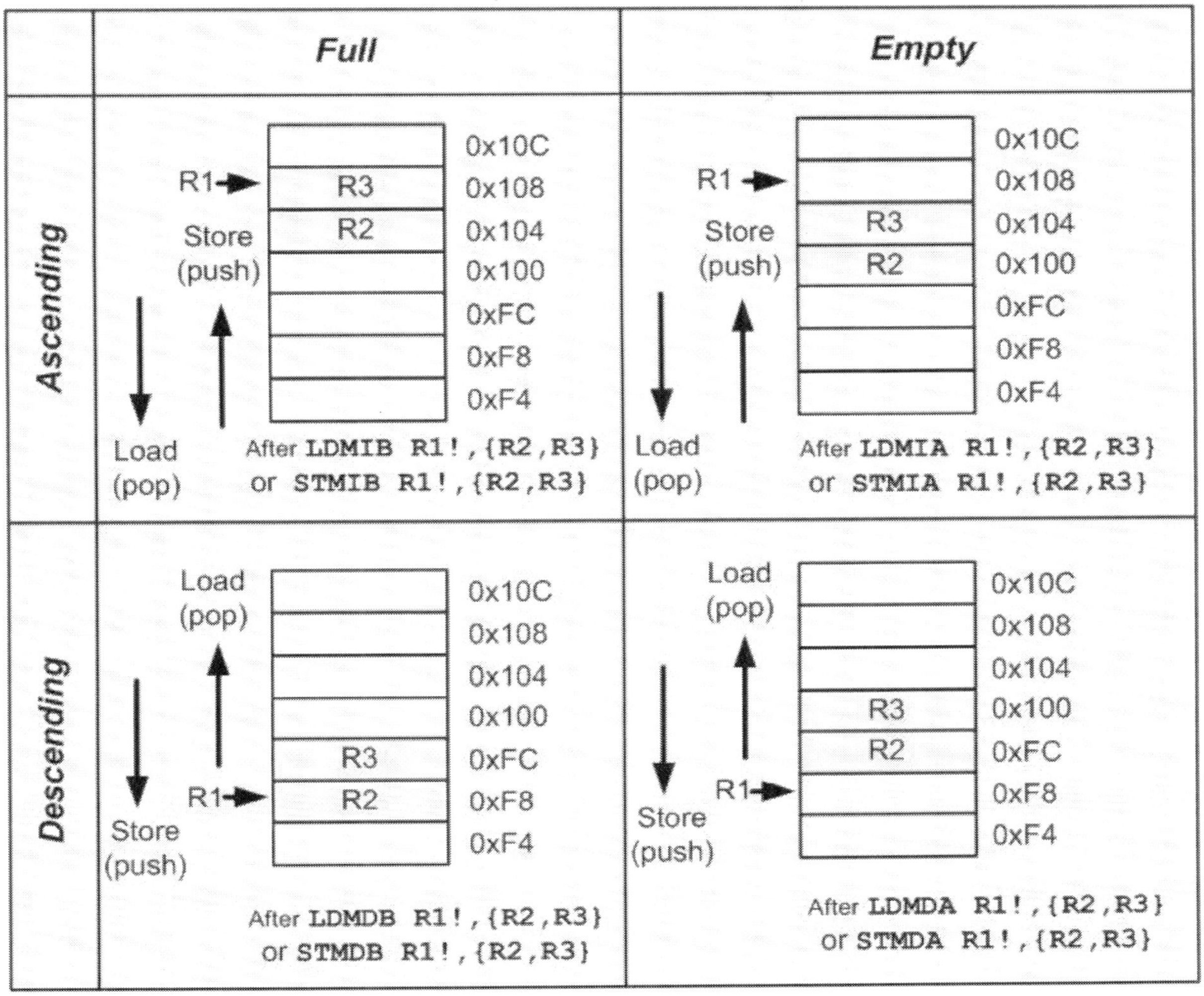

Figure 6-8: Four General Stack Structure

To implement a Full Ascending stack we have to use STMIB because the stack pointer should increment on store instruction and it should be incremented before storing each register because it should point to full location. On the other hand, we have to use LDMDA for pop instruction because the stack pointer should decrement on load instruction and it should be decremented before loading each full location because it was pointing to an empty location before decrementing. Table 6-5 lists appropriate load and store instruction for each stack structure. It is difficult and prone to error to remember which load and store should be used with each stack structure.

Stack Structure	Load	Store	Load (alternate Names)	Store (alternate Names)
Full Ascending	LDMDA	STMIB	LDMFA	STMFA
Full Descending	LDMIA	STMDB	LDMFD	STMFD
Empty Ascending	LDMDB	STMIA	LDMEA	STMEA
Empty Descending	LDMIB	STMDA	LDMED	STMED

Table 6-5: The four stack structures and the options of LDM and STM instructions

To solve this problem, each of load and store options has alternate name which is easy to remember when it is used for stack operation. The last two columns of Table 6-5 list the alternate names.

The stack structure used by ARM for PUSH, POP instructions and interrupt handling is a Full Descending stack using R13 as the stack pointer. To support a Full Descending stack, STMDB and LDMIA pair of instructions should be used.

STMDB

Below shows the syntax for some of the usages of STMDB.

```
STMDB R11!, {R0, R1, R2, R3}
```

Store R0 through R3 onto memory pointed to by R11 and update R11 with the final address. Registers may be listed with comma separation.

```
STMDB R8!, {R0-R7}
```

Store R0 through R7 onto memory pointed to by R8 and update R8 with the final address. Registers may be listed as a range from R0 to R7 inclusive.

```
STMDB R7!, {R0, R5, R3}
```

Store R0, R3, R5 onto memory pointed to by R7 and update R7 with the final address. Register list does not have to be in numerical order.

```
STMDB R11!, {R0-R3, R8, R7}
```

Store R0, R1, R2, R3, R7, and R8 onto memory pointed to by R11 and update R7 with the final address. List of single registers and register range may be mixed.

LDMIA

Below shows the syntax for LDMIA. Their syntax is similar to STMDB.

```
LDMIA R11!, {R0, R1, R2, R3}
LDMIA R8!, {R0-R7}
LDMIA R7!, {R0, R5, R3}
LDMIA R11!, {R0-R3, R8, R7}
```

As you saw in the examples, the register list does not have to be in numeric order. When the registers are pushed on to the stack, the higher numbered register is pushed first so that the resulting stack has lower numbered register with lower address and higher numbered register with higher address. When the registers are popped off the stack, the lower address data goes into the lower numbered register. If you use a pair of load/store instructions from Table 6-5, the saved values will return to the proper registers.

Example 6-19 shows how we can use STMDB and LDMIA to simplify a code and prevent unwanted errors.

Example 6-19

Modify the Example 6-18 using the LDM and STM instructions.

Solution:

```
        ; initialize the SP to point to
Stack_Top equ 0x40007f80

        AREA    EXAMPLE_6_19, CODE, READONLY

        ; initialize the SP to point to the last location of RAM
        ; Assume Stack_Top = 0x40008000
        LDR     R13, =Stack_Top    ; load SP
        LDR     R0, =0x125   ; R0 = 0x125
        LDR     R1, =0x144   ; R1 = 0x144
        MOV     R2, #0x56    ; R2 = 0x56
        BL      MY_SUB       ; call a subroutine
        ADD     R3, R0, R1   ; R3 = R0 + R1 = 0x125 + 0x144 = 0x269
        ADD     R3, R3, R2   ; R3 = R3 + R2 = 0x269 + 0x56 = 0x2BF
HERE    B       HERE         ; stay here

MY_SUB
        ; save R0, R1, and R2 on stack before they are used
        STMDB   R13!, {R0, R1, R2}

        ; -------- modify R0, R1, and R2
        MOV     R0, #0       ; R0 = 0
        MOV     R1, #0       ; R1 = 0
        MOV     R2, #0       ; R2 = 0
        ; --------

        ; restore the original registers contents from stack
        LDMIA   R13!, {R0, R1, R2}

        BX      LR           ; return to caller

        END
```

PUSH and POP

We can also use the PUSH and POP pseudo-instructions to do the same thing. PUSH is an alias of "STMDB R13!" And POP is an alias of "LDMIA R13!".

ARM allows use of any general register and R13 to be used as stack pointer. But when PUSH and POP are used the stack pointer is limited to only R13 and full ascending stack.

Copying a block of data with LDM and STM

So far, we have seen using STM and LDM instructions for stack. These instructions may be used to copy a block of data too.

To copy a block of data, we bring into the CPU's register a word of data from memory and then write it out from the register to a location in RAM. In that case we copy one word (4 bytes) at a time. So, to copy 10 words we have to set a counter to 10 for a loop iteration. We can use the LDM and STM to do the same thing with much less coding. Using LDM and STM instructions to copy a block of data, we need a register for the source address and another one for the destination address. Example 6-20 uses R11 and R12 for source and destination addresses, respectively. The registers R0–R9 are used as temporary storage for data before they are copied to the destination, that gives us 10 words (40 bytes) transfer at a time.

Notice that in the STM and LDM instructions without suffix, they operate with the default increment afterward (IA) mode. When using the same mode for STM and LDM, the order of the data in the source is maintained in the destination.

Example 6-20

These two lines of code copy a block of 10 words (40 bytes) memory from source to destination. The registers R11 and R12 are used for source and destination addresses. To copy more data, these two lines may be put in a loop and add the writeback ("!") to the register.

```
LDM   R11, {R0-R9}   ; Load R0 thru R9 from memory pointed to by R11
STM   R12, {R0-R9}   ; Store R0 thru R9 to memory pointed to by R12
```

Accessing to the data on the stack

It is conventional to allocate a block of memory on the stack each time a subroutine is called. This block of memory is commonly referred as the stack frame of the subroutine call. The parameters are pushed onto the stack by the caller. At the beginning of the subroutine, the return address is pushed onto the stack from the linked register (R14) if nested function calls are anticipated. The subroutine then moves the stack pointer to leave a block of memory space for the local variables. At this point, the stack pointer is copied to another register to be used for access into the stack frame. This register is called the frame pointer.

The code in the subroutine needs to read the values in the parameters and read/write the local variables, all of them within the stack frame. The frame point is used with base plus offset addressing mode described in the previous section to read and write the entries in the stack frame.

The stack limit and nested calls in ARM

As mentioned earlier, we can define the stack anywhere in the read/write memory. So, in the ARM the stack can be as big as its RAM except the statically allocated variables. The other dynamic memory allocation often used in high level language is heap. Both stack and heap grow as needed and shrink when the memory is no longer useful. When heap is used, it is often put at the other end of the memory of the stack. Both stack and heap grow toward each other. In most of the system, there is no hardware checking for their collision and software checking has high negative impact on the performance and therefore rarely implemented. Programmer must be vigilant about the memory allocation for stack and the run-time usage.

In ARM, the stack is used for subroutine calls and interrupt handling. We must remember that upon calling a subroutine from the main program using the BL instruction, R14, the linker register, keeps track of where the CPU should return to after completing the subroutine. Now, if we have another call inside the subroutine using the BL instruction, then it is our job to store the original R14 on the stack. Failure to do that will end up crashing the program. For this reason, we must be very careful when manipulating the stack contents.

Each subroutine may use some registers to hold data temporarily. The subroutine has no knowledge whether the caller left any data in the registers that need to be preserved. So each subroutine should preserve any register it is going to use and restore them before return.

Review Questions

1. The ______ register is the default stack pointer.
2. How deep is the size of the stack in the ARM?
3. Write a program that pushes R5, R6, R7, and R8 into the stack.
4. Write a program that pops R5, R6, R7, and R8 from the stack.
5. What does the following program do?

```
LDR    R5, =0x40000000
LDM    R5, {R1, R4}
LDR    R5, =0x50000000
STM    R5, {R1, R4}
```

Section 6.4: ARM Bit-Addressable Memory Region

ARM memory/peripheral is byte-addressable, that means the smallest size of memory access by the CPU is a single byte (8-bit). This presents an issue. In order to modify a single bit in the memory or peripheral, the whole byte where the bit resides is read, the bit is modified using AND, OR, or exclusive-OR operation, then the whole byte is written back. This is a procedure commonly referred to as the Read-Modify-Write (RMW) operation. One problem with RMW is that it incurs three steps and generally three separate instructions. In a multi-tasking environment, two RMW operations to the same byte may occur simultaneously, one interrupts the other. In that case, the second write will wipe out the modification of the first write.

There are software techniques to mitigate the issue of RMW but ARM introduced the "bit-banding" option for Cortex-M in hardware. It is generally available in M3 and M4 controllers though the manufacturers have the option to decide whether they implement it or not in the controllers.

Bit-banding is a feature that creates an alias word address for each bit of the selected memory and peripheral regions. Writing to the bit-banded alias address will change only the corresponding bit in the memory or peripheral without affecting all other bits of the same byte. Reading from the bit-banded alias address will return only the value of the addressed bit. Although internally writing to bit-banded memory or peripheral is still implemented in a read-modify-write in hardware, it is done with a single write instruction and therefore an "atomic" operation that will not be interrupted by the other instruction.

Since bit-banded alias addresses are word-size addresses. They are read and written in word size. Writing a word to a bit-banded alias address will transfer Bit 0 of the word to the selected bit. All other bits in the word have no effect. Reading from a bit-banded alias address will return the bit value in Bit 0 of the word. All other bits will be 0.

Bit-addressable (bit-banded) memory region

Since bit-banding assigns each bit with a word address and each word has 32 bits, bit-banding requires 32 times the address space than the regular memory addressing. Of the 4GB memory space of the ARM, only few small regions of memory or peripheral are bit-addressable, or the bit-banded regions. Recall bit-banding is created to mitigate the issues of Read-Modify-Write, so none of the read-only memory is bit-banded only the RAM and peripheral regions.

The bit-banded RAM and peripheral locations vary among the family members and manufacturers. The ARM Cortex-M generic manual defines the address regions of bit-banding as 0x20000000 to 0x200FFFFF for SRAM and 0x40000000 to 0x400FFFFF for peripherals. We will use these address regions for the discussion in the rest of this section. Notice they are located at the lowest 1 MB address space of SRAM and peripherals. See Table 6-1 in Section 6-1. It must be also noted that the bit-banded (bit-addressable) regions are the only region that can be accessed in both bit and byte/halfword/word formats while the other area of memory must be accessed in byte/halfword/word size.

For the ARM Cortex-M, the bit-banded SRAM has addresses of 0x20000000 to 0x200FFFFF. This 1M bytes bit-addressable region is given 32M-byte bit-banded alias addresses of 0x22000000 to 0x23FFFFFF. The higher addresses are called alias address because they are addressing the exact same memory as the lower direct addressed SRAM, only each word address represents a single bit in the lower address. Because each bit occupies a word (4-byte) address in the bit-banded alias address region, to find out the alias address of a bit, the following formula is used:

$$\text{Bit alias address} = \text{Bit alias base address} + \text{Byte offset } \times 32 + \text{Bit number } \times 4$$

For example, to calculate the bit alias address of bit 3 of 0x20000004

Bit alias base address = 0x22000000

Byte offset = 0x20000004 – 0x20000000 = 4

Bit number = 3

Bit alias address = 0x22000000 + 4 * 32 + 3 * 4 = 0x22000000 + 128 + 12 = 0x22000000 + 0x8C

= 0x2200008C

Therefore, the bit addresses 0x22000000 to 0x2200001F are for the first byte of SRAM location 0x20000000, and 0x22000020 to 0x2200003F are the bit addresses of the second byte of SRAM location 0x20000001, and so on. See Figure 6-9.

SRAM Byte addresses	SRAM Bit addresses (We use these addresses to access the individual bits)							
	D7	D6	D5	D4	D3	D2	D1	D0
200FFFFF	23FFFFFC	F8	F4	F0	EC	E8	E4	23FFFFE0
200FFFFE	23FFFFDC	D8	D4	D0	CC	C8	C4	23FFFFC0
200FFFFD	23FFFFBC	B8	B4	B0	AC	A8	A4	23FFFFA0
200FFFFC	23FFFF9C	98	94	90	8C	88	84	23FFFF80
200FFFFB	23FFFF7C	78	74	70	6C	68	64	23FFFF60
200FFFFA	23FFFF5C	x8	x4	x0	xC	x8	x4	23FFFF40
200XXXXX	2XXXXXXC	X8	X4	X0	XC	X8	X4	2XXXXXX0
20000008	2200011C	118	114		...		104	22000100
20000007	220000FC	F8	F4	F0	EC	E8	E4	220000E0
20000006	220000DC	D8	D4	D0	CC	C8	C4	220000C0
20000005	220000BC	B8	B4	B0	AC	A8	A4	220000A0
20000004	2200009C	98	94	90	8C	88	84	22000080
20000003	2200007C	78	74	70	6C	68	64	22000060
20000002	2200005C	58	54	50	4C	48	44	20000040
20000001	2200003C	38	34	30	2C	28	24	22000020
20000000	2200001C	18	14	10	0C	08	04	22000000

Figure 6-9: SRAM bit-addressable region and their alias addresses

Since each byte of SRAM has 8 bits, we need an address for each bit. This means we need at least 8M address locations to access 8M bits, one address for each bit. However, to make the addresses word-aligned the ARM provides 4-byte alias address for each bit. For example, 0x22000000 to 0x2200001F is assigned to a single byte location of 0x20000000. That means we have 0x22000000 to 0x23FFFFFF (total of 32M locations, as alias addresses) for 1M bytes of address.

Bit map for SRAM

From Figure 6-9 once again notice the following facts:

1. The bit address 0x22000000 is assigned to D0 of SRAM location of 0x20000000.
2. The bit address 0x22000004 is assigned to D1 of SRAM location of 0x20000000.
3. The bit address 0x22000008 is assigned to D2 of SRAM location of 0x20000000.
4. The bit address 0x2200000C is assigned to D3 of SRAM location of 0x20000000.
5. The bit address 0x22000010 is assigned to D4 of SRAM location of 0x20000000.
6. The bit address 0x22000014 is assigned to D5 of SRAM location of 0x20000000.
7. The bit address 0x22000018 is assigned to D6 of SRAM location of 0x20000000.
8. The bit address 0x2200001C is assigned to D7 of SRAM location of 0x20000000.

Notice that SRAM locations 0x20000000 – 0x200FFFFF are both byte-addressable and bit-addressable. The only difference is when we access it in byte (or halfword or word) we use direct addresses 0x20000000 to 0x200FFFFF, but when they are accessed in bit, they are accessed via their alias addresses of 0x22000000 to 0x23FFFFFF. The reason they are called aliases is because it is the same physical memory but accessed by two different addresses. It is like a same person but different names (aliases) See Examples 6-21 through 6-23.

Example 6-21

The generic ARM chip has the following address assignments. Calculate the space and the amount of memory given to each region.

(a) Address range of 0x20000000–200FFFFF for SRAM bit-addressable region

(b) Address range of 0x22000000–23FFFFFF for alias addresses of bit-addressable SRAM

Solution:

(a) 200FFFFF – 20000000 = FFFFF bytes. Converting FFFFF to decimal, we get 1,048,575 + 1 = 1,048,576, which is equal to 1M bytes.

(b) 23FFFFFF – 22000000 = 1FFFFFF bytes. Converting 1FFFFFF to decimal, we get 33,554,431 + 1 = 33,554,432, which is equal to 32M bytes.

Example 6-22

Write a program to set HIGH the D6 of the SRAM location 0x20000001 using a) byte address and b) the bit alias address.

Solution:

a)

```
LDR   R1, =0x20000001    ; load the address of the byte
LDRB  R2, [R1]           ; get the byte
ORR   R2, R2, #2_01000000      ; make D6 bit high
           ; (binary representation in Keil for 0b01000000)
STRB  R2, [R1]     ; write it back
```

b) From Figure 6-9 we have address 0x22000038 as the bit address of D6 of SRAM location 0x20000001.

```
LDR   R1, =0x22000038    ; load the alias address of the bit
MOV   R2, #1             ; R2 = 1
STR   R2, [R1]           ; Write one to D6
```

Example 6-23

Write a program to set LOW the D0 bit of the SRAM location 0x20000005 using a) byte address and b) the bit alias address.

Solution:

a)

```
LDR    R1, =0x20000005      ; load the address of byte
LDRB   R2, [R1]             ; get the byte
AND    R2, R2, #2_11111110     ; make D0 bit low
STRB   R2, [R1]             ; write it back
```

b) From Figure 6-9 we have address 0x220000A0 as the bit address of D0 of SRAM location 0x20000005.

```
LDR R2, =0x220000A0      ; load the alias address of the bit
MOV R0, 0                ; R0 = 0
STR R0, [R2]             ; write zero to D0
```

Peripheral I/O port bit-addressable region

The general purpose I/O (GPIO) and peripherals such as ADC, DAC, RTC, and serial COM port are widely used in the embedded system design. In many ARM-based trainer boards we see the connection of LEDs, switches, and LCD to the GPIO pins of the ARM chip. In such trainers the vendor provides the details of I/O port and peripheral connections to the ARM chip in addition to their address map. As we discussed earlier, the ARM Cortex-M3 and M4 have set aside 1M bytes of address space to be used bit-banding (bit-addressable) I/O and peripherals. The address space assigned to bit-banded peripherals and GPIO is 0x40000000 to 0x400FFFFF with bit-banded alias addresses of 0x42000000 to 0x43FFFFFF. Examine your trainer board data sheet for the bit-banded addresses implemented on the ARM chip.

Bit map for I/O peripherals

From Figure 6-10 once again notice the following facts.

1. The bit address 0x42000000 is assigned to D0 of peripherals location of 0x40000000.
2. The bit address 0x42000004 is assigned to D1 of peripherals location of 0x40000000.
3. The bit address 0x42000008 is assigned to D2 of peripherals location of 0x40000000.
4. The bit address 0x4200000C is assigned to D3 of peripherals location of 0x40000000.
5. The bit address 0x42000010 is assigned to D4 of peripherals location of 0x40000000.
6. The bit address 0x42000014 is assigned to D5 of peripherals location of 0x40000000.
7. The bit address 0x42000018 is assigned to D6 of peripherals location of 0x40000000.
8. The bit address 0x4200001C is assigned to D7 of peripherals location of 0x40000000.

Peripherals Byte addresses	Peripherals Bit addresses. (We use these addresses to access the individual bits)						
	D7	D6	D5	D4	D3	D2	D1	D0
400FFFFF	43FFFFFC	F8	F4	F0	EC	E8	E4	43FFFFE0
400FFFFE	43FFFFDC	D8	D4	D0	CC	C8	C4	43FFFFC0
400FFFFD	43FFFFBC	B8	B4	B0	AC	A8	A4	43FFFFA0
400FFFFC	43FFFF9C	98	94	90	8C	88	84	43FFFF80
400FFFFB	43FFFF7C	78	74	70	6C	68	64	43FFFF60
400FFFFA	43FFFF5C	x8	x4	x0	xC	x8	x4	43FFFF40
400XXXXX	4XXXXXXC	X8	X4	X0	XC	X8	X4	4XXXXXX0
40000008	4200011C	118	114		...		104	42000100
40000007	420000FC	F8	F4	F0	EC	E8	E4	420000E0
40000006	420000DC	D8	D4	D0	CC	C8	C4	420000C0
40000005	420000BC	B8	B4	B0	AC	A8	A4	420000A0
40000004	4200009C	98	94	90	8C	88	84	42000080
40000003	4200007C	78	74	70	6C	68	64	42000060
40000002	4200005C	58	54	50	4C	48	44	42000040
40000001	4200003C	38	34	30	2C	28	24	42000020
40000000	4200001C	18	14	10	0C	08	04	42000000

Figure 6-10: Peripherals bit-addressable region and their alias addresses.

When accessing a peripheral port in a single-bit manner, we must use the address aliases of 0x42000000 – 0x43FFFFFF.

Review Questions

1. True or false. All bytes of SRAM in ARM are bit-addressable.
2. True or false. All bits of the I/O peripherals in ARM are bit-addressable.
3. True or false. All ROM locations of the ARM are bit-addressable.
4. Of the 4G bytes of memory in the ARM, how many bytes are bit-addressable? List them.
5. How would you check to see whether bit D0 of location 0x20000002 is high or low?
6. Find out to which byte each of the following bits belongs. Give the address of the RAM byte in hex.

   (a) 0x23000030 (b) 0x23000040 (c) 0x23000048
   (d) 0x4200003C (e) 0x43FFFFFC

Section 6.5: ADR, LDR, and PC Relative Addressing

In indexed addressing modes, any registers including the PC (R15) register can be used as the pointer register. For example, the following instruction reads the contents of memory location PC+4:

```
LDR   R0, [PC, #4]
```

In this way, the data which has a known distance from the current executing line can be accessed. As discussed in Chapter 4, the PC register points 8 bytes (2 instructions) ahead of executing instruction. As a result, "LDR R0, [PC, #4]" accesses a memory location whose address is 4+8 bytes ahead of the current instruction. Generally speaking, the address of the memory location which is being accessed using "LDR R0, [PC, offset]" can be found using this formula: the address of current instruction + 8 + offset. For instance, if "LDR R0, [PC, #4]" is located in address 0x10 the effective address is: 0x10 + 8 + 4 = 0x1C.

Because all ARM instructions have the same 4-byte size, calculating the offset from current PC is straight forward, it is still a tedious job that needs be done every time new instructions are inserted or deleted. There are two pseudo-instructions using PC relative addressing mode, ADR and LDR with "=" to make programming easier.

The ADR Pseudo-instruction

The ADR pseudo-instruction uses the PC relative addressing mode to load a register with an address. It has the syntax of

```
ADR   Rn, Label
```

The assembler calculates the offset from the current PC value to the line where Label is and translates the pseudo-instruction into:

```
ADD   Rn, PC, #offset
```

For example, see the following program:

```
      AREA  LOOKUP_EXAMPLE, READONLY, CODE

      ADR   R2, OUR_FIXED_DATA      ; R2 points to OUR_FIXED_DATA
      LDRB  R0, [R2]                ; load R0 with the contents
                                    ; of memory pointed to by R2
      ADD   R1, R1, R0              ; add R0 to R1
HERE  B     HERE                    ; stay here forever
OUR_FIXED_DATA
      DCB   0x55, 0x33, 1, 2, 3, 4, 5, 6
      END
```

See Figure 6-11. At compile time, the ADR is replaced with "ADD R2, PC, #0x08". Since the instruction is at address 0x00, the instruction accesses location 0 + 8 + 0x08 = 0x10. As shown in the Figure, where 0x10 is the address of OUR_FIXED_DATA.

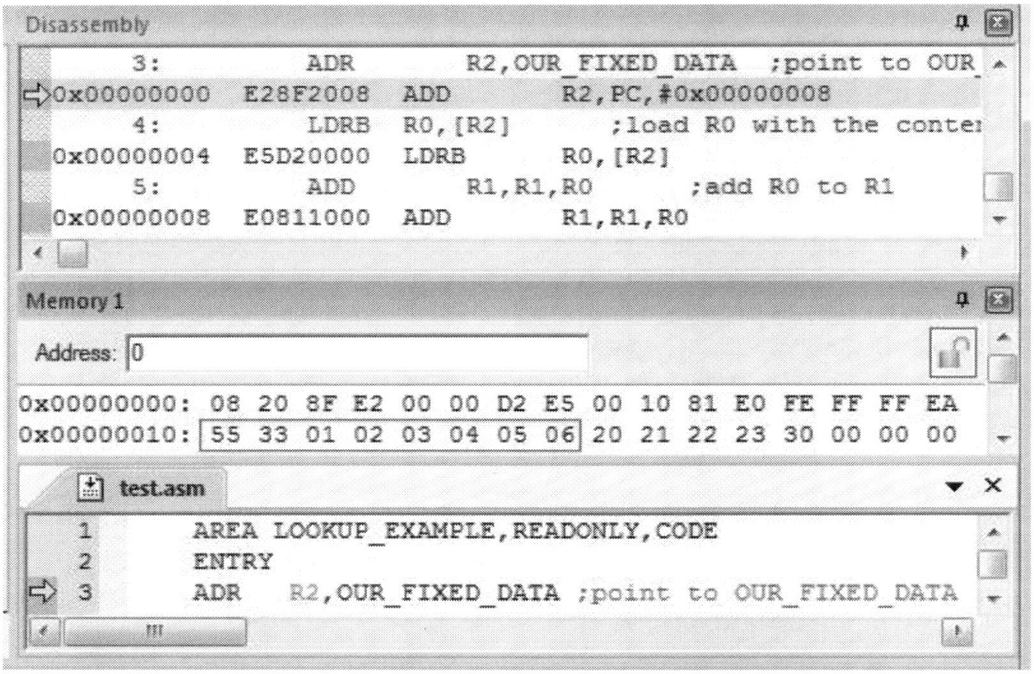

Figure 6-11: Memory Dump for ADR Instruction

Implementing the LDR Pseudo-instruction

ARM instructions are 32-bit long. It is impossible to incorporate a 32-bit immediate data in a 32-bit instruction. To load a register with a 32-bit immediate data, the ARM assembler stores the value as a constant data in program memory and accesses it using the LDR instruction and the PC relative addressing mode. Figure 6-12 shows the implementation of Program 6-2. For example, 0x12345678 is stored in memory locations 0x10–0x13, and the LDR directive is replaced with LDR R0, [PC, #0x0008]. Since PC=0, the LDR R0, =0x1234567 is located at address 0x000000. Now we have 0+8+8=16=0x10.

Program 6-2: LDR Directive

```
        AREA   EXAMPLE, READONLY, CODE

        LDR    R0, =0x12345678
        LDR    R1, =0x86427531
        ADD    R2, R0, R1
H1      B      H1
        END
```

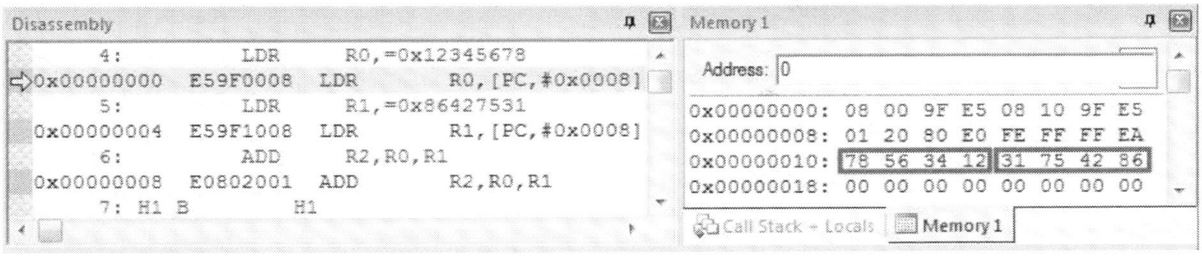

Figure 6- 12: Memory Dump for LDR Instruction

The memory region that the assembler reserved to store the constant data for LDR pseudo-instruction is called the "Literal pool." Literal pool is normally located at the end of the current section. (Section is terminated either by END or by another AREA directive.) The LDR instruction with immediate offset allows a range of -4095 to 4095. It is a good programming practice not to write a program section longer than 1000 instructions. Just in case you have a need to have a long section that the distance from the LDR instruction to the end of the section is beyond the range, ARM assembler allows you to designate a location within the section for an additional literal pool using LTORG directive. Remember, you should not designate a location for literal pool where the program execution may encounter and attempt to execute the constant data as instructions.

The same way for the LDR R1, =0x86427531 is located in ROM address 0x00000004. Therefore, we have 4+8+8=20=0x14, which is the address of the data 0x86427531.

Review Questions

1. Which register is used as the pointer in PC relative addressing mode?
2. Which directive is more optimized ADR or LDR? Why?

Problems

Section 6.1: ARM Memory Map and Memory Access

1. What is the bus bandwidth unit?
2. Give the variables that affect the bus bandwidth.
3. True or false. One way to increase the bus bandwidth is to widen the data bus.
4. True or false. An increase in the number of address bus pins results in a higher bus bandwidth for the system.
5. Calculate the memory bus bandwidth for the following systems.
   (a) ARM of 100 MHz bus speed and 0 WS
   (b) ARM of 80 MHz bus speed and 1 WS
6. Indicate which of the following addresses is word aligned.

(a) 0x1200004A	(b) 0x52000068	(c) 0x66000082
(d) 0x23FFFF86	(e) 0x23FFFFF0	(f) 0x4200004F
(g) 0x18000014	(h) 0x43FFFFF3	(i) 0x44FFFF05

7. Show how data is placed after execution of the following code using (a) little endian and (b) big endian.

```
LDR   R2, =0xFA98E322
LDR   R1, =0x20000100
STR   [R1], R2
```

8. True or false. In ARM, instructions are always word aligned.
9. True or false. In a word aligned address the lower digit of the address is 0, 4, 8, or C.
10. Show how many memory cycles does it take to fetch the following data into register

```
LDR   R1, =0x20000004
LDRD  [R1], R2
```

11. Show how many memory cycles does it take to fetch the following data into register

```
LDR   R1, =0x20000102
LDRD  [R1], R2
```

12. Show how many memory cycles does it take to fetch the following data into register

```
LDR   R1, =0x20000103
LDRD  [R1], R2
```

13. Show how many memory cycles does it take to fetch the following data into register

```
LDR   R1, =0x20000006
LDRH  [R1], R2
```

14. Show how many memory cycles does it take to fetch the following data into register

```
LDR   R1, =0x20000C10
LDRB  [R1], R2
```

Section 6.2: Advanced Indexed Addressing Mode

15. True or false. Writeback is by default enabled in pre-indexed addressing mode.
16. Indicate the addressing mode in each of the following instructions
    (a) LDR R1, [R5], R2, LSL #2 (b) STR R2, [R1, R0]
    (c) STR R2, [R1, R0, LSL #2]! (d) STR R9, [R1], R0
17. Which addressing mode uses the register as pointer to data location?
18. True or false. In the preindexed addressing mode with write back the value of register does not change after the instruction is executed.
19. How many Indexed addressing modes do we have in ARM? Name them.
20. In LDR Rd,[Rm,#k}, what is the range of values that K can take?
21. In LDR Rd,[Rm,#k], what is the size of k in bits?
22. In which addressing mode the value of register does not change after the instruction is executed.
23. True or false. In the preindexed addressing mode only a fixed value can be used as offset.

24. True or false. In the preindexed addressing mode both fixed value and a register can be used as offset.
25. What IA, IB, DA and DB stands for?
26. Which instructions are used to load and store multiple registers?

Section 6.3: Stack and Stack Usage in ARM

27. True or false. In ARM the R13 is designated as stack pointer.
28. When BL is executed, how many locations of the stack are used?
29. When B is executed, how many locations of the stack are used?
30. In ARM, stack pointer is a__________ bit register.
31. Describe how the action associated with the return operation is performed in ARM.
32. Give the size of the stack in ARM.
33. In ARM, which address is saved when BL instruction is executed.
34. Explain the LDMIA operation and its impact on the SP.
35. Explain the LDMIB operation and its impact on the SP.
36. Explain the STMIA operation and its impact on the SP.
37. Explain the STMIB operation and its impact on the SP.
38. What is an ascending stack?
39. What is the difference between an empty and a full stack?
40. Write an instruction that stores R0 in a full descending stack.
41. Write an instruction that loads R9 from an empty descending stack.
42. Explain the difference between LDM and LDR instructions.
43. Explain how the difference between STM and STR instructions

Section 6.4: ARM Bit-Addressable Memory Region

44. Give the bit-addressable SRAM region address for generic ARM.
45. What bit addresses are assigned to byte address of 0x20000004?
46. What bit addresses are assigned to byte address of 0x20000010?
47. What bit addresses are assigned to byte address of 0x200FFFFF?
48. What bit addresses are assigned to byte address of 0x20000020?
49. What bit addresses are assigned to byte address of 0x40000008?
50. What bit addresses are assigned to byte address of 0x4000000C?
51. What bit addresses are assigned to byte address of 0x40000020?
52. The following are bit addresses. Indicate where each one belongs.

    (a) 0x2200004C (b) 0x22000068 (c) 0x22000080

    (d) 0x23FFFF80 (e) 0x23FFFF00 (f) 0x4200004C

    (g) 0x42000014 (h) 0x43FFFFF0 (i) 0x43FFFF00

53. Of the 4G bytes of memory locations in the ARM, how many of them are also assigned a bit address as well? Indicate which bytes those are.
54. True or false. The bit-addressable region cannot be accessed in byte.

55. True or false. The bit-addressable region cannot be accessed in word.
56. Write a program to see whether the D7 bit of RAM location 0x20000020 is high. If so, send a 1 to D1 of RAM location 0x20000000.
57. Write a program to see whether the D7 bit of I/O location 0x40000000 is low. If so, send a 0 to the D0 of location 0x400FFFFF.

Section 6.5: ADR, LDR, and PC Relative Addressing

58. Assuming that the instruction "LDR R2, [PC, #8] is located in address 0x300, calculate the address of the memory location which is accessed.
59. Using PC relative addressing mode, write an LDR instruction that accesses a memory location which is 0x20 bytes ahead of itself.
60. Why ADR is called pseudo-instruction?

Answers to Review Questions

Section 6.1

1. 4 bytes
2. Compilers ensure that codes are word aligned.
3. little endian
4. 1/66 MHz = 15.15 ns is the bus clock period. Since the bus cycle time of zero wait states is 2 clocks, we have 2 × 15.15 = 30.3 ns
5. 1/100 MHz = 10 ns is the bus clock period. 50 ns - 10 ns = 40 ns. The Number of WS is 40 ns / 10 ns = 4.
6. False, most of the ARM devices use little endian as default.

Section 6.2

1. Register
2. Preindexed, postindexed and preindexed with write back.
3. True
4. In the preindexed write back the calculated value is written back to the pointing register. That is not the case for preindexed mode.
5. !

Section 6.3

1. R13
2. The stack can be as big as its RAM
3. STM R13, {R5-R8}
   SUB R13, R13, #16
4. ADD R13, R13, #16
   LDM R13, {R5-R8}
5. It copies the contents of locations 0x40000000–0x4000000F into locations 0x50000000–0x5000000F using the LDM and STM instructions.

Section 6.4

1. False
2. False
3. False
4. 2MBytes; locations 0x20000000 to 0x200FFFFF of SRAM and 0x40000000 to 0x400FFFFF of GPIO

5.

```
    LDR   R0, =0x22000040
    LDR   R1, [R0]
    CMP   R1, #0
    BNE   L1
    ...
L1:
```

6.

(a) 0x23000030 - 0x22000000 = 0x1000030; 0x1000030 / 0x20 = 0x80001; thus it is in location 0x20000000 + 0x80001 = 0x20080001

(0x1000030 % 32) / 4 = (48 % 32) / 4 = 16 / 4 = 4; it is D4 of 0x20080001.

(b) 0x1000040 / 0x20 = 0x80002; it is in location 0x20080002

(0x1000040 % 0x20) / 4 = 0; it is D0 of location 0x20080002

(c) 0x1000048 / 0x20 = 80002; it is in location 0x20080002

(0x1000048 % 0x20) / 4 = 2; it is D2 of location 0x20080002

(d) 0x4200003C - 0x42000000 = 0x03C; 0x03C / 0x20 = 0x01

(0x3C % 0x20) / 4 = 0x1C / 4 = 7; it is D7 of 0x40000001

(e) 0x43FFFFFC – 0x42000000 = 0x1FFFFFC; 0x1FFFFFC / 0x20 = 0xFFFFF

(0x1FFFFFC % 0x20) / 4 = 0x1C / 4 = 7; D7 of 0x400FFFFF

Section 6.5

1. PC (R15)
2. ADR, To implement the LDR directive the value is stored in memory; as a result, it uses more memory while the ADR uses no memory.

Chapter 7: ARM Pipeline and CPU Evolution

This chapter will look at pipeline evolution in ARM while examining other CPU enhancements. In Section 7.1 the ARM's pipelines are studied. Section 7.2 explores various processors enhancements.

Section 7.1: ARM Pipeline Evolution

There are many ways available to processor designers to increase the processing power of the CPU. Here we list some of them that are used in ARM.

1. Increase the clock frequency of the chip. One drawback of this method is that the higher the frequency, the more the power consumption and the more difficult and expensive the design of the microprocessor and circuit board.
2. Increase the number of data buses to bring more information (code and data) into the CPU to be processed. For example, Von Neumann architecture in ARM7 has been replaced by Harvard architecture in newer versions. See Chapter 6.
3. Change the internal architecture of the CPU to overlap the execution of several instructions. This requires significant amount of circuit to implement. There are two trends for this option, pipeline and superscalar. In pipeline, the process of fetching and executing instructions is split into several smaller steps and these steps are done in parallel. In superscalar, the whole execution unit is duplicated so that instructions may be executed in parallel.
4. Combining more than one core in a single processor is another way of improving the speed of high end processers. Cortex-A series of ARM supports up to four cores.

More about pipelining

In the early CPUs everything is running in series. At any given moment, it is either fetching the instruction or executing it. It could not do both at the same time. While the buses were fetching the instructions or data, the CPU was sitting idle waiting for the instruction or data to arrive, and in the same way, when the CPU was executing an instruction, buses were sitting idle.

With pipelining, while the CPU is executing an instruction, the busses may be fetching the next instruction or data. This way at any given moment, more than instructions may be processed. See Figure 7-1.

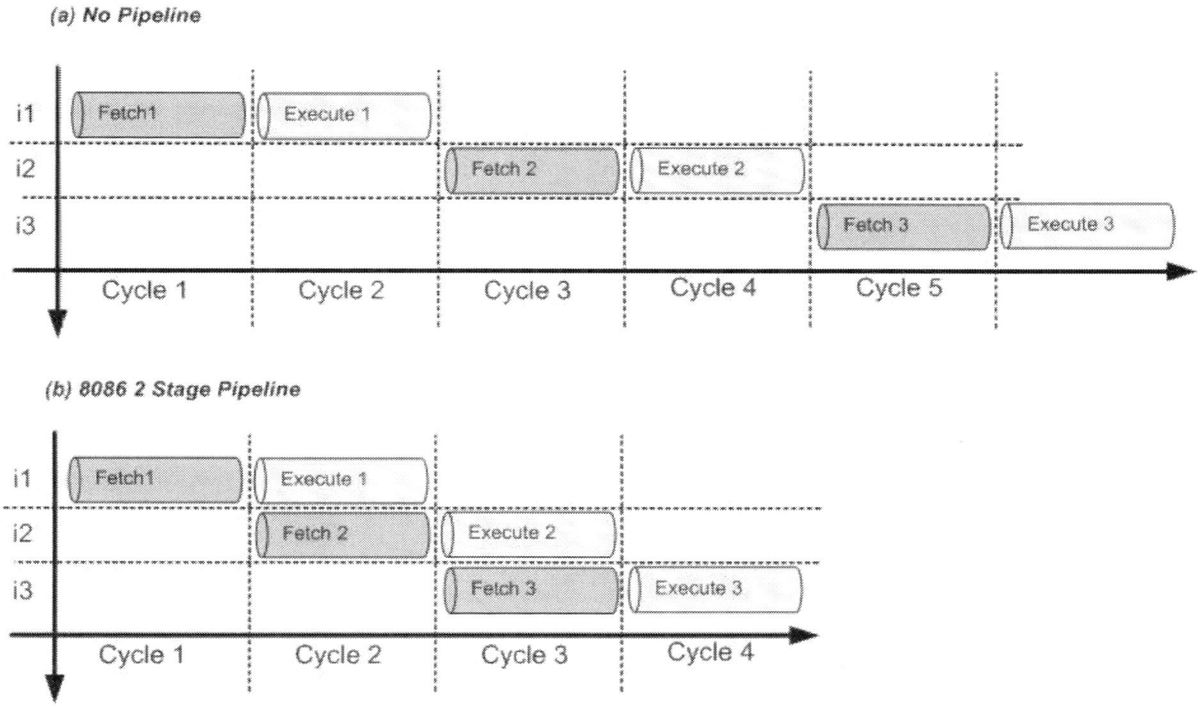

Figure 7-1: Non-Pipelined Instruction Execution vs. 2-stage Pipeline

The number of instructions being processed at a given time depends on the number of pipeline stages, commonly termed as the pipeline depth. Some designers use as many as 8 stages of pipelining. One limitation of pipelining is that the speed of the execution is limited to the slowest stage of the pipeline. Compare this to making pizza. You can split the process of making pizza into many stages, such as flattening the dough, putting on the toppings, and baking, but the process is limited to the slowest stage, baking, no matter how fast the rest of the stages are performed. What happens if we use two or three ovens for baking pizzas to speed up the process? This may work for making pizza but not always for executing instruction, since we must make sure that the sequence of instructions is kept intact and that there is no out-of-step execution in some cases. For example, if one instruction is modifying register R3 and the next instruction is using the data in R3, the execution of the second instruction must wait for the previous one to finish before it can start.

For the concept of pipelining to work, while executing one instruction, the following instructions are being fetched and decoded at the same time. In some circumstances, the CPU must flush out the pipeline. For example, when a branch (B, BL, BNE, BCS, and so on) instruction is executed, the CPU starts to fetch next instruction from a new memory location and the instructions in the pipeline that was fetched previously must be discarded. In this case, the execution unit needs to wait until the bus unit fetches the new instruction. This is called a branch penalty. The penalty is extra cycles to fetch and decode the instructions from the target location of the branch instead of executing the instructions already in the pipeline. Some of the newer CPUs have more stages in their pipeline. For example, a 3-stage pipeline may divide the code execution to Fetch, Decode and Execute stages. When the number of stages in a pipeline increases, more stages need be flushed out when a branch is taken. Examine Example 7-1 to see how branch penalty slows down the execution. Next, you will see how branch prediction may reduce the branch penalty.

Example 7-1

How many cycles does it take for a 3-stage pipelined CPU to run 3 iterations of the following code?

```
      MOV   R1, #0
L1    ADD   R2, R2, #1
      B     L1
      MOV   R3, #3
      MOV   R4, #4
```

Solution:

For the first instruction (MOV R1, #0), it takes 3 cycles to pass through the stages of pipeline and be executed. After the third cycle, one instruction is executed in each cycle. When the Branch instruction is executed in cycle 5, the CPU flushes the pipeline because the fetch and decode instruction in cycles 4 and 5 are not used. It causes two clock cycles of branch penalty. The same scenario happens each time the CPU executes a branch. As we can see in the figure, it takes 13 cycles to run 7 instructions.

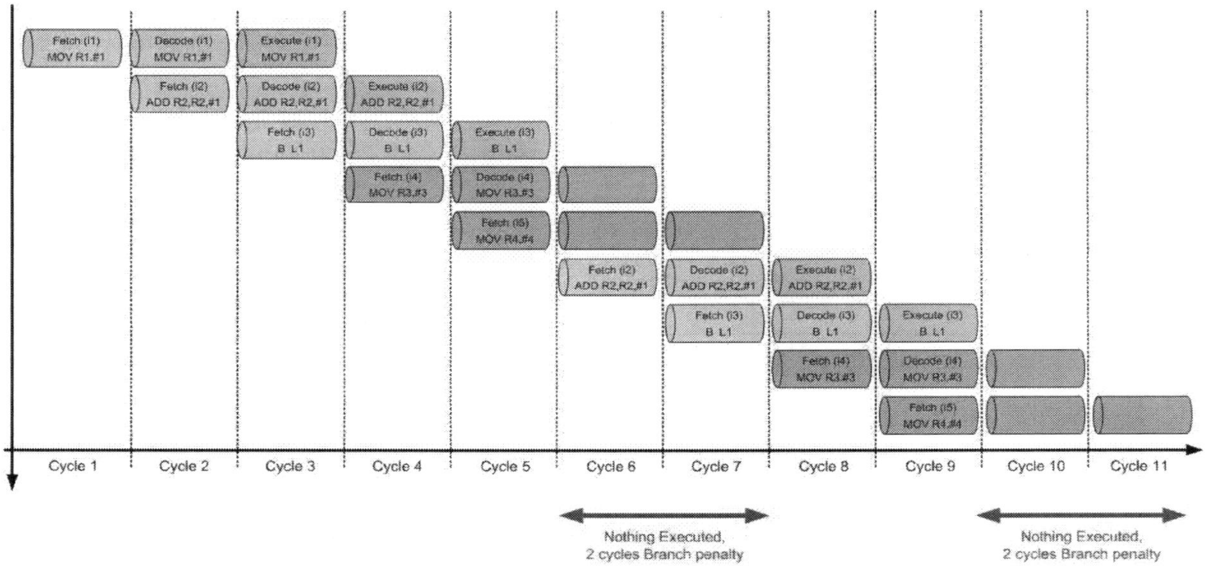

In the best case scenario, every cycle an instruction is executed, it takes 7 cycles to run 7 instructions. In the worst case scenario, each instruction takes three cycles and 7 instructions will take 21 cycles to complete. So even with branch penalty, 13 cycles are still much shorter than 21 cycles. There are ways to mitigate branch penalty. We will discuss one strategy often used by designer next.

Branch prediction

Some processors have the capability to fetch code from both possible locations of a branch and have them advanced through the pipelines. When the branch decision is made, the correct path is kept and the instructions in the wrong path is discarded from the pipeline.

Some CPUs make prediction of whether the branch will take place or not and fill the pipeline with the instructions from the predicted path. If the prediction is incorrect, the pipeline is flushed and the new instructions are fetched, otherwise, the pipeline keeps flowing without penalty. Remember, if there is no branch prediction strategy, the pipeline is in essence predicting that the branch will not take place. Any prediction strategy that yields better odds is an improvement over the default. You may wonder how we can predict whether the branch is going to take place or not. A very simple and effective strategy is assuming that backward branch is always taken and forward branch is always not taken. Backward branch is usually used in a loop that has many iterations. The chance of taking the branch backward is more often than not. On the other hand, a forward branch is often used to skip a few instructions in rare cases, therefore the branch is less often taken. There are more sophisticated strategies to predict branch direction and they are beyond the scope of this book.

See Example 7-2 for an example of how correct predictions of branch may improve the performance.

Example 7-2

Show how many cycles does it take for a 3-stage pipelined CPU to run 3 iterations of the code in Example 7-1. Assume that the branch prediction unit has predicted all branches correctly.

Solution:

It takes 9 cycles to run 7 instructions. In cycles 4 to 8 instructions are predicted by branch prediction unit.

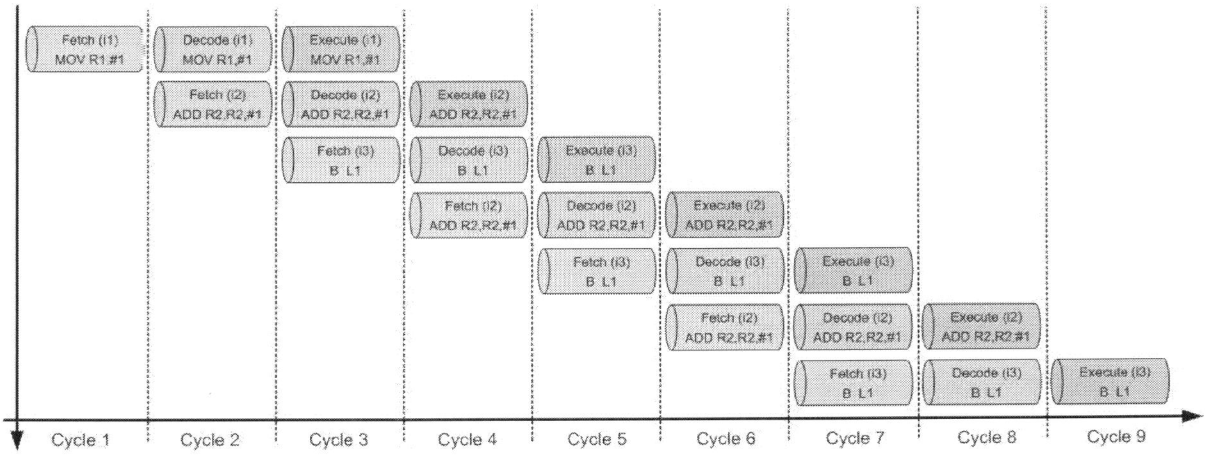

3-stage pipeline in ARM7

Since the introduction of the 8086 microprocessor in 1978, processor designers have come to rely more and more on the pipelining to increase the processing power of the CPU. ARM7 used the concept of pipelining with three stages of fetch, decode, and execute. See Example 7-3.

Example 7-3

Show how the following code is executed in ARM7.

```
MOV   R4, R5
ADD   R1, R2, R3
SUB   R6, R7, R8
```

Solution:

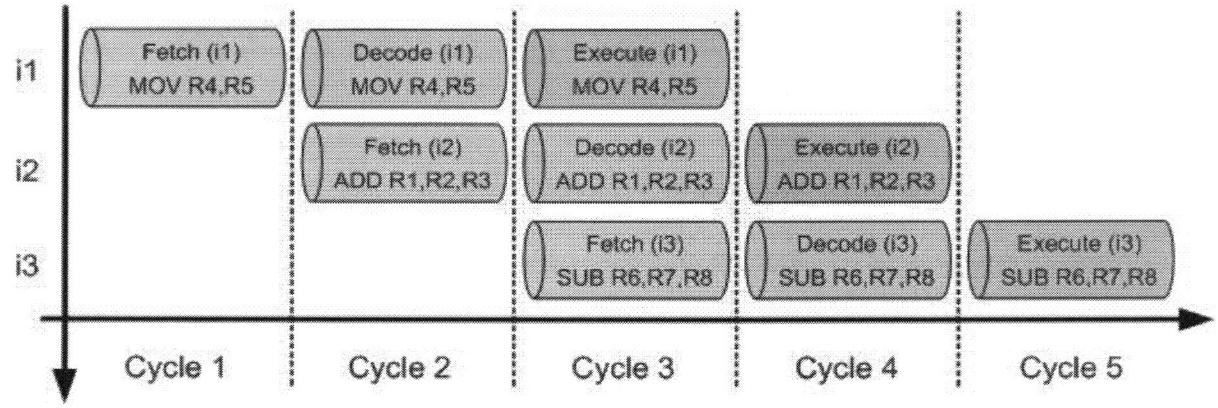

5-stage pipeline in ARM9

As we mentioned earlier the ARM7 has a 3-stage pipeline. As shown in Figure 7-2, the ARM9 has extended the pipeline to 5 stages. They are:

1. Fetch
2. Decode
3. Execute
4. Memory
5. Write

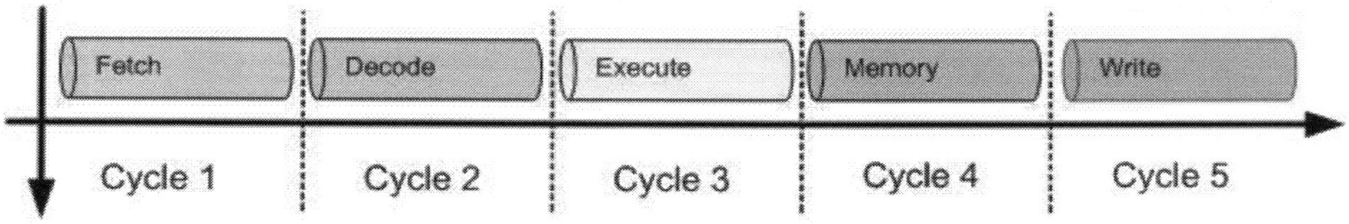

Figure 7- 2: 5-Stage Pipeline in ARM9

Fetch: In the Fetch stage the instructions are fetched from memory and placed in the queue and wait to be decoded. In this stage the Program Counter (PC) is also incremented by 4 since the ARM instructions are 4-byte long.

Decode: In the decode stage the instruction is decoded and the register file is also accessed to get everything ready for the Execute stage.

Execute: In this stage, any effective address calculation and sign extending of a byte or a half-word are done. In the instructions such as Load and Store this stage gets everything ready for the next stage of memory access. In instructions such as "ADD R1, R2, R3" in which all the resources needed for the execution of the instruction are ready before it comes to this stage, the registers are added and it goes directly to the write-back stage to write the result to the register file.

Memory: For instructions such as Load and Store in which external memory accesses are needed, the memory stage fetches the data from the external memory and has the data inside the CPU ready for the next stage of the write-back. If an instruction does not need to access memory, this stage is bypassed and the result is forwarded to the last stage of write-back.

Write: Also called write-back is the stage in which the instruction is completed by writing the result to the register file and retiring the instruction. As we just stated, if an instruction does not need to access memory, write-back is the stage right after the execute stage, meaning for many instructions we really have only 4 stages in the pipeline.

3-stage vs. 5-stage pipeline

In the 3-stage pipeline of ARM7, the execution, the memory access, and the writing of the result to register file are all performed by the Execute stage. In the 5-stage pipeline, the CPU decouples the memory access and execute stage. With the two new stages of memory and write-back, the ARM9 increases the processing power of the CPU by allowing the CPU to work concurrently on 5 instructions instead of 3 instructions at a given time. This is a major enhancement of the ARM9 over ARM7.

Review Questions

1. What is pipelining?
2. What is the speed limitation of pipeline?
3. What is superscalar?
4. True or false. The 5-stage pipeline has better performance than the 3-stage pipeline.
5. Give the names of the 5 stages in the pipeline of ARM9.

Section 7.2: Other CPU Enhancements

There are many other ways available to microprocessor designers to increase the processing power of the CPU. Next, we examine some of them.

Superscalar CPUs

Another unique feature of the many of new CPUs is its superscalar architecture. Superscalar CPU has multiple execution units. Using the pizza making analogy from the previous section, in addition to using several ovens to bake pizza that may result in out-of-order execution, we add more pizza makers so each oven has a full team of personnel to work on the dough and add the topping. This eliminates the possibility of out-of-order execution for each execution unit.

A large number of transistors are used to put more than one execution unit inside the CPU. As the instructions are fetched, they are issued to these execution units. Figure 7-3 shows the concept of superscalar.

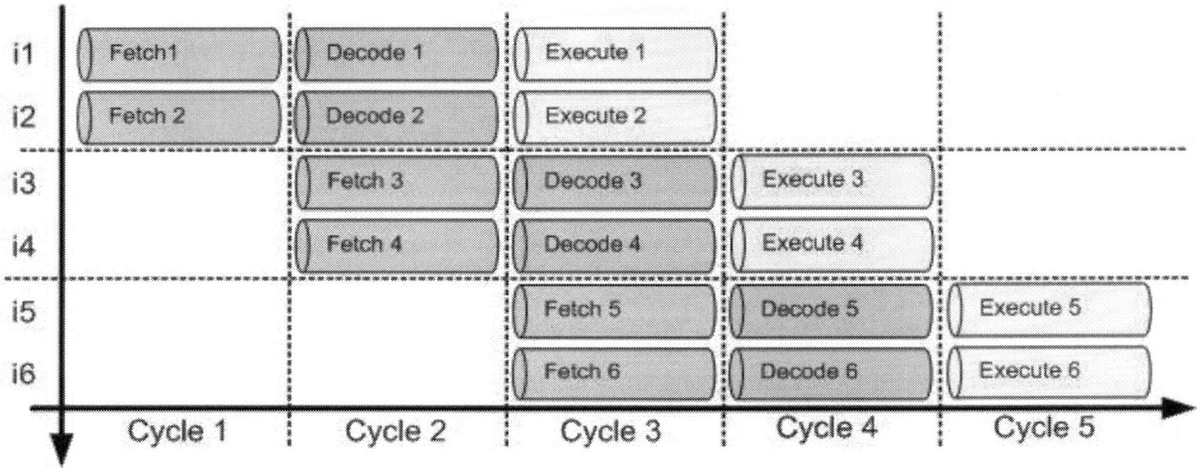

Figure 7- 3: Superscalar CPUs

Issuing two instructions at the same time to different execution units can work only if the execution of one does not depend on the other one, in other words, if there is no data dependency. As an example, look at the following instructions.

```
ADD   R1, R2, R3
SUB   R4, R1, R5
AND   R6, R7, R8
MOV   R9, R10
```

In the above code, the ADD and SUB instructions cannot be issued to two execution units since R1, the destination of the first instruction, is used immediately by the second instruction. This is called *read-after-write dependency* since the SUB instruction needs to read the R1 contents, but it must wait until after the ADD is finished writing the result into R1. The problem is that ADD will not write into R1 until the last stage of the pipeline. This prevents the SUB instruction from advancing in the pipeline, therefore causing the pipeline to stall until the ADD finishes writing the result to the register and then the

SUB instruction can advance through the pipeline. This kind of data dependency raises the clock count for the SUB instruction. What if the instructions are rescheduled as in the follow sequence?

```
ADD   R1, R2, R3
AND   R6, R7, R8
SUB   R4, R1, R5
MOV   R9, R10
```

If they are rescheduled as shown above, each can be issued to separate execution units, allowing parallel execution of both instructions by two different units of the CPU. Since the clock count for each instruction is one, having two execution units leads to executing two instructions at the same time, thereby using only one clock cycle for two instructions. In the case of the above program, if it is run on the CPU with superscalar it will take only 2 clocks instead of 4, assuming that two instructions are paired together. This reordering of instructions to take advantage of the two internal execution units of the CPU can be done by compiler or CPU itself and is called *instruction scheduling*. Currently, some compilers are being equipped to do instruction scheduling to remove dependencies. The process of issuing two instructions to the two execution units is commonly referred to as *instruction pairing* or *dual issue*.

Superpipelined and superscalar

Some microprocessors use a 10-stage pipeline for the CPU. In contrast to the 5-pipestage, although each pipe stage of the 10-pipestage performs less work, there are more stages. This means that in such processors, more instructions can be worked on and finished at a time. These CPUs with their 10- or 12-stage pipeline are referred to as *superpipelined*. Since they also have multiple execution units capable of working in parallel, they are also superscalar. Another advantage of the pipelined concept is that it can achieve a higher clock rate (frequency) with the given transistor technology. They also use what is called out-of-order execution to increase the performance of the CPU. This is explained next.

Decoupling and out-of-order execution

In CPU architecture, when one of the pipeline stages is stalled, the prior stages of fetch and decode are also stalled. In other words, the fetch stage stops fetching instructions if the execution stage is stalled, due, for example, to a delay in memory access. This dependency of fetch and execution has to be resolved in order to increase CPU performance. That is exactly what many designers have done with the CPU and is called *decoupling* the fetch and execution phases of the instructions. In these processors, instructions are fetched from memory and placed into a pool called the *instruction pool*. See Figure 7-4.

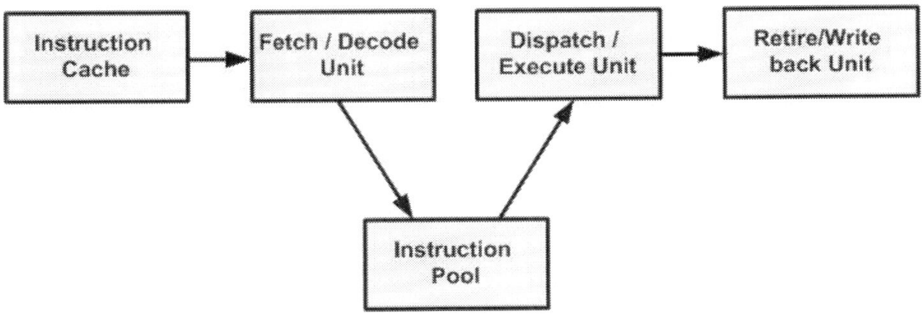

Figure 7- 4: CPU Instruction Execution

This fetch/decode of the instructions is done in the same order as the program was coded by the programmer (or compiler). However, when they are placed in the instruction pool they can be executed in any order as long as the data needed is available. In other words, if there is no dependency, the instructions may be executed out of order, not in the same order as the programmer coded them. Such a speculative execution can go 20–30 instructions deep into the program. It is the job of the retire unit to provide the results to the programmer's (visible) registers (e.g., R0, R1) according to the order in which the instructions were coded. Again, it is important to note that the instructions are fetched in the same order that they were coded, but executed out of order if there is no dependency, and ultimately retired in the same order as they were coded. This out-of-order execution can boost performance in many cases. Look at Example 7-4.

Example 7-4

The following ARM code (a) sets the pointer for three different arrays, and the counter value, (b) gets each element of ARRAY_1, adds a fixed value of 100 to it, and stores the result in ARRAY_2, and (c) complements the element and stores it in ARRAY_3. Analyze the execution of the code in light of the out-of-order execution and branch prediction capabilities of an ARM CPU.

```
(i1)          LDR   R1, =ARRAY_1  ;load pointer
(i2)          LDR   R2, =ARRAY_2  ;load pointer
(i3)          LDR   R3, =ARRAY_3  ;load pointer
(i4)          MOV   R4, #COUNT    ;load the counter
(i5)   AGAIN  LDR   R5, [R1]      ;load the element
(i6)          ADD   R5, R5, #100  ;add the fix value
(i7)          ADD   R1, R1, #4    ;update the pointer
(i8)          STR   R5, [R2]      ;store the result
(i9)          ADD   R2, R2, #4    ;update the pointer
(i10)         MVN   R5, R5        ;complement the result
(i11)         STR   R5, [R3]      ;and store it
(i12)         ADD   R3, R3, #4    ;update the pointer
(i13)         SUBS  R4, R4, #4    ;
(i14)         BNE   AGAIN         ;stay in the loop
(i15)
```

Solution:

The fetch/decode unit fetches and puts instructions into the pool. Since there is no dependency for instructions i1 through i4, they are dispatched, executed, and retired. Notice that the pointer values of i1 to i4 are immediate values; therefore, they are embedded into the instruction when the fetch/decode unit gets them. Now i5 is a memory fetch that can take many clock cycles, depending on whether the needed data is located in cache or main memory. Meanwhile i6, i8, i10, and i11 must wait until the data are available. However, i7, i9, and i12 can be executed out of order. More importantly, the BNE instruction is predicted to go to the target address of AGAIN and i5, i6, ... are dispatched once more for the next iteration. This time the memory fetch will take very few clock cycles since in the previous data fetch, the CPU read some bytes of data into the cache. This process will go on until the last round of looping where R4 becomes zero and falls through to i15. At this time, due to mis-prediction, the instructions i5, i6, i7, ... (start of the loop) are removed and the whole pipeline restarts with instructions starting at i15 and so on.

Due to the fact that memory fetches (due to cache misses) can take many clock cycles and result in underutilization of the CPU, out-of-order execution is a way of finding something to do for the CPU. Simply put, the idea of out-of-order execution is to look deep into the stream of instructions and find the ones that can be executed ahead of others, provided that resources are available. Again, it is important to note that these processors will not immediately provide the results of out-of-order executions to programmer-visible registers such as R0, R1, and so on, since it must maintain the original order of the code. Instead, the results of out-of-order executions are stored in the pool and wait to be retired in the same order as they were coded. Therefore, programmer-visible registers are updated in the same sequence as expected by the programmer.

Register renaming

There are some cases in which instructions are not really dependent on each other but there is a kind of implicit dependency called *register dependency*. See Example 7-5.

Example 7-5

For the following code, indicate the instructions that can be executed in parallel or out of order.

```
(i1) LDR  R4, [R2]        ; load R4 from memory pointed to by R2
(i2) ADD  R3, R4, R7      ; R4+R7--->R3
(i3) ADD  R6, R8, R10     ; R8+R10--->R6
(i4) SUB  R5, R1, R9      ; R1-R9--->R5
(i5) ADD  R6, R12, #1     ; R12+1---->R6
```

Solution:

Instruction i2 cannot be executed until the data is brought into R4 from memory (either cache or main memory DRAM). Therefore, i2 is dependent on i1 and must wait until the R4 register has the data. However, instructions i3 and i4 can be executed out of order and parallel with each other since there is no dependency among them. Notice that i5 is not really dependent on i3 because i5 does not use any of data generated by i3. But i5 and i3 cannot be executed out of order or in parallel because R6 is modified by both of i3 and i5. This kind of dependency is called register dependency and is solved by a method called register renaming.

In the following code none of the instructions can be executed in parallel because of using R1 in all instructions:

```
MOV   R1, #5
ADD   R3, R1, #2
MOV   R1, #6
ADD   R4, R1, #2
```

If you examine the above code carefully you will see that the first two lines of code are independent from the second two lines of code and we can remove the implicit dependency by changing R1 to another register such as R2 in the last two lines of code:

```
MOV   R1, #5
ADD   R3, R1, #2
MOV   R2, #6
ADD   R4, R2, #2
```

Renaming the registers before issuing the instructions to execution unit is done in many of new advanced CPU and it is called register renaming.

Putting them all together in an ARM CPU

In Figure 7-5 you can see a top-level diagram of the ARM Cortex A9 processor. It has most of the parts discussed in this chapter.

Bus frequency vs. internal frequency in CPU

Frequently you may see an advertisement for a 1-GHz or 2-GHz CPUs. It is important to note that the stated frequency is the internal frequency of the CPU and not the bus frequency. This is due to the fact that designing a 1-GHz circuit board is very difficult and expensive. Such a design requires a very fast logic family and memory in addition to a massive simulation to avoid crosstalk and signal radiation. At the same time, most of the peripherals and the memory cannot run at that high speed either.

Review Questions

1. True or false. The branch prediction task is performed by circuitry inside the CPU.
2. Why some CPUs are called superscalar processor?
3. Instruction scheduling is done by ________.
4. Out of order execution is arranged by ________.

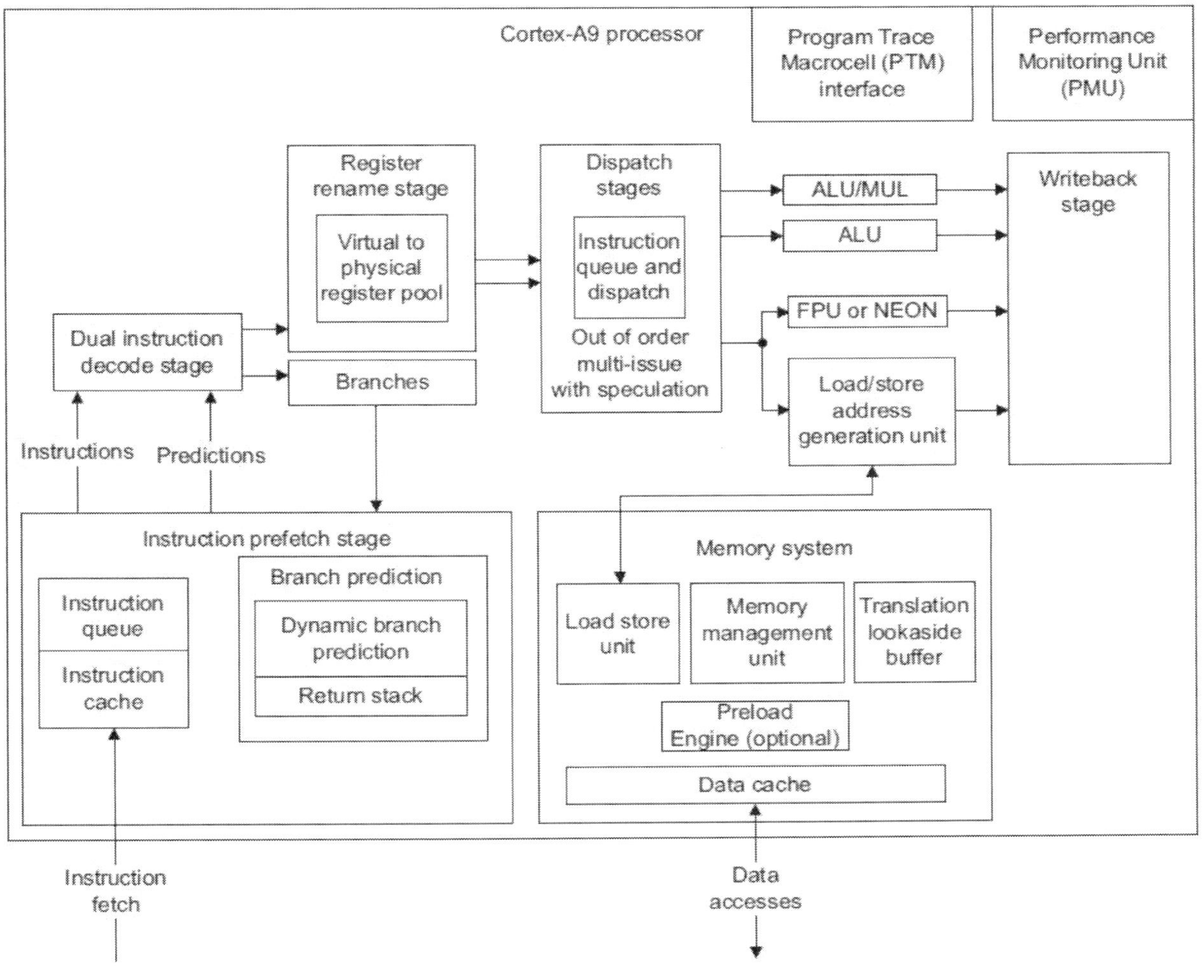

Figure 7- 5: Top-level diagram of the ARM Cortex A9 processor

Problems

Section 7.1: ARM Pipeline Evolution

1. The ARM7 uses a pipeline of _______ stages.
2. Give the names of the pipeline stages in the ARM7
3. The ARM9 uses a pipeline of _______ stages.
4. Give the names of the pipeline stages in the ARM9

Section 7.2: Other CPU Enhancements

5. The number of pipeline stages in a pipeline system is ________ (less, more) than in a superscalar system.
6. Which has one or more execution units, pipeline or superscalar?
7. Which part of on-chip cache in the ARM is write protected, data or code?

8. What is instruction pairing, and when can it happen?
9. What is data dependency, and how is it avoided?
10. True or false. Instructions are fetched according to the order in which they were written.
11. True or false. Instructions are executed according to the order in which they were written.
12. True or false. Instructions are retired according to the order in which they were written.
13. The visible registers R0, R1, and so on, are updated by which unit of the CPU?
14. True or false. Among the instructions, STRs (store) are never executed out of order.

Answers to Review Questions

Section 7.1

1. In pipelining, the process of fetching and executing instructions is split into several small steps and these steps are done in parallel. In this way, the executions of several instructions are overlapped.
2. The speed of the execution is limited to the slowest stage of the pipeline.
3. In superscaling, the entire execution unit has been doubled
4. True
5. Fetch, decode, execute, memory, write back

Section 7.2

1. True
2. Since they have two or more execution units (pipelines) capable of executing multiple instructions within one clock cycle.
3. circuitry inside the CPU and the compiler
4. the CPU

Chapter 8: ARM and Thumb Instructions

The original ARM instructions were all 32-bit long. There are certainly advantages of having all the instructions of the same size and 32 bits are more than enough to cover all the needs of encoding the instructions except the instructions with 32-bit immediate data. The only issue is that the programs with 32-bit instructions occupy much more memory than the programs using 16-bit or 8-bit data. The increased mobile applications of ARM Cortex-A and Cortex-R processors and the small microcontrollers using ARM Cortex-M core all demand smaller footprint of program memory. Smaller memory not only reduces the cost of the system it also saves the power consumption which is a critical constraint of a battery power device.

The Thumb instruction set was created to answer the demand for smaller program size. All the Thumb instructions are 16-bit long. With shorter instructions, some of the features of the instructions have to be eliminated and the ranges of the immediate values reduced. To accomplish the same task, sometimes more than one Thumb instructions are needed to replace an ARM instruction. In case an ARM instruction is replaced by two Thumb instructions, the total memory usage still have no loss. So the overall saving of the memory could be around 35%.

It might be necessary to have some clarifications here. When we say 32-bit instructions and 16-bit instructions in this chapter, we are talking about the instruction encoding length. A 32-bit instruction here means the instruction is encoded by 32 bits and a 16-bit instruction means the instruction is encoded by 16 bits. In other context, 32-bit instruction might imply the instruction operates on 32-bit data and 16-bit instruction operates on 16-bit data, which is not what we discuss in this chapter. Besides the new 64-bit ARM architecture, all the ARM and Thumb instructions are capable of operating on 32-bit registers and 32-bit data in the memory.

Section 8.1: The Thumb Instructions

To fit the instructions into 16 bits, restrictions are imposed on the instructions.

Register usages

There are 16 registers in the ARM CPU. The top three registers have dedicated special usages (SP, LR, and PC). The rest of the 13 registers are general purpose registers. To encode 16 registers, 4 bits are necessary. ARM data processing instructions are three-operand instruction, so to encode three registers, 12 bits are needed. That leaves only four bits, too few to encode the rest of the instructions. Two approaches were taken to reduce the register encodings in the instructions: Thumb instructions are limited to two register operands and three bits are used to encode the registers. These reduce the bit usage for register operand from 12 (3 x 4) bits down to 6 (2 x 3) bits.

The data processing instructions in Thumb may have only two register operands, one of the source registers must be the same as the destination register such as:

```
ADDS R4, R4, R5   ; add R5 to R4 and set flags in CPSR
```

The first 8 registers (R0 – R7) are called the low registers and the other 8 registers (R8 – R15) are called high registers. When three bits are used for register encoding, they can only address 8 registers so the low registers are used. There are very few Thumb instructions that use the high registers. They are ADD, BX, CMP, and MOV.

Usage of the barrel shifter

In the ARM CPU, a barrel shifter is situated between the second operand source registers and the ALU. The content of the source can be shifted by up to 31 bits before it is operated by the ALU. The following instruction shifts R2 left by 6 bits then add it to R1.

```
ADD R1, R1, R2, LSL #6
```

In Thumb 16-bit instruction, there are no bits left to specify the shift so the content of the source register always bypasses the barrel shifter. You will not be able to specify a shift with the source register.

Immediate Data Range Reduced

Immediate data is the literal value encoded with the instruction. Reducing the instruction from 32-bit to 16-bit format limits the number of bits that can be used for immediate data.

The immediate data in ARM data processing instructions consists of 8-bit data and 4-bit rotate number for a total of 12 bits. The 16-bit Thumb instruction has only 8-bit immediate data without any rotation available.

We mentioned earlier that Thumb data processing instructions may have only two register operands. They could have immediate data in addition to the two registers but there are only three bits left in the instruction for the immediate data so the range is limited to 0-7 like:

```
ADDS R1, R2, #6     ; add 6 to R2, store sum in R1 and set
```

The logical instructions in Thumb are not allowed to have immediate data at all. See the following examples.

Example 8-1

Rewrite the following ARM instruction in Thumb.

```
ADDS    R1, R2, #100
```

Solution:

Thumb ADD instruction can have only three bits for immediate data, which is not enough for the immediate value 100. Furthermore, Thumb data processing instructions cannot have three operands. The immediate data needs to be moved to the destination register first then the other source register is added to the destination register.

```
MOVS    R1, #100
ADDS    R1, R2
```

Example 8-2

Rewrite the following ARM logical instruction in Thumb.

```
ANDS    R4, #0x00FF
```

Solution:

Thumb logical instructions do not allow immediate data. The immediate data needs to be moved to an unused register first.

```
MOVS    R5, #0x00FF
ANDS    R4, R5
```

Processor Status Register Update

The data processing instructions may update the NZCV bits (Negative, Zero, Carry, oVerflow) of the current processor status register (CPSR) according to the result of the instruction execution. In ARM instructions, the default is no CPSR update. To update the CPSR by the instruction, an 'S' suffix should be added to the instruction such as ADDS. If no 'S' suffix is added, the instruction execution will not affect the NZCV bits of the CPSR. This is done to improve the performance of pipeline.

In Thumb, the data processing instructions always update the NZCV bits of CPSR. It seems that there is no point of adding the 'S' suffix to the Thumb instruction since it is not an option. In fact, the older assemblers (and some of the current ones) do not require the 'S' suffix in the assembly source file. The Unified Assembly Language (UAL) imposes the use of 'S' suffix on Thumb instructions.

Conditional Execution

All the ARM instructions can be executed conditionally, that is the instruction is executed only when the condition is met by the NZCV bits of the CPSR. To specify that an instruction is conditionally executed, the abbreviation of the condition such as EQ, NE, CS, CC, ... etc. are added as suffix to the instruction. For example, SUBCS means the SUB instruction is executed only when the 'C' bit of CPSR is set otherwise the instruction is not executed.

In Thumb, the only instruction that may be executed conditionally is the branch instruction like BNE, BPL.

Example 8-3

Rewrite the following ARM instruction in Thumb.

```
SUBNE   R1, R1, R2
```

Solution:

The only instruction that may be executed conditionally is branch.

```
        BEQ     skip
        SUB     R1, R1, R2
skip:
```

Branch Range

The ARM branch and conditional branch instructions (B, BL) may carry 24 bits immediate data to specify the offset of the branch destination from the current program counter, as such, they have the range of ±32MB. Obviously, 16-bit Thumb instructions will not be able to fit that many bits of offset in the instruction.

With Thumb, branch instructions B, BL carry 11 bit offset and has a range of ±2KB while conditional branch instructions carry only 8 bit offset with the range of -252 to +258. To deal with shorter conditional branch range, programs should be written in short functions so that the branch destinations can always be reached. Between the functions, the BL instruction is used. The branch with link, BL, instruction is a rare 32-bit instruction in Thumb (or is encoded in a two 16-bit instruction pair) and has a range of ±4MB.

Another way to branch to a long distance is to use BX instruction with register offset such as "BX R0".

Data Transfer Addressing Mode

The available addressing mode in Thumb is a subset of ARM.

For register indirect with immediate offset (such as LDR R1, [R2, #24]), the ARM instructions allow 12 bits of signed offset (positive and negative offset). But in Thumb using general purpose registers, only 5 bits are allocated for offset and only positive offsets are allowed. If PC or SP are used as the indirect register, 8 bits are allocated for offset.

To make the most use of the bits allocated for offset, Thumb requires that the offsets are aligned to the size of the transfer. In word transfer instructions, a byte offset of 120 is stored as 30 (instead of 120 byte offset, 30 word offset is used). Therefore, with 5 bits (0-31) the possible offset can have range of 0-124 for word transfer and with 8 bits (0-255) the possible offset can have range of 0-1020 for word transfer. At the meantime, writing offset that is not aligned to the transfer size is prohibited.

One implication of shorter offset range that may not be obvious is the use of pseudo-instruction to load a 32-bit literal value like LDR R4, =12345678. The assembler will put the literal value at the end of the file (which is called the *literal pool*) and use the instruction LDR R4, [PC, #offset] to load the value into the register. If the file becomes too long, the offset may exceed the limit of 1020 (maximum offset using PC). To work around this problem, you may designate a location in the middle of the source file for the assembler to put the current literal pool for all the current literal values. The assembler directive to specify the location of the current literal pool is LTORG in Keil and .pool in GNU. You may designate as many literal pools as you like but they must be between functions where program execution does not cross.

Thumb does not support auto-increment with write-back mode. Pre-increment with write-back instructions like LDR R0, [R2, R3]! are not allowed, neither are post-increment instructions like LDR R1, [R2], #12 since post-increment instructions always perform write back.

Invoking the shifter for the register offset like LDR R1, [R2, R3, LSL #2] is not allowed in Thumb mode.

Example 8-4

Rewrite the following ARM instructions in Thumb.

```
LDR R0, [R2, R3]!
LDR R1, [R2], #12
```

Solution:

Since Thumb instructions does not do write-back for auto-increment, the write-back has to be done in separate instruction.

```
ADDS R2, R3
LDR  R0, [R2]
LDR  R1, [R2]
ADDS R2, #12
```

Stack Operation

ARM has instructions for multiple register transfer with auto-increment and auto-decrement that allows the program to use any one of the general registers to be used as a stack pointer. Thus has multiple stack pointers and multiple stacks.

The only multiple register transfer instructions supported by Thumb are STM and LDM (which are equivalent of STMIA and LDMIA). Because both instructions do auto-increment afterward, these store/load multiple pair cannot be used for stack operation.

To create a stack using Thumb instructions, we have to use the dedicated stack operation PUSH and POP. The PUSH {register list} does the same as STMDB SP!, {register list} and the POP {register list} does the same as LDMIA SP!, {register list}. So, in Thumb there can have only one active stack at a time and the dedicated stack pointer SP register must be used.

Performance

The obvious benefit of Thumb instruction set is the reduction of the program memory usage, which could be an important factor for some systems. The other benefit of Thumb instruction is on the system with 16-bit instruction memory bus. In these systems, 16-bit Thumb instructions only need one memory access while 32-bit ARM instructions require two memory cycles.

There are negative performance impacts of using Thumb instructions. First, because the Thumb instructions are more restricted than the equivalent of the ARM instructions, sometimes we need additional instructions to accomplish the same task as explained previously. Most of the instructions take one clock cycle to execute. Having an additional instruction means one extra clock cycle to execute.

The other impact is the increase of pipeline hazard because all the Thumb data processing instructions may alter the CPSR. The conditional branch instruction has to wait for all the previous data processing instructions to clear the pipeline. This impact should be minor because typically the conditional branch instruction is right after the instruction that sets the CPSR bits.

Review Questions

1. Thumb instructions are _____-bit wide while ARM instructions are _____-bit wide.
2. True or False. If an ARM program takes 4K bytes of ROM space, the Thumb version of the same programs takes approximately 2K-3K bytes but definitely less than 4K bytes.
3. Compare the maximum size of immediate data in ARM and Thumb.
4. True or false. Although the ARM registers are 32-bit wide, Thumb uses only the lower 16-bit of it.
5. The thumb instructions are (subset, superset) of ARM.

Section 8.2: Thumb-2 Technology

The Thumb-2 technology was introduced to bring the Thumb instruction set to cover all the ARM instructions in their entirety. When an ARM instruction cannot be encoded in 16-bit, it is encoded in 32-bit. In doing so, the restrictions on the Thumb instructions are eliminated and no additional instructions need to be added and therefore improves the performance of the program while preserving the program memory saving.

With the Thumb-2 technology, the programmer may write the assembly code in ARM and have the code assembled into Thumb-2 instructions without change. ARM Cortex-M3, M4, and M7 implemented the Thumb-2 technology. The ARM assembly programs can be reassembled and run on them. On the other hand, ARM Cortex-M0 and M0+ only implemented the 16-bit Thumb instructions. ARM assembly programs need to be rewritten to run on them.

Although the Thumb instructions may be encoded in 32-bit with Thumb-2, their encodings are not the same as the ARM instruction encodings. One distinct difference is the encoding of the immediate data in data processing instructions. Recall ARM data processing instructions allows 8-bit immediate data with even bits or right rotate. The Thumb-2 data processing instructions allows 8-bit immediate data with any number of bits left shift, even or odd. In addition, they allow repetitive byte patterns 0x00XY00XY, 0xXY00XY00, and 0xXYXYXYXY.

The Thumb-2 technology allows the mixture of 16-bit encoding and 32-bit encoding. This poses a new demand for the CPU – the instruction fetch has to handle unaligned 32-bit instructions in the memory, that is the 32-bit instructions stored in the memory not aligned on the 32-bit word boundary.

In the following example the same program is written using ARM, Thumb, and Thumb-2 instructions. See the codes and compare the disassembled programs.

Example 8-5

In this example, a subroutine to enable the coprocessor is implemented in three different processors using three different encoding of the instructions.

ARM Instructions

Here are the five lines of code in ARM7 using LPC2368 as the platform.

```
LDR     R0, =0xE000ED88
LDR     R1, [R0]
ORR     R1, R1, #0xF00000
STR     R1, [R0]
BX      LR
```

In the disassembled code below, you will see that each instruction is encoded in a 32-bit word. The sixth line is the literal pool that supplies the immediate data for the first instruction. A total of 24 bytes are used.

```
0x00000000  E59F000C  LDR    R0,[PC,#0x000C]
0x00000004  E5901000  LDR    R1,[R0]
0x00000008  E381160F  ORR    R1,R1,#0x00F00000
0x0000000C  E5801000  STR    R1,[R0]
0x00000010  E12FFF1E  BX     R14
0x00000014  E000ED88  DCD    0xE000ED88
```

Thumb Instructions

For Thumb instruction, an ARM Cortex M0+ (NXP MKL25Z) is used as the platform. To perform the same task in Thumb code, some instructions need to be modified. First Thumb code does not take immediate data for "ORR" so the third instruction has to be expanded into three instructions. Secondly, the data processing instructions MOVS, LSLS, ORRS need to have the 'S' suffix.

```
LDR     R0, =0xE000ED88
LDR     R1, [R0]
MOVS    R2, #0xF
LSLS    R2, #20
ORRS    R1, R1, R2
STR     R1, [R0]
BX      LR
```

In the disassembled code below, you see each instruction is translated into a 16-bit code. The last two lines are the literal pool that supplies the immediate data for the first instruction. The line before them is a two byte padding to make sure the literal pool aligns at a 32-bit word boundary. A total of 20 bytes are used compared to 24 bytes in ARM but 7 instructions instead of 5 instructions are needed.

```
0x00000008 4803      LDR     r0,[pc,#12]   ; @0x00000018
0x0000000A 6801      LDR     r1,[r0,#0x00]
0x0000000C 220F      MOVS    r2,#0x0F
0x0000000E 0512      LSLS    r2,r2,#20
0x00000010 4311      ORRS    r1,r1,r2
0x00000012 6001      STR     r1,[r0,#0x00]
0x00000014 4770      BX      lr
0x00000016 0000      DCW     0x0000
0x00000018 ED88      DCW     0xED88
0x0000001A E000      DCW     0xE000
```

Thumb2 Instructions

For Thumb2 instruction, an ARM Cortex M4 (TI TM4C123) is used as the platform. For the Thumb2 code, the original five ARM instructions can be used.

```
LDR     R0, =0xE000ED88
LDR     R1, [R0]
ORR     R1, R1, #0xF00000
STR     R1, [R0]
BX      LR
```

As you see in the disassembled code below, line 1, 2, 4, and 5 are identical to the 16-bit Thumb code above. When the ORR instruction in line 3 could not be coded in 16-bit Thumb code, a 32-bit code is generated. This 32-bit code is different from the 32-bit ARM code above for the same instruction.

The last two lines are the literal pool. Since the literal pool starts at a 32-bit word boundary, no padding was added. With Thumb2, only 16 bytes are used and still maintaining 5 instructions. It saves the code space without sacrificing the performance.

```
0x00000008 4802       LDR     r0,[pc,#8]   ; @0x00000014
0x0000000A 6801       LDR     r1,[r0,#0x00]
0x0000000C F4410170   ORR     r1,r1,#0xF00000
0x00000010 6001       STR     r1,[r0,#0x00]
0x00000012 4770       BX      lr
0x00000014 ED88       DCW     0xED88
0x00000016 E000       DCW     0xE000
```

Instruction Decoding

Because the Thumb instruction set is a subset of ARM instruction set, there is not a Thumb instruction decoder, rather a mapping circuit is used to map each Thumb instruction to an ARM instruction for the ARM decoder. The same decoder decodes the ARM instruction fetched from the memory when the processor is in ARM state or from the Thumb-ARM instruction mapping circuit when in Thumb state.

ARM Cortex-M cores accept only the Thumb instructions while ARM Cortex-A and Cortex-R accept both ARM and Thumb instructions. Cortex-M0 and Cortex-M0+ use only 16-bit Thumb instructions. Cortex-M3, M4, and M7 use 16-bit and 32-bit Thumb-2 instructions.

Switch between ARM state and Thumb state

ARM Cortex-A and Cortex-R run both ARM instructions and Thumb instructions. When decoding ARM instructions, the instruction fetch feeds the decoder directly. When Thumb instructions are fetched, the CPU need to decide whether it is a 32-bit instruction or a 16-bit instruction. If the instruction is 16-bit in a 32-bit memory bus, it needs to pick the high half-word or the low half-word. The instruction then needs to be mapped to ARM instruction before it is decoded. Because the instruction fetch paths are different for ARM instructions and Thumb instructions, the CPU has an ARM state and a Thumb state. The current state is reflected in bit 5 (T bit) of the Current Processor Status Register (CPSR).

To switch between ARM state and Thumb state, the program needs to use the BX instruction. Putting ARM or Thumb (or .arm/.thumb in GNU assembler) directives in the code only tells the assembler to assemble the code into the respective encoding. The directives have no effect in program execution. One common way to switching instruction state is to use the BX instruction.

The operand of the BX instruction is the branch destination address. Since the instructions are either 16-bit or 32-bit and they must be aligned to 16-bit boundary, bit 0 is not used in the address. If the bit 0 of the operand of the BX instruction is a '1', the T bit of CPSR is set after the branch and the CPU enters Thumb state or remains in Thumb state if it was already in Thumb state. If the bit 0 of the operand of the BX instruction is a '0', the T bit of CPSR is cleared after the branch and the CPU enters ARM state or remains in ARM state if it was already in ARM state.

Example 8-6

Write the code to switch from ARM state to Thumb state and back.

Solution:

```
        ARM
        ADR     R4, thumbfunc+1     ; Put the destination address in R4
                                    ; and set bit 0
        BLX     R4                  ; Branch to subroutine in Thumb state
                                    ; with return address and state in LR
stay:   B       stay


        THUMB
thumbfunc:
        PUSH    {LR}                ; Preserve the content of link register
        ...
        POP     {LR}                ; Restore the content of link register
        BX      LR                  ; return to caller in their state
```

Example 8-6 shows a way of switching from ARM state to a subroutine in Thumb state. The address of the branch destination is put in register R4 with bit 0 set using pseudo-instruction ADR. The next instruction BLX puts the return address with the current state in bit 0 in register LR then branches to the function thumbfunc in Thumb state.

When returning from the subroutine, using BX LR will put the return address from LR into PC and set or clear the T bit in CPSR according to bit 0 of LR. The program execution will return to the caller and resume its original instruction state.

If the syntax of "**`ADR R4, thumbfunc+1`**" is not accepted by the assembler, it can be replaced by the two instructions:

```
LDR R4, thumbfunc
ADD R4, R4, #1
```

While the program execution stays in the same instruction state, subroutine calls should use BL and the instruction state will stay the same. If instructions BX or BLX must be used, make sure bit 0 of the register containing the branch destination address is properly set or cleared for the destination instruction state, otherwise an illegal instruction fault will occur when executing the instruction in the wrong state.

Review Questions

1. True or false. While Thumb uses limited number of ARM instructions, Thumb 2 uses all the ARM instructions
2. Which ARM Cortex-M supports Thumb 2 instructions?
3. True or false. ARM Cortex M0/M+ supports the Thumb 2 instructions.
4. ARM assembly codes can be reassembled in (Thumb, Thumb2) and run without any changes.

Problems

Section 8.1: The Thumb Instructions

1. What are low registers and high registers?
2. What is the major difference between high and low registers in Thumb programming?
3. How many bits are used for immediate data of a MOV instruction in ARM and Thumb?
4. "MOV R5, #2000" does not fit into a 16-bit Thumb instruction. How do you put 2000 in register R5?
5. True or false. Using Thumb instructions always slows down the program execution?
6. Thumb program has (smaller, larger) footprint (program size).
7. Why do we want programs to have smaller foot print?
8. True or false. In original ARM, the instructions were 32-bit wide.
9. True or false. In Thumb mode, the instructions are 32-bit wide.
10. True or false. The Thumb code is generally 35% larger in size than the same program in ARM.
11. The Thumb instructions use (16-bit or 32-bit) ARM register.
12. Most Thumb instructions use _______ register set.
13. Compare the size of immediate data in original ARM and Thumb instructions.

14. In Thumb code, how do we bring into CPU a 32-bit data?
15. Rewrite the ARM instruction "ADD R4, R5, #200" in Thumb.

Section 8.2: Thumb-2 Technology

16. What instruction sets are used in ARM Cortex-M0, M0+, M3, and M4?
17. What instructions are used to switch between ARM state and Thumb state?
18. True or false. Most the ARM instructions also exist in Thumb-2.
19. Thumb2 instructions can be (16-bit, 32-bit, both).
20. What is the advantage of Thumb2 over Thumb?
21. True or false. In Thumb, the ARM instruction that could not be encoded in 16-bit may be encoded using multiple Thumb (16-bit) instructions.
22. True or false. In Thumb2, the ARM instruction that could not be encoded in 16-bit are encoded using multiple Thumb2 (16-bit) instructions.
23. At a given time, how do we know if we are in ARM state or Thumb state?

Answers to Review Questions

Section 8.1

1. 16, 32
2. True
3. 0xFFF in ARM and 0xFF in Thumb
4. False. Even though the Thumb instructions are 16-bit, the working registers are 32-bit just like ARM instructions
5. Subset

Section 8.2

1. True
2. ARM Cortex M3, M4 and M7
3. False
4. Thumb2

Chapter 9: ARM Floating-point Arithmetic

So far, all the arithmetic we discussed are all integer arithmetic but in real world not all the problems can be solved by integer arithmetic. There are three methods that are commonly used: rational number approximation, fixed point arithmetic, and floating-point arithmetic.

Rational number approximation is used when an integer result is desirable, fixed-point arithmetic is used when a desired number of digits of the fraction is known, and floating-point arithmetic covers all situations but costs more CPU time.

We will discuss in details in the next three sections.

Section 9.1: Rational Number Approximation

If the number involved is a rational number (a number that can be expressed by p/q where p and q are integers) and an integer is sufficient for the result then the arithmetic statement may be written as multiply p then divided by q. For example, if we wish to multiply X by 0.75, we may multiply X by 3 then divide the product by 4. To preserve most of the precision, the multiply should be performed before divide.

If the number involved is an irrational number, most of the time, a rational number approximation may provide fairly precise result. For example, $e = 2.7182818285$ can be expressed by $193/71$ with 0.001% error and by $1457/536$ with 0.000065% error.

Example 9-1

Write a program to calculate the area of a circle with less than 1% error. The radius of the circle is in register R0 and area should be left in R0.

Solution:

With area of a circle $= \pi r^2$, π may be expressed by $22/7$ with 0.04% error.

```
MUL     R0, R0, R0
MOV     R1, #22
MUL     R0, R0, R1
MOV     R1, #7
UDIV    R0, R0, R1
```

Because the result is truncated to an integer, the actual error may be more than 0.04%.

Example 9-2

Write a program to calculate the area of a circle with less than 1 ppm (part per million) error. The radius of the circle is in register R0.

Solution:

With area of a circle $= \pi r^2$, π may be expressed by $355/113$ with 0.08 ppm error.

```
MUL     R0, R0, R0
LDR     R1, =355
MUL     R0, R0, R1
LDR     R1, =113
UDIV    R0, R0, R1
```

Because the result is truncated to an integer, the actual error may be more than 0.08 ppm.

Review Questions

1. Circle the rational number.

   a) 5/9 b) $\sqrt{5}$ c) π d) 3/10 e) log(3) f) 6/13
2. In a given program we need to calculate the value (W x 0.75). How would you represent it in rational number?
3. True or false. In using rational number for Z multiply by 0.8, we divide by 5 first then multiply by 4.
4. True or false. In using rational number for Z multiply by 0.6, we multiply by 6 first then divide by 10.
5. Rational number is defined as ratio of two _____ numbers.

Section 9.2: Fixed Point Arithmetic

In the previous section, a floating-point number is expressed in a ratio of two integers. This method yields reasonable high precision of the result if an integer is sufficient for the result.

In other applications, a desired number of digits is required for the fraction. For example, a digital thermometer may display only one digit of the fraction, a cash register may display only two digits of fraction. In these situations, fixed point arithmetic may be used. Fixed point arithmetic requires much less CPU time than floating-point arithmetic, especially when the processor does not have a hardware floating-point unit.

In fixed point arithmetic, a number is represented by multiplying a scaling factor to it. The scaling factor could be any number but usually is decimal (power of 10) or binary (power of 2). Decimal scaling factors give more precise value but binary scaling factors is faster in computation because multiply or divide by the scaling factor can be done with the shift operation in the ARM instruction operand. We will start with decimal scaling factor because it is more intuitive to describe.

If the scaling factor is 100, the number n is represented by $100 \times n$. For instance, if you want to display distances in meter with precision of 0.01, you can store values in centimeter. Instead of storing 4.23 meters you can store 423 and display the value with 2 digits of fraction.

To add or subtract two fixed point numbers, it is adequate to just add or subtract them. If we are adding m and n in fixed point format with the scaling factor of 100, the arithmetic will be

$$100 \times m \ + \ 100 \times n \ = \ 100 \times (m + n)$$

For example, when we add 4.50 meters to 3.24 meters the result becomes 7.74 meters. If we do the same calculation in centimeters 450cm + 324cm becomes 774cm = 7.74 meters.

In multiplication, the resulting product needs to be divided by the scaling factor to get the proper fixed-point representation.

$$100 \times m \ \times \ 100 \times n \ / \ 100 = \ 100 \times 100 \times (m \times n) \ / \ 100 = 100 \times (m \times n)$$

When performing division, the numerator needs to be multiplied by the scaling factor before the division to yield the proper result.

$$100 \times (100 \times m) \ / \ (100 \times n) \ = \ 100 \times (m \ / \ n)$$

Example 9-3

Represent π in fixed point format with the scaling factor of 100000.

Solution:

The fixed point representation of π with scaling factor of 100000 is

$3.14159 \times 100000 = 314159.$

Example 9-4

If the sales tax rate is 7.25% (for every dollar you pay for the merchandize, you need to pay 7.25 cents of tax), how much sales tax do you owe when you buy a logic probe for $36.50 and a resistor kit for $7.99. Calculate the tax using fixed point arithmetic.

Solution:

Using dollar for unit, two digits of fraction are needed. The tax rate of 7.25% will be represented by the ratio of (7.25 / 100). Also 7.25 needs two digits of fraction. Therefore, the decimal scaling factor of 100 will be used.

$36.50 will be represented by 3650,
$7.99 will be represented by 799,

7.25 will be represented by 725,
100 will be represented by 10000.

First add the price of the two items together:

$$3650 + 799 = 4449$$

Then multiply the sum by 725 and divide it by 10000:

$$4449 \times 725 \;/\; 10000 = 322$$

Notice that after the multiplication, the product needs to be divided by the scaling factor and before the division the number needs to be multiply by the scaling factor. These two operations cancel each other out and are omitted from the operation above.

Divide 108 by the scaling factor 100 yield the quotient 3 with the remainder 22. The tax you owe is $3.22.

Example 9-5

Write an assembly program to perform the arithmetic operations in Example 9-4.

Solution:

```
LDR R0, =3650          ; price of logic probe
LDR R1, =799           ; price of resistor kit
LDR R2, =725           ; tax rate in %
LDR R3, =10000         ; 100
ADD R0, R0, R1         ; add the prices together
MUL R0, R0, R2         ; multiply the tax rate
UDIV R0, R0, R3
MOV R2, R0             ; save a copy to calculate remainder
MOV R1, #100           ; divide by the scaling factor
UDIV R0, R0, R1        ; to get the integer part
MLS R1, R0, R1, R2     ; get the remainder
```

Binary scaling factor is commonly used because instead of multiply left shift is used and instead of divide right shift is use. With the barrel shifter in the data path between the registers and the ALU, the ARM shift operation can be done in conjunction with other instructions without additional time required. The binary fixed point arithmetic operations are identical to the decimal counterpart with the exception of the multiply and divide using shift operations.

Binary fixed-point arithmetic is used extensively in ARM CMSIS DSP library. The shorthanded notation of q7, q15, or q31 is used to denote the number of bits used for the fraction part of the coefficients. The lengths of the integer part are not specified because these coefficients are all less than 1.

Example 9-6

TI Tiva C ARM microcontroller has Universal Asynchronous Receiver and Transmitter (UART) modules for data communication. The rate data is transmitted is determined by two registers IBRD and FBRD, which hold the integer part and fraction part of the clock divisor. The IBRD and FBRD registers are 16-bit and 6-bit long respectively.

The data rate (Baud rate) is determined by the system clock divided by 16 then divided by the values of IBRD and FBRD.

$$Baud\ rate = \frac{System\ clock\ /\ 16}{IBRD.FBRD}$$

Therefore,

$$IBRD.FBRD = \frac{System\ clock\ /\ 16}{Baud\ rate}$$

If the System clock is running at 16 MHz, write an assembly program to calculate the values to put in IBRD and FBRD for the Baud rate in register R0.

Solution:

Because the fraction part is 6 bit long, fixed point arithmetic with a scaling factor of $2^6 = 64$ will be used.

```
MOV R1, R0, LSL #6      ; convert Baud rate to fixed-point into R1
LDR R0, =1000000*64     ; load R0 with (System clock / 16)
MOV R0, R0, LSL #6      ; multiply numerator by scaling factor
UDIV R0, R0, R1         ;    before divide

AND R1, R0, #0x3F       ; extract 6-bit fraction
MOV R0, R0, ASR #6      ; shift 6-bit right to get integer part
```

Assume we are to calculate the IBRD and FBRD values for the Baud rate of 115200 in example 9-6 with 2^6 scaling factor,

$$IBRD.FBRD = \frac{System\ clock\ /\ 16}{Baud\ rate} = \frac{1000000}{115200} = \frac{1000000 \times 64}{115200 \times 64} = \frac{64000000}{7372800}$$

To perform a fixed-point division, we need to multiply the numerator with the scaling factor first, so

$$\frac{64000000 \times 64}{7372800} = \frac{4096000000}{7372800} = 555$$

or 10 0010 1011 in binary. This is a fixed-point representation with 2^6 as the scaling factor, so the integer part is 1000 in binary or 8 in decimal and the fraction part is 101011 in binary or 43 in fraction.

Review Questions

1. True or false. Using the integer ALU to do the floating-point arithmetic takes less time if we use fixed point number representation.
2. To preserve three digits of fraction through the calculations, what decimal scaling factor should we use to represent the numbers in fixed point format?
3. Show the calculation of (4.36 + 7.34)/1.06 in fixed number arithmetic using 100 as decimal scaling factor.
4. True or false. In performing division for fixed point numbers, the numerator is multiplied by the scaling factor after division is performed.
5. Why is binary scaling factor often used in fixed number representation in ARM?

Section 9.3: Floating-point Arithmetic

IEEE 754 Floating-Point Standards

At the beginning, real numbers (numbers with decimal points and fractions) were represented differently in binary forms by different computers. This made data incompatible between different machines and it was very difficult to move the data from one computer to be processed by another one. In the early 1980s, an IEEE committee established a set of standards (IEEE 754-1985 Standards) for the floating-point data formats, rounding rules, arithmetic operations, and exception handling. This standard, much of which was contributed by Intel based on the 8087 math coprocessor, has since adopted by almost all the computer manufacturers. Over the years, there were several revisions of IEEE 754 but most of the original formats are still included.

The current revision of IEEE 754 defines five binary encodings and three decimal encodings of different sizes and precisions. The 32-bit single-precision and 64-bit double-precision binary formats are the most commonly used. C programming language defines data type **float** for the 32-bit single-precision encoding and **double** for the 64-bit double-precision encoding. These two common data types are used by other popular programming languages such as C++ and Java. We will discuss these two formats in details here.

IEEE 754 single-precision floating-point numbers

IEEE single-precision floating-point numbers use 32 bits of data to represent any real number range 2^{-126} to 2^{127}, for both positive and negative numbers. This translates approximately to a range of 1.18×10^{-38} to 3.4×10^{38} in decimal numbers, again for both positive and negative values. Assignment of the 32 bits in the single-precision format is shown in Figure 5-3.

Figure 9-1: IEEE 754 Single-precision Floating-point Numbers

In this format, bit 31 is the sign bit. If it is 0, the number is positive, if it is 1, the number is negative.

The exponent field has 8 bits spanning from bit 30 to bit 23. It may hold the exponent from -126 to +127. To simplify the encoding, the exponent field does not have a sign bit, rather the exponent is added to a bias of 127 (0x7F in hexadecimal) before storing in this field. This is referred as a biased exponent. So, the exponents from -126 to +127 are encoded as 1 to 254. The biased exponent field has two special values, 0 and 255. When it is 0 and the significand is 0, the number is zero or negative zero depending on the sign bit. When the biased exponent is 255, it is either infinity or not a number depending on the value in the significand.

The significand field is bit 22 to bit 0. It holds the fraction part of the normalized binary number. The number is called normalized when the integer part is a 1. For example, 7.25 is encoded in binary as 111.01. To normalize it, the radix point (or commonly referred as decimal point) is moved two digits to the left to yield 1.1101 E 10. The fraction part will be 1101.

Converting a decimal floating-point number to IEEE754 single-precision format involves the following steps.

1. If the number is positive, bit 31 is 0. If the number is negative, bit 31 is 1.
2. The real number is converted to its binary form.
3. The binary number is normalized to 1.xxxx E yyyy
4. The bias 127 (0x7F) is added to the exponent portion, yyyy, to get the biased exponent, which is placed in bits 30 to 23.
5. The significand, xxxx, is placed in bits 22 to 0.

Examples 9-7, 9-8, and 9-9 demonstrate this process.

Example 9-7

Convert 9.75_{10} to IEEE754 single-precision floating-point format.

Solution:

Sign bit 31 is 0 for positive
Decimal 9.75 = binary 1001.11
which is normalized to 1.00111 E 3
Exponent bits 30 to 23 are 1000 0010 after adding the bias (3 + 0x7F = 0x82)
Significand bits 22 to 0 are 00111000000000000000000
Putting them all together gives the following binary form, under which is written the hex form:

0100	0001	0001	1100	0000	0000	0000	0000
4	1	1	C	0	0	0	0

This can be verified by using an assembler such as Keil.

Example 9-8

Convert 0.078125_{10} to IEEE754 single-precision floating-point format.

Solution:
Sign bit 31 is 0 for positive
Decimal 0.078125 = binary 0.000101
which is normalized to 1.01 E –4
Exponent bits 30 to 23 are 0111 1011 after adding the bias (-4 + 0x7F = 0x7B)
Significand bits 22 to 0 are 01000000000000000000000
Putting them all together gives the following binary form, under which is written the hex form:

0011	1101	1010	0000	0000	0000	0000	0000
3	D	A	0	0	0	0	0

Example 9-9

Convert -96.27_{10} to IEEE754 single-precision floating-point format.

Solution:
Sign bit 31 is 1 for negative
Decimal 96.27 = binary 1100000.01000101000111101
which is normalized to 1.10000001000101000111101 E 6
Exponent bits 30 to 23 are 1000 0101 after adding the bias (6 + 0x7F = 0x85)
Significand bits 22 to 0 are 10000001000101000111101
Putting them all together gives the following binary form, under which is written the hex form:

1100	0010	1100	0000	1000	1010	0011	1101
C	2	C	0	8	A	3	D

It must be noted that conversion of the decimal portion 0.27 to binary can be continued beyond the point shown above, but because the fraction part of the single-precision is limited to 23 bits, this was all that was shown. For that reason, double-precision FP numbers are used in some applications to achieve a higher degree of precision.

IEEE 754 double-precision floating-point numbers

Double-precision floating-point numbers can represent numbers in the range 2.3×10^{-308} to 1.7×10^{308}, both positive and negative. A total of 52 bits (bits 51 to 0) are used for the significand, 11 bits (bits 62 to 52) are for the exponent, and finally, bit 63 is for the sign. The conversion process is the same as for single-precision in that the real number must first be normalized as 1.xxxxxxx E YYYY, then YYYY is added to 1023 (0x3FF) to get the biased exponent. See Figure 9-2 and Example 9-10.

Figure 9-2: IEEE 754 Double-precision Floating-point Numbers

Example 9-10

Convert 152.1875_{10} to IEEE754 double-precision floating-point format.

Solution:

Sign bit 63 is 0 for positive
Decimal 152.1875 = binary 10011000.0011
which is normalized to 1.00110000011 E 7
Exponent bits 62 to 53 are 10000000110 after adding the bias (7 + 0x3FF = 0x406)
Significand bits 52 to 0 are 00110000011000.....000
Putting them all together gives the following binary form, under which is written the hex form:

0100	0000	0110	0011	0000	0110	0000	0000	0000	...	0000
4	0	6	3	0	6	0	0	0	...	0

IEEE 754 half-precision floating-point numbers

In the 2008 revision of IEEE 754 floating-point standards, half-precision floating-point number format is added. The half-precision number format occupies 16 bits of the memory. It can represent numbers in the range 6.10×10^{-5} to 6.55×10^{4}, both positive and negative. A total of 10 bits (bits 9 to 0) are used for the significand, 5 bits (bits 14 to 10) are for the exponent and bit 15 is for the sign. The conversion process is the same as for single-precision in that the real number must first be normalized as 1.xxxxxxx E YYYY, then YYYY is added to 15 (0x0F) to get the biased exponent. See Figure 9-3.

Figure 9-3: IEEE 754 Half-precision Floating-point Numbers

Review Questions

1. Single-precision IEEE FP standard uses _________ bits to represent data.
2. Double-precision IEEE FP standard uses ________ bits to represent data.
3. To get the biased exponent portion of IEEE single-precision floating-point data we add ________ to the exponent.
4. To get the biased exponent portion of IEEE double-precision floating-point data we add ________ to the exponent.
5. True or false. In the absence of a floating-point processor, the general-purpose processor must perform all math calculations.

Section 9-4: Floating-point Coprocessor in ARM

The arithmetic operations between numbers of floating-point format can be carried out by the integer arithmetic unit of the CPU. For example, if we are to multiply two floating-point numbers, the operations can be done by:

- Extract the sign bits and determine the sign of the product.
- Extract the biased exponents, remove the bias and add them together.
- Extract the fractions, add 1 to them and multiply them as fixed-point numbers.
- Convert the sign, exponent, and fraction of the product back to floating-point format.

There are library functions to perform these floating-point arithmetic operations using integer arithmetic instructions in both Keil and GNU toolchains. As you can see from the steps above, it takes many integer instructions to perform a single floating-point operation. To speed up the floating-point arithmetic operations, hardware floating-point coprocessor is often added to the high-performance processor. For ARM CPU, there are two coprocessors, VFP and NEON, that may be incorporated in the chip to perform floating-point operations.

A coprocessor has its own instruction decoder, register bank, and arithmetic logic unit but it does not perform instruction fetch. It sits on the memory bus watch the CPU fetching instructions. When a coprocessor instruction is fetched by the CPU and the coprocessor is present, the CPU does not try to execute the instruction rather the coprocessor decodes the instruction and execute it. If the coprocessor instruction is fetched and the coprocessor is not present, it generates an illegal instruction exception and the CPU may call the library functions. This way it may maintain certain degree of portability of the code.

The ARM Vector Floating-point (VFP) performs single-precision and double-precision arithmetic operations that are fully compliant to IEEE 754 standard. The "Vector" in the name implies that it may perform operations over multiple data in one instruction. These operations are performed sequentially so the performance is not very significantly better than non-vectored operations. The vectored operations were removed from VFP in the later versions but the "V" in the name and as the prefix of the instructions stays. The Advanced SIMD (Single Instruction Multiple Data), code name NEON, is the ARM extension to provide high performance for media applications and digital signal processing. NEON performs SIMD over integers, fixed-point numbers, and single-precision floating-point numbers. It does not do double-precision floating-point operations.

ARM Cortex-M4 and Cortex-M7 have optional IEEE 754-2008 compliant floating-point unit. Cortex-M4 option is single-precision only. Cortex-M7 has a single-precision option and a single/double-precision option. Neither of them supports vector mode.

For the rest of the chapter, we will limit the discussions to the 32-bit single-precision floating-point operations.

Floating-point Registers

There are 32 single-precision (32-bit) data registers in VFPv2. These registers are named S0, S1, S2, ..., S31. For 64-bit operations, these registers are renamed D0, D1, D2, ..., D15. Register D0 is actually the concatenation of S0 and S1, D1 is S2 and S3, and so on. NEON shares the same floating-point register bank.

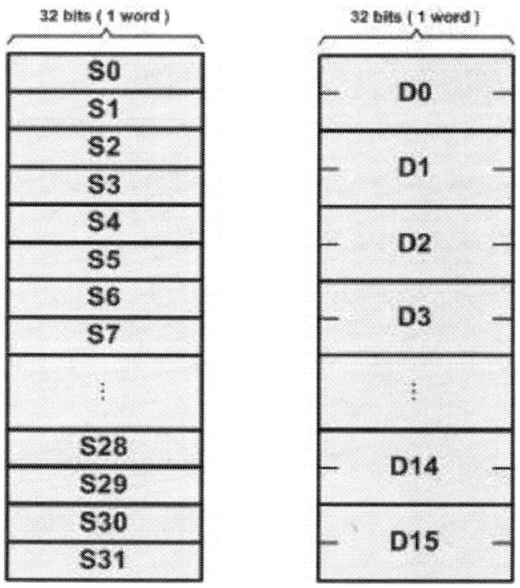

Figure 9-4: ARM Floating-point data Register Bank

The floating-point unit also has a status and control register (FPSCR). The layout of bits in the FPSCR are listed in Figure 9-5 and Table 9-1.

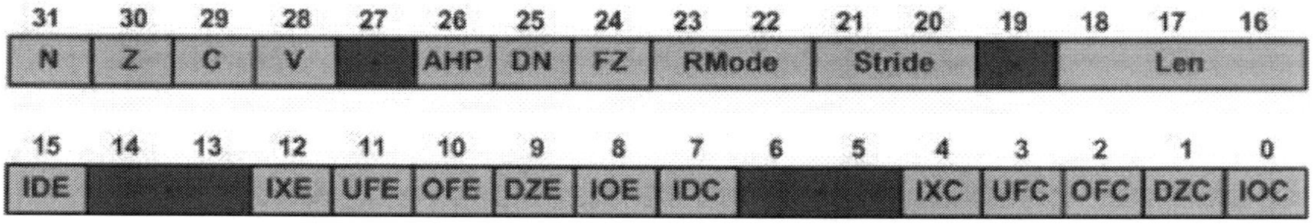

Figure 9-5: ARM Floating-point status and control register (FPSCR)

Bits	Name	Function
31-28	N, Z, C, V	Negative, Zero, Carry, Overflow flags
25	DN	Default NaN mode control
24	FZ	Flush-to-zero mode control
23-22	RMode	Rounding Mode control
21-20	Stride	Step size in vector
18-16	Len	Length of the vector
15, 12-8		Exception trap enable bits
		IDE — Input subnormal exception enable
		IXE — Inexact exception enable
		UFE — Underflow exception enable
		OFE — Overflow exception enable
		DZE — Division by zero exception enable
		IOE — Invalid operation exception enable
7, 4-0		Cumulative exception bits
		IDC — Input subnormal exception flag
		IXC — Inexact exception flag
		UFC — Underflow exception flag
		OFC — Overflow exception flag
		DZC — Division by zero exception flag
		IOC — Invalid operation exception flag

Table 9-1: ARM Floating-point status and control register bit assignments

Bits 31-28 contain the Negative, Zero, Carry, Overflow flags. They are set or cleared by very few VFP instructions, most notably the compare instruction VCMP. Most of the VFP/NEON instructions can be conditionally executed just like the ARM instructions. To do so, the condition is appended to the end of the instruction. But their conditional execution is based on the status of the NZCV bits of the CPU current program status register (CPSR) not the NZCV bits of the FPSCR register. In order to control the program flow by the condition flags of the floating-point unit, the NZCV bits of the FPSCR need to be copied into the NZCV bits of CPSR. The instruction VMRS may be used to do that, which will be described in more details later.

Format Modifiers of Floating-point Instructions

Because the floating-point instructions involve arguments of different sizes of integers, fixed-point numbers, and floating-point numbers, it is necessary to specify the format of the arguments in the instruction. The format modifiers are appended after the instruction with a '.' separator. For example, ".F32" specifies a single-precision floating-point number.

Floating-point Data Movement Instructions

VPF instructions that moves the data are VMOV, VLDR, VSTR, VLDM, VSTM, VPOP, VPUSH, VMRS, and VMSR. Most of them are similar to their integer counterpart.

VMOV Instruction

VMOV instruction is used to move data among the registers, these include between the ARM registers and the floating-point registers, and between two floating-point registers. VMOV instructions only copies the content of the registers. They do not modify the content while moving data between ARM integer registers and floating-point registers. Moving an integer from an ARM register to a floating-point register does not change its encoding to floating-point format. The same holds when moving a floating-point number from a floating-point register to an ARM register. The content of the source register stays the same after the VMOV instruction. The following three instructions demonstrate the three single-precision VMOV:

```
VMOV.F32    S1, R1    ; copy content of R1 to S1
VMOV.F32    S2, S1    ; copy content of S1 to S2
VMOV.F32    R2, S2    ; copy content of S2 to R2
```

In VFPv3 and later, the VMOV instruction also support moving an immediate value. The immediate value is followed by a '#' sign and must be written in decimal. The immediate value may be integer or floating-point but they are loaded as floating-point format in the register. Due to the available bits to carry the immediate value, the range of the values are limited to $(+/-)n \times 2^{-r}$, where n and r are integers and $16 \leq n \leq 31 and\ 0 \leq r \leq 7$. The following two are sample instructions of VMOV with immediate value:

```
VMOV.F32    S1, #2        ; load S1 with 2.0
VMOV.F32    S2, #0.125    ; load S2 with 0.125
```

VLDR and VSTR Instructions

Unlike their corresponding integer instructions, VLDR and VSTR addressing mode is rather limited. It accepts register indirect mode with constant offset. A sample instruction may look like:

```
VLDR.F32    S2, [R2, #4]     ; R2 holds the base address
VSTR.F32    S2, [R3, #-4]    ; R3 holds the base address
```

The constant offset must be multiple of 4.

VLDR and VSTR Pseudo-instructions

Like LDR, VLDR also accept a 32-bit/64-bit literal value as immediate data to be loaded into the register. The literal value is stored in the literal pool by the assembler and the addressing mode is using PC as the base register and the current PC value to the data in the literal pool as the constant offset.

```
VLDR.F32    S1, =1.41421356
```

The assembler also allows VLDR and VSTR to have pre-increment with write-back and post-increment address modes even though the instructions do not. With these addressing modes, the assembler actually converts them to VLDM and VSTM instructions that will be described below. For example,

```
VLDR.F32   S3, [R4], #4
```

Is converted to

```
VLDMIA     R4!, {S3}
```

and

```
VLDR.F32   S3, [R4, #-4]!
```

Is converted to

```
VLDMDB     R4!, {S3}
```

VLDM, VSTM, VPOP and VPUSH Instructions

VLDM and VSTM are instructions for loading or storing multiple floating-point registers. By default, the mode is IA (increment afterward), the address is incremented by the size of the data after each transfer. For single-precision register transfer, the address is incremented by 4. The alternative mode is DB (decrement before). When DB mode is desired, the suffix DB must be appended to the end of the instruction. Suffix IA is optional since IA mode is the default. The base register must be an ARM register. The final address after the transfer may be written back to the base register by appending a '!' to the base register in the instruction. With write-back, these two instructions allow the use of any ARM general purpose registers to be used as a stack pointer for stack operations.

The list of registers to be loaded or stored are listed within a pair of parentheses. The registers may be listed singly with comma separated or written as a range with a '-' in between. All the registers must be the same data type and also match the data type specified by the instruction. This sample instruction stores single-precision registers S2, S5, S7, S8, S9, and S10 starting from address in R7. The final address is written back to R7.

```
VSTM.F32     R7!, {S2, S5, S7-S10}
```

The following instruction restores the registers from where they were saved in the previous instruction:

```
VLDMDB.F32  R7!, {S2, S5, S7-S10}
```

When the dedicated stack pointer register, SP, is used as the base register and update is specified, "VLDM SP!," can be written as VPOP and "VSTMDB SP!," can be written as VPUSH.

VMRS and VMSR Instructions

VMRS moves the VFP system register content to one of the ARM registers (except PC). VMSR moves one of the ARM register content to a VFP system register.

The following instruction is used to copy the NZCV bits of the VFP status register to the ARM CPSR so that the conditional execution of the instructions will be based on the status of the floating-point processor.

```
VMRS    APSR_nzcv, FPSCR
```

Floating-point Data Conversion Instructions

The ARM floating-point processor is capable of handling the conversions between different data type format such as integer, fixed-point, half-precision, single-precision, and double-precision. Different variant of VFP covers different data types. Not all VPFs cover all these data types. We will limit the discussion to single-precision and integer conversion in this section.

The syntax of the conversion instruction looks like:

```
VCVT.type.type    Sd, Sm
```

Where Sd is the destination floating-point register and Sm is the source floating-point register. For single-precision floating-point, the type is F32. For integer, the type may be U32 for unsigned 32-bit integer or S32 for signed 32-bit integer. The following instructions convert a signed integer in S0 to a single-precision floating-point number in S1 then convert it back to a signed integer in S2.

```
VCVT.F32.S32    S1, S0
VCVT.S32.F32    S2, S1
```

Floating-point Data Processing Instructions

See Table 9-2. There are three unary operations: VABS (absolute), VNEG (negate), and VSQRT (square root). The absolute and negate instructions simply change the sign bit of the operand regardless of the rest of the number even if the value is not a number (NaN).

There are four binary operations: add, subtract, multiply and divide. A wealth of variations of multiply instruction, including multiply and accumulate (MLA) and multiply and subtract (MLS) are available for digital signal processing. MLA and MLS may be fused (single rounding after add or subtract). All multiply instructions can have the final result negated before storing in the destination register with adding an 'N' in the instruction.

And lastly the compare instruction, VCMP, is used to compare two numbers and set the NZCV bits in FPSCR register accordingly. The first operand of VCMP must be a floating-point register, the second operand may be a floating-point register or an immediate value of 0. In order for the NZCV bits of FPSCR to affect the program, they have to be copied into a general-purpose register for bit analysis or to the ARM CPSR register for conditional execution. The content of FPSCR is copied to ARM register by the VMRS instruction.

AAPCS of Floating-point

The ARM Architecture Procedure Call Standard (AAPCS) allows the use of the lower half of the floating-point registers (S0-S15 or D0-D8) for parameter passing and return value if they are the data types of these registers. The parameters are loaded in the registers starting from the lowest number. Keil ARMcc (v5.06) does use them.

The lower half of the floating-point register bank is used for parameter passing and return value and are not required to be preserved through function calls. The upper half of the floating-point register bank (S16-S31 or D8-D15) needs to be preserved through the function calls.

The NZCV bits of the FPSCR are not preserved across public function call interface.

Mnemonic	Function	Description
VABS	Absolute	Obtain the absolute value of the operand
VNEG	Negate	Negate the value of the operand
VSQRT	square root	Obtain the square root of the operand
VADD	Add	Add the operands
VSUB	Subtract	Subtract the second operand from the first operand
VDIV	Divide	Divide the first operand by the second operand
VMUL	Multiply	Multiply the two operands
VNMUL	multiply negate	Multiply the two operands then negate the result
VMLA	multiply and accumulate	Multiply the two operands then add the result to the destination register and store the final result in the destination register
VNMLA	multiply and accumulate negate	Multiply the two operands then add the result to the destination register, negate the final result and store it in the destination register
VMLS	multiply and subtract	Multiply the two operands then subtract the result from the destination register and store the final result in the destination register
VNMLS	multiply and subtract negate	Multiply the two operands then subtract the result from the destination register, negate the final result and store it in the destination register
VFMA	fused multiply and accumulate	Same as VMLA except using fused operation (single rounding at the final result)
VFMS	fused multiply and subtract	Same as VMLS except using fused operation
VFNMA	fused multiply and accumulate negate	Same as VNMLA except using fused operation
VFNMS	fused multiply and subtract negate	Same as VNMLS except using fused operation
VCMP	Compare	Subtract the second operand from the first operand and set the NZCV bits of FPSCR

Table 9-2: Floating-point data processing instructions

Assembler Directives for floating-point numbers

There are four assembler directives to allocate memory and define initial content for floating-point numbers. DCFS is used to allocate single-precision numbers and DCFD is used for double-precision numbers. The directives insert up to three byte padding before the first number to ensure four-byte alignment of all the floating-point numbers since the floating-point instructions fetching these numbers expect them to be word-aligned. If alignment is not required, DCFSU and DCFDU may be used instead to turn off the alignment to save memory. See the following examples.

Example 9-11

Write a program to calculate the area of a circle with single-precision floating-point format. The radius of the circle is in register S0 and area should be left in S0.

Solution:

This the same problem as Example 9-1 but in floating-point format. The area of a circle is πr^2.

```
VMUL.F32    S0, S0, S0          ; calculate r^2
VLDR.F32    S1, =3.1415926      ; load pi
VMUL.F32    S0, S0, S1          ; multiply pi
```

Example 9-12

Write a program to add two floating-point numbers in the memory and save the result in the memory.

Solution:

Operands are defined as

```
operand1        DCFS    0.69314718
operand2        DCFS    1.41421356
```

Result is defined as

```
sum             SPACE   4
```

The code is

```
LDR         R3, =operand1       ; load address of operand1
VLDR.F32    S0, [R3]            ; load operand1 in S0
LDR         R3, =operand2       ; load address of operand2
VLDR.F32    S1, [R3]            ; load operand1 in S0
VADD.F32    S0, S0, S1          ; add operand2 to operand1
LDR         R3, =sum            ; load address of sum
VSTR.F32    S0, [R3]            ; store the result in sum
```

Example 9-13

Write a function to calculate the square root of a number in S0 register. Return the square root in S0.

Solution:

The VFP does have a square root instruction. This task can be easily accomplished by an instruction:

```
        VSQRT.F32    S0, S0
```

To illustrate the use of floating-point instructions, we will demonstrate the use of the Newtonian iteration to calculate the square root. With Newtonian iteration, it starts with a guess x_0 (in this example we use N/2 as the first guess). From it the guess x_1 is calculated using the formula:

$$x_{k+1} = \frac{\left(x_k + \frac{N}{x_k}\right)}{2}$$

The value should converge very quickly. The iteration stops when the two consecutive values are identical.

```
; Function to calculate square root by Newtonian iteration
; register assignments:
; S0 - N
; S1 - Xk
; S2 - N/Xk
; S3 - Xk+1
; S4 - 2.0
;

sqRoot  VMOV.F32    S4, #2          ; S4 holds constant 2.0
        VDIV.F32    S1, S0, S4      ; initial guess Xk = N/2
loop    VDIV.F32    S3, S0, S1      ; N/Xk
        VADD.F32    S3, S1          ; Xk + N/Xk
        VDIV.F32    S3, S4          ; Xk+1 = (Xk + N/Xk)/2
        VCMP.F32    S3, S1          ; compare Xk and Xk+1
        VMRS        APSR_nzcv, FPSCR
        VMOV.F32    S1, S3          ; Xk+1 becomes Xk of next iteration
        BNE         loop            ; if not the same, reiterate,
        VMOV.F32    S0, S1          ; else, return square root in S0
        BX          LR
```

Review Questions

1. True or false. The VFP in ARM Cortex supports only the single precision FP arithmetic.
2. Which ARM Cortex family has single precision FP only?
3. Which ARM Cortex family supports both single and double precision FP?
4. True or false. In ARM VFP single precision FP, the VFP registers are 64-bit wide.
5. Name the ARM VFP single precision FP registers.

Problems

Section 9.1: Rational Number Approximation

1. What is a rational number?
2. Show how we get 0.001% error for 193/71 for e = 2.7182818285
3. In a given program, we need scale the output of the ADC, W, by a factor of 0.72. How would you represent it in rational number?
4. True or false. In using rational number for Z multiply by 0.923, we divide by 13 first then multiply by 12.
5. True or false. In using rational number for Z multiply by 0.4, we multiply by 2 first then divide by 5.
6. Circle the rational number.
   (a) 5/12 (b) 1.5 (c) e^2 (d) 3/7 (e) $\sqrt{3}$ (f) 6/13
7. In Example 9-1, show how we got 0.04% error.
8. In Example 9-2, show how we got 1ppm error.

Section 9.2: Fixed Point Arithmetic

9. What is a fixed-point number?
10. What is advantage of using fixed-point number?
11. True or false. We use scaling factor of 2 in binary and scaling factor of 10 in base 10 numbers.
12. What is the fixed-point representation of 3.333 if the scaling factor is 1000?
13. What is the fixed-point representation of 3.333 if the scaling factor is 2^6?
14. If x = 25.74 and y = 71.35, use scaling factor of 100 and calculate the sum of x and y.
15. Using the same values of x and y and the scaling factor in above problem, calculate x / y.

Section 9.3: Floating-point Arithmetic

16. What is the disadvantage of using an integer processor to perform floating-point operations?
17. Show the bit assignment of the IEEE single-precision standard.
18. Convert (by hand calculation) each of the following real numbers to IEEE single-precision standard. (a) 15.575 (b) 89.125 (c) –1022.543 (d) –0.00075
19. Show the bit assignment of the IEEE double-precision standard.
20. In single-precision FP (floating-point), the biased exponent is calculated by adding ________ to the ________ portion of a scientific binary number.
21. In double-precision FP, the biased exponent is calculated by adding ________ to the ________ portion of a scientific binary number.
22. Convert the following to double-precision FP. (a) 12.9823 (b) 98.76123
23. Indicate the data directive used for the following data types. (a) single-precision FP (b) double-precision FP

Section 9.4: Floating-point Coprocessor in ARM

24. True or false. All of the ARM chips come with the FPU.
25. Write and run an ARM VFP program to calculate $= (2.4x + 3.7y)/2.0$, where x =3.12 and y =5.43.

26. Write and run an ARM VFP assembly program to calculate $y = 7.2x^2 + 8.5x + 12.34$, where $x = 1.25$.
27. Write and run an ARM VFP assembly program to calculate the area of a circle if r = 25.5.
28. Write and run an ARM VFP assembly program to calculate $4(\pi r^3)/3$ if r = 25.5.

Answers to Review Questions

Section 9.1

7. a, d, and f
8. (W x 3) / 4
9. False, always multiply before divide when using integer arithmetic.
10. True
11. Integer

Section 9.2

1. True
2. 1000
3. The numbers will be represented by 436, 734, and 106 with 100 as the scaling factor. The calculation will be (436 + 734) x 100 / 106 = 1104, which represents 11.04.
4. False, the numerator should be multiplied by the scaling factor **before** division.
5. Multiply and divide by a number that is power of 2 can be carried out by left shift or right shift. With the barrel shifter in the ARM CPU, the shift can be incorporated with other instructions without additional computing time. On the other hand, multiply and divide instructions take much more CPU time to perform.

Section 9.3

1. 32
2. 64
3. 0x7F
4. 0x3FF
5. True

Section 9.4

1. False
2. ARM Cortex M4
3. ARM Cortex M7
4. False
5. S0-S31

Appendix A: ARM Cortex-M3 Instruction Description

Section A.1: List of ARM Cortex-M3 Instructions

ADC Add with Carry

ADD Add

ADR Load PC-Relative Address

AND Logical AND

ASR Arithmetic Shift right

B Branch (unconditional jump)

Bxx Branch Conditional

BFC Bit Field Clear

BFIBit Field Insert

BIC Bit Clear

BKPT Breakpoint

BL Branch with Link (this is Call instruction)

BLX Branch Indirect with Link

BX Branch Indirect (BX LR is used for Return)

CBNZ Compare and Branch on Non-Zero

CBZ Compare and Branch on Zero

CDP Coprocessor Data processing

CLREX Clear Exclusive

CLZ Count Leading Zero

CMN Compare Negative

CMP Compare

CPSID Change processor ID and Disable Interrupt

CPSIE Change Processor State and Enable Interrupt

DMB Data Memory Barrier

DSB Data Synchronization Barrier

EOR Exclusive OR

ISBInstruction Synchronization Barrier

IT If-Then Condition Block

LDC	Load Coprocessor
LDM	Load Multiple registers
LDMDB	Load Multiple registers and Decrement Before each access
LDMEA	Load Multiple registers from Empty Ascending
LDMFD	Load Multiple registers Full Descending
LDMIA	Load Multiple registers and Increment after each Access
LDR	Load Register
LDR Rx, =Value	Load Register with 32-bit value
LDRB	Load Register Byte
LDRH	Load Register Halfword
LDRSB	Load Register signed Byte
LDRSH	Load Register Signed Halfword
LDRT	Load Register with Translation
LSL	Logical Shift Left
LSR	Logical Shift Right
MCR	Move to Coprocessor from ARM Register
MLA	Multiply Accumulate
MLS	Multiply and Subtract
MOV	Move (ARM7)
MOV	Move (ARM Cortex)
MOVT	Move Top
MOVW	Move 16-bit constant
MRC	Move to ARM Register from Coprocessor
MRS	Move to general Register from Special register
MSR	Move to Special register from general Register
MUL	Unsigned Multiplication
MVN	Move Negative
NOP	No Operation
ORN	Logical OR Not
ORR	Logical OR
POP	POP register from Stack
PUSH	PUSH register onto stack

RBIT	Reverse Bits
REV	Reverse byte order in a word
RV16	Reverse byte order in 16-bit
REVSH	Reverse byte order in bottom halfword and sign extend
ROR	Rotate Right
RRX	Rotate Right with extend
RSB	Reverse Subtract
SBC	Subtract with Carry (Borrow)
SBFX	Sign Bit Field extract
SDIV	Signed Divide
SEV	Send Event
SMLAL	Signed Multiply Accumulate Long
SMULL	Signed Multiply Long
SSAT	Sign Saturate
STM	Store Multiple
STMDB	Store Multiple register and Decrement Before
STMEA	Store Multiple register Empty Ascending
STMIA	Store Multiple register Empty Ascending
STMFD	Store Multiple register Full Descending
STR	Store Register
STRB	Store Register Byte
STRD	Store Register Double (two words)
STRH	Store Register Halfword
STRT	Store Register
SUB	Subtract
SUBS	Subtract
SVC	supervisor Call (Software Interrupt)
SXTB	Sign Extend byte
SXTH	Sign Extend Halfword
TBB	Table Branch Byte
TBH	Table Branch halfword
TEQ	Test Equivalence

TST	Test
UBFX	Unsigned Bit filed extract
UDIV	Unsigned Divide
UMLAL	Unsigned Multiply with Accumulate
UMULL	Unsigned Multiply Long
UXBT	Zero extend a byte
UXTH	Zero extend halfword
WFE	Wait for event
WFI	Wait for interrupt

Section A.2: ARM Instruction Description

ADC   Add with Carry
Flags: Unaffected.

Format: ADC Rd, Rn, Op2   ; Rd = Rn + Op2 + C

Function: If C = 1 prior to this instruction, then after execution of this instruction, Op2 is added to Rn plus 1 and the result is placed in Rd. If C = 0, Op2 is added to Rn plus 0. Used widely in multiword additions. After the execution the flags are not updated. The ADCS instruction updates the flags.

Example 1:

```
LDR   R0, =0xFFFFFFFB          ;  R0=0xFFFFFFFB
LDR   R1, =0xFFFFFFFF          ;  R1=0xFFFFFFFF
MOV   R2, #3                   ; R2=3
MOV   R3, #4                   ; R3=4
ADDS  R4, R0, R1               ; R4=R0+R1, C=1
ADC   R5, R2, R3               ; R5=R2+R3+C=R2+R3+1
```

ADD   ADD
Flags: Unaffected

Format: ADD Rd, Rn, Op2   ; Rd = Rn + Op2

Function: Adds source operands together and places the result in destination. This will not update the flags. To update the flags we must use ADDS.

Example 1:

```
LDR   R0, =0xFFFFFFFF          ; R0=0xFFFFFFFB
MOV   R1, #0x5                 ; R1=0x5
ADD   R2, R0, R1
      ; R2=R0+R1=0xFFFFFFFB+0x5=00000000
      ; flags unchanged
```

Example 2:

```
        LDR    R0, =0xFFFFFFFF          ; R0=0xFFFFFFFF
        ADD    R2, R0, #0xF1
               ; R2=R0+0xF1=R1=0xFFFFFFFF+0xF1=000000F0
               ; flags unchanged
```

ADR Load PC-Relative Address

Flags: Unaffected:

Format: ADR Rd, label ; Rd= address of label

Function: This allows loading into Rd register an address relative to the current PC (program counter). The label target address must be within the -4,095 to +4,096 bytes from the address in PC register. That is no farther than 1024 instructions in either direction of backward or forward.

Example:

```
               ADR    R3, MyMessage
HERE           B      HERE
MyMessage      DCB    "Hello"
```

AND Logical AND

Flags: Unaffected

Format: AND Rd, Rn, Op2 ; Rd= Rn ANDed Op2

Function: Performs logical AND on the operands, bit by bit, storing the result in the destination. This will not update the flags. To update the flags, we must use ANDS. Notice that C flag is updated during calculation of Op2 when LSR or LSL are used.

Inputs		Output
X	Y	X AND Y
0	0	0
0	1	0
1	0	0
1	1	1

Example 1:

```
        MOV    R0, #0x39     ; R0=0x39
        MOV    R1, #0x0F     ; R1=0x0F
        AND    R2, R1, R0    ; R2=09
                             ; 39   0011 1001
                             ; 0F   0000 1111
                             ; --   ---------
                             ; 09   0000 1001   Flags unchanged
```

Example 2:

```
        MOV    R0, #0x37     ; R0=0x37
        AND    R1, R0, #0x0F       ; R1 = R0 ANDed 0x0F = 07
                             ; 37   0011 0111
```

```
                    ; 0F  0000 1111
                    ; --  ---------
                    ; 07  0000 0111  Flags unchanged
```

ASR Arithmetic Shift right

Flags: Unaffected. Except C

Format: ASR Rd, Rm, Rn

Function: As each bit of Rm register is shifted right, the LSB is removed and the empty bits filled with the sign bit (MSB). The number of bits to be shifted right is given by Rn and the result is placed in Rd register. The flags are unchanged. To update the flags, use ASRS instruction.

Example 1:

```
    LDR   R2, =0xFFFFFF82
    ASR   R0, R2, #6   ; R0=R2 is shifted right 6 times
                       ; now, R0 = 0xFFFFFFFE
```

Example 2:

```
    LDR   R0, =0x2000FF18
    MOV   R1,  #12
    ASR   R2, R0, R1   ; R2=R0 is shifted right R1 number of times.
                       ; now, R2 = 0x0002000F
```

Example 3:

```
    LDR   R0, =0x0000FF18
    MOV   R1,  #16
    ASR   R2, R0, R1   ; R2=R0 is shifted right R1 number of times
                       ; now, R2 = 0x00000000
```

ASR arithmetic shift is used for signed number shifting. ASR essentially divides Rm by a power of 2 for each bit shift.

B Branch (unconditional jump)

Flags: Unchanged.

Format: B target ; jump to target address

Function: This instruction is used to transfer control unconditionally to a new address. The difference between B and BL is that the BL instruction saves the address of the next instruction to LR (the link register, R14). For ARM7, the target address is calculated by (a) shifting the 24-bit signed (2's comp) offset left two bits, (b) sign-extend the result to 32-bit, and (c) add it to contents of PC (program counter). This means the target address could be within the –32M bytes to +32M bytes of address space from the current program counter. For ARM Cortex M3. the target address must be within –16MB to +16 MB address space from current instruction.

Bxx Branch Conditional

Flags: Unaffected.

Format: Bxx target ; jump to target upon condition

Function: Used to jump to a target address if certain conditions are met. In ARM7, the target address cannot be more than –32MB to +32MB bytes away. For ARM Cortex M3. the target address must be within –16MB to +16 MB address space from current instruction. The conditions are indicated by the flag register. The conditions that determine whether the jump takes place can be categorized into three groups:

1. flag values,
2. the comparison of unsigned numbers, and
3. the comparison of signed numbers.

Each is explained next.

1. "B condition" where the condition refers to flag values. The status of each bit of the flag register has been decided by execution of instructions prior to the jump. The following "B condition" instructions check if a certain flag bit is raised or not.

Instruction		Condition
BCS	Branch if Carry Set	jump if C=1
BCC	Branch if Carry Clear	jump if C=0
BEQ	Branch if Equal	jump if Z=1
BNE	Branch if Not Equal	jump if Z=0
BMI	Branch if Minus/Negative	jump if N=1
BPL	Branch if Plus/Positive	jump if N=0
BVS	Branch if Overflow	jump if V=1
BVC	Branch if No overflow	jump if V=0

2. "B condition" where the condition refers to the comparison of unsigned numbers. After a compare (CMP Rn, Op2) instruction is executed, C and Z indicate the result of the comparison, as follows:

	C	Z
Rn > Op2	1	0
Rn = Op2	1	1
Rn < Op2	0	0

Since the operands compared are viewed as unsigned numbers, the following "B condition" instructions are used.

Instruction		Condition
BHI	Branch if Higher	jump if C=1 and Z=0
BEQ	Branch if Equal	jump if C=1 and Z=1
BLS	Branch if Lower or same	jump if C=0 or Z=1

In reality, the "CMP Rn, Op2" is a subtract instruction (Rn-Op2). After the subtraction the result is discarded and flags are changed according to the result. Notice in ARM the subtract affects the C flag setting differently from the x86 and other CPUs. See the SUB instruction.

3. "B condition" where the condition refers to the comparison of signed numbers. In the case of the signed number comparison, although the same instruction, "CMP Rn, Op2", is used, the flags used to check the result are as follows:

Rn > Op2	V=N or Z=0
Rn = Op2	Z=1
Rn < Op2	V inverse of N

Consequently, the "B condition" instructions used are different. They are as follows:

Instruction		
BGE	Branch Greater or Equal	jump if N=1 and V=1 or N=0 and V=0 (V=N)
BLT	Branch Less than	jump if N=1 and V=0 or N=0 and V=1 (N not equal to V)
BGT	Branch Greater than	jump if Z=0 and either N=1 and V=1 or N=0 and V=0 (N=V)
BLE	Branch Less or Equal	jump if Z=1 or N=1 and V=0. Or N=0 and V=1 (Z=1 or N not equal to V)
BEQ	Branch if Equal	jump if Z = 1

All "B condition" instructions are short jumps, meaning that the target address cannot be more than -32M bytes backward or +32M bytes forward from the PC of the instruction following the jump. In ARM Cortex M3 it is 16MB in each direction. What happens if a programmer needs to use a "B condition" to go to a target address beyond the -32MB to +32MB range? The solution is to use the "BX condition, Rm" since Rm can be 32-bit address and covers the entire 4GB address space of the ARM. This is shown next.

```
            LDR   R4, =MYTARGET
            ADDS  R1, R2, R3
            BXEQ  R4    ; branch to address held by R4 if Z=1
MYTRGT      SUBS  R7, #4
            NOP
            NOP
            ....
```

	C	Z	N	V
Rn > Op2	0	0	0	N
Rn = Op2	0	1	0	N
Rn < Op2	1	0	1	Inverse of N

BFC Bit Field Clear

Flags: Unaffected.

Format: BFC Rd, #LSB, #Width

Function: Clears selected bits of Rd. The start location of the Rd bit is indicated by #LSB and must be in the range of 0–31. How many bits should be cleared is indicated by #Width and must be in the range of 1–32.

Example 1:

```
LDR   R1, =0xFFFFFFFF   ; R1=0xFFFFFFFF
BFC   R1, #2, #14       ; now R1=0xFFFF0003
```

Example 2:

```
LDR   R2, =0x999999999  ; R2=0x99999999
BFC   R2, #8, #24       ; now R2=0x00000099
```

BFI Bit Field Insert

Flags: Unaffected.

Format: BFI Rd, Rn, #LSB, #Width

Function: Selected bits of Rn are copied to Rd. The start location of the Rd bit is indicated by #LSB and must be in the range of 0 – 31. How many bits should be copied is indicated by #Width and must be in the range of 1–32. The start bit location of Rn is always bit 0 (D0).

Example:

```
LDR   R1, =0xABCDABCD   ; R1=0xABCDABCD
LDR   R2, =0x12345678   ; R2=0x12345678
BFI   R1, R2, #4, #8    ; now R1=0xABCDA78D
```

BIC Bit Clear

Flags: Unaffected.

Format: BIC Rd, Rn, Op2 ; Rd=Rn ANDed with NOT of Op2

Function: Selected bits of Rn are cleared and placed in Rd. The Op2 provides the bits selection. If the selected bits in Op2 are high, then corresponding bits in Rn are cleared and the result is placed in Rd. If the selected bits in Op2 are low the corresponding bits in Rn are left unchanged and the result is placed in Rd. In reality, the BIC performs the AND operation on the bits of Rn with the complement of the bits in Op2. The BIC will not update the flags. To update the flags, we must use BICS.

Inputs		Output
X	Y	X AND (NOT Y)
0	0	0
0	1	0
1	0	1
1	1	0

Example:

```
      LDR   R1, =0xFFFFFF00    ; R1=0xFFFFFF00
      LDR   R2, =0x99999999    ; R2=0x9999999
      BIC   R3, R2, R1         ; now R3=0x00000099
```

BKPT Breakpoint

Flags: Unaffected.

Format: BKPT #imme_value

Function: used by compiler to insert breakpoint into programs. Upon execution of the BKPT instruction the program enters the Debug mode. See your ARM compiler for more information

BL Branch with Link (this is Call instruction)

Flags: Unchanged.

Format: BL Subroutine_Addr ; transfer control to a subroutine

Function: Transfers control to a subroutine. This instruction saves the address of the instruction after the BL in R14 (link register). At the end of the subroutine the control to the instruction after the BL is achieved by copying the LR (R14) register to PC. In ARM7, the target address cannot be more than –32MB to +32MB bytes away. For ARM Cortex M3. the target address must be within –16MB to +16 MB address space from current instruction.

Example:

```
      LDR   R7, =20000000
      BL    DELAY         ; Call subroutine MY_DELAY
      ADD   R3, #4              ; address of this instruction is saved in R14
      ...
      ...
DELAY SUBS  R7, #4
      NOP
      NOP
      MOV   PC, R14             ; Return, could have used "BX LR" instruction
```

BLX Branch Indirect with Link

Flags: Unaffected.

Format: BLX Rm ; transfer control to a subroutine whose

; address is given by Rm

Function: Transfers control to a subroutine whose address is given by the Rm register. This instruction saves the address of the instruction after the BL in R14 (link register). At the end of the subroutine the control to the instruction after the BL is achieved by copying the LR (R14) register to PC. One can use "BX LR" as return instruction. Notice the difference between this instruction and "BL Target_Addr" instruction. In the "BL Target_Addr" instruction the target address of the subroutine is given right there. However, in the "BLX Rm" instruction, the target address of the subroutine is held by register Rm.

Example:

```
      ADR   R2, DELAY
      BLX   R2          ; Call subroutine pointed to by R2
      ADD   R3, #4      ; address of this instruction is saved in R14
      ...
      ...
DELAY SUBS  R1, #4
      NOP
      NOP
      BX    LR          ; return
```

BX Branch Indirect (BX LR is used for Return)

Flags: Unchanged.

Format: BX Rm ; BX LR is used for Return from a subroutine

Function: The most widely usage of this instruction is in the form of "BX LR" for the purpose of return instruction at the end of subroutine.

Example:

```
      LDR   R1, =20000000
      BL    DELAY       ; Call subroutine MY_DELAY
      ADD   R3, #4      ; address of this instr. is saved in R14
      ......
DELAY SUBS  R1, #4
      NOP
      NOP
      BX    LR          ; return to caller
```

CBNZ Compare and Branch on Non-Zero

Flags: Unchanged.

Format: CBNZ Rn, Target

Function: Transfers control to the target location if Rn is not equal to zero. The Rn must be in the range of R0–R7 and target address cannot be farther than 130 bytes away from the instruction. This instruction compares the Rn with zero and jumps only if Rn is not zero. The comparison has no effect on flags. This can be used for loops in which the body of the loop is no more than 20 instructions.

Example 1:

```
      MOV   R1, #10     ; R1=10
L1    NOP
      NOP
      NOP
      SUB   R1, R1, #1  ; R1=R1-1
      CBNZ  R1, L1
```

CBZ Compare and Branch on Zero

Flags: Unaffected.

Format: CBZ Rn, Target

Function: Transfers control to the target location if Rn is zero. The Rn must be in the range of R0–R7 and target address cannot be farther than 130 bytes away from the instruction. This instruction compares the Rn with zero and jumps only if Rn is zero. The comparison has no effect on flags. This can be used to test a register value after reading a port.

Example 1:

```
      LDR   R0, =MYPORT_ADR    ; R0 = MYPORT address
HERE  LDR   R2, [R0]           ; read from MYPORT
      CBZ   R2, HERE           ; keep reading MYPORT until it is zero
```

CDP Coprocessor Data processing

See ARM Cortex-M Manual.

CLREX Clear Exclusive

See ARM Cortex-M Manual.

CLZ Count Leading Zero

Flags: Unchanged.

Format: CLZ Rd, Rn

Function: Scans the Rn register contents from most significant bit (D31) toward least significant bit (D0) until it finds the first HIGH. The number of binary zero bits before it encounters the first binary HIGH is placed in Rd.

Example:

```
      LDR   R3, =0x01FFFFFF
      CLZ   R1, R3             ; R1=7 since there are 7 zeros before the first
binary 1
```

CMN Compare Negative

Flags: Affected: V, N, Z, C.

Format: CMN Rn, Op2 ; sets flags as if "Rn + Op2"

; Notice, the Rn -(-Op2)=Rn+Op2

Function: Compares Rn register value with the negative of Op2 value. This is done by Rn - (negative of Op2) which is Rn - (-Op2) = Rn + Op2. The Rn and Op2 operands are not altered. In other words, the CMN adds the Op2 to Rn (Rn+Op2) and sets the flags accordingly. This is the same as ADDS instruction except the operands are unchanged and the result is discarded. See Bxx instruction for possible cases of comparison.

CMP Compare

Flags: Affected: V, N, Z, C.

Format: CMP Rn, Op2 ; sets flags as if "Rn-Op2"

Function: Compares two operands. The operands are not altered. Performs comparison by subtracting the Op2 operand from the Rn and updates flags as if SUBS were performed. As we can see in SUBS, the CMP perform the operation of Rn + 2's comp of Op2 and sets the flags according to the result. See Bxx instruction for possible cases of comparison.

CPSID Change processor ID and Disable Interrupt

Flags: Unaffected

Format: CPSID iflag ; iflag is i in PRIMASK or f in FAULTMASK

Function: Used for disabling the interrupt flags in PRIMASK or FAULTMASK registers. See ARM Cortex manual.

CPSIE Change Processor State and Enable Interrupt

Flags: Unaffected

Format: CPSIE iflag ; iflag is i in PRIMASK or f in FAULTMASK

Function: Used for enabling the interrupt flags in PRIMSK or FAULTMASK registers. See ARM Cortex manual.

DMB Data Memory Barrier

Flags: Unaffected

Format: DMB

Function: It makes sure that all the explicit memory accesses prior to DMB instruction are completed before the explicit memory accesses after the DMB. See ARM Cortex manual.

DSB Data Synchronization Barrier

Flags: Unaffected

Format: DSB

Function: It makes sure that all the explicit memory accesses prior to DSB instruction are completed before the DSB instruction is executed. See ARM Cortex manual.

EOR Exclusive OR

Flags: Unaffected

Format: EOR Rd, Rn, Op2

Function: Performs logical Ex-OR on the Rn and Op2 operands, bit by bit, storing the result in the Rd. This will not update the flags. Use EORS instruction to updates the flags.

Inputs		Output
X	Y	X EOR Y
0	0	0
0	1	1
1	0	1
1	1	0

Example 1:

```
MOV   R0, #0xAA   ; R0=0xAA
EOR   R2, R0, #0xFF      ; now, R2=0x55
                  ; AA  1010 1010
                  ; FF  1111 1111
                  ; --  ---------
                  ; 55  0101 0101   flags unchanged
```

Example 2:

```
LDR   R0, =0xAAAAAAAA    ; R0=0xAAAAAAAA
LDR   R1, =0x55555555    ; R1=0x55555555
EOR   R2, R1, R0         ; R2=0xFFFFFFFF
                         ; AA  1010 1010
                         ; 55  0101 0101
                         ; --  ---------
                         ; FF  1111 1111   flags unchanged
```

The "EOR Rd, Rx, Rx" can be used to clear Rd.

Example 3:

```
MOV   R1, #0x55
EOR   R2, R1, R1  ; R2=0
                  ; 55  0101 0101
                  ; 55  0101 0101
                  ; --  ---------
                  ; 00  0000 0000   flags unchanged
```

To complement the bits of Rn, EX-OR it with 0xFF.

Example 4:

```
LDR   R0, =0xAAAAAAAA    ; R0=0xAAAAAAAA
LDR   R1, =0xFFFFFFFF    ; R1=0xFFFFFFFF
EOR   R2, R1, R0         ; R2=0x55555555
                         ; AA  1010 1010
                         ; FF  1111 1111
                         ; --  ---------
                         ; 55  0101 0101   flags unchanged
```

ISB Instruction Synchronization Barrier

Flags: Unaffected.

Format: ISB

Function: It flushes the pipeline to make sure the instructions executed right after the ISB instruction are fetched fresh from the cache or memory.

IT If-Then Condition Block
Flags: Unaffected

Format: See ARM manual

Function: It allows the execution of up to four instructions after the IT to be conditional.

LDC Load Coprocessor
See the ARM Manual

LDM Load Multiple registers
Flags: Unaffected.

Format: LDM Rn, {Rx, Ry, ...}

Function: Loads into registers from consecutive memory locations. The starting address of memory location is given by Rn register. The destination registers separated by comma and placed in braces. In the ARM Cortex, the stack is descending meaning that as information is pushed onto stack the stack pointer is decremented. This IA (Increment the address after each Access) is the default for loading (Poping). This instruction is widely used for Poping (loading) multiple words from descending stack into CPU registers.

Example:

```
; Assume the following memory locations with the contents:
; 12000=(46)
; 12001=(10)
; 12002=(38)
; 12003=(82)
; 12004=(56)
; 12005=(50)
; 12006=(58)
; 12007=(15)
; 12008=(63)
; 12009=(60)
; 1200A=(68)
; 1200B=(39)
; 1200C=(79)
; 1200D=(70)
; 1200E=(75)
; 1200F=(92)

LDR   R7, =0x12000
LDM   R7, {R0, R2, R4}
; now, R0=0x82381046, R2=0x15585056, ...
; the contents of memory locations 0x12000-0x12003 are
```

```
; moved to register R0, and the contents of memory
; locations 0x12004-0x12007 are moved to register
; R2, and so on. Therefore we have R0=0x82381046,
; R2=0x15585056, and R4=0x39686063.
```

LDMDB Load Multiple registers and Decrement Before each access

Flags: Unaffected.

Format: LDMDB Rn, {Rx, Ry, ...}

Function: This is the same as LDMEA (load multiple registers from Empty Ascending) used for cases in which the stack is ascending. See LDMEA instruction.

LDMEA Load Multiple registers from Empty Ascending

Flags: Unaffected.

Format: LDMEA Rn, {Rx, Ry, ...}

Function: Loads into registers from consecutive memory locations. The starting address of memory location is given by Rn register. The destination registers separated by comma and placed in braces. In the ARM Cortex, the default for stack is descending meaning that as information are pushed onto stack the stack pointer is decremented. The IA (Increment the address after each Access) is the default. If we change the default of descending stack to ascending stack, then we have to use the EA (Empty Ascending). The ascending stack means as information are pushed onto stack the stack pointer is incremented. The LDMEA is used for Popping (loading) multiple words from ascending stack into CPU registers.

LDMFD Load Multiple registers Full Descending

Flags: Unaffected.

Format: LDMFD Rn, {Rx, Ry, ...}

Function: This is the same as LDM and LDMIA.

LDMIA Load Multiple registers and Increment after each Access

Flags: Unaffected.

Format: LDM Rn, {Rx, Ry, ...}

Function: This is the same as the LDM instructions. In the ARM Cortex, the stack is descending meaning that as information are pushed onto stack the stack pointer is decremented. This IA (Increment the address after each Access) is the default. We use this for Popping (loading) multiple words from descending stack into CPU registers.

LDR Load Register

Flags: Unaffected.

Format: LDR Rd, [Rx] ; load into Rd a word from memory location pointed to be Rx

Function: Loads into destination register the contents of four memory locations. The [Rx] points to address of memory location. This is widely used to load 32-bit data from memory into Rd register of the ARM since in the "MOV Rd, #immediate_value" the immediate value cannot be larger than 0xFF.

Example:

```
; Assume the following memory locations with the contents:
; 12000=(46)
; 12001=(10)
; 12002=(38)
; 12003=(82)
LDR R0, =0x12000
LDR R1, [R0]
; now, R1=82381046.
```

LDR Rx, =Value Load Register with 32-bit value

Flags: Unaffected.

Format: LDR Rd, =32_bit_value ; load Rd with 32-bit value

Function: Loads into destination register a 32-bit immediate value. This is widely used to load 32-bit immediate value into Rd register of the ARM since in the "MOV Rd, #immediate_value" the immediate value cannot be larger than 0xFF.

Example:

```
LDR    R0, =0x1200000      ; R0=0x1200000
LDR    R1, =0x2FFFF        ; R1=0x2FFFF
LDR    R0, =0xFFFFFFFF     ; R0=0xFFFFFFFF
LDR    R1, =200000000      ; R1=200000000
```

LDRB Load Register Byte

Flags: Unaffected.

Format: LDRB Rd, [Rx] ; load into Rd a byte from memory location pointed to be Rx

Function: Loads into destination register the contents of a single memory location indicated by Rx.

Example:

```
; Assume the following memory locations with the contents:
; 12000=(46)
; 12001=(10)
; 12002=(38)
; 12003=(82)
LDR   R0, =0x12000
LDRB  R1, [R0]
; now, R0=00000046
```

LDRH Load Register Halfword

Flags: Unaffected.

Format: LDRH Rd, [Rx] ; load into Rd a 2-byte from memory location pointed to be Rx

Function: Loads into destination register the contents of the two consecutive memory locations (halfword) indicated by Rx.

Example:

```
; Assume the following memory locations with the contents:
; 12000=(46)
; 12001=(10)
; 12002=(38)
; 12003=(82)
LDR   R0, =0x12000
LDRH  R1, [R0]
; now, R0=00001046
```

LDRSB Load Register signed Byte

Flags: Unaffected.

Format: LDRSB Rd, [Rx]

Function: Loads into Rd register a byte from memory location pointed to by Rx and sign-extends the byte to 32-bit word. That means the sign (D7) of the byte is copied to all the upper 24 bits of the Rd register.

Example 1:

```
; Assume the following memory locations with the contents:
; 12000=(85)
; 12001=(10)
; 12002=(38)
; 12003=(82)
LDR   R0, =0x12000
LDRB  R1, [R0]     ; now  R1=FFFFFF85 because MSB of 85 is 1
```

Example 2:

```
; Assume the following memory locations with the contents:
; 12000=(15)
; 12001=(20)
; 12002=(3F)
; 12003=(82)
LDR   R0, =0x12000
LDRB  R1, [R0]     ; now, R1=00000015 because MSB of 15 is 0
```

LDRSH Load Register Signed Halfword

Flags: Unaffected.

Format: LDRSH Rd, [Rx]

Function: Loads into Rd register a half-word (2-byte) from memory location pointed to by Rx and sign-extends it to 32-bit word. That means the sign (D15) of the 16-bit operand is copied to all the upper 16 bits of the Rd register.

Example 1:

```
; Assume the following memory locations with the contents:
; 12000=(46)
; 12001=(F3)
; 12002=(38)
; 12003=(82)
LDR   R0, =0x12000
LDRB  R1, [R0]     ; now, R0=FFFFF346 because MSB of F3 is 1
```

Example 2:

```
; Assume the following memory locations with the contents:
; 12000=(4F)
; 12001=(23)
; 12002=(18)
; 12003=(B2)
LDR   R0, =0x12000
LDRB  R1, [R0]     ; now, R1=0000234F because MSB of 23 is 0
```

LDRT Load Register with Translation

Flags: Unaffected

Format: LDRT Rd, [Rx]

Function: Loads into Rd register a byte from memory location pointed to by Rx and zero-extends the byte to 32-bit word. That means a zero is copied to all the upper 24 bits of the Rd register. Used for unprivileged memory access.

Example:

```
; Assume the following memory locations with the contents:
; 12000=(46)
; 12001=(10)
; 12002=(38)
; 12003=(82)
LDR   R0, =0x12000
LDRB  R1, [R0]     ; now, R1=00000046
```

LSL Logical Shift Left

Flags: Unaffected.

Format: LSL Rd, Rm, Rn

Function: As each bit of Rm register is shifted left, the MSB is removed and the empty bits are filled with zeros. The number of bits to be shifted left is given by Rn and the result is placed in Rd register. The LSL does not update the flags.

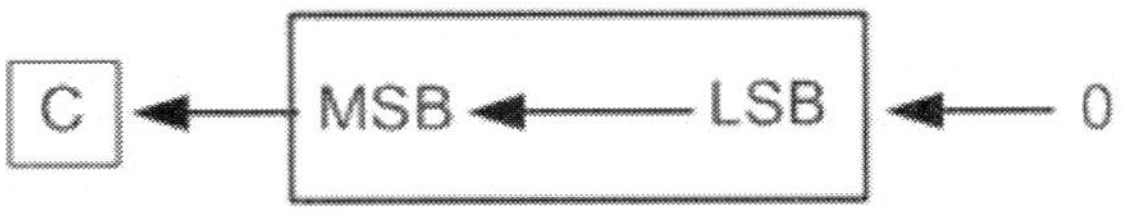

Example 1:

```
        LDR     R2, =0x00000010
        LSL     R0, R2, #8    ; R0=R2 is shifted left 8 times
                              ; now, R0= 0x00001000, flags not changed
```

Example 2:

```
        LDR     R0, =0x00000018
        MOV     R1, #12
        LSL     R2, R0, R1    ; R2=R0 is shifted left R1 number of times
                              ; now, R2= 0x000018000, flags not changed
```

Example 3:

```
        LDR     R0, =0x0000FF18
        MOV     R1, #16
        LSL     R2, R0, R1    ; R2=R0 is shifted left R1 number of times
                              ; now, R2= 0xFF180000, flags not changed
```

The logical shift left used for unsigned number shifting. LSL essentially multiplies Rm by a power of 2 for each bit shift.

LSR Logical Shift Right

Flags: Unaffected.

Format: LSR Rd, Rm, Rn

Function: As each bit of Rm register is shifted right, the LSB is removed and the empty bits are filled with zeros. The number of bits to be shifted left is given by Rn and the result is placed in Rd register. The LSR does not update the flags.

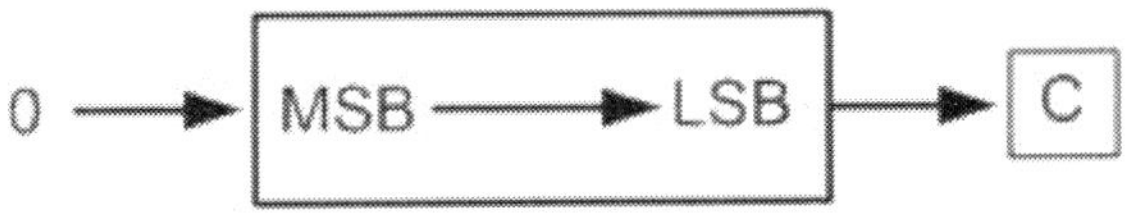

Example 1:

```
        LDR     R2, =0x00001000
        LSR     R0, R2, #8    ; R0=R2 is shifted right 8 times
                              ; now, R0= 0x00000010, C=0
```

Example 2:

```
        LDR     R0, =0x000018000
        MOV     R1, #12
        LSR     R2, R0, R1    ; R2=R0 is shifted right R1 number of times
                              ; now, R2= 0x00000018, C=0
```

Example 3:

```
        LDR     R0, =0x7F180000
```

```
        MOV    R1, #16
        LSR    R2, R0, R1   ; R2=R0 is shifted right R1 number of times
                            ; now, R2=0x00007F18, C=0
```

The logical shift right used for shifting unsigned numbers. LSR essentially divides Rm by a power of 2 for each bit shift.

MCR Move to Coprocessor from ARM Register
See ARM Manual.

MLA Multiply Accumulate
Flags: Unaffected

Format: MLA Rd, Rs1, Rs2, Rs3 ; Rd= (Rs1 × Rs2) + Rs3

Function: Multiplies an unsigned word held by Rs1 by a unsigned word in Rs2 and the result is added to Rs3 and placed in Rd.

Example:

```
        MOV    R0, #0x20    ; R0=0x20
        MOV    R1, #0x50    ; R1=0x50
        MOV    R2, #0x10    ; R2=0x10
        MLA    R4, R0, R1, R2     ; now R4= (0x20 × 0x50)+10= 0xA10
```

MLS Multiply and Subtract
Flags: Unaffected

Format: MLS Rd, Rm, Rs, Rn ; Rd= Rn -(Rs × Rm)

Function: Multiplies an unsigned word held by Rm by an unsigned word in Rs and the result is subtracted from Rn and placed in Rd.

Example:

```
        MOV    R0, #0x20    ; R0=0x20
        MOV    R1, #0x50    ; R1=0x50
        LDR    R2, =0x1000  ; R2=0x1000
        MLS    R4, R0, R1, R2     ; now R4= 0x1000-(0x20×0x50)=0x600
```

MOV Move (ARM7)
Flags: Unaffected.

Format: MOV Rd, #imm_value ; Rd=imm_Value < 0x200

Function: Load the Rd register with an immediate value. The immediate value cannot be larger than 0xFF (0–255). After the execution the flags are not updated. The MOVS instruction updates the flags.

Example 1:

```
        MOV    R0, #0x25    ; R0=0x25
```

```
MOV    R1, #0x5F    ; R1=0x5F
```

To load the ARM register with value larger than 0xFF we must use the "LDR Rd, = 32_bit_data." For example, we can use LDR R2, =0xFFFFFFFF.

Example 2:

```
LDR    R0, =0x2000000         ; R0=0x2000000
```

MOVT Move Top

Flags: Unaffected.

Format: MOVT Rd, #imm_value ; imm_value < 0x10000

Function: Loads the upper 16-bit of Rd register with an immediate value. The immediate value cannot be larger than 0xFFFF (0–65535). The lower 16-bit of the Rd register remains unchanged.

Example:

```
LDR    R0, =0x25579934    ; R0=0x25579934
MOVT   R0, #0xAAAA        ; R0=0xAAAA9934
```

MOVW Move 16-bit constant

Flags: Unaffected.

Format: MOVW Rd, #imm_value   ; imm_value < 0x10000

Function: Load the Rd register with an immediate value. The immediate value cannot be larger than 0xFFFF (0–65535).

Example:

```
MOVW   R1, #0x5555 ; R1=0x5555
```

To load the ARM register with value larger than 0xFFFF we must use the "LDR Rd, = 32_bit_data." For example we can use LDR R2, =0xFFFFFFF.

MRC Move to ARM Register from Coprocessor

See ARM manual

MRS Move to general Register from Special register

Flags: Unaffected.

Format: MRS Rd, special_reg   ; copy special_reg to Rd

Function: Copies the contents of a special function register to a general-purpose register. This instruction along with the MSR is widely used to modify the special function registers such as CONTROL, PRIMASK, and ISPR. This is the only way we can access the special function registers.

Example:

```
MRS    R1, CONTROL ; R1=CONTROL
```

```
AND    R1, #0x00    ; mask the lower 8 bits
MSR    CONTROL, R1
```

MSR Move to Special register from general Register

Flags: Unaffected.

Format: MSR special_reg, Rn ; copy special_reg to Rn

Function: Copies the contents of a general-purpose register to special function register. This instruction along with the MRS is widely used to modify the contents of special function registers such as CONTROL, PRIMASK, and ISPR. This is the only way we can access the special function registers.

Example:

```
MRS    R1, CONTROL ; R1=CONTROL
AND    R1, #0x00   ; mask the lower 8 bits
MSR    CONTROL, R1 ; mask the lower 8 bits of CONTROL reg.
```

MUL Unsigned Multiplication

Flags: Affected: N, Z, Unaffected: C, V

Format: MUL Rd, Rn, Rm ; Rd = Rn × Rm

Function: Multiplies a word in register Rn by a word in register Rm and places the result in Rd.

Example 1:

```
MOV    R0, #100     ; R0=100
MOV    R1, #200     ; R1=200
MUL    R3, R0, R1   ; R3 = R0 x R1 = 100 x 200 =20000
```

Example 2:

```
LDR    R0, =10000   ; R0=10000
LDR    R1, =20000   ; R1=20000
MUL    R3, R0, R1   ; R3 = R0 x R1= 10000 x 20000 = 200000000
```

MVN Move Negative

Flags: Unaffected.

Format: MVN Rd, Op2 ; Rd = 1's comp. of Op2

Function: Places in Rd the negation (the 1's complement) of Op2. Each bit of Op2 is inverted (logical NOT) and placed in Rd while flags remain unchanged.

Example 1:

```
MOV    R0, #0xAA    ; R0=0xAA
MVN    R2, R0       ; now, R2=0xFFFFFF55
```

Example 2:

```
LDR    R0, =0xAAAAAAAA   ; R0=0xAAAAAAAA
MVN    R1, R0            ; R1=0x55555555
```

Example 3:

```
MVN   R0, #0x0F    ; R0=0xFFFFFFF0
```

Example 4:

```
MVN   R2, #0x0     ; R0=0xFFFFFFFF widely used to load Rx with all 1s
```

NOP No Operation

Flags: Unaffected.

Format: NOP

Function: Performs no operation. Sometimes used for timing delays to waste clock cycles. Updates PC (program counter) to point to next instruction following NOP. In some ARM CPUs, the pipeline removes the NOP before it reaches the execution stage.

ORN Logical OR Not

Flags: Unaffected.

Format: ORN Rd, Rn, Op2 ; Rd = Rn ORed with 1's comp of Op2

Function: Performs the OR operation on the bits of Rn with the complement of the bits in Op2. The ORN will not update the flags. To update the flags, we must use ORNS.

Inputs		Output
A	B	A OR (NOT B)
0	0	1
0	1	0
1	0	1
1	1	1

Example 1:

```
LDR   R1, =0xFFFFFF00    ; R1=0xFFFFFF00
LDR   R2, =0x99999999    ; R2=0x9999999
ORN   R3, R2, R1         ; now R3=0x999999FF
```

Example 2:

```
MOV   R1, #0                     ; R1=0
LDR   R0, =0xFFFFFFFF            ; R0=0xFFFFFFFF
ORN   R2, R1, R0         ; now, R2=0x0
```

ORR Logical OR

Flags: Unaffected

Format: ORR Rd, Rn, Op2 ; Rd= Rn ORed Op2

Function: Performs logical OR on the bits of Rn and Op2, and places the result in Rd. Often used to turn a bit on. ORR will not update the flags.

Example 1:

```
        MOV     R0, #0xAA     ; R0=0xAA
        ORR     R2, R0, #0x55       ; now, R2=0xFF
```

Example 2:

```
        LDR     R0, =0x00010203     ; R0=00010203
        LDR     R1, =0x30303030
        ORR     R2, R0, R1          ; R2=0x30313233
```

Example 3:

```
        LDR     R0, =0x55555555     ; R0=0x55555555
        LDR     R1, =0xAAAAAAAA     ; R0=0xAAAAAAAA
        ORR     R2, R1, R0          ; R1=0xFFFFFFFF
```

POP POP register from Stack

Flags: Unaffected.

Format: POP {reg_list} ; reg_reg = words off top of stack

Function: Copies the words pointed to by the stack pointer to the registers indicated by the reg_list and increments the SP by 4, 8, 12, 16, ... depending on the number of registers in the reg_list.

Example:

```
        POP     {R1}            ; POP the top word of stack to R1
        POP     {R1, R4, R7}         ; POP the top 3 words of stack to R1, R4, R7
        POP     {R2-R6}         ; POP the top 5 words of stack to R2-R6
        POP     {R0, R5}        ; POP the top 2 words of stack to R0 and R5
        POP     {R0-R7}         ; POP the top 8 words of stack to R0-R7
```

The POP instruction is synonyms for LDMIA.

PUSH PUSH register onto stack

Flags: Unaffected.

Format: PUSH {reg_list} ; PUSH reg_list onto stack

Function: Copies the contents of registers stated in reg_list onto the stack and decrements SP by 4, 8, 12, 16, ... depending on the number of registers in reg_list.

Example:

```
        PUSH    {R1}            ; PUSH the R1 onto top of stack
        PUSH    {R1, R4, R7}         ; PUSH R1, R4, R7 onto top of stack
        PUSH    {R2-R6}         ; PUSH the R2, R3, R4, R5, R6 onto top of stack
        PUSH    {R0, R5}        ; PUSH the R0 and R5 onto top of stack
        PUSH    {R0-R7}         ; PUSH the R0 through R7 onto top of stack
```

The PUSH instruction is synonyms for STMDB.

RBIT Reverse Bits

Flags: Unaffected.

Format: RBIT Rd, Rn ; Reverse the bit order of Rn and place in Rd

Function: Reverses the bit position order of the 32-bit value in Rn register and place the result in Rd.

Example:

```
MOV   R1, #0x5F
RBIT  R2, R1            ; now, R2=0xF5000000
```

REV Reverse byte order in a word

Flags: Unaffected

Format: REV Rd, Rn ; Reverse the byte of Rn and place it in Rd

Function: Reverses the byte position order of the 32-bit value in Rn register and places the result in Rd. This can be used to convert from little endian to big endian or from big endian to little endian.

Example:

```
LDR   R1, =0x12345678
REV   R2, R1            ; now, R2=0x78564312
```

RV16 Reverse byte order in 16-bit

Flags: Unaffected

Format: REV16 Rd, Rn ; Reverse the bits if Rn and place it in Rd

Function: Reverses the 16-bit position order of the 32-bit value in Rn register and places the result in Rd. This can be used to convert 16-bit little endian to big endian or from 16-bit big endian to little endian.

Example:

```
LDR   R1, =0x559922FF
RV16  R2, R1            ; now, R2=0x22FF5599
```

REVSH Reverse byte order in bottom halfword and sign extend

Flags: Unaffected

Format: REVSH Rd, Rn ; Rd=Reverse the byte and sign extend Rn

Function: Reverses the 16-bit position order of Rn register and after sign extending to 32-bit it is placed in Rd. This can be used to convert a signed 16-bit little endian to 32-bit signed big endian or from signed 16-bit big endian to 32-bit signed little endian.

Example:

```
LDR   R1, =0x559922FF
REVSH R2, R1            ; now, R2=0x22FF5599
```

ROR Rotate Right

Flags: Unaffected.

Format: ROR Rd, Rm, Rn ; Rd=rotate Rm right Rn bit positions

Function: As each bit of Rm register shifts from left to right, they exit from the right end (LSB) and enter from left end (MSB). The number of bits to be rotated right is given by Rn and the result is placed in Rd register. The ROR does not update the flags.

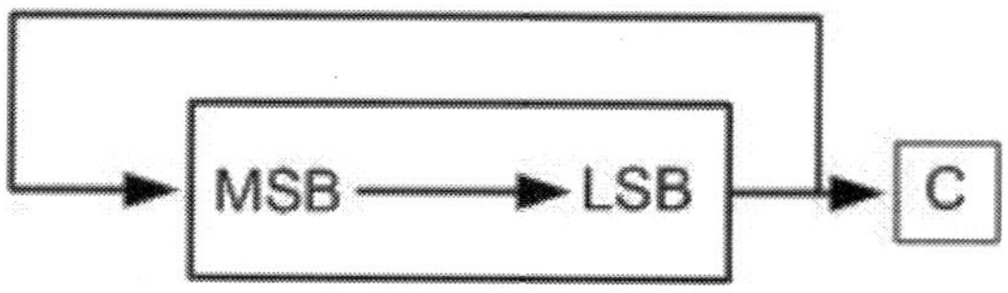

Example 1:

```
LDR   R2, =0x00000010
ROR   R0, R2, #8   ; R0=R2 is rotated right 8 times
                   ; now, R0 = 0x10000000, C=0
```

Example 2:

```
LDR   R0, =0x00000018
MOV   R1, #12
ROR   R2, R0, R1   ; R2=R0 is rotated right R1 number of times
                   ; now, R2 = 0x01800000, C=0
```

Example 3:

```
LDR   R0, =0x0000FF18
MOV   R1, #16
ROR   R2, R0, R1   ; R2=R0 is rotated right R1 number of times
                   ; Now, R2 = 0xFF180000, C=0
```

RRX Rotate Right with extend

Flags: Unaffected.

Format: RRX Rd, Rm ; Rd=rotate Rm right 1 bit position

Function: Each bit of Rm register is shifted from left to right one bit. The RRX does not update the flags.

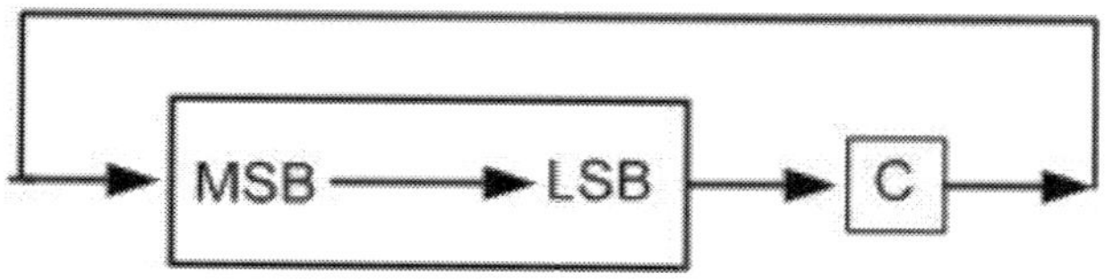

Example:

```
LDR   R2, =0x00000002
RRX   R0, R2       ; R0=R2 is shifted right one bit
                   ; now, R0=0x00000001
```

RSB Reverse Subtract

Flags: Unaffected

Format: RSB Rd, Rn, Op2 ; Rd = Op2 - Rn

Function: Subtracts the Rn from the Op2 and puts the result in the Rd. The RSB has no effect on flags. The steps for subtraction performed by the internal hardware of the CPU are as follows:

1. Takes the 2's complement of the Rn
2. Adds this to the Op2
3. Places the result in Rd

The Op2 and Rn operands remain unchanged by this instruction.

Example:

```
LDR    R0, =0x55555555    ; R0=0x55555555
LDR    R1, =0x99999999    ; R1=0x99999999
RSB    R2, R0, R1   ; R2=R1-R0
       ; For "RSB R2, R0, R1" we have:
       ; R2=R1-R0=0x99999999 - 0x55555555 =
       ; R2=0x99999999 + 2's comp of 0x55555555
       ; R2=0x99999999 + 0xAAAAAAAB = 0x44444444
       ;   0x99999999
       ; - 0x55555555
       ;   ---------------
       ;   0x44444444
```

SBC Subtract with Carry (Borrow)

Flags: Unaffected

Format: SBC Rd, Rn, Op2 ; Rd = Rn – Op2 – (1– C)

Function: Subtracts the Op2 operand from the Rn, placing the result in Rd. If C = 0, it subtracts 1 from the result; otherwise, it operates like SUB. The SBC has no effect on flags. This is used widely for multiword (64-bit) subtraction.

Example:

```
LDR    R0, =0x55555555    ; R0=0x55555555
LDR    R1, =0x99999999    ; R1=0x99999999
SUBS   R2, R0, R1   ; R2=R0 - R1
MOV    R3, #0x09    ; R3=0x09
SBC    R4, R3,#03   ; R4=R3 - 0x3
             ; For SUBS we have:
             ; R2=R1 - R0 = 0x55555555 - 0x99999999 =
             ; R2=0x55555555 + 2's comp of 0x99999999
             ; R2=0x55555555 + 0x66666667 = 0xBBBBBBBC  C=0
             ; For SBC we have:
             ; R4=R3-0x3=0x09 - 0x3 -(1 - C) = 9 - 3 - 1
             ; R4= 0x9 +2'comp. of -4 = 0x9 + 0xFFFFFFFC = 0x05
```

```
;    0x0000000955555555
; -  0x0000000399999999
```

SBFX Sign Bit Field extract

Flags: Unaffected

Format: SBFX Rd, Rn, #LSB, #Width

Function: Extracts the bit field from the Rn register and then after sign extending it is placed in Rd. The #LSB indicates which bit and #Width indicates how many bits.

Example 1:

```
LDR   R0, =0x00000543     ; R0=0x00000543
SBFX  R2, R0, #8, #4      ; now, R2=0x00000005
```

Example 2:

```
LDR   R0, =0x00000C43     ; R0=0x00000C43
SBFX  R2, R0, #4, #8      ; now, R2=0xFFFFFFC4
```

SDIV Signed Divide

Flags: Unaffected

Format: SDIV Rd, Rn, Rm ; Rd= Rn/Rm

Function: Divides a signed integer word in Rn by another signed integer word in Rm. The quotient result is placed in Rd. If value in Rn register is not divisible by the value in Rm register, the result is rounded to zero and placed in Rd. Divide by zero causes interrupt type 3.

Example:

```
LDR   R0, =-20000 ; R0=-20000
LDR   R1, =-1000  ; R1=-1000
SDIV  R2, R0, R1  ; now, R2 = -2000/-1000= 2
```

SEV Send Event

Flags: Affected.

Format: SEV

Function: Sends signal to all the processors in the multiprocessors system. See the ARM Cortex manual.

SMLAL Signed Multiply Accumulate Long

Flags: Unaffected

Format: SMLAL Rdlo, Rdhi, Rn, Rm ; Rdhi:Rdlo=(Rm × Rn) + (Rdhi:Rdlo)

Function: Multiplies signed words in Rn and Rm register, adds the 64-bit result to Rdhi:Rdlo register, and saves the final result in Rdhi:Rdlo. The Rdlo (low) and Rdhi(high) are the lower word and higher word of a 64-bit value.

Example 1:

```
LDR     R0, =0
LDR     R1, =0x23
LDR     R2, =-5000
LDR     R3, =-4000
SMLAL        R0, R1, R2, R3     ; now, R3:R2= (R3:R2)+ (R1 × R0)
                    ; = 0x2300000000 + (-5000 × -4000)
                    ; = 0x2300000000 + 20000000
                    ; = 0x23000000 + 0x1312D00 = 0x2301312D00
                    ; => R0 = 0x1312D00 and R1 = 0x23
```

SMULL Signed Multiply Long

Flags: Unaffected

Format: SMULL Rdlo, Rdhi, Rn, Rm ; Rdhi:Rdlo = Rm × Rn

Function: Multiplies signed words in Rn and Rm register, and saves the result in Rdhi:Rdlo. The Rdl (low) and Rdh(high) are the lower word and higher word of a 64-bit value.

Example:

```
LDR     R0, =-20000 ; R0=-20000 (signed 2's comp)
LDR     R1, =-1000000      ; R0=-100000 (signed 2's comp)
SMLAL R2, R3, R0, R1      ; now, R3:R2= R1 × R0 = -20000 × -1000000 =
              ; 20000000000 =0x4A817C800 => R3 = 0x4 and
              ; R2 = 0xA817C800
```

SSAT Sign Saturate

Flags: Unaffected.

Format: SSAT Rd, #n, Rm, shift#

Function: Used for saturation operation. See ARM Cortex manual.

STM Store Multiple

Flags: Unaffected.

Format: STM Rn, {Rx, Ry, ...}

Function: Stores registers Rx, Ry, ... into consecutive memory locations. The starting address of memory location is given by Rn register. The source registers are separated by comma and placed in braces. In the ARM Cortex, the default stack is descending meaning that as information are pushed onto stack the stack pointer is decremented. This IA (Increment the address After each access) is the default. This instruction is widely used for Pushing (storing) multiple registers into ascending stack.

Example:

```
LDR     R7, =0x12000
LDR     R0, =0x82381046     ; R0=0x82381046
LDR     R2, =0x15585056     ; R2=0x15585056
LDR     R4, =0x39686063     ; R4=0x39686063
```

```
STM   R7, {R0, R2, R4}        ; now, R2=0x15585056, ..
; The contents of registers R0, R2, and R4 are stored into
; consecutive memory locations starting at an address given by R7.
; The R0 contents are stored into memory locations 0x12000-0x12003,
; the R2 contents are stored into memory locations 0x12004 through
; 0x12007, and so on. This is shown below.
; 12000=(46)
; 12001=(10)
; 12002=(38)
; 12003=(82)
; 12004=(56)
; 12005=(50)
; 12006=(58)
; 12007=(15)
; 12008=(63)
; 12009=(60)
; 1200A=(68)
; 1200B=(39)
```

STMDB Store Multiple register and Decrement Before

Flags: Unaffected.

Format: STMDB Rn, {Rx, Ry, ...}

Function: Stores registers Rx, Ry, ... into consecutive memory locations. The starting address of memory location is given by Rn register. The source registers are separated by comma and placed in braces. In the ARM Cortex, the default stack is descending meaning that as information are pushed onto stack the stack pointer is decremented. Since IA(Increment the address After each access) is the default we need to use DB (Decrement the address Before each access) is to overwrite the default. This instruction is widely used for Pushing (storing) multiple registers into Descending stack.

Example:

```
LDR   R7, =0x12000
LDR   R0, =0x39686063    ; R0=0x39686063
LDR   R2, =0x15585056    ; R2=0x15585056
LDR   R4, =0x82381046    ; R4=0x82381046
STMDB R7, {R0, R2, R4}
; The contents of registers R0, R2, and R4 are stored into
; consecutive memory locations starting at an address given by R7.
; The R0 contents are stored into memory locations 0x11FFF-0x11FFC,
; the R2 contents are stored into memory locations 0x11FFB
; through 0x11FF8, and so on. This is shown below.
; 11FF4=(46)
; 11FF5=(10)
; 11FF6=(38)
; 11FF7=(82)
; 11FF8=(56)
; 11FF9=(50)
; 11FFA=(58)
; 11FFB=(15)
```

```
        ; 11FFC=(63)
        ; 11FFD=(60)
        ; 11FFE=(68)
        ; 11FFF=(39)
```

STMEA Store Multiple register Empty Ascending

Flags: Unaffected.

Format: STMEA Rn, {Rx, Ry, ...}

Function: This is same as STM.

STMIA Store Multiple register Empty Ascending

Flags: Unaffected.

Format: STMIA Rn, {Rx, Ry, ...}

Function: This is same as STM.

STMFD Store Multiple register Full Descending

Flags: Unaffected.

Format: STMFD Rn, {Rx, Ry, ...}

Function: This is another name for STMDB. The FD is for pushing onto Full Descending stacks

STR Store Register

Flags: Unaffected.

Format: STR Rd, [Rx] ; Store Rd into memory location pointed to be Rx

Function: Stores Rd register into four consecutive memory locations. The [Rx] points to starting address of memory location. This is widely used to store 32-bit register into memory locations.

Example:

```
        LDR   R1, =0x82381046    ; R1=0x82381046
        LDR   R0, =0x12000       ; R0=0x12000
        STR   R1, [R0]           ; now,
                                 ; 12000=(46)
                                 ; 12001=(10)
                                 ; 12002=(38)
                                 ; 12003=(82)
```

STRB Store Register Byte

Flags: Unaffected.

Format: STRB Rd, [Rn]

Function: Stores the lowest byte of the Rd register into a single memory location indicated by Rn.

Example:

```
LDR    R1, =0x82381046    ; R1=0x82381046
LDR    R0, =0x12000              ; R0=0x12000
STRB   R1, [R0]                  ; now, 12000=(46)
```

STRD Store Register Double (two words)

Flags: Unaffected.

Format: STRD Rd, [Rn]

Function: Stores two registers of Rd and Rd+1 into 8 consecutive memory locations indicated by Rn. Rd can be R0, R2, R4, R6, R8, R10, or R12.

Example:

```
LDR    R2, =0x12000
LDR    R0, =0x82381046    ; R0=0x82381046
LDR    R1, =0x15585056    ; R1=0x15585056
STRD   R0, R1, [R2] ; store R0 and R1 into memory locations starting
                    ; at an address given by R2. Now, we have:
; 12000=(46)
; 12001=(10)
; 12002=(38)
; 12003=(82)
; 12004=(56)
; 12005=(50)
; 12006=(58)
; 12007=(15)
```

STRH Store Register Halfword

Flags: Unaffected.

Format: STRH Rd, [Rn]

Function: Stores the lower 2 bytes of the Rd register into two consecutive memory locations indicated by Rn.

Example:

```
LDR    R1, =0x82381046    ; R1=0x82381046
LDR    R0, =0x12000       ; R0=0x12000
STRB   R1, [R0]           ; now, 12000=(46), and  12001=(10)
```

STRT Store Register

Flags: Unaffected

Format: STRT Rx, [Rn]

Function: Stores Rx register into memory location pointed to by Rx. This is the same as STR but is used for unprivileged memory access. See ARM Cortex manual.

Example:

```
LDR   R1, =0x82381046    ; R1=0x82381046
LDR   R0, =0x12000       ; R0=0x12000
STRT  R1, [R0]
                         ; now, 12000=(0x82381046)
```

SUB Subtract

Flags: Unaffected

Format: SUB Rd, Rn, Op2 ; Rd = Rn – Op2

Function: Subtracts the Op2 from the Rn and puts the result in the Rd. Has no effect on flags. The steps for subtraction performed by the internal hardware of the CPU are as follows:

1. Takes the 2's complement of the Op2
2. Adds this to the Rn
3. Place the result in the Rd

The Rd and Op2 operands remain unchanged by this instruction.

Example:

```
LDR   R0, =0x55555555    ; R0=0x55555555
LDR   R1, =0x99999999    ; R1=0x99999999
SUB   R2, R1, R0         ; R2=R1-R0
                 ; For "SUB R2, R1, R0" we have:
                 ; R2=R1-R0=0x99999999 - 0x55555555 =
                 ; R2=0x99999999 + 2's comp of 0x55555555
                 ; R2=0x99999999 + 0xAAAAAAAB = 0x44444444
                 ;   0x99999999
                 ; - 0x55555555
                 ;   -------------
                 ;   0x44444444
```

SVC supervisor Call (Software Interrupt)

Flags: Unaffected.

Format: SVC #imm_value

Function: It is used by application software to get services from operating systems (OS). This is like the SWI (software interrupt) instruction in ARM7.

SXTB Sign Extend byte

Flags: Unaffected.

Format: SXTB Rd, Rm

Function: Converts a signed byte in Rm into a signed word by copying the sign bit (D7) of Rm into all the bits of Rd. Used widely to convert a signed byte in Rm to a signed word to avoid the overflow problem in signed number arithmetic.

Example:

```
        MOV    R1, #0xFB     ; R1=0xFB which is 2's complement of -5
        SXTB   R0, R1        ; now, R0=0xFFFFFFFB
                             ; R1= 0000 0000 0000 0000 0000 0000 1111 1011
                             ; now R0=0xFFFFFFFB
                             ; R0 = 1111 1111 1111 1111 1111 1111 1111 1011
```

SXTH Sign Extend Halfword

Flags: Unaffected.

Format: SXTH Rd, Rm

Function: Converts a signed halfword in Rm into a signed word by copying the sign bit (D15) of Rm into all the bits of Rd. Used widely to convert a signed halfword (16-bit) in Rm to a signed word to avoid the overflow problem in signed number arithmetic.

Example:

```
        ; assume R1=0xFFFB which is 2's complement of -5
        SXTH   R0, R1       ; now, R0=0xFFFFFFFB
        ; R1= 0000 0000 0000 0000 1111 1111 1111 1011
        ; now, R0=0xFFFFFFFB
        ; R0 = 1111 1111 1111 1111 1111 1111 1111 1011
```

TBB Table Branch Byte

Flags: Unaffected.

Format: TBB [Rn, Rm]

Function: Branches forward using table of single byte offset using PC-relative addressing mode. Rn has starting address of the table and Rm is an index into the table. See ARM Cortex M3 manual.

TBH Table Branch halfword

Flags: Unaffected.

Format: TBH [Rn, Rm, LSL #1]

Function: Branches forward using table of halfword offset using PC-relative addressing mode. Rn has starting address of the table and Rm is an index into the table. The "LSL # 1" shifts left the address once to make it halfword aligned address. See ARM Cortex M3 manual.

TEQ Test Equivalence

Flags: Affected: N and Z

Format: TEQ Rn, Op2 ; performs Rn Ex-OR Op2

Function: Performs a bitwise logical Ex-OR on Rn and Op2, setting flags but leaving the contents of both Rn and Op2 unchanged. While the EORS instruction changes the contents of the destination and the flag bits, the TEQ instruction changes only the flag bits. This is widely used to see if two registers are equal.

Example 1:

```
      TEQ   R1, R2       ; check to see if R1=R2. If so Z=1. R1 and R2
                         ; remain unchanged
```

Example 2:

```
      TEQ   R2, #0x01    ; check to see if D0 of R2 is 1, if so Z=1. R2
                         ; remains unchanged
```

Example 3:

```
      TEQ   R1, #0xFF    ; check to see if D7_D0 of R1 are 1s,
                         ; if so Z=1. R1 remains unchanged
```

TST Test

Flags: Affected: N and Z

Format: TST Rn, Op2 ; performs Rn AND Op2

Function: Performs a bitwise logical AND on Rn and Op2, setting flags but leaving the contents of both Rn and Op2 unchanged. While the ANDS instruction changes the contents of the destination and the flag bits, the TST instruction changes only the flag bits. To test whether a bit of Rn is 0 or 1, use the TST instruction with an Op2 constant that has that bit set to 1 and all other bits cleared to 0.

Example 1:

```
      TST   R1, #0x01    ; check to see if D0 of R1 is zero, if so Z=1.
                         ; R1 remain unchanged
```

Example 2:

```
      TST   R1, #0xFF    ; check to see if any bits of R1 is zero, if so
                         ; Z=1. R1 remain unchanged
```

UBFX Unsigned Bit field extract

Flags: Unaffected.

Format: UBFX Rd, Rn, #LSB, #Width

Function: Extracts the bit field from the Rn register and then zero extends it and places in Rd. The #LSB indicates from which bit and #Width indicates how many bits.

Example 1:

```
      LDR   R0, =0x00077555    ; R0=0x00077555
      UBFX  R2, R0, #8, #4     ; now, R2=0x00000005
```

Example 2:

```
      LDR   R0, =0x12345678    ; R0=0x12345678
      UBFX  R2, R0, #8, #12    ; now, R2=0x00000456
```

UDIV Unsigned Divide

Flags: Unaffected

Format: UDIV Rd, Rn, Rm ; Rd= Rn/Rm

Function: Divides an unsigned integer word in Rn by another unsigned integer word in Rm. The quotient result is placed in Rd. If value in Rn register is not divisible by the value in Rm register, the result is rounded to zero and placed in Rd. Divide by zero causes exception interrupt.

Example 1:

```
LDR   R0, =100     ; R0=100
LDR   R1, =2000
UDIV  R2, R1, R0   ; now, R2=R1/R0=2000/100=20
```

Example 2:

```
LDR   R0, =20000   ; R0=20000
UDIV  R2, R0, #100       ; now, R2=2000/100=20
```

UMLAL Unsigned Multiply with Accumulate

Flags: Unaffected

Format: UMLAL RdLo, RdHi, Rn, Rm ; RdHi:RdLo=(Rm × Rn) + (RdHi:RdLo)

Function: Multiplies unsigned words in Rn and Rm register, adds the 64-bit result to RdHi:RdLo registers, and saves the final result in RdHi:RdLo. The RdLo (low) and RdHi(high) are the unsigned lower word and higher word of the 64-bit value.

Example:

```
LDR   R0, =20000   ; R0=20000
LDR   R1, =1000
LDR   R2, =5000
LDR   R3, =4000
UMLAL R2, R3, R0, R1     ; now, R3:R2= R1 × R0 + R3:R2
```

UMULL Unsigned Multiply Long

Flags: Unaffected

Format: UMULL RdLo, RdHi, Rn, Rm ; RdHi:RdLo = Rm × Rn

Function: Multiplies unsigned words in Rn and Rm registers, and saves the result in RdHi:RdLo. The RdLo (low) and RdHi(high) are the lower word and higher word of a 64-bit value.

Example:

```
LDR   R0, =20000   ; R0=20000
LDR   R1, =10000   ; R1=10000
LDR   R2, =50000   ; R2=50000
LDR   R3, =40000   ; R3=40000
UMULL R2, R3, R0, R1     ; now, R3:R2= R1 × R0
```

UXBT Zero extend a byte

Flags: Unaffected

Format: UXBT Rd, Rm

Function: Zero extends a byte in Rm and places in Rd. Used widely to convert a byte in Rm to word for signed number operations.

Example:
```
        MOV    R1, #0xFB     ; R1=0xFB
        UXBT   R0, R1        ; now, R0=0x00000000FB
                      ; R1= 0000 0000 0000 0000 0000 0000 1111 1011
                      ; now R0=0x000000FB
                      ; R0 = 0000 00000 0000 0000 0000 0000 1111 1011
```

UXTH Zero extend halfword

Flags: Unaffected

Format: UXTH Rd, Rm

Function: Zero extends a halfword in Rm and places in Rd. Used widely to convert a halfword in Rm to word for signed number operations.

Example:
```
        ; assume R1=0xFFFB
        UXTH   R0, R1        ; now, R0=0x00000FFFB
                      ; R1= 0000 0000 0000 0000 1111 1111 1111 1011
                      ; now, R0=0x0000FFFB
                      ; R0 = 0000 0000 0000 0000 1111 1111 1111 1011
```

WFE Wait for event

Flags: Unaffected

Format: WFE

Function: Used by power management. See ARM Cortex M3 manual.

WFI Wait for interrupt

Flags: Unaffected

Format: WFI

Function: Suspends execution until one of the following events occurs:

1. a non-masked interrupt occurs and is taken,
2. an interrupt masked by PRIMASK becomes pending,
3. a Debug Entry request.

See ARM Cortex manual.

Appendix B: ARM Assembler Directives

Section B.1: List of ARM Assembler Directives

ALIGN

AREA

DCB directive (define constant byte)

DCD directive (define constant word)

DCW directive (define constant half-word)

ENDP or ENDFUNC

ENTRY

EQU (Equate)

EXPORT or GLOBAL

EXTRN (External)

FUNCTION or PROC

INCLUDE

RN (equate)

Section B.2: Description of ARM Assembler Directives

Directives, or as they are sometimes called, pseudo-ops or pseudo-instructions, are used by the assembler to translate Assembly language programs into machine language. Unlike the microprocessor's instructions, directives do not generate any opcode; therefore, no memory locations are occupied by directives in the final hex version of the assembly program. To summarize, directives give directions to the assembler program to tell it how to generate the machine code; instructions are assembled into machine code to give instructions to the CPU at execution time. The following are descriptions of the some of the most widely used directives for the ARM assembler. They are given in alphabetical order for ease of reference.

ALIGN

Format:

```
ALIGN        n      ; n is any power of 2 from 2^0 to 2^31
```

This is used to make sure data is aligned in 32-bit word or 16-bit half word memory address. If n is not specified, ALIGN sets the current location to the next word (four byte) boundary. The following uses ALIGN to make the data word and half word aligned:

```
ALIGN   4           ; The next instruction is word (4 bytes) aligned
ALIGN               ; The next instruction is word (4 bytes) aligned
```

```
ALIGN    2          ; The next instruction is half word (2 bytes) aligned
```

Notice that, this ALIGN directive should not be confused with the ALIGN attribute of the AREA directive.

AREA

Format:

```
AREA         sectionname        attribute, attribute, ...
```

The AREA directive tells the assembler to define a new section of memory. The memory can be code or data and can have attributes such as ReadOnly, ReadWrite, and so on. This is widely used to define one or more blocks of indivisible memory for code or data to be used by the linker. Every assembly language program has at least one AREA.

The following line defines a new area named MY_ASM_PROG1 which has CODE and READONLY attributes:

```
AREA   MY_ASM_PROG1        CODE, READONLY
```

Among widely used attributes are CODE, DATA, READONLY, READWRITE, COMMON, and ALIGN. The following describes these widely used attributes.

CODE is an attribute given to an area of memory used for executable machine instruction. Since it is used for code section of the program it is by default READONLY memory. In ARM Assembly language we use this area to write our instructions.

DATA is an attribute given to an area of memory used for data and no instruction (machine instructions) can be placed in this area. Since it is used for data section of the program it is by default a READWRITE memory. In ARM Assembly language we use this area to set aside SRAM memory for scratch pad and stack.

READWRITE is an attribute given to an area of memory which can be read from and written to. Since it is READWRITE section of the program it is by default for DATA. In ARM Assembly language we use this area to set aside SRAM memory for scratch pad and stack.

READONLY is an attribute given to an area of memory which can only be read from. Since it is READONLY section of the program it is by default for CODE. In ARM Assembly language we use this area to write our instructions for machine code execution.

COMMON is an attribute given to an area of DATA memory section which can be used commonly by several program codes. We do not initialize the COMMON section of the memory since it is used by compiler exclusively. The compiler initializes the COMMON memory area with all zeros.

ALIGN is another attribute given to an area of memory to indicate how memory should be allocated according to the addresses. When the ALIGN is used for CODE and READONLY it aligned in 4-bytes address boundary by default since the ARM instructions are all 32-bit (4-bytes) word. The ALIGN attribute of AREA has a number after like ALIGN=3 which indicates the information should be placed in memory with addresses of 2^3, that is 0x50000, 0x50008, 0x50010, 0x50020, and so on. This ALIGN attribute of the AREA should not be confused with the ALIGN directive.

DCB directive (define constant byte)

Format:

```
label       DCB    n              ; n between -128 to 256 , byte or string
```

The DCB directive allocates a byte size memory and initializes the values for reading only.

```
MYVALUE     DCB    5                 ; MYVALUE = 5
MYMSAGE     DCB    "HELLO WORLD"     ; string
```

DCD directive (define constant word)

Format:

```
label             DCD    n
```

The DCD directive allocates a word size memory and initializes the values for reading only. The data is 32 bit aligned.

```
MYDATA      DCD    0x200000, 0xF30F5, 5000000, 0xFFFF9CD7
```

DCW directive (define constant half-word)

Format:

```
label             DCB    n
```

The DCW directive allocates a half-word size memory and initializes the values for reading only.

```
MYDATA      DCW    0x20, 0xF230, 5000, 0x9CD7
```

END

The END directive tells the assembler that it has reached the end of the program (not the end of the source file). All the text beyond the END directive is ignored by the assembler.

ENDP or ENDFUNC

The ENDFUNC or ENDP directive informs the assembler that it has reached the end of a function. ENDFUNC and ENDP are the same. See FUNCTION or PROC directives.

ENTRY

The ENTRY directive shows the entry point of a program to the assembler. Each program must have one entry point. *The newer versions of ARM Linker have alternative methods of specifying the program entry point that overwrite this directive.*

EQU (Equate)

To assign a fixed value to a name, one uses the EQU directive. The assembler will replace each occurrence of the name with the value assigned to it.

```
DATA1 EQU   0x39         ; the way to define hex value
PORTB EQU   0xF0018000   ; SFR Port B address
SUM1  EQU   0x40000120   ; assign RAM location to SUM1
```

Unlike data directives such as DCB, DCD, and so on, EQU does not assign any memory storage; therefore, it can be defined at any time and at any place, and can even be used within the code segment.

EXPORT or GLOBAL

To inform the assembler that a name or symbol will be referenced by other modules (in other files), it is marked by the EXPORT or GLOBAL directives. If a module is referencing a name outside itself, that name must be declared as EXTRN (or IMPORT). Correspondingly, in the module where the variable is defined, that variable must be declared as EXPORT or GLOBAL in order to allow it to be referenced by other modules. See the EXTRN directive for examples of the use of both EXTRN and EXPORT.

EXTRN (External)

The EXTRN directive is used to indicate that certain variables and names used in a module are defined by another module. In the absence of the EXTRN directive, the assembler would search for the definition and give an error when it couldn't find it. The format of this directive is:

```
      EXTRN       name
```

The following example shows how the EXPORT and EXTERN directives are used:

```
      ; from the main program:
      EXTRN MY_FUNC
      ...
      BL    MY_FUNC
      ...
      ; ---------------------------------------
      ; MY_FUNC is located in a different file:
      AREA  OUR_EXAMPLE,CODE,READONLY
      EXTRN       DATA1
      EXPORT       MY_FUNC
MY_FUNC     FUNCTION
      ...
      LDR   R1,=DATA1
      ...
      ENDFUNC
```

Notice that the EXTRN directive is used in the main procedure to show that MY_FUNC is defined in another module. This is needed because MY_FUNC is not defined in that module. Correspondingly, MY_FUNC is defined as GLOABAL in the module where it is defined. EXTRN is used in the MY_FUNC module to declare that operand DATA1 has been defined in another module. Correspondingly, DATA1 is declared as GLOBAL in the calling module.

FUNCTION or PROC

Often, a group of Assembly language instructions will be combined into a procedure so that it can be called by another module. The FUNCTION and ENDFUNC directives are used to indicate the beginning and end of the procedure. *Some versions of Keil uVision debugger require the code to be enclosed in PROC/ENDP pair to be single stepped.* See the following example:

```
MY_FUNC      FUNCTION
             ...
             ...
             ENDFUNC
```

INCLUDE

When there is a group of macros written and saved in a separate file, the INCLUDE directive can be used to bring them into another file.

RN (Register Naming)

This is used to define a name for a register. The RN directive does not set aside a separate storage for the name, but associates a register with that name. The following code shows how we use RN:

```
VAL1  RN    R1    ; define VAL1 as a name for R1
VAL2  RN    R2    ; define VAL2 as a name for R2
SUM   RN    R3    ; define SUM as a name for R3

      AREA   PROG_2_1, CODE, READONLY
      ENTRY
      MOV   VAL1, #0x25         ; R1 = 0x25
      MOV   VAL2, #0x34         ; R2 = 0x34
      ADD   SUM, VAL1, VAL2     ; add R2 to R1 and place it in R3
HERE  B     HERE
      END
```

Appendix C: Macros

What is a macro and how is it used?

There are applications in Assembly language programming where a group of instructions performs a task that is used repeatedly. For example, you might need to add three registers together. So it does not make sense to rewrite them every time they are needed. Therefore, to reduce the time that it takes to write these codes and reduce the possibility of errors, the concept of macros was born. Macros allow the programmer to write the task (set of codes to perform a specific job) once only and to invoke it whenever it is needed, wherever it is needed.

MACRO definition

Every macro definition must have three parts, as follows:

```
                MACRO
[$label]                macroName parameter1, parameter2, ..., parameterN
        ...     ...
        ...     ...
                MEND
```

The MACRO directive indicates the beginning of the macro definition and the MEND directive signals the end. What goes in between the MACRO and MEND directives is called the body of the macro. The name must be unique and must follow Assembly language naming conventions. The parameters are names, or parameters, or even registers that are mentioned in the body of the macro. After the macro has been written, it can be invoked (or called) by its name, and appropriate values are substituted for parameters. For example, you might want to have an instruction that adds three registers. The following is a macro for the purpose:

```
MACRO
ADD3VAL     $DEST, $ARG1, $ARG2, $ARG3
ADD         $DEST, $ARG1, $ARG2
ADD         $DEST, $DEST, $ARG3
MEND
```

The above code is the macro definition. Note that parameters $DEST, $ARG1, $ARG2, and $ARG3 are mentioned in the body of the macro. To distinguish parameters, they must start with $. In the following example, the macro is invoked by its name with the user's actual data:

```
AREA OURCODE, READONLY, CODE
MOV   R1, #5
MOV   R2, #2
ADD3VAL     R0, R1, R2, #5
```

The instruction "ADD3VAL R0, R1, R2, #5" invokes the macro.

The assembler expands the macro by providing the following code in the .LST file:

```
3 00000008 E0810002       ADD    R0, R1, R2
4 0000000C E2800005       ADD    R0, R0, #5
```

Default Values for parameters

We can define default values for parameters as shown below:

```
MACRO
ADD3VAL      $DEST, $ARG1=R3, $ARG2, $ARG3=#5
ADD          $DEST, $ARG1, $ARG2
ADD          $DEST, $DEST, $ARG3
MEND
```

To use the default value, we put a '|' instead of the parameter while invoking the macro:

```
ADD3VAL      R0, R1, R2, |
```

The above code uses the default value of $ARG3 which is set to #5.

Using labels in macros

In the discussion of macros so far, examples have been chosen that do not have a label or name in the body of the macro. This is because if a macro is expanded more than once in a program and there is a label in the label field of the body of the macro, the same label would be generated more than once and an assembler error would be generated. To address the problem, we can give a unique label to the macro when we invoke it, as shown below:

```
        MACRO
$lbl    OUR_MACRO
        CMP  R1,#5
        BEQ  $lbl
        MOV  R1, #1
$lbl
        MEND

        AREA        OURCODE, READONLY, CODE
        ENTRY
        MOV  R1, #3
label1       OUR_MACRO
        MOV  R1, #5
label2       OUR_MACRO
HERE    B    HERE
```

The assembler expands the macro by providing the following code in the .LST file:

```
20 00000000                        AREA OURCODE, READONLY, CODE
21
22 00000000 E3A01003                 MOV  R1, #3
23 00000004             label1       OUR_MACRO
 3 00000004 E3510005                 CMP  R1, #5
 4 00000008 0A000000                 BEQ  label1
 5 0000000C E3A01001                 MOV  R1, #1
 6 00000010             label1
24 00000010 E3A01005                 MOV  R1, #5
25 00000014             label2       OUR_MACRO
 3 00000014 E3510005                 CMP  R1, #5
```

```
  4 00000018 0A000000          BEQ label2
  5 0000001C E3A01001          MOV R1, #1
  6 00000020          label2
 26 00000020 EAFFFFFE
                      HERE   B   HERE
```

In cases that there is more than one label in a macro the lines can be labeled as shown below:

```
      MACRO
$lbl        OUR_MACRO
      CMP   R1, #5
      BEQ   $lbl.equal
      MOV   R1, #1
      B     $lbl.next
$lbl.equal
      MOV   R1, #2
$lbl.next
      MEND

      AREA  OURCODE, READONLY, CODE

      MOV   R1, #3
label1      OUR_MACRO
      MOV   R1, #5
label2      OUR_MACRO
HERE  B     HERE
```

The assembler expands the macro by providing the following code in the .LST file:

```
 13 00000000                    AREA OURCODE, READONLY, CODE
 14
 15 00000000 E3A01003          MOV R1, #3
 16 00000004          label1  OUR_MACRO
  3 00000004 E3510005          CMP R1, #5
  4 00000008 0A000001          BEQ label1equal
  5 0000000C E3A01001          MOV R1, #1
  6 00000010 EA000000          B   label1next
  7 00000014          label1equal
  8 00000014 E3A01002          MOV R1, #2
  9 00000018          label1next
 17 00000018 E3A01005          MOV R1, #5
 18 0000001C          label2  OUR_MACRO
  3 0000001C E3510005          CMP R1, #5
  4 00000020 0A000001          BEQ label2equal
  5 00000024 E3A01001          MOV R1, #1
  6 00000028 EA000000          B   label2next
  7 0000002C          label2equal
  8 0000002C E3A01002          MOV R1, #2
  9 00000030          label2next
 19 00000030 EAFFFFFE
                      HERE   B   HERE
```

Conditional macros

We can pass condition into macros, as well:

```
        MACRO
$lbl    OurMacro$cond
        CMP   R1, #5
        B$cond     $lbl.equal
       MOV    R1, #1
$lbl.equal
        MEND

        AREA OURCODE, READONLY, CODE

        MOV  R1, #3
label1       OurMacroEQ   ; in the macro check equality
        MOV  R1, #3
label2       OurMacroLO   ; in the macro check if is lower
HERE    B    HERE
```

The assembler expands the macro by providing the following code in the .LST file:

```
   10 00000000                    AREA OURCODE, READONLY, CODE
   11
   12 00000000 E3A01003            MOV   R1, #3
   13 00000004          label1      OurMacroEQ
    3 00000004 E3510005            CMP   R1, #5
    4 00000008 0A000000            BEQ   label1equal
    5 0000000C E3A01001            MOV   R1, #1
    6 00000010          label1equal
   14 00000010 E3A01003            MOV   R1, #3
   15 00000014          label2   OurMacroLO
    3 00000014 E3510005            CMP   R1, #5
    4 00000018 3A000000            BLO   label2equal
    5 0000001C E3A01001            MOV   R1, #1
    6 00000020          label2equal
   16 00000020 EAFFFFFE
                         HERE          B     HERE
```

Notice that the first B$cond is substituted with BEQ while the second B$cond is substituted with BLO since the conditions EQ and LO are used respectively.

INCLUDE directive

Assume that there are several macros that are used in every program. Must they be rewritten every time? The answer is no if the concept of the INCLUDE directive is known. The INCLUDE directive allows a programmer to write macros and save them in a file, and later bring them into any file. For example, assuming that some widely used macros were written and then saved under the filename "MYMACRO1.S", the INCLUDE directive can be used to bring this file into any ".asm" file and then the program can call upon any of the macros as many times as needed. In the following example the ADD3VAL macro is defined in the MyMACRO.s file and it is used in the example.asm file.

prog.asm

```
        AREA OURCODE,READONLY,CODE
        INCLUDE MyMacro.s
        ENTRY
        MOV R1,#5
        MOV R2,#2
        ADD3VAL R0,R1,R2,#5
H1      B   H1
        END
```

MyMacro.s

```
        MACRO
        ADD3VAL $DEST,$ARG1,$ARG2,$ARG3
        ADD $DEST,$ARG1,$ARG2
        ADD $DEST,$DEST,$ARG3
        MEND
        END
```

Figure C. 1: Defining a Macro in an Include File

Macros vs. subroutines

Macros and subroutines are useful in writing assembly programs, but each has limitations. Macros increase code size every time they are invoked. For example, if you call a 10-instruction macro 10 times, the code size is increased by 100 instructions; whereas, if you call the same subroutine 10 times, the code size is only that of the subroutine instructions. On the other hand, a function call takes 3 clocks and the return instruction takes 3 clocks to get executed. So, using functions adds around 6 clock cycles. The subroutines might use stack space as well when called, while the macros do not.

Appendix D: Flowcharts and Pseudocode

Flowcharts

If you have taken any previous programming courses, you are probably familiar with flowcharting. Flowcharts use graphic symbols to represent different types of program operations. These symbols are connected together into a flowchart to show the flow of execution of a program. The more commonly used symbols are as follows:

Start and End points

Start and End points are commonly represented as rounded rectangles or ovals containing the words "Start" or "End". Small circle is another way to show them.

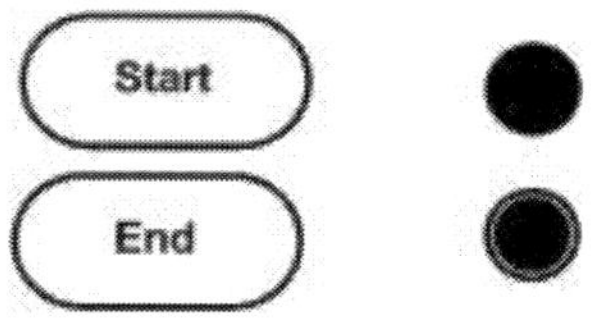

Figure D- 1: Start and End Points

Decisions

The conditions are represented in diamonds.

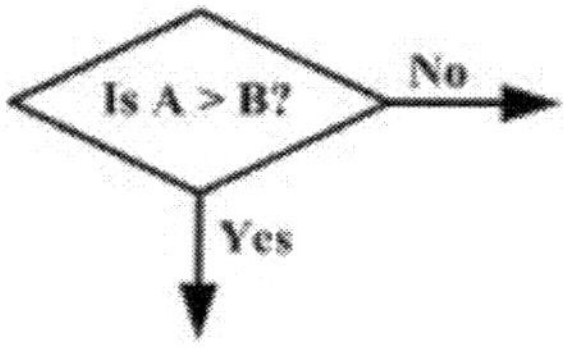

Figure D- 2: a Decision that Compares A with B

Process

The processing steps are represented using rectangles.

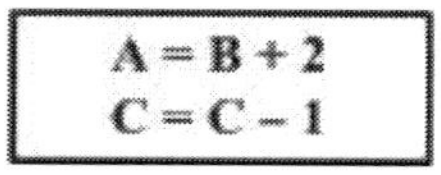

Figure D- 3: a Process Sample

Inputs and outputs

Inputs and outputs are represented as parallelogram.

Figure D- 4: an Output Sample

Subroutines

Calling subroutines are represented as shown below

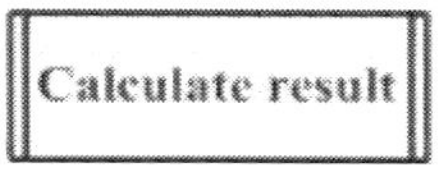

Figure D- 5: a Subroutine Call Sample

Pseudocode

Flowcharting has been standard practice in industry for decades. However, some find limitations in using flowcharts, such as the fact that you can't write much in the little boxes, and it is hard to get the "big picture" of what the program does without getting bogged down in the details. An alternative to using flowcharts is pseudocode, which involves writing brief descriptions of the flow of the code. Figures D-6 through D-10 show flowcharts and pseudocode for commonly used control structures.

Structured programming uses three basic types of program control structures: sequence, control, and iteration. Sequence is simply executing instructions one after another. Figure D-6 shows how sequence can be represented in pseudocode and flowcharts.

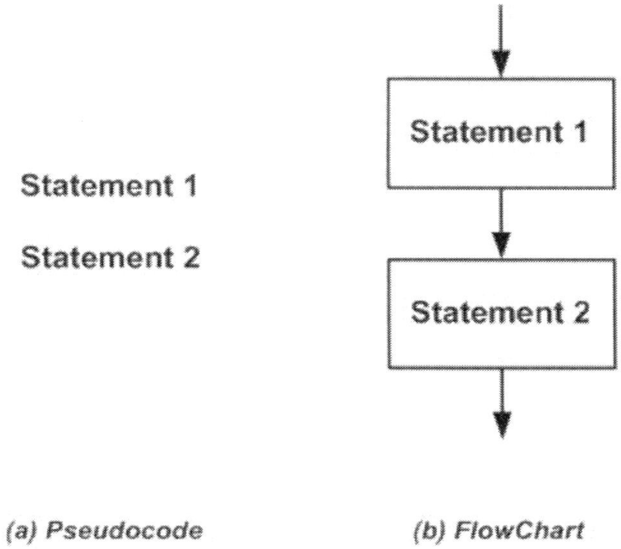

Figure D- 6: SEQUENCE Pseudocode versus Flowchart

Note in Figures D-6 through D-11 that "statement" can indicate one statement or a group of statements.

Figure D-7 through D-9 show two control programming structures: IF-THEN-ELSE and IF-THEN in both pseudocode and flowcharts.

```
IF (condition) THEN
      Statement 1
ELSE
      Statement 2
```

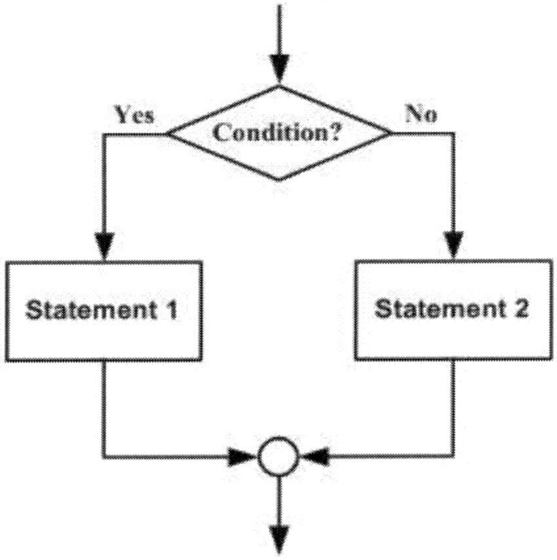

Figure D- 7: IF THEN ELSE Pseudocode versus Flowchart

```
IF (A = B) THEN
      C = 2
ELSE
      C = 5
```

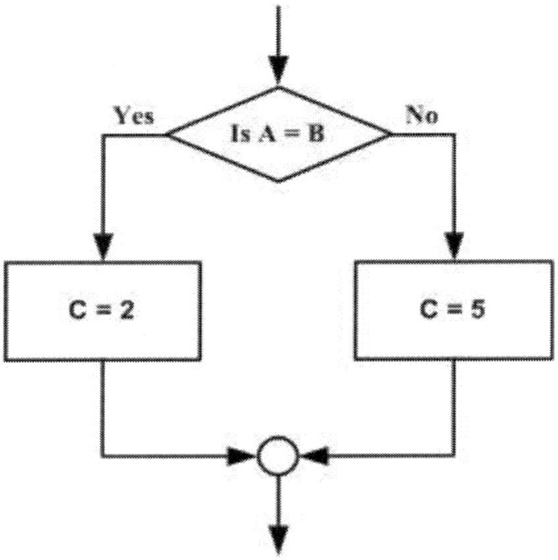

Figure D- 8: an IF THEN ELSE Sample

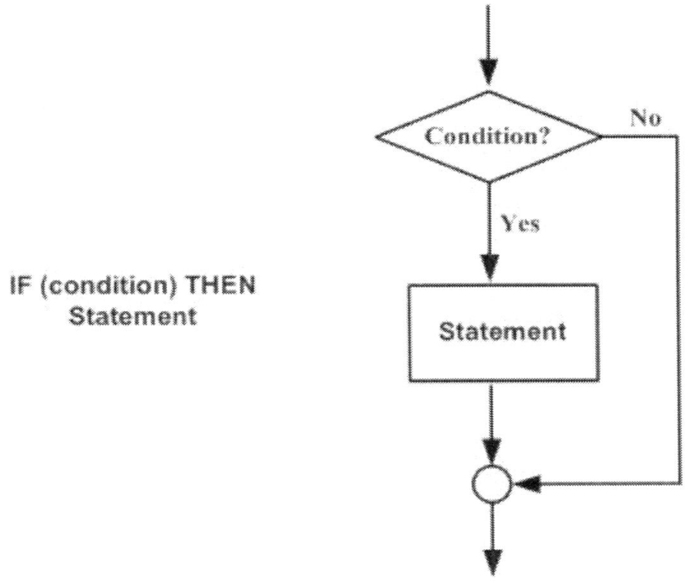

Figure D- 9: IF THEN Pseudocode versus Flowchart

Figures D-10 and D-11 show two iteration control structures: REPEAT UNTIL and WHILE DO. Both structures execute a statement or group of statements repeatedly. The difference between them is that the REPEAT UNTIL structure always executes the statement(s) at least once, and checks the condition after each iteration, whereas the WHILE DO may not execute the statement(s) at all because the condition is checked at the beginning of each iteration.

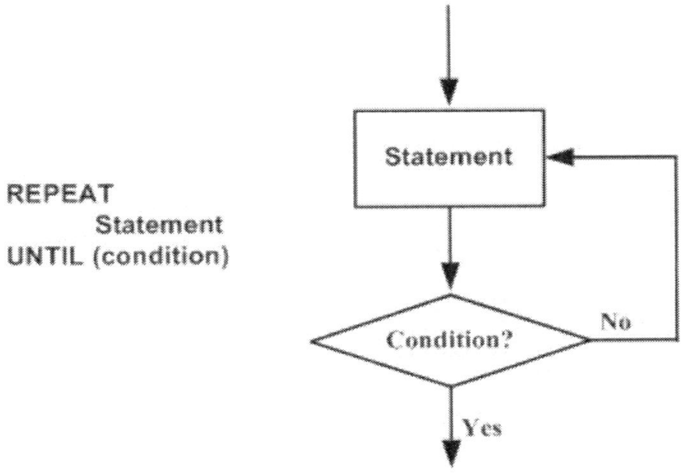

Figure D- 10: REPEAT UNTIL Pseudocode versus Flowchart

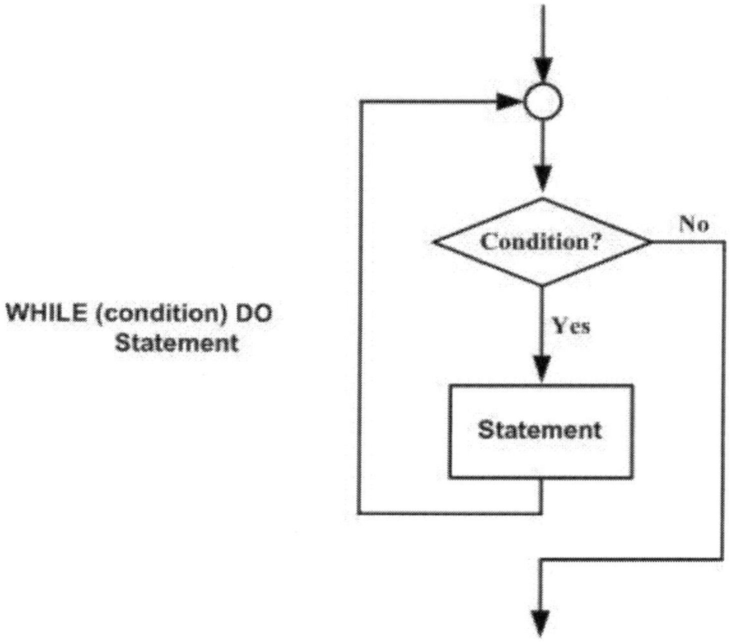

Figure D- 11: WHILE DO Pseudocode versus Flowchart

Program D-1 finds the sum of numbers between 1 and 10. Compare the flowchart versus the pseudocode for Program D-1 (shown in Figure D-12). In this example, more program details are given than one usually finds. For example, this shows steps for initializing and changing values. Another programmer may not include these steps in the flowchart or pseudocode. It is important to remember that the purpose of flowcharts or pseudocode is to show the flow of the program and what the program does, not the specific Assembly language instructions that accomplish the program's objectives. Notice also that the pseudocode gives the same information in a much more compact form than does the flowchart. It is important to note that sometimes pseudocode is written in layers, so that the outer level or layer shows the flow of the program and subsequent levels show more details of how the program accomplishes its assigned tasks.

Program D-1

```
int main ()
{
        int sum = 0;
        int value = 1;

        do{
                sum = sum + value;
                value++;
        }while(value <= 10);

        printf ("%d", sum);
}
```

```
value = 1
sum = 0
REPEAT
  sum = sum + value
  value = value + 1
UNTIL (value > 10)
Display sum
```

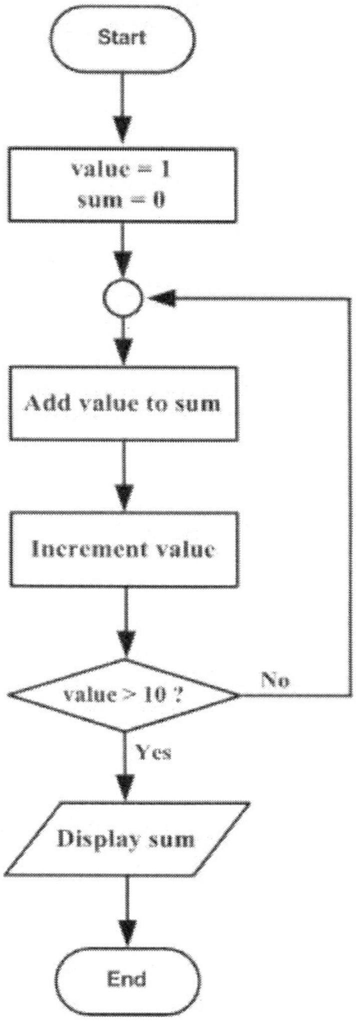

Figure D-12: Pseudocode versus Flowchart for Program D-1

Appendix E: Passing Arguments into Functions

There are different ways to pass arguments (parameters) to functions. Some of them are:

- through registers
- through memory using references
- using stack

E.1: Passing arguments through registers

In the following program the BIGGER function gets two values through R0 and R1. After comparing R0 and R1, it returns the bigger value through R0.

Program E-1

```
        AREA   OUR_PROG, CODE, READONLY

        MOV    R0, #5        ; R0 = 5
        MOV    R1, #7        ; R1 = 7
        BL     BIGGER        ; BIGGER(5, 7)
HERE    B      HERE   ; stay here

        ; =======================================
        ; BIGGER returns the bigger value
        ; Parameters:
        ;      R0 and R1: the values to be compared
        ; Returns:
        ;      R0: containing the bigger value
        ; =======================================
BIGGER
        CMP    R0, R1
        BHI    L1            ; if R0 > R1 go to L1
        MOV    R0, R1        ; R0 = R1
L1      BX     LR            ; return

        END
```

This is a fast way of passing arguments to the function.

E.2: Passing through memory using references

We can store the data in memory and pass its address through a register. In the following program the STR_LENGTH function gets the address of a zero-ended string through R0 and returns the length of the string through R1.

Program E-2

```
        AREA   OUR_PROG, CODE, READONLY
```

```
      ADR    R0, OUR_STR ; R0 = addr. of OUR_STR
      BL     STR_LENGTH  ; STR_LENGTH(&OUR_STR)
HERE  B      HERE  ; stay here

OUR_STR DCB "HELLO!"
      ALIGN 4
      ; ========================================
      ; STR_LENGTH returns the length of string
      ; Parameters:
      ;     R0: address of the string
      ; Returns:
      ;     R0: the length of string
      ; ========================================
STR_LENGTH
MOV   R1, R0              ; move string pointer to R1
      MOV    R0, #0              ; use R0 as string length counter
L_BEGIN
      LDRB  R2, [R1]            ; fetch a character from string
      CMP   R2, #0
      BXEQ  LR              ; return if character is null (end of string)
      ADD   R1, R1, #1  ; point to next character in string
      ADD   R0, R0, #1          ; increment the counter
      B     L_BEGIN

      END
```

E.3: Passing arguments through stack

Passing through the stack is a flexible way of passing arguments. To do so, the arguments are pushed onto the stack just before calling the function and popped off after returning. In Program E-3, the BIGGER function gets two arguments through the stack and returns the bigger value in R0.

Program E-3

```
      AREA  OUR_PROG, CODE, READONLY

      ; init stack pointer
      LDR SP, =(0x40000000+(16*1024))

      MOV   R0, #5
      PUSH  {R0}          ; push Arg1
      MOV   R0, #7
      PUSH  {R0}          ; push Arg2

      BL    BIGGER              ; BIGGER(5, 7)
      ADD   SP, SP, #8  ; adjust the stack pointer to remove the arguments

HERE  B     HERE          ; stay here
```

```
        ; ========================================
        ; BIGGER returns the bigger value
        ; Parameters:
        ;     values to be compared on stack
        ; Returns:
        ;     R0: the bigger value
        ; ========================================
BIGGER
        LDR    R0, [SP, #4]       ; R0 = arg1
        LDR    R1, [SP, #0]       ; R1 = arg2

        CMP    R0, R1
        MOVLO  R0, R1        ; if R0 < R1 move R1 into R0
L1      BX     LR            ; return

        END
```

This method of passing arguments is used in x86 computers because they have very few general-purpose registers. In ARM CPU, the arguments are passed in the first four registers if there are four or fewer arguments. If there are more than four arguments, the first four are passed in the first four registers and the rest are passed on the stack.

It is important to remember that after returning from the call, the caller must clear the arguments on the stack.

E.4: AAPCS (ARM Application Procedure Call Standard)

The AAPCS provides a standard for implementing the functions and the function calls so that the codes made by different compilers and different programmers can work with each other. Some of the rules of the standard are:

- The arguments must be sent through R0 to R3. Each register cannot hold more than one argument. If there more than four words are needed, the first four words are sent in R0 to R3, the rest are passed on the stack.
- The return value must be returned in R0 (and R1 if the return value is 64-bit).
- The functions can use R4 to R8, R10 and R11 for temporary storage (Thumb code can only use R4 to R7). But their values must be saved upon entering the function and restored before returning. To do so, we push the registers before using them and pop them before returning from the function.
- The stack must be used as Full Descending

In Program E-4 the above rules are considered.

Program E-4

```
      AREA  OUR_PROG, CODE, READONLY

      ; init stack pointer
; (change it according to your chip)
      LDR SP, =(0x40000000+(16*1024))

      MOV   R0, #20
      BL    DELAY ; DELAY(20)
HERE  B     HERE  ; stay here

      ; =======================================
      ; DELAY waits for a while
      ; Parameters:
      ;     R0: the amount of wait
      ; Returns:
      ;     none
      ; =======================================
DELAY
      CMP   R0, #0
      BXEQ  LR           ; return if zero

      PUSH  {R5}         ; save R5

      LDR   R5, =5000000       ; R5 = 5000000
L1    SUBS  R5, R5, #1   ; R5=R5-1
      BNE   L1           ; go to L1 if R5 is not zero

      POP   {R5}         ; restore R5
      BX    LR           ; return

      END
```

More information

For more information about AAPCS see the following article or search "AAPCS" on the Internet:

http://infocenter.arm.com/help/topic/com.arm.doc.ihi0042e/IHI0042E_aapcs.pdf

Appendix F: ASCII Codes

Dec	Hex	Ch	Dec	Hex	Ch	Dec	Hex	Ch	Dec	Hex	Ch
0	00		32	20		64	40	@	96	60	`
1	01	☺	33	21	!	65	41	A	97	61	a
2	02	☻	34	22	"	66	42	B	98	62	b
3	03	♥	35	23	#	67	43	C	99	63	c
4	04	♦	36	24	$	68	44	D	100	64	d
5	05	♣	37	25	%	69	45	E	101	65	e
6	06	♠	38	26	&	70	46	F	102	66	f
7	07	•	39	27	'	71	47	G	103	67	g
8	08	◘	40	28	(	72	48	H	104	68	h
9	09	○	41	29	)	73	49	I	105	69	i
10	0A	◙	42	2A	*	74	4A	J	106	6A	j
11	0B	♂	43	2B	+	75	4B	K	107	6B	k
12	0C	♀	44	2C	,	76	4C	L	108	6C	l
13	0D	♪	45	2D	-	77	4D	M	109	6D	m
14	0E	♫	46	2E	.	78	4E	N	110	6E	n
15	0F	☼	47	2F	/	79	4F	O	111	6F	o
16	10	►	48	30	0	80	50	P	112	70	p
17	11	◄	49	31	1	81	51	Q	113	71	q
18	12	↕	50	32	2	82	52	R	114	72	r
19	13	‼	51	33	3	83	53	S	115	73	s
20	14	¶	52	34	4	84	54	T	116	74	t
21	15	§	53	35	5	85	55	U	117	75	u
22	16	▬	54	36	6	86	56	V	118	76	v
23	17	↨	55	37	7	87	57	W	119	77	w
24	18	↑	56	38	8	88	58	X	120	78	x
25	19	↓	57	39	9	89	59	Y	121	79	y
26	1A	→	58	3A	:	90	5A	Z	122	7A	z
27	1B	←	59	3B	;	91	5B	[	123	7B	{
28	1C	∟	60	3C	<	92	5C	\	124	7C	|
29	1D	↔	61	3D	=	93	5D	]	125	7D	}
30	1E	▲	62	3E	>	94	5E	^	126	7E	~
31	1F	▼	63	3F	?	95	5F	_	127	7F	⌂

Index

Made in United States
Troutdale, OR
11/03/2026

56847567R00184